THE Glasgow GUIDE

GUIDED
WALKS
THROUGH
OLD
AND
NEW
GLASGOW

To Helen
love
David.

DAVID WILLIAMS

CANONGATE BOOKS LTD

Other books by David Williams
Iceland: the Visitor's Guide (1985, Stacey International, London)
Mývatn: a Paradise for Nature Lovers (1988, Örn og Örlygur, Reykjavík)
A guide to the Southern Upland Way (1989, Constable, London)
Essential Iceland (1996, Automobile Association, Basingstoke)
Tour Guide Scotland (1996, Automobile Association, Basingstoke)

First published in Great Britan in 1998
by Canongate Books Ltd,
14 High Street
Edinburgh EH1 1TE

ISBN 0 86241 840 2

British Library Cataloguing-in-Publication Data
A catalogue record for this book is available on request from the
British Library.

Design: JW Graphics

Maps: Jim Lewis

Photographs: All the photographs in the book are by David Williams
and were supplied by the David Williams Picture Library.

Cover portrait of David Williams courtesy of Fotek Portraits Ltd,
Swindon.

Frontis: Glasgow University

Printed and bound in Great Britain by Butler & Tanner, Frome

Contents

Acknowledgements

A great number of people have helped me in the preparation of this book and my thanks go to all the curators, administrators, countryside rangers, librarians, architects, ministers and members of numerous organisations who gave me so much information and advice. The staff of many departments of Glasgow City Council were always helpful, especially the curators of the city's museums, the librarians of the Mitchell Library's Glasgow Room and members of the Parks Department. Thanks also to the staff of Glasgow University Archives, the National Trust for Scotland, British Waterways, Historic Scotland, Glasgow West Conservation Trust and the Greater Glasgow & Clyde Valley Tourist Board. The curators of the city's smaller museums and the custodians of all the other places I visited were also very helpful in supplying me with information.

It is always a difficult task to name individual people as so many others were kind enough to give assistance, but special mention must go to the following: Maggie Coffield, Bob Crawford, Tom Davidson Kelly, Jim Dick, Margaret Kirk, Ranald MacInnes, David Mullane, David Nicklin, Mark O'Neill, Doreen Reid, Daniel Robbins, Helen Rowbottom and Gordon Urquhart. In particular, I would like to thank Margaret Kirk for all her help and patience during the years I worked on this book.

Kelvingrove Art Gallery and Museum

Introduction

For many years I have had an interest in Glasgow's buildings and this was encouraged by the city's 'Doors Open' days when numerous buildings had their doors opened to anyone who wanted to view their architectural treasures. Every building tells a story and much of the history of Glasgow can be discovered by looking at our buildings as in many cases they reflect the achievements and aspirations of those who worked, lived or met in them. Many of our most important buildings celebrate great achievements in the fields of science, engineering, commerce and architecture, and numerous famous people such as the scientists Lord Kelvin and James Watt, shipbuilder Sir William Pearce and architect Charles Rennie Mackintosh are connected with buildings and institutions which are described in the book.

The guidebook is arranged in a series of thirteen walks which take the reader around many of the most interesting parts of the city. Over six hundred sights are described and the history of many of them is related. The city's principal graveyards are also dealt with, with information on some of their best-known monuments and the story of the people who are buried there.

In the last few years there has been a growing awareness of the work of the city's most successful architects and, as a special tribute to two of them, there are individual chapters on Charles Rennie Mackintosh and

Kelvingrove Art Gallery and Museum

Alexander Thomson. Mackintosh's work is well known and widely appreciated in many countries and Thomson's buildings are gaining recognition as exceptionally important examples of how Classical designs could be used in grand Victorian architecture.

As well as dealing with things we can see – like buildings, statues and sculptures – the walks also allow the reader to discover how people have lived and worked in the city over the last few hundred years. The story of the Tobacco Lords, the shipbuilding industry, life in the city's tenements and the successes of our football teams are all woven into the text in order to describe the lives of countless generations of Glaswegians. A number of the walks also allow the reader to learn more about the literature of Glasgow, from William Miller's children's poem *Wee Willie Winkie* to the far more serious work of Hugh MacDiarmid, and there are numerous quotations from writers from previous centuries which tell us more about how our forebears lived.

Edward Burt visited Glasgow in 1726 and was so delighted with what he saw that he wrote *Glasgow is, to outward appearance, the prettiest and most uniform Town that I ever saw; and I believe there is nothing like it in Britain*. Burt's comment may have been made nearly three centuries ago but Glasgow is still a fascinating city to walk around and I hope this book helps the reader enjoy many hours of exploration.

CHAPTER I

The City of Glasgow

G lasgow is not an ancient city (though the Romans did establish forts nearby during their occupation of this part of Scotland), but its history as a relatively important community can be traced back nearly nine hundred years. Bishop John Achaius began building the first cathedral around 1124 on a site where the city's patron saint, St Mungo, was said to have erected a wooden church and from then on Glasgow's role as a religious centre ensured its political prominence in the West of Scotland. It also developed as a market town and thus played a pivotal role in the local economy.

After the cathedral was destroyed by fire in 1172 a new building was erected and a tomb was established for St Mungo. The city's original centre (where High Street meets Rottenrow) was close to the cathedral and from there High Street ran downhill to where Glasgow Cross now stands; a fishing community developed in the area between this latter cross and the River Clyde. The medieval city was legally established as a 'burgh of barony' with the bishop as the feudal superior and thus the person who was able to control the social, commercial and political life of the whole community. Scotland's other principal religious centre, St Andrews, had founded a university in 1413 and in the 1450s Glasgow's Bishop Turnbull was granted a papal Bull which led to the formation of the University of Glasgow. This was based in the old part of the city until the late nineteenth century when it moved to the West End.

By the fifteenth century Glasgow had established itself as a prominent trading centre and its trading activities were under the control of the city's Merchant Guild, the precursor of today's Merchants' House whose headquarters are in George Square. The craftsmen were organised in a quite different body, the Trades House, whose offices are in Stockwell Street, and these two bodies played an important role in developing trade and industry. They also held influential positions within the burgh's administration and were involved in charitable work, especially looking after the widows and families of their deceased members.

The Protestant Reformation of 1560 ushered in important changes in the social and political life of Scotland and for over a hundred years there was repeated turmoil as the various factions fought against each other. Locally, this led to the Battle of Langside (1568) between the forces of Mary, Queen of Scots and Regent Moray, and as a result of her defeat the young queen fled to England where she was eventually beheaded in 1587. The crowns of Scotland and England were united in 1603 and in the decades that followed the attempts by the British monarchy to impose its religious ideas on the country were violently opposed and resulted in terrible bloodshed. During these 'Covenanting Times' (named after the various documents called the National Covenants), Glasgow took measures to defend itself and the inhabitants were ordered to carry guns and be prepared to counter any attack by government troops. While these matters of state and religion provided an almost never-ending series of disputes and panics, Glasgow's growth and subsequent overcrowding led to other crises. In 1652 a serious fire destroyed eighty tenement 'closes' (the shared entrance doorways in a building) and after another fire in the 1670s the council gave notice that stone, not timber, should be used for the exterior walls of new buildings. Diseases took their toll too, and the bubonic plague caused many deaths in 1574, 1584-5, 1605-6 and 1646-7.

By 1660 the city's population had reached 14,678 and many were involved in trading with European countries such as Ireland, France, Holland and Norway. Apart from importing iron, wood, salt and beef and exporting goods such as coal, malt, barley and clothes, ships were used to carry re-exported goods to other countries such as Irish tallow to France. The importance of this trade was that it laid the basis for the city's subsequent role as a world-wide shipper. However, at this stage of Glasgow's trading activities, there were few exports of locally-produced items as manufacturing was yet to become important to the city. Trade brought prosperity to Glasgow and in 1656 Thomas Tucker reported to Oliver Cromwell that *this town, seated in a pleasant and fruitful soil, and consisting of four streets handsomely built in form of a cross, is one of the most considerable burghs of Scotland, as well for the structure as trade of it.* Unfortunately the River Clyde's shallowness in Glasgow precluded the building of a decent harbour and although a quay was built at Broomielaw in 1662, the bulk of the city's goods were landed at Port Glasgow, much farther downstream. The east coast town of Leith was the country's principal port (due to its proximity to mainland Europe) but from the end of the sixteenth century the Clyde's importance for trading was increased dramatically as west coast ports were able to develop trading links with the Americas. Subsequently, tobacco trading with Virginia was established and this began the process whereby Glasgow was to gain its undoubted success as one of the world's greatest trading and manufacturing cities.

The English Navigation Acts of 1660 and 1663 prohibited Scotland from trading with English colonies and for a while this curtailed the Scots' activities. Undaunted, a huge proportion of the country's capital was invested in setting up a Scottish colony in Darien in Central America but for numerous reasons this ended in complete disaster in 1701, leading to the loss of one quarter of the country's liquid assets. Scotland was greatly weakened by what has been called 'The Darien Disaster' and the English were blamed for this severe blow to the home economy. Scotland was thus in a poor bargaining position when it discussed possible union with England, but the union took effect in 1707 and one benefit it brought was the ending of discrimination against Scottish traders. From then on Glasgow's merchants took full advantage of the new opportunities that opened up. The city's location on the west coast gave it a clear advantage over its London rivals and in 1726 Daniel Defoe noted that London-based ships faced real dangers *especially in time of war, when the* [English] *channel is throng'd with privateers, and when the ships wait to go in fleets for fear of enemies; whereas the Glasgow men are no sooner out of the Firth of Clyde… and are oftentimes at the capes of Virginia before the London ships get clear of the channel.* The commercial exploits of the small but very powerful group of Tobacco Lords brought tremendous wealth to the city and their role is described on pp.47 and 93. Fortunately, by the time of the American War of Independence (1776-83) these merchants had already widened their commercial interests and were thus able to survive the war's disruption. Some had invested in Scotland's manufacturing industry as they could sell the products in their stores in the Americas; others had put their profits into emergent industries such as textiles, coal mining and ironworks. They also helped finance the local canals, notably the Forth and Clyde Canal which was planned to link the east and west coasts of the country.

Glasgow's population grew steadily during the eighteenth century and by 1801 it reached 48,256 (83,769, including the suburbs). The city grew in a westward direction to accommodate the incomers and many

The Tobacco Laird's House in Miller Street

new and important streets were laid out such as Miller Street (1762), Queen Street (1777) and Buchanan Street (1786). While the better-off inhabitants moved westwards into these newly-developed areas, the old centre of the city around High Street crumbled into decay, producing some of Europe's worst slums. The grossly overcrowded East End became a centre for new industries such as cloth-making and many people were involved in producing linen and cotton goods which were exported all over the world by merchants such as David Dale. Various districts in and around Glasgow specialised in weaving. The weavers became one of the earliest groups of workers to organise themselves and the story of the weavers' revolt of 1787 is told on p.366. By this time a number of other industries had also become successful, such as sugar refining and rum making, and new industries such as potteries and breweries were also being established.

By 1834 there were one hundred and thirty-four cotton mills within the Glasgow area and the development of these large economic units was just one result of the Industrial Revolution. With the harnessing of the power of coal (for producing steam), the scene was set for building large factories which had no need to be close to streams for their motive power. Thus the city expanded quickly, large factories were built and workers herded into tenement houses close to the factories in which they worked. Cotton now took the place of tobacco as the city's great source of wealth but the fundamental difference between the two commodities was that processing cotton into cloth required the labour of many local people. New industries were built up alongside the cotton mills and these included bleaching and dyeing; in turn, these encouraged the construction of chemical works to provide their raw materials.

Much of the city's production was sent overseas and this led to the enlargement of the quays in Glasgow to the extent that by the middle of the nineteenth century there were four kilometres (two and a half miles) of quays in the city. The Clyde had been considerably deepened in order to allow ships to reach the city centre and this, together with the demand for new ships, led to shipyards being erected beside the river. Previously, the city had relied on vessels built in the Americas or in England but now many of the Glasgow-owned vessels could be constructed locally. Indeed, such was the expansion of shipbuilding in Glasgow and in other Clydeside towns that in 1851 Clydeside accounted for eighty-five percent of Britain's total tonnage; the development of the River Clyde's shipbuilding industry is described on p.153. Scotland's iron industry was begun in 1759 when the Carron Company began its operations near Falkirk, and Central Scotland's coal and ironstone industries were able to provide the ironworks with these two vital raw materials; in turn, these factories supplied iron, and later, steel, to the shipyards and engineering factories. Although many of these large enterprises were spread throughout the industrial West of Scotland, Glasgow had important coalmines within its boundaries and a large ironworks (known as 'Dixon's Blazes') was established in 1839 by William Dixon at Crown Street in the Gorbals; it was only demolished in the early 1960s.

The River Clyde and the Kvaerner Govan Shipyard

By the mid-nineteenth century the city had grown into a busy, noisy, smelly and very unhealthy place. The factories produced copious amounts of noxious gases and liquid waste was often poured into the rivers or left to soak into the ground. Solid waste was piled up near the factories. The old tenements, especially those in the East End, were grossly overcrowded and an 1863 report by the city's Medical Officer of Health reported that *64 Havannah Street is not surpassed by any close in the city for filth, misery, crime and disease; it contains 59 houses, all inhabited by a most wretched class of individuals; several of these houses do not exceed 15 feet square, yet they are forced to contain a family of sometimes six persons.* Disgusting conditions like these could only be tackled by wholescale rehousing and a few years later the City Improvement Trust was given the task of dealing with the worst areas. In many ways they were very successful in their work and numerous tenements which they erected are still standing, such as in the High Street and Saltmarket.

As well as taking on the daunting task of improving the city's housing stock, the 'city fathers' set about establishing what has sometimes been called 'municipal socialism' (although many of the most influential councillors were highly successful capitalists!). As well as being responsible for such matters as education, housing, parks and all the other local government services we have today, at various times the council operated the public transport system (including the trams and the Underground), the Municipal Telephone System and they even controlled the production and distribution of gas and electricity. Perhaps the most lauded example of how the council worked to improve the lot of the people was the provision of a clean water supply. This large project lasted from 1856 to 1859 and involved building a pipeline which brought water from Loch Katrine to Glasgow; the city's gratitude was marked by the erection of the Stewart Memorial Fountain in

Kelvingrove Park (see p.202). In 1905 Frederic Clemson Howe, an American professor of Civic Administration, visited the city and was quite astounded by all the municipal enterprises. He reported that the council *runs several farms upon which it uses the street refuse as fertilizer. It has brought them to a high state of fertility, and produces provisions for its departments. Even from this source it has a net income of $3,000 a year. It has a wonderful system of sewage disposal which is nearing completion. The River Clyde has always been a foul-smelling stream, but the city is expending millions to purify it through the destruction of its sewage and the use of the sludge as fertilizer. The city fire department has a big workshop at the central station where it builds all of its own apparatus, just as the tramway department erects its own cars... Thus Glasgow looks after her people. She is as frugal as a Scotch parent.*

As the city grew in importance, the council began the process of annexing the surrounding suburbs. The early seventeenth-century boundary had remained unchanged for two hundred years but in the mid-nineteenth century various burghs, such as Anderston, Calton and Gorbals were taken over. At the end of the century the city swallowed even larger burghs such as Govan, Partick, Hillhead and Pollokshields and this process continued well into the twentieth century though some areas (such as Rutherglen which was annexed in 1975) are no longer within Glasgow. But local traditions still remain, particularly in the older parts of the city, even though the huge housing developments of the 1960s and 1970s led to large numbers of people leaving the traditional tenement areas for the peripheral housing schemes such as Drumchapel, Easterhouse and Castlemilk.

The city's heyday was in the late Victorian period. By that time, Glasgow had built up an enormously powerful industrial and commercial base and was able to sell 'high-tech' manufactured goods all over the world; in addition, these exports (from steel nails to massive railway locomotives) were transported abroad in Clyde-built ships and the financial and insurance arrangements were often made by Glasgow banks and insurance companies. Glasgow was now 'The Second City of the Empire' and since Britain was at that time the greatest imperialist power the world had ever seen, many Glaswegians saw themselves as citizens of the second most important city in the world. The Victorians were brimful with confidence. They had found success in manufacturing and trading, they had conquered much of the world and they celebrated their achievements by erecting often ostentatious buildings in which to work, live and meet. The glories of ancient empires were recalled through the prominent statuary on the bigger buildings. The City Chambers in George Square, the Clyde Navigation Trust at Broomielaw and the St Andrew's Halls near Charing Cross are all well-known buildings which are decorated with large statues depicting Greek gods as well as other Classical statues representing the Arts, Sciences and the achievements of Glasgow and the British Empire. The leading citizens saw Glasgow as a city with a very international perspective and this was reflected in the two International Exhibitions (1888 and 1901) which were held in Kelvingrove Park; these are described on p.197.

In the late-Victorian period the city's middle class had never had it so good; they lived in substantial stone houses, they had leisure time to enjoy and well-stocked 'warehouses' (department stores) in which to buy the luxuries that others could only dream about. Some of these large shops, such as Wylie & Lochhead in Buchanan Street, stocked high-quality goods from all around the world but many of their expensive household goods, such as furniture and carpets were made either by themselves or by other Scottish manufacturers. These firms were involved in making furnishings for the luxury ships which were built on the Clyde and they used this expertise to be able to supply customers with the contents of complete dining rooms or parlours, no matter whether the purchaser lived in Glasgow or wanted to have everything shipped abroad to some far-flung corner of the Empire.

But times – and fortunes – change. At the turn of the twentieth century British industry and commerce were losing out to their rivals and in 1908 *The Times* reported that over 16,000 people in Govan were *on the verge of starvation.* Various radical and left wing organisations grew in strength during this period and leaders such as John Maclean (whose life is described on p.52) drew huge crowds to rallies and demonstrations. The First World War eased some problems, exacerbated others and created new ones. There were fights against rent rises and various strikes took place in big engineering factories such as Albion Motors and Beardmore's and these gave rise to the working-class leaders known as the 'Red Clydesiders' and influential organisations such as the Clyde Workers' Committee. Social unrest continued after the war, with one of the most serious events being 'Black Friday' (31 January 1919) when troops were brought onto the streets after a huge demonstration (see p.81).

The shipbuilding industry had been expanded rapidly during the war and this led to postwar overcapacity and subsequent closures of some of the yards. This had a knock-on effect and by 1922 there were 80,000 people unemployed in the city. The anger and frustration at this senseless waste of people's skills was reflected in the results of the 1922 General Election when ten of the city's fifteen parliamentary seats were won by the Independent Labour Party. Many of the hopes raised by election of these MPs were dashed, though there were some improvements in the quality of life, but the Glasgow economy continued to decline and it reached another crisis in the Depression of the 1930s. However, with the prospect of another war looming on the horizon, the city's economy began to pick up in the late 1930s, and as well as local yards getting extra orders for naval ships, the Rolls-Royce aeroplane engine factory was built in Hillington. During the war the city was a target for enemy bombers, though it was the nearby town of Clydebank which took the brunt of the death and destruction, and relatively few Glasgow buildings or factories were damaged. One notable exception was Alexander Thomson's Queen's Park Church.

Although the shipyards were busy in the postwar period building much-needed replacements for ships sunk during the hostilities, they

George Square

were increasingly unable to compete with foreign competitors and the whole Clydeside industry faced a great crisis which is described on p.154. This situation was mirrored by many other industries in the West of Scotland, due in great measure to the lack of investment over many decades. And so a once-great world-class centre of engineering excellence slowly withered, leaving today only a handful of big factories which are carrying on the proud tradition of first-class workmanship that was so prevalent a century ago. Employment patterns have thus changed dramatically during the past few decades, with jobs in the service sector replacing many of those lost in manufacturing. In recent years Glasgow has also become a popular tourist destination and the city attracts many visitors who come to see the museums, galleries and our fine heritage of Victorian buildings. The city's new claim to being Britain's premier shopping centre (after London) also attracts countless people (including many from abroad) who come for a weekend's 'shop-'till-you-drop' visit.

Glasgow is not alone in Europe in having to cope with the relatively sudden loss of heavy industry and many commentators have noted that it has been remarkably successful in coping with what some call the 'post-industrial age'. However, no amount of clever marketing can erase the fact that Glasgow still suffers from high unemployment, poor housing and a unwanted reputation as a city where many suffer (or will suffer) illness due to an exceptionally unhealthy diet. But in some ways the loss of traditional industries has been beneficial as the noise, grime and pollution have decreased dramatically. This has resulted in the air being cleaner, the people generally healthier and the stone-cleaned buildings sparkling in the sunlight. And, yes, street cafés are becoming more common.

CHAPTER 2

Practical Information

GETTING INFORMATION

Scottish Tourist Board
Address: PO Box 705, Edinburgh EH4 3EU.
Tel: 0131-332 2433
General tourist information about Scotland, accommodation, transport to and in Scotland, maps, books, etc.

Greater Glasgow & Clyde Valley Tourist Board
Address: 11 George Square, Glasgow G2 1DY.
Tel: 0141-204 4400
(Referred to as the Tourist Information Centre throughout the book.) General tourist information about the Glasgow area, accommodation, transport to and in the city, details of museums and art galleries (including opening times), etc. It also acts as a Bureau de Change; other services are mentioned elsewhere in this chapter. The office is passed in Walk 3 (see p.88).

Newspapers
The Herald, Evening Times and the *Daily Record* for news, 'what's on', etc. These papers are published daily, except Sunday.

The *Scottish Sunday Mail* is published each Sunday.

Magazines
The List gives information and listings covering what's on, entertainment, restaurants and other 'tourist information'. Available fortnightly at newsagents.

The Glasgow Galleries Guide gives details of lots of local galleries and museums. Available in many of the galleries. Free.

Bookshops
The main bookshops are John Smith (St Vincent Street and Byres Road), Waterstones (Sauchiehall Street) and Dillons (Argyle Street). These have collections of books on Scotland and Glasgow. The Tourist Information Centre also sells books and maps.

There are a number of second-hand bookshops, many of which are in the West End. Contact the Tourist Information Centre for information.

Libraries
The main reference library is the Mitchell Library (see p.135). There are numerous local lending libraries around the city and the most convenient in the city centre is Stirling's Library at 62 Miller Street.

TRANSPORT IN GLASGOW

• Transport information can be obtained from the Tourist Information Centre and the Travel Centre in St Enoch Square (see p.143). Handy pocket maps of the main transport routes are available.

• The most straightforward way of getting around many of the tourist areas is by using the Underground system. It consists of fifteen stations serving the city centre, the West End and the area just south of the River Clyde.

• The two major railway stations (both of which are main-line termini) are Central Station and Queen Street Station and these are about a ten minute walk apart. Both of these also have through low-level lines which serve the local areas and these allow the city to be crossed quickly. In addition, the Cathcart Circle serves the South Side and this is linked to other railway lines at Central Station. There is a bus service between the two main railway stations.

• The city's bus system is confusing with lots of variously coloured buses going to places inside and well outside the city. The pocket transport route map available from the Tourist Information Centre and the Travel Centre includes details of bus routes and numbers.

• The terminus for long-distance coaches is Buchanan Bus Station.

• Special discount tickets are available on the public transport systems. Enquire at the Tourist Information Centre or the Travel Centre for details.

• There are sight-seeing tours around Glasgow on open-top buses. The Tourist Information Centre has details of these and it also sells tickets.

• There are numerous taxis. The black Hackney carriages have ranks in many places, notably the two main railway stations and the bus station; they can also be hailed from the street.

• Visitors flying to Glasgow should note that Glasgow Airport is about 11km (7 miles) west of the city and Prestwick Airport is about 43km (27 miles) south-west of the city. Glasgow Airport has a bus service to and from Glasgow's Buchanan Bus Station. Prestwick Airport has a railway service to and from Glasgow Central Station. Glasgow Airport has a Tourist Information Centre which can assist with travel information and booking accommodation; this office is linked to the main office in George Square.

ACCOMMODATION

• There is a wide variety of accommodation available in the city, from small bed and breakfast establishments to large hotels. The Tourist Information Centre can provide information on most of these places and can also book accommodation. The office can also book accommodation in other parts of the country.

- The main areas for hotels are the city centre and the West End and the biggest concentration of large hotels is in the area to the west of Buchanan Street.

- During university holidays the students' halls of residence are available. Contact the three universities (Glasgow, Strathclyde and Caledonian) through the Tourist Information Centre.

- The Youth Hostel is situated on Woodlands Hill (see p.222). It is part of the IYHA.

EATING AND DRINKING

- Glasgow is well served by numerous eating and drinking places. Many types of cuisine are available and visitors will find that Glasgow can justifiably boast the title 'Curry capital of Europe' as there are so many good restaurants serving food from the Indian sub-continent. Italian and Chinese restaurants are also greatly in evidence. Indeed, visitors seeking genuine Scottish food using traditional ingredients may sometimes have quite a search in front of them!

- Many pubs provide meals at lunchtime and during the early evening. In addition, many small restaurants offer 'pre-theatre' meals in the early evening which are rather cheaper than their normal menus.

Italian Centre pavement café

- 'High tea' is a very well-known Scottish tradition. Taken in the late afternoon, it generally consists of a hot main course, tea or coffee, and a plateful of cakes.

- The city's (and the country's) favourite fast food is a fish supper: what English visitors would call 'fish and chips'.

- The best-known areas for restaurants and pubs are the city centre and the West End. All the introductions to the walks give some indication of areas that have interesting eating places.

- The walks go past many pubs of interest and a number of these are described in the guide. The reasons for being mentioned include the interest of the building, the interior decoration or because it is a nice example of a good Glasgow pub.

- Non-smokers may well find that a lot of the city's pubs and restaurants are exceptionally smoky.

SPECIAL EVENTS AND PUBLIC HOLIDAYS

The calendar shown on p.15 gives some of the regular annual events as well as public holidays. These dates can vary, notably if a holiday period overlaps a weekend, so use this list as a general guide only. Please note that many shops and other services will remain open on some of the public holidays. Contact the Tourist Information Centre for further details.

The Botanic Gardens

Month	Special events	Public holidays
January	New Year's Day: the city recovers from Hogmanay. Big sales in the shops. Celtic Connections music festival.	January 1 and 2
February	-	-
March	-	-
April	Easter	Good Friday and Easter Monday
May	West End Festival	Holiday weekends: first and third weekends. (Monday holiday)
June	School holidays start at the very end of the month and last until mid August.	-
July	'Glasgow Fair' is in the second half of the month. International Jazz Festival	Fair Monday
August	World Pipe Band Championships	-
September	'Doors Open' day (see p.17)	September Weekend (last weekend: Monday holiday)
October	Schools close for a week.	-
November	-	-
December	Christmas Festivities Christmas Carnival at the SECC Hogmanay (New Year's Eve)	December 25 and 26

FACILITIES FOR THE DISABLED

•   Glasgow is a hilly city and is not particularly wheelchair-friendly, though more facilities are being made available. Many public buildings (including museums) have ramps and lifts available but these are not always very obvious. Ask at the Tourist Information Centre for general advice and specific information.

•   The introductions to all the walks give some information on the terrain, and warn where the route negotiates hills. Most of the walks through parks give alternative routes which avoid these difficulties as far as possible.

Public toilets

Public toilets can be few and far between. However, they can be found in the two major railway stations, the bus station, museums and art galleries, the bigger parks, major shops and shopping centres. In addition, there are public toilets at St Vincent Place, Cathedral Square Gardens and Sauchiehall Street (at West Campbell Street).

Shopping

• The main 'traditional' shopping streets (with their Walk Numbers) are: Argyle Street (3), Buchanan Street (3) and Sauchiehall Street (4). Other streets off these often have a number of shops of interest.

• Other streets (or small districts) with a number of 'interesting' shops (with their Walk Numbers) include: the Merchant City (1), Parnie Street (2) for galleries, Argyll Arcade (3) for jewellery, Bath Street (4) for antiques, West Regent Street (3) for galleries, Byres Road (7), De Courcey's Arcade (7), Hillhead (7) for bookshops and Great Western Road (7).

• The city now has a number of covered shopping centres and the best known (with their Walk Numbers) are: Princes Square (3), Buchanan Galleries (3) and the St Enoch Centre (5).

• There is a weekend street market at 'The Barras'. Walk Number (2).

• Many city centre shops open late on Thursdays and also on Sundays.

• The banks in the city have various opening hours but they are generally open around 09.00-17.00 Monday to Friday. Foreign currencies can be exchanged in banks, the Tourist Information Centre and some travel agents.

Safety

• Personal safety is always a very important issue, particularly in a major city. For all the friendliness of Glaswegians, visitors should take the usual precautions with their own safety and the security of their belongings.

• Most of the walks go through relatively busy areas where readers should not feel vulnerable. However, great care should be exercised when the streets are quiet, in the late evening or when going through parks. Parts of the Kelvin Walkway and the Forth and Clyde Canal can be particularly quiet at times.

• Particular care must be observed while walking through the various graveyards as some of them have very few visitors.

• Visitors from outside Britain should be aware that the emergency services (police, fire and ambulance) can be reached by telephone by dialling 999.

BINOCULARS

Lots of the city's Victorian buildings are decorated with marvellous statues and other architectural details, many of which can only be appreciated with the use of binoculars. They are also remarkably useful for studying stained-glass windows and for reading worn descriptions on plaques and gravestones. There are lots of opportunities for bird-watching on the Kelvin Walkway and the Forth and Clyde Canal.

MISCELLANEOUS

•   The 'City Centre Representatives' are a group of people whose job it is to help visitors (and locals!). They can assist with directions and general information and they are easily spotted by their bright red jackets. They can usually be seen in Argyle Street, Buchanan Street, George Square and Sauchiehall Street.

•   Walking tours around the city are available. In addition, the Charles Rennie Mackintosh Society organises walks around the city to see some of the architect's work. Contact the Tourist Information Centre for details.

•   'Doors Open' day is not just a day, but a whole weekend in September in Glasgow! This is when scores of buildings open their doors to let the public see behind the scenes. It is possible to visit churches, court cells, offices, theatres, fire stations and many fascinating places which are closed for most of the year to the general public. Contact the Tourist Information Centre for further information.

GLASGOW AT A GLANCE

This list gives the names of the more important places that are described in the guide and the interiors of many of these buildings are described in the text. The most interesting of these places (a very subjective choice!) are shown in bold. All the parks and graveyards are listed here, but not all the works of Alexander Thomson or Charles Rennie Mackintosh (see pp.397 and 410 respectively for complete lists). Churches no longer used for religious purposes are indicated by brackets round their names.

Most of the buildings have been included because there is public access to them but a few are listed for their architectural or cultural interest. See the list on p.335 for information on buildings that are open to the public.

Walk	Museums and Galleries	Important Public Buildings	
1 High Street, Strathclyde University and the Merchant City	**St Mungo Museum of Religious Life and Art** (17) **Provand's Lordship** (67) Collins Gallery (41)	Strathclyde University (29)–(45) City Halls (54)	
2 Glasgow Green and the River Clyde	**People's Palace** (15) Glasgow Print Studio (46) Sharmanka (49)		
3 The City Centre	**Gallery of Modern Art** (28) Glasgow Herald Building (31) The Piping Centre (53)	**City Chambers** (8) Glasgow Royal Concert Hall (57)	
4 Blythswood Hill, Garnethill and Charing Cross	Centre for Contemporary Arts (10) McLellan Galleries (11) **Tenement House** (26) Royal Highland Fusiliers Museum (38) Police Museum (48)	**Glasgow School of Art** (13) Mitchell Library (42)	
5 North Clydeside and Anderston		SECC (30)	
6 Glasgow University and Kelvingrove Park	**Hunterian Museum** (11) Zoology Museum (35) **Hunterian Art Gallery** (37) **Mackintosh House** (39) **Kelvingrove Art Gallery and Museum** (69) **Museum of Transport** (70)	**Glasgow University** (9)–(44)	
7 The West End and the Botanic Gardens			
8 The Kelvin Walkway			
9 The Forth and Clyde Canal			
10 Pollokshields, Bellahouston Park and Govan	Scotland Street School (2) House for an Art Lover (16)		
11 Pollok Country Park and The Burrell Collection	Pollok House (7) **The Burrell Collection** (9)		
12 Queen's Park			
13 Cathcart and Linn Park	Holmwood (18)		
Not on any walk	Fossil Grove 602 Squadron Museum Provan Hall Springburn Museum		

Religious Buildings	Parks	Graveyards	Miscellaneous
Glasgow Cathedral (54)		**Glasgow Necropolis** (15) Glasgow Cathedral Graveyard (53) St David's (Ramshorn Kirk) Graveyard (45)	Tolbooth Steeple (2) Trades Hall (52) Tron Steeple (58)
(St Andrew's Parish Church (8)) (St Andrew's-by-the-Green (9)) St Andrew's Roman Catholic Cathedral (38)	**Glasgow Green** (9)-(25)	St Andrew's-by-the Green Graveyard (7) Calton Burial Ground (18)	The Barras (0) Merchants' Steeple (44)
			George Square (1)
	Garnethill Park (17)		Willow Tea Rooms (13)
St Vincent Street Free Church of Scotland (31)			Clyde Navigation Trust Building (11) **PS Waverley** (16) SS Glenlee (24)
Glasgow University War Memorial Chapel (22)	**Kelvingrove Park** (46)-(47)		
St Mary's Episcopal Cathedral (84) (Dowanhill Church (59))	**Botanic Gardens** (34)-(47)		**Great Western Terrace** (51)
(Queen's Cross Church (29))			Kelvin Aqueduct (8) Maryhill Locks (10) Spiers Wharf (39)
Govan Old Parish Church (39)	Maxwell Park (7) Bellahouston Park (13)-(18) Elder Park (45)-(50)	Govan Old Parish Church Graveyard (40)	Haggs Castle (6) Rangers Football Club (19)
	Pollok Country Park (1)-(16)		
	Queen's Park (3)-(10)		
	Linn Park (8) and (10)-(14)	Cathcart Old Parish Church Graveyard (4)	
		Sighthill Cemetery Southern Necropolis	Celtic Football Club Crookston Castle Scottish Mask and Puppet Centre

CHAPTER 3

How to use
this Guide

Glasgow's architecture attracts visitors from around the world and many of the city's finest buildings (especially those of the Victorian era) are described in the book. Unfortunately, most people walking casually past them often fail to raise their eyes above the horizontal and so many of the buildings' finest features, including their statuary, are not even glanced at. Fortunately, the recent stone-cleaning of many of the city's buildings has meant that the black layer of soot has been removed and now they can be seen in all their (almost original) glory. The book's text describes many of the statues, emblems, mottoes and other carvings that can be seen and these are generally described from left to right as the reader sees them.

The book contains thirteen walks that visit many of the city's most interesting places. The routes are designed to go through areas where there are shops, pubs and eating places which may appeal to the reader.

Chapters 6, 8 and 9 of the book deal with graveyards, Alexander Thomson and Charles Rennie Mackintosh respectively. Nine of the city's graveyards, all of Thomson's and Mackintosh's buildings (and also some of their other works) are described in the book.

Unless otherwise stated, all churches belong to the established church, the Church of Scotland.

CHOOSING A WALK

The choice of which walks to follow obviously depends on the reader's personal interests and the time that is available. If you are a visitor to the city and your time is limited to only one, two or three days then the following suggestions can be considered.

- Look at the table entitled 'Glasgow at a glance' (see p.18) and the list in Chapter 5 (see p.335) to select which particular places are of interest.

- Use each walk's map and the general map on p.24 to plan a route that will link up the places you would like to visit.

Alternatively, the following suggestions could be considered.

- Combine parts of Walk 1, Walk 2 and Walk 3 to explore the centre of the city. This could include the Cathedral area, George Square, the Merchant City, the River Clyde at Clyde Street and the shopping area of Buchanan Street. A number of important museums and galleries are in these areas.

- Combine parts of Walk 6 and Walk 7 to explore the West End and to visit Glasgow University, Kelvingrove Park and the Botanic Gardens. A number of important museums and galleries are in these areas.

- Follow Walk 11 which combines The Burrell Collection and Pollok House with a walk round the city's biggest park.

INTRODUCTIONS TO EACH WALK

The description of each walk is preceded by a brief summary of useful information relating to the walk. The following table indicates what kind of information is given under each heading.

Main places of interest	A list of the highlights of the walk in the order they are encountered; their numbers on the walk's map are also given. The list includes all the buildings, parks and graveyards listed in 'Glasgow at a glance' (p.18). The most important places are shown in bold type. Church buildings no longer used as churches are listed in parentheses.
Circular/linear	A circular walk starts and finishes at the same place, allowing readers to choose their own starting point if wished. Only Walks 8, 9 and 10 are not circular.
Starting point	This is usually a prominent place in the city or a station.
Finishing point	This is usually a prominent place in the city or a station.
Distance	This is given to the nearest 0.5 kilometre (and 0.5 mile).
Terrain	This gives an indication of whether pavements or paths are used and whether the route is hilly. Note that most hills in the parks can be avoided by following low-level alternative routes.
Public transport	This gives a list of all the underground and railway stations that are on (or near) the route, though not all of them are specifically mentioned in the text. The bus system is very complex and is not referred to.

The stations are part of the following systems:
1. The Glasgow Underground.
2. Stations connected with Queen Street Railway Station (denoted by 'Q').
3. Stations connected with Central Railway Station (denoted by 'C').

Sections	All the walks are divided into a number of sections and these are listed. Details of any detours are also noted. There are, as far as possible, natural divisions in the walk; they are not designed to be equal in length.
Architects	This lists all the buildings and other works by Alexander Thomson and Charles Rennie Mackintosh that are encountered during the walk. Those that are a short distance off the main route are indicated by brackets. All Place Numbers are given. Chapters 8 and 9 provide a fuller description of the life and work of these two famous architects.
Nearby walks	All other nearby walks are listed. The general map on p.24 shows all the walks and this map can be used to link parts of walks together.
Refreshments	This suggests a few specific places or areas where refreshments may be obtained. Galleries, museums and other particular buildings of interest which have catering facilities are specifically mentioned but it should be noted that inclusion here does not mean that a full meals service is necessarily available.
Notes	This gives various miscellaneous pieces of information that may be useful when planning the walk.

GENERAL NOTES

- Each walk has been carefully planned to go past as many interesting places as possible, hence the zigzags in many of the walks.

- Only in a few places does the guide specifically suggest which side of the road to walk along, leaving it up to the reader to decide which side gives the better view of the places of most personal interest.

- Small detours are suggested in the main body of the text but longer detours (more than about 250m (0.5 miles)) have been moved to the end of the particular walk the detour is in. The small detours are usually just down a street to see one or two particular buildings while a long detour visits a number of places of interest.

- Most of the buildings are given a Place Number and this number is used in the text and on each walk's map.

- Many of the buildings' descriptions include a note of its date of construction and the architect (or architectural practice) who designed it. Further information on the city's most prominent architects is given in Chapter 7.

- Inscriptions on buildings and plaques are quoted in italics in the text.

- The Glossary of Architectural Terms at the back of the book (see p.417) explains many of the architectural expressions used in the text.

- Where applicable, the opening times for museums, galleries and other places to visit are given on p.337.

Using the maps

- All prominent and interesting buildings or points of interest marked on maps have a number which corresponds to their number in the text of the walk.

- A dark line shows the general direction of the walk. Detours are also shown while the route of neighbouring walks is indicated by a dotted line.

- Statues are marked in the key to the map with an (S). Sculptures and works of art are given in italics.

- The location of Underground and railway stations is indicated. Railway lines are not marked.

- Car parks are marked, but in certain cases these are situated on waste land which may be subject to changing land use or development. A number of the car parks indicated charge for parking.

- Some paths are shown in the major parks.

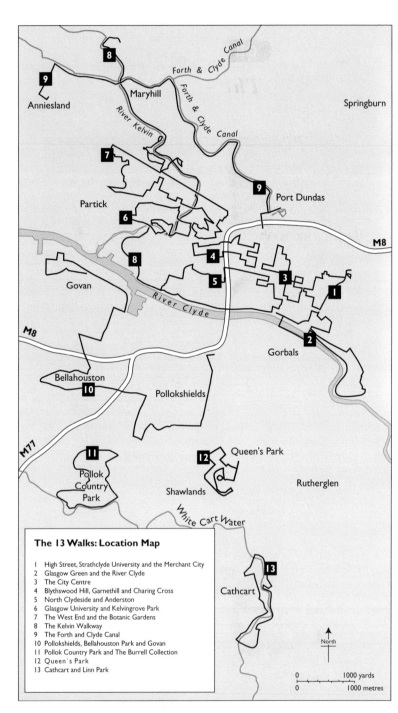

The 13 Walks: Location Map

1. High Street, Strathclyde University and the Merchant City
2. Glasgow Green and the River Clyde
3. The City Centre
4. Blythswood Hill, Garnethill and Charing Cross
5. North Clydeside and Anderston
6. Glasgow University and Kelvingrove Park
7. The West End and the Botanic Gardens
8. The Kelvin Walkway
9. The Forth and Clyde Canal
10. Pollokshields, Bellahouston Park and Govan
11. Pollok Country Park and The Burrell Collection
12. Queen's Park
13. Cathcart and Linn Park

North

0   1000 yards

0   1000 metres

CHAPTER 4

The Walks

Lampost in Cathedral Precinct showing the symbols used on the Glasgow coat of arms

High Street, Strathclyde University and the Merchant City

A walk up High Street, the city's most historic thoroughfare, to the Cathedral, Glasgow's oldest building. The route then goes through the modern campus of Strathclyde University and into the Merchant City, a maze of streets dominated by great Victorian warehouses built at the height of Glasgow's trading prosperity.

Glasgow Cathedral

Main places of interest	Tolbooth Steeple ❷ (17th-century building) **Glasgow Necropolis** ⓯ (Victorian graveyard) **St Mungo Museum of Religious Life and Art** ⓱ Glasgow Cathedral Graveyard ㉓ **Glasgow Cathedral** ㉔ (Glasgow's oldest building) **Provand's Lordship** ㉗ (Glasgow's oldest house) Strathclyde University ㉘-㊺ Collins Gallery ㊶ (Strathclyde University art gallery) St David's (Ramshorn Kirk) Graveyard ㊻ Trades Hall ㊾ (18th-century building by Robert Adam) City Halls ㊼ (large public halls) Tron Steeple ㊽ (16th-century structure)
Circular/linear	circular
Starting point	Glasgow Cross ❶
Finishing point	Glasgow Cross ❶
Distance	3 km (2 miles)
Terrain	a long hill to the cathedral; paths and steps through Strathclyde University campus; steep hill down to the Merchant City then fairly level pavements
Public transport	High Street Railway Station (Q) Argyle Street Railway Station (C)
Sections	Glasgow Cross to Cathedral Precinct Cathedral Precinct Cathedral Precinct to George Street via Strathclyde University George Street to Glasgow Cross via the Merchant City
Architects	Thomson: Glasgow Necropolis Graveyard ⓯ (monument) Mackintosh: Glasgow Necropolis Graveyard ⓯ (monument) Martyrs' Public School ㉖
Nearby walks	❷, ❸
Refreshments	St Mungo Museum of Religious Life and Art; many places in the Merchant City
Notes	Be aware of safety advice (see p.16) as both graveyards can be very quiet at times.

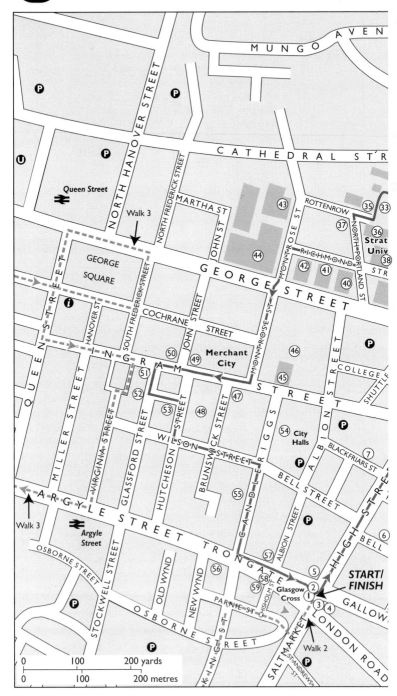

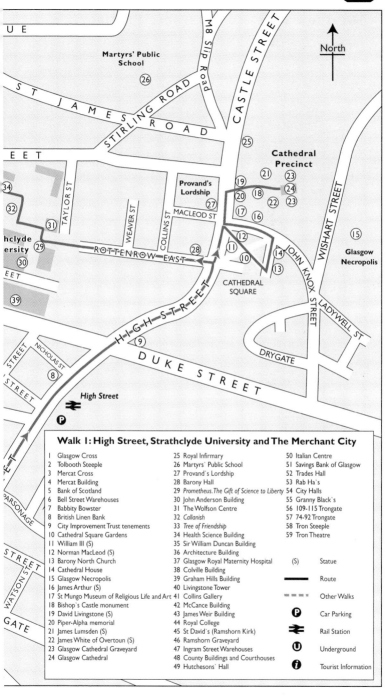

Walk 1: High Street, Strathclyde University and The Merchant City

GLASGOW CROSS TO CATHEDRAL PRECINCT

Glasgow Cross ❶ is one of the city's most historic sites, though most of its present buildings are relatively modern. Five important streets meet here: High Street, Gallowgate, London Road, Saltmarket and Trongate, making this a busy and very important junction. High Street was the city's main street from medieval times. It ran from the Cathedral towards the river; Gallowgate was the route to Edinburgh, passing Gallows Muir (the hanging place); London Road led southwards to England; the Saltmarket was where salt sellers were established; Trongate followed the north bank of the River Clyde towards the important town of Dumbarton.

The seven-storey **Tolbooth Steeple** ❷ (1625-7, John Boyd) is the Cross's most important feature and it is topped by a clock and a stone crown. This was once part of a much larger building, the Tolbooth, which provided accommodation for the Town Clerk's office, the council hall and the city prison. The debtors' prison had a steady stream of inmates who elected their own provost and generally ran the place like an exclusive club. They produced their own regulations, including one from 1789 which stated: 'It is firmly and irrevocably agreed upon that the members of these rooms shall not permit the jailor or turnkeys to force any person or persons into their apartments, who are thought unworthy of being admitted.' There was even a rule about celebrating freedom: 'Every member, when liberated, shall treat his fellow-prisoners with one shilling's worth of what liquor they think proper.'

The Tolbooth provided the backdrop to many of the city's dramas and it was here that witches, thieves and murderers were summarily dealt with, by hanging if necessary. It also had a special platform from which proclamations were read, important in the days before general literacy. The paved area (the 'plainstanes') in front of the Tolbooth was the 'in place' to be seen and here the rich paraded in their finery, particularly the Tobacco Lords (whose activities are described on pp.47 and 93), attired in red cloaks and sporting gold-topped canes.

The cross developed as a communications hub, with stagecoaches from Edinburgh and London bringing visitors and news, and a reading room in the Tolbooth providing newspapers. However, as the city expanded and moved westwards, the Tolbooth was abandoned and eventually demolished, leaving the steeple as an isolated reminder of bygone days. This tragic loss of an important building was the result of the work of the City Improvement Trust which had the unenviable task of ridding the city of its slums.

The **Mercat Cross** ❸ (1930, Edith Burnet Hughes (née Burnet)) stands at the south-eastern corner of Glasgow Cross. Market crosses like this are found all over Scotland to mark the places where markets were legally held and this example represents one removed from Glasgow Cross in 1659. A town's cross was often its symbolic centre as markets and other communal events took place beside it and the absence of such an important monument must have caused a bit of a dent in civic pride.

Glasgow Cross: The Tolbooth Steeple

The new cross was paid for by Dr William Black and his wife and its inauguration on 24 April 1930 was a day of great pomp and ceremony. The next day's *Glasgow Herald* reported that:

> *Probably not since 1649 when Charles II was proclaimed King to the accompaniment of a carillon from the city bells, has the Mercat Cross been the centre of such striking ceremonial. . . The gold, scarlet, and blue robes of the Lyon King of Arms and his heralds and pursuivants struck a note of brilliance, and stood out in bold relief against the black and ermine gowns of the Lord Provost and Magistrates. . . That pomp and circumstance, those gorgeous robes, the royal greeting, the arresting sound of the trumpets, the whole magnificent pageant, belonged not to that day alone, but to centuries of that past life which has made us a great nation.*

The structure is in the form of an octagonal tower with the cross (which is topped by a heraldic unicorn holding a shield) rising high above it. On the tower's western side a plaque declares that this is *The Mercat Cross of Glasgow built in the year of grace 1929*. Above that is the coat of arms of the city with its motto *Let Glasgow flourish*. On the tower's eastern side there is a badge (with a thistle and a St Andrew's Cross) and the Latin phrase *Nemo me impune lacessit* ('No-one provokes me with impunity'). This is the motto of Scotland and can be translated as 'Wha daur meddle wi' me?' in Scots. Above that is an unidentified coat of arms (with a lion, a knight's head and a shield on which is a St Andrew's Cross) and a Latin phrase.

Behind the cross stands the tall and many-sided **Mercat Building** ❹ (1925-28, A. Graham Henderson). This unusual building has a pair of giant columns above which is a space with the shape of a semi-dome; at the top is a winged head on the prow of a boat. Six large statues of semi-clad male and female figures decorate the building's front and sides. These figures are seated or crouched and hold various tools or other artefacts associated with Glasgow's trades.

On the opposite corner of Glasgow Cross stands the **Bank of Scotland** ❺ (1922, A. Graham Henderson), whose curved frontage allows space for traffic going round the Tolbooth Steeple. It is built in the same style as the Mercat Building.

Walk up **High Street.** This was the most important thoroughfare of the medieval city as it ran downhill from the Cathedral to Glasgow Cross. The city gradually expanded eastwards and westwards from here. In the centuries that followed, industry generally developed in the eastern side of the city while commercial premises and better housing were found in the west. Weather played an important part in this differentiation: since the wind most frequently blows from the south-west, those who could afford to move westwards did so to be upwind of the factories' noxious fumes. For the same reasons, Glasgow's numerous hills almost inevitably have the more expensive houses at their summit where the breeze keeps the air fresher and cleaner.

To the west of High Street is a great collection of warehouses (precursors of today's department stores) in what has become known as the **Merchant City** (for a description of its development see p.47). With Glasgow's changing fortunes many of these became dilapidated after the Second World War but have now been renovated and converted into blocks of flats; this, in turn, has helped to revitalize the area. A good example of new life being breathed into old buildings can be seen on the right, at 105-69 Bell Street, where the massive **Bell Street Warehouses** ❻ (1882-3), originally built for the Glasgow and South Western Railway, have been converted into houses.

Continue up High Street and on the left, in Blackfriars Street, stands the pub **Babbity Bowster** ❼ (*c.* 1794, Robert and John Adam). It was originally built as a house and it still has its original Roman Doric doorway. The building was derelict before its conversion to a pub in 1984-5 and the restoration won well-deserved awards. The 'Babbity Bowster' is an old Scottish dance.

To the east of High Street stood the medieval **Glasgow University** (often referred to as the Old College), originally founded in 1451 by Bishop William Turnbull. In 1460 it was given land here adjacent to the Blackfriars Monastery and later gifts of adjoining land enabled a large set of buildings and a garden to be built in the seventeenth century.

In the 1870s the land was sold to build a huge railway goods yard and most of the university buildings were destroyed, though a fine staircase and parts of the main front of the building were transferred to the new university site in the West End. Glasgow would today be a very different place if the university hadn't sold out to the railway developers and moved to a suburb which at that time wasn't even in Glasgow. Today, the railway goods yard has moved out but street names like College Street and Blackfriars Street act as reminders of the area's history.

Few of the buildings in this part of High Street have much ornate decoration, but there is a curiosity at 215 High Street. This is the former **British Linen Bank ❽** (1905, Salmon, Son & Gillespie), which has some Renaissance styling, a cupola roof and a crowstepped gable. Pallas, the Greek goddess of wisdom and weaving, tops the building, a suitable figure for the original occupier. Further information on the history of the bank is given on p.290.

At the side of the building is a plaque inscribed *On this site stood the house in which the poet Campbell lived. Born 1777. Died 1844.* Thomas Campbell's statue stands in George Square (see p.85). The plaque also shows a gabled house and people dressed in early nineteenth-century styles.

The north-eastern corner of the junction of High Street and George Street/Duke Street is overlooked by the five-storey **City Improvement Trust tenements ❾** (1900-01; Burnet, Boston & Carruthers). This bears the inscription *City Improvement Trust*, the name of the body which was charged with the task of cleaning up the squalid living conditions that existed in the city in the second half of the nineteenth century. Learning from visits to Paris, to see the work of Baron Haussmann, the trustees were very successful in adapting the traditional tenement house style to rehouse many thousands of people.

High Street curves round and climbs quite steeply through a canyon of tenements up to Rottenrow, which is met on the left. This spot was originally known as the **Bell o' the Brae** and a village developed here in medieval times. Tradition has it that around 1297, during the Scottish Wars of Independence, William Wallace's forces attacked and defeated a force of English soldiers here, with Wallace personally dispatching Earl Percy, the English Governor.

High Street now leads to the historic group of buildings in the Cathedral Precinct.

CATHEDRAL PRECINCT

The **Cathedral Precinct** starts at Rottenrow as the High Street becomes Castle Street, named after the Bishop's Castle (sometimes known as the Bishop's Palace) which once stood near here. The Cathedral buildings enjoyed a strong hillside site, though the crown of the hill was occupied by the castle, a dominating position which reflected the political power of the Church and its bishops. The first records of the castle are from 1258 but the only part that remains is found beside the St Mungo Museum.

The building on the left at Rottenrow is the former Barony Parish Church, now the Barony Hall of the University of Strathclyde, whose campus lies to the west. The church is described on p.45. On the right as you walk past it are the **Cathedral Square Gardens** ❿ (1879, John Carrick).

On the west side of the garden is an equestrian statue of **King William III** ⓫, curiously dressed in Roman attire. Intriguingly, the horse's tail is said to be designed to move in the wind by means of a ball and socket joint. In front of the plinth is a plaque declaring *In commemoration of the Tercentenary of the Glorious Revolution of 1688-89*. This refers to the removal of the Catholic King James II of Britain (VII of Scotland) and his replacement by the Protestant Queen Mary and Prince William of Orange. English and Latin inscriptions extol the many virtues of 'King Billy' and reflect the very partisan attitudes of the subscibers to this monument, which was erected in 1735.

Continue walking past the statue then turn sharp right to follow a wide path through the gardens. On the left is a statue of **Norman MacLeod** ⓬ (1812-72) by John G. Mossman (1881-2). He was minister of the Barony Parish Church from 1851 to 1872 as well as chaplain to Queen Victoria. He served as Moderator of the Church of Scotland and was the author of a number of books, including the interesting *Reminiscences of a Highland Parish* (1867) about everyday life in west and north-west Scotland.

Continue through the gardens and pass a colourful **mosaic** on the left. It has a large dove of peace and contains the words *Let peace flourish*.

At the eastern end of the gardens is the former **Barony North Church** ⓭ (1878-80, John Honeyman), now the Glasgow Evangelical Church. This is Italian Renaissance in style and is unusual for a Glasgow church as it has a number of prominent statues: St Paul and St Peter are in niches in the two towers while St Mathew, St Mark, St Luke and St John grace the balustrade. At their feet lie, respectively, the heads of a man, a lion, a calf and an eagle.

Turn left and at the end of the street stands the former **Cathedral House** ⓮ (1894-6, Campbell Douglas & Morrison), now the Cathedral House Hotel. This was originally built to accommodate former prisoners by the Discharged Prisoners' Aid Society. The infamous Duke Street Prison, which was closed in 1955 and demolished in 1958, stood not very far away from here.

Cross John Knox Street. On the northern side of it (and opposite Cathedral House) is the side entrance to the **Glasgow Necropolis** ⓯. This is described separately on p.351 in Chapter 6. Look downhill to see the brightly coloured pipes and other industrial equipment which belong to the Wellpark Brewery, said to have been founded as far back as 1556 by the Tennent family.

Turn left and walk up John Knox Street. On the right is a statue of **James Arthur** ⑯ (1819-85). He was one of many successful merchants who was involved in exporting great quantities of the city's manufactured goods. The sculptor was G. A. Lawson (1893).

Keep following John Knox Street to its junction with Castle Street. Here stands the **St Mungo Museum of Religious Life and Art** ⑰ (1989-92, Ian Begg), which is housed in a modern building in Scots Baronial style. The museum also serves as a visitor centre for the cathedral. The design of the building has caused much heated debate over whether it should have been built in this or a more modern style.

This remarkable museum deals with various religious philosophies and uses the city's art collections to illustrate these themes. The first gallery on the first floor contains **religious works of art**, some of them quite outstanding. The best known is the painting *Christ of St John of the Cross* (1951) by the Spanish surrealist painter Salvador Dali (1904-89) – a haunting image with dramatic lighting and a remarkable perspective. The painting was purchased in 1952 by the Director of Glasgow's museums, Tom John Honeyman, at a cost of £9200. At the time, this was regarded as a terrible extravagance by some people but it has become one of the city's most popular paintings. The windows in this gallery are used to display various stained-glass panels, a number of which are from former Glasgow churches built around the turn of the nineteenth century; other panels date back to the fourteenth or fifteenth centuries and were

St Mungo Museum of Religious Life and Art

collected by Sir William Burrell (see p.308). Hinduism is represented here by a large and beautifully made eighteenth- or nineteenth-century bronze figure of the Hindu god Shiva. This depicts him as the Lord of the Dance performing on top of a black dwarf who represents ignorance. Muslim art, in the form of a modern calligraphic design *The attributes of divine perfection* by Ahmed Moustafa (1943–), follows the Muslim tradition that its art should use the letters of the Arabic alphabet instead of showing living creatures. Of much greater vintage is a brightly coloured Egyptian mummy mask dating from about 500BC.

The next gallery on this floor deals with **religious life** and contains a bewildering array of artefacts used by people of various beliefs while celebrating rites of passage or during festivals. Buddhism, Christianity, Hinduism, Islam, Judaism and Sikhism are each dealt with in individual displays and there are other exhibits from lesser-known cultures. The artefacts range from a bizarre Mexican dancing skeleton (1992) to various types of bridal wear, but it is the sheer diversity of ways various cultures have of celebrating similar events that makes this section particularly thought-provoking. However, it is not just the peaceful and sociable nature of life that is dealt with here, and the bloody conflicts perpetrated by, or against, people of different religious persuasions are depicted as examples of humanity's intolerance.

The top floor gallery deals with the **history of religion** in Glasgow and the West of Scotland. The displays cover a considerable period of time and the artefacts include very old items such as a Roman altar found near the Antonine Wall (see p.180). Many of the more modern objects are items used in ceremonies or mementoes of the campaigns of religious organizations such as the temperance movement (described on p.62).

The might of the Roman Catholic Church in Scotland was toppled by the sixteenth-century protestant Reformation, ushering in the national Church of Scotland. The numbers of Catholics decreased dramatically and in 1778 it was reported that there were only thirty known Catholics in Glasgow. This number increased substantially with the nineteenth-century influx of poor from Ireland and the Scottish Highlands, a change which produced terrible tensions in the city, many of them exacerbated by blatant discrimination against Catholics. Today, most of these problems have abated, but the continued existence of denominational schools and the intense rivalry between Rangers and Celtic football fans perpetuate the two separate traditions. In the twentieth century, Scotland's links with other countries in the British Empire led to a new wave of immigrants, this time mainly from Asia, coming to the city and bringing their cultures with them.

There is a good view of the museum's Zen Garden, Glasgow Cathedral and the Glasgow Necropolis from the top gallery's picture window.

The museum's **Zen Garden**, *Where we are* (1993) by Yasutaro Tanaka, stands behind the building. Its raked gravel bed and undulating mossy 'islands' are punctuated by large boulders. Zen gardens are full of Buddhist symbolism and are designed according to strict rules. In essence, their traditional simplicity and use of natural materials helps the uncluttered mind to contemplate.

Walk a short distance up Castle Street then turn right at the award-winning landscaped area between the museum, the Cathedral and the Royal Infirmary. This L-shaped space is decorated by ornate lampstandards depicting the four elements (fish, bird, tree and bell) from the city's coat of arms. This open space has a number of interesting statues and memorials.

Close to the pavement is a bronze **three-dimensional model** of the area showing all the nearby buildings of interest. Then, looking as if it is coming up from underneath the museum, there is a slightly raised platform of sandstone blocks which is part of the old Bishop's Castle. Keep following the northern wall of the museum to find the site of the castle's well. Just a few paces from here stands the granite **Bishop's Castle monument** ⓲ which carries an engraving of the Castle and the Cathedral, together with the inscription *To mark the site of the bishop's palace which was built in the thirteenth century and was finally removed in 1792.*

Walk back to Castle Street to see the imposing statue of **David Livingstone** ⓳ (1813-73). The scenes engraved on the plinth depict events during his travels in Africa. Livingstone studied medicine and divinity in Glasgow's Anderson's College (see p.212) and in 1841 he started the first of his three great explorations of Africa. He first travelled northward from Cape Town through the Kalahari Desert, then west to the Atlantic Ocean, then east following the Zambesi River to the Indian Ocean, on which he 'discovered' the Victoria Falls. He returned to Africa in 1858 and it was on his last expedition, which started in 1866, that a number of groups set out in search of him, including one led by Henry Morton Stanley, who eventually found him, hailing him with the well-known phrase 'Doctor Livingstone, I presume?'. On his death, Livingstone's body was carried by his party 2400km (1500 miles) to the coast. The statue was sculpted by John G. Mossman (1875-9).

Just to the south of this statue is the **Piper–Alpha memorial** plaque ⓴ to the 167 men who lost their lives on 6 July 1988 when a large North Sea oil platform exploded after a massive gas leak.

Now walk towards the Cathedral. The statue of **James Lumsden** ㉑ (1778-1856) is on the left, sheltering beneath the tall Royal Infirmary (see below), its position a reflection of the work he did for this important institution. He was Lord Provost of the city in the middle of the nineteenth century, a time of great economic expansion, and in 1838 he was one of the founders of the Clydesdale Bank which was started in order to finance the expansion of Glasgow's merchants' world-wide activities. John G. Mossman sculpted this statue in 1862.

Walk through the open area on the right between the museum and the Cathedral. This leads to the statue of **James White of Overtoun** ㉒ (1812-84) by John G. Mossman and Frank Leslie (1890). White was involved in the manufacturing of chemicals and his family's Shawfield Chemical Works was one of the biggest of its kind in Britain. The chemical works were, by any standards, a horribly dangerous place and scant attention was paid to the conditions and wages of the employees. Men laboured twelve hours a day and since relatively little money was spent on mechanisation, they worked closely with very corrosive materials; indeed, the men were called 'White's canaries' on account of the yellow dust that stuck to their clothes. The local community suffered too: the fumes were noxious, a discharge pipe let greenish-yellow liquid into the Clyde and waste material was dumped on the site for future generations to worry about.

In the 1890s the firm was under the control of White's son, Lord Overtoun (1843-1908), who was involved in all sorts of religious and good causes, as well as being a powerful figure in the Liberal Party (his peerage was from Gladstone). In 1899 (while he was preparing an ostentatious religious revival campaign) his workers went on strike for a wage increase and Keir Hardie (editor of *Labour Leader*) weighed in on their behalf. The dispute became a *cause célèbre* and widened into a crusade against working conditions and the effects of Overtoun's factory on the health of his workers and the local community. Stories like these should be remembered when celebrating the 'success' of Glasgow's manufacturing industries. There was a price to pay.

Directly behind the statue is the elaborate main entrance gate to the Glasgow Necropolis, which is described on p.351.

Glasgow Cathedral Graveyard ㉓ (see p.360) lies around the Cathedral and also to its north, under the shadow of the Royal Infirmary – hardly a reassuring sight when patients look out the windows!

To the east of the cathedral is a steep-sided ravine through which ran the (now-culverted) Molendinar Burn. Beyond it is the Glasgow Necropolis.

Glasgow Cathedral ㉔ stands behind the museum. The history of this site goes back to the fifth century when the missionary St Ninian consecrated a graveyard here. In the sixth century a priest, who later became St Mungo, buried a holy man by the name of Fergus here. St Mungo later became Glasgow's bishop, founded a religious community and built a church in which he was himself buried in *c*. 612. His shrine later became a place of pilgrimage and much later he was 'elevated' to the role of patron saint of Glasgow and his deeds became celebrated on the city's coat of arms (a full description of these is given on p.415). The earliest stone church on this site was erected in the eleventh century, to be succeeded by a new building consecrated in 1197. The thirteenth century saw large extensions (the Quire, the Lower Church and the two Chapter Houses) which essentially form the core of the building as it is today. Two large towers were later erected at the west end but these were demolished in the 1840s.

With the Cathedral, the Bishop's Castle and all the ancillary buildings, this seat of Church power wielded much influence up to the sixteenth-century Protestant Reformation. After that, the cathedral was divided in order to accommodate three smaller churches and the power and wealth of the Church waned considerably. Today it is Scotland's most important thirteenth-century building and it is the city's most impressive structure, but one which has far less general significance to the city than it had in previous centuries.

The Cathedral is entered by a door in its southern side which leads into the **Nave**. The view of the Nave is at first dominated by two rows of large pillars which support the bulk of the building. Light floods in through the upper and lower sets of windows, but the eye is soon attracted to the stained-glass windows, especially at the western end. Here, Adam and Eve are the main figures in a depiction of the Creation. The fine timber ceiling dates from around the fourteenth century. In the Nave's north-western corner lies the Old Bell, gifted in the first half of the sixteenth century. On the north wall are various memorials, including a very fine plaque to Peter Lowe, whose contribution to medicine is described on p.361. One plaque on the wall is to **Sir William Smith** (1854-1914) who founded the Boys' Brigade in 1883. He had, as the *Hillhead Album* notes, 'a heritage of upright living firmly disciplined by exemplary military service', and he decided to use paramilitary methods to 'subdue' his (presumably unruly) Sunday School pupils in the Woodside Mission Hall. The combination of military-style church parades and plenty of sporting activity was very appealing to many boys and his ideas caught on. Soon there were companies throughout Scotland, and the organisation became so successful internationally that in the 1970s it had over 250,000 members world-wide.

The nave's southern wall has many military memorials and one prominent plaque on this side is dedicated to Dr Andrew Ure (1778-1857). He was obviously a very talented and busy person as he was *for many years Professor of Chemistry, Mechanics, Natural Philosophy and* Materia Medica [medicine] *at the Andersonian University of Glasgow.* The university was presumably a bit short of staff! Towards the eastern end of the nave stands a wooden pulpit and beyond that stairs on either side go to the North and South Transepts which are dominated by their fine twentieth-century windows commemorating various land, sea and air forces. The eastern end of the Nave is divided from the Quire by the Quire Screen which probably dates from the fifteenth century. The figures above it may represent the Seven Deadly Sins or the Seven Ages of Man. The organ sits above this.

Go through the Quire Screen to the **Quire**, which is essentially a chapel dating from the middle of the thirteenth century. It is lit by numerous stained-glass windows, with the eastern set featuring the four evangelists: Matthew, Mark, Luke and John. The oak ceiling has numerous painted bosses which symbolise the life of Christ. In the Quire's **Chancel**, the wooden pulpit dates from 1595 when it was made for the nearby (and long-gone) Barony Church. The lectern is in the form of an eagle which was made in France in the seventeenth century. The carved communion table, with a relief showing the Last Supper, is nineteenth-century Scottish.

The **Ambulatory** is behind the Chancel, with each of its four chapels incorporating a pair of stained-glass windows. The southern chapel is that of St Stephen and St Lawrence and it is dominated by the painted monument to Archbishop James Law (1615-32). The Chapel of St Martin has a display of pewter communion plates and flagons, and a Bible of 1617.

A door by the Ambulatory's northern chapel leads to the **Upper Chapter House** or Sacristy. This well-proportioned room was added in the mid-thirteenth century and rebuilt in the fifteenth century. Light floods in through its nineteenth-century stained-glass windows, showing off its fine stonework and tiled floor. On the southern wall is a carved royal coat of arms (c. 1810). The Scottish unicorn holds the English Cross of St George, while the English lion holds the Scottish Cross of St Andrew. Its mottoes are *Nemo me impune lacessit* ('No-one provokes me with impunity') and *Honi soit qui mal y pense* ('Evil be to him who evil thinks').

Head back to the nave and descend the North Transept stairs to reach the **Lower Church**. To the left of the stairs is the Covenanters' Memorial, commemorating nine men who were hanged and beheaded at Glasgow Cross in 1684; this gravestone was originally in the Cathedral's graveyard. The Covenanting period is described on p.371. Just beyond this memorial are the two Bishops' Castle Stones. These two blocks were originally placed on the castle's gateway by Archbishop Gavin Dunbar (1524-47). They carry the coat of arms of Dunbar, James Houston (the sub-dean) and King James V. The Lower Church has a forest of stone pillars and four of them, situated below the position of the pre-Reformation altar, guard the **Chapel and Tomb of St Mungo**. This marks St Mungo's original burial place; later, probably in the twelfth century, his remains were moved upstairs behind the Choir's High Altar. To the west of the tomb is the St Kentigern Tapestry (St Kentigern is another name for St Mungo). The middle panel contains the four important St Mungo symbols: a fish with a ring in its mouth, a bird, a tree and a bell. Glasgow's coat of arms is based on these four elements. Two thirteenth-century floor slabs lie in front of the tapestry. In the northern part of the chapel are nineteenth-century German stained-glass panels, a great number of which were installed in the windows in 1859-64; most have been removed and some of them are on display here.

In the north-eastern corner of the Lower Church, a carved doorway leads down to the **Lower Chapter House** which was built in the thirteenth century. A stone bench runs along the walls and by the eastern wall is a canopied seat, topped by the arms of Bishop William Lauder (1408-25).

Leave the Lower Chapter House to look at the four chapels in the eastern wall of the Lower Church. The second chapel, which is decorated with richly coloured stained-glass windows, is the **Chapel of St Peter and St Paul**. To its right lies the headless effigy of Robert Wishart (c. 1240-1316). He became bishop in 1271 but the quiet monastic life was not for him. Bishops held an important political position in the country and he joined William Wallace and Robert the Bruce in their fight against the English during the Wars of Independence. He was captured twice, in 1297 and 1306. Next to it is the **Chapel of St Andrew**. St Andrew, Scotland's patron saint, was one of Christ's apostles who preached in Asia Minor and Russia (he is also patron saint of Russia). Tradition has it that he was crucified at Patras in Greece on an X-shaped cross, hence the shape of the white cross on Scotland's flag. His relics are said to have been moved to St Andrews on Scotland's east coast, later giving the city its name, and giving the country its reason for adopting him. In the south-eastern corner is the **Chapel of St John the Evangelist**. St Mungo's well is sited here and he is depicted in the window above it, baptizing the child of Rhydderch, King of Strathclyde. Fragments of parts of the building, dating from the thirteenth century onwards, are displayed here. When the Cathedral was divided into three churches, the lower church was occupied by the Barony Church; when its members left in 1801 the floor of the eastern side (where the four small chapels are) was covered with soil to a depth of 1.5m (5ft) and used as a burial ground. The parts of the pillars above the soil were then painted black and decorated with white 'tears', an old Scots mourning custom.

Head westwards along the south aisle. Just before the St Kentigern Tapestry is passed, the lid of a twelfth- or thirteenth-century tomb chest can be seen on the left. It has the worn outline of a human figure on it. The corner of the wall nearest the chest has a shaft which is much more decorated than other shafts nearby; this, and the wall, are late twelfth century and are the oldest parts of the Cathedral.

Leave the Lower Church by following the south aisle. Turn left halfway up the stairs to the nave and enter the **Blacader Aisle** which was built by Archbishop Robert Blacader (1483-1508). This is a bright and airy room, its ceiling's ribs decorated with carved bosses carrying foliage, coats of arms and grotesque faces. The stained-glass windows add splashes of colour to the white walls and pillars.

Leave the Cathedral and head towards Castle Street; on the right is the huge bulk of the **Royal Infirmary** ㉕ which all but dwarfs the Cathedral. This enormous complex was built in stages on land previously occupied for centuries by the Bishop's Castle. The first infirmary building was started in 1792 to a design of Robert and James Adam but this was replaced in 1907 by a 1901 design of James Miller. Square towers, cupolas and balustrades are a feature of this massive structure, to which large additions were made in the 1970s and 1980s. The infirmary has been associated with Glasgow University since its inception and much important work has been done here, the most famous being that by Joseph Lister (1827-1912) who pioneered the principle of antiseptic surgery. He discovered how carbolic acid could be used to keep wounds, dressings and equipment germ-free, thus saving countless deaths from post-operative diseases such as gangrene. His pioneering work is fully described on p.203. This was also a leading hospital in the development of the diagnostic uses of X-rays.

A statue of the enthroned Queen Victoria is on the southern side of the Infirmary; she is holding an orb and a sceptre, symbols of royal power. The orb is a sphere (representing the universe) and this Roman symbol has a Christian cross placed on top of it. The sceptre (an ornamented rod or staff) is also an ancient (pre-Christian) symbol representing authority.

Follow the perimeter of the building to its main entrance in Castle Street. It can now be seen that the Infirmary is made up of a number of impressive buildings, the northernmost of which is the Robert and James Dick Block (1909). Opposite its entrance is the single-storey Lister Lecture Theatre (1926-7) and a plaque on the theatre wall marks the spot where he worked; the phrase on the plaque *Opifer per orbem* means 'Bringing aid throughout the world'.

Some of the oldest parts of the Infirmary can be seen just a short distance farther up Castle Street. An archway carries the date *MDCCCXXXII* (1832) and leads into the hospital complex. Beside it stands the former **Blind Asylum** (1879, William Landless), the most striking part of which is a tall and slim hexagonal clock tower. It, and other parts of the building, are awash with Scots Baronial features such as turrets, shields and waterspouts. A statue of Christ (1881, Charles Grassby) which shelters from the weather under a stone canopy, looks over the street. His hand is raised as if giving a blessing and a child is by his knee, having his sight restored. Below this is the inscription *A.D. 1881 Presented by Sir Charles Tennant Bart*. A doorway a little farther up Castle Street carries the inscription *Private entrance* in highly elaborate script.

From the Blind Asylum, look westwards to the red three-storey former **Martyrs' Public School** ㉖ (1895-8, Charles Rennie Mackintosh); it is easily recognized by the three unusual-looking ventilators on its roof. It is described on p.412.

Walk back down Castle Street to the St Mungo Museum, then cross the road to reach **Provand's Lordship** ㉗. This is the city's oldest house and is now one of Glasgow's museums, exhibiting furniture and living conditions in medieval times. It was originally built in 1471 by Bishop Andrew Muirhead to house the chaplain of the nearby St Nicholas Hospital. The Cathedral was served by numerous clergy who lived in manses around the precinct and received their financial support (or 'prebend') from various surrounding parishes. This house was supported by the lands of Provan (to the east of here) so the canon living here was called the Lord of Provan and the house became known as Provand's Lordship. His country house was Provan Hall (described on p.344).

Much of the building's exterior is medieval, with rubble-built walls and traditional crow-stepped gables. However, the western extension was added in the seventeenth century; the windows are probably seventeenth or eighteenth century in origin and the northern end was altered in the nineteenth century. There are few external decorations but there is an old sundial on the southern gable. In 1670 it was extended by the tailor who then occupied the building; since then it has had many functions,

Provand's Lordship

including accommodating the local hangman in a lean-to which was built for him. It has also served as an alehouse and as a barber's shop. Inevitably, the building's fabric deteriorated over the centuries but it was 'saved' early in the twentieth century and, in 1970, it was taken over as a city museum.

The main part of the building has three floors, each with three rooms, and these contain many interesting items of furniture dating from the sixteenth, seventeenth and eighteenth centuries; some of these were originally collected by Sir William Burrell. There are also numerous paintings (mainly portraits), some stained-glass windows and various interesting bits of 'Glaswegiana'. On the first floor is a reconstruction of the furnished chamber of Cuthbert Simson who lived here as a chaplain at the beginning of the sixteenth century. Tall visitors should take care when entering the rooms as the doorways' stone lintels are very low!

Behind the house is the **St Nicholas Garden** (1995). This contains a Physic Garden with herbs and other plants which were used in fifteenth-century medicine. Within it is the Knot Garden whose shape is based on an ancient Celtic knot design. Thirteen grotesque heads are displayed on the walls of the surrounding cloister. These are the well-known Tontine Faces, many of which were originally part of the external decoration of the Tontine Building which was erected around 1760 beside the Tolbooth at Glasgow Cross. The original ten faces were sculpted by Mungo Naismith and were supposed to be based on particular people in Glasgow. The faces were removed around 1867 and the story of their disappearance, recovery, re-use, loss and so on is a delight (or frustration) to local historians; to make matters even more complex, new faces have been added at various times! Three sculpted coats of arms are also on display at the north-western corner of the garden. The one on the left has two shields: the upper has the arms of the

Earl of Argyll on his marriage to Elizabeth Stewart and the lower celebrates the marriage of a Campbell to a Stewart. The middle sculpture shows the arms of Scotland and comes from the mansion of Silvercraigs. Finally, the Glasgow coat of arms on the right came from the Old College in High Street.

An open garden stands farther to the west (and beyond the museum's perimeter wall). Within it is a bronze three-dimensional plan of the Cathedral area, a finely carved sundial and an orchard.

Walk back down Castle Street to the Barony Hall and turn right at Rottenrow.

CATHEDRAL PRECINCT TO GEORGE STREET VIA STRATHCLYDE UNIVERSITY

Strathclyde University has its John Anderson Campus on the hilly ground that lies at the top of Rottenrow. Readers needing more information should visit the university's Village Office which is well signposted.

The university traces its history back to **John Anderson** (1726-96) who was Professor of Natural Philosophy (Physics) at Glasgow University from 1757 to his death. During his tenure he had many clashes with the extremely conservative university establishment and he rebelled against what he considered was academic elitism. He founded classes which were aimed at encouraging working people to study the practical applications of science and he emphasised that *useful learning* was the stated aim of this revolutionary educational advance, implying that the other professors' courses were not particularly useful at all! However, he went further than simply establishing lecture courses, and his will contained detailed plans for what later became Anderson's University (1796), a science-based institute which held its first meetings in the Grammar School buildings in George Street. Gradually the new university's breadth of subjects developed and included arts and medicine (the history of this faculty is described on p.212). During the next century there were numerous splits, amalgamations and many changes of name, and in 1912 it became the Royal Technical College, better known as 'The Tech'. This advance led to students being able to sit degree examinations. In 1964 this became Strathclyde University and since then it has developed into one of the country's foremost universities, building on a long-standing reputation for excellence in the applied sciences.

The university's longest-established teaching building is on George Street (see p.46) and over the last few decades much of the land lying between it and the Cathedral has been taken over and new buildings have been erected. It has to be said that few of these are of great architectural merit, but a walk through the campus offers an interesting glimpse into how a city-centre site can be gradually transformed in order to cater for the diverse needs of a large university community. In addition, two interesting churches have been taken over: the Barony Parish Church (see below) and the Ramshorn Kirk. In the 1990s, Jordanhill College of Education joined Strathclyde as a Faculty of Education and this has given the university a new and extensive parkland campus in the west of the city.

The former Barony Parish Church (1886-9, J. J. Burnet and J. A. Campbell), stands at the bottom of Rottenrow. It is now the ceremonial **Barony Hall** **28** of the university. This very fine Gothic building is constructed in a warm red sandstone and is loosely modelled on the cathedral in Gerona, northern Spain. It has been described as possibly the most important Victorian Gothic church in Scotland, though students sitting examinations might not always take the opportunity to enjoy the design. Its basic plan is T-shaped, with additions such as the prominent porch in the south-eastern angle. The height of the southern end is accentuated by three tall, narrow windows which are flanked by buttresses. There is no tower or spire but the roof does have a French-inspired flèche.

Ascend Rottenrow and pass the red-brick students' halls of residence to a large galvanized steel sculpture**, *Prometheus. The Gift of Science to Liberty*** **29** (1994, Jack Sloan). Beside it, a plaque quotes *And fire has proved for men a teacher in every art, their grand resource* (Aeschylus, *Prometheus Bound*). In Greek mythology, Prometheus stole fire from heaven for the human race.

Pass to the right of the statue and climb some steps. On the left is the **John Anderson Building** **30** (1968-71, Building Design Partnership). This houses the department of Natural Philosophy, known elsewhere as Physics.

On the right is **The Wolfson Centre** **31** (1970-1, Morris & Steedman), the bio-engineering centre.

A small **park** is now reached and this is decorated by a sculpture comprising a set of rusted steel posts. This is *Callanish* **32** (1971, Gerald Laing), based on the famous circle of standing stones on Lewis which dates back to the third millennium BC.

In the centre of the park is a *Tree of Friendship* **33**, an Indian Bean Tree planted in 1996 to mark the 125th anniversary of the birth of the Indian nationalist leader Mahatma Gandhi (1869-1948), the world's best-known pacifist leader who did so much to help win independence from Britain.

Go anticlockwise round the park, later following a little stream. The building to the north of the park is the **Health Science Building** **34** (1996-8, Riach and Hall).

At the end of the path round the park, the building on the right is the **Sir William Duncan Building** **35** (1974-5, G. R. M. Kennedy & Partners), home of the Strathclyde Graduate Business School.

On the the left is the **Architecture Building** ❻ 1964-7, Frank Fielden & Associates); interestingly, Fielden was the Professor of Architecture when he designed this.

Here the route reaches the junction of Rottenrow and North Portland Street. The large sandstone building at this corner, the only building mentioned in this section that is not part of the university, is the **Glasgow Royal Maternity Hospital** ❼ (1903, Robert A. Bryden). The history of Glasgow's maternity hospitals goes back to 1792 and a number of premises were used until this site was taken over in 1858. While it might seem a misfortune for Glasgow's babies to start their life in a place called Rottenrow, its name may have been derived from 'Route de roi' ('the king's way'). However, there are many other possible derivations of the name, enough to keep local historians arguing for a very long time!

Turn left, down the very steep North Portland Street. On the left is the **Colville Building** ❽ (1964-7, Sir Robert Mathew, Johnson -Marshall & Partners) which is used by Strathclyde University's engineering departments.

Below that is the **Graham Hills Building** ❾ (1960-1, Arthur Swift & Partners), used by languages and arts.

Turn right at Richmond Street. At the corner is the tall **Livingstone Tower** ❿ (1965-8), in which are located languages, arts, mathematics and computing. It is named after David Livingstone (whose exploits are described on p.37).

Following that is the **Collins Building** (1973) in which is housed the **Collins Gallery** ⓸. This small gallery was founded in 1973 and it holds temporary exhibitions of contemporary art by both Scottish and non-Scottish artists. It is named in memory of W. Hope Collins (1903-67), a member of the publishing family whose history is described on p.62.

Pass the **McCance Building** ⓺ (1962-3, Covell Matthews & Partners) which houses the university's administration departments. Montrose Street is now met.

On the right (on the other side of the road) is the **James Weir Building** ⓻ (engineering).

Turn left and walk down Montrose Street to meet George Street. The massive red sandstone building on the right is the **Royal College** ⓸ (1901, David Barclay). This six-storey block, with its handsome wrought-iron gates, is used by various science and engineering departments. The large examination hall and a swimming pool are both housed within the building.

GEORGE STREET TO GLASGOW CROSS VIA THE MERCHANT CITY

Cross George Street and continue down Montrose Street, passing to the left of the rear of the City Chambers (this is described in Walk 3 on p.81). The route now leads into the heart of the **Merchant City**, so-called because of the merchants who lived or set up business here in the eighteenth and nineteenth centuries. Much of the wealth needed for this westward expansion of the city from the High Street area came from the tobacco trade which was controlled by a few exceptionally rich men who imported entire tobacco crops from planters in places such as Virginia and Maryland in the Americas. The crops were then sold on to buyers in England and continental Europe, especially France. These men imported about half of all the tobacco coming into Britain, greatly incurring the wrath and jealousy of English merchants. Glasgow's export trade in locally made linen, ironware and other items ensured that the city's shipowners had full cargoes in both directions across the Atlantic and this two-way traffic allowed the blossoming of the city's manufacturing industries. However, the American War of Independence of 1776-83 led to the bankruptcy of some of these 'merchant princes'.

Much of the area was laid out in 1770-90 but it didn't remain residential for very long as the wealthy continued their westward movement away from the encroaching noise and smell of the city's expanding industrial areas. However, merchants such as Archibald Ingram, John Glassford and James Buchanan are still remembered by the streets named after them.

The route now meets **Ingram Street**, named after Archibald Ingram (1704-70), a very wealthy merchant and provost of Glasgow in 1762-4. He was also a patron of the Foulis brothers (see p.363).

Turn left to reach Strathclyde University's Ramshorn Theatre, formerly the **St David's (Ramshorn Kirk)** ⓯ (1824-6, Thomas Rickman). The name 'Ramshorn' comes from the 'Lands of Ramshorn and Meadowflat' which were given to the Bishop of Glasgow in 1241 by King Alexander. The origin if the name is uncertain but may come from the sheep which were grazed here.

The height of the church is partly due to the fact that it is built over a crypt which houses the contents of graves which were disturbed when the church was built on the old graveyard. Inside, the tall Gothic windows are filled with magnificent stained glass. On the west side of the tower is a plaque commemorating Sir John A. MacDonald (1815-91) who was born in the Ramshorn parish and whose family emigrated to Kingston, Ontario in Canada in 1820. He became involved in politics and became Prime Minister of Upper Canada in 1857 and the country's Prime Minister in 1867-73 and 1878-91. On the eastern wall of the church is a large memorial plaque to three men called John Anderson, father, son and grandson. The father was the minister of the church in 1720 and the grandson was the founder of what became Strathclyde University.

The **St David's (Ramshorn Kirk) Graveyard** ⑯ is described on p362.

Head westwards along Ingram Street to Brunswick Street and at the junction is the fanciful former **Ingram Street Warehouses** ⑰ (1845-56, Robert Billings). This sports a mass of fussy gables, turrets, oriel windows and a decorated corner tower which faces diagonally across the street. This nineteenth-century warehouse has been converted into flats.

Continue along Ingram Street to the massive former **County Buildings and Courthouses** ⑱ (1841 and 1868-71, Clark & Bell) which take up a whole block. When the Tolbooth was declared too small for council use, a new building was erected here. Initially, the offices were built on the southern part of the site with their entrance on Wilson Street. Its very fine facade is dominated by a Greek Ionic portico standing above a classical frieze. The frieze contains representations of the work of the justice system and includes a chained prisoner and some solemn-looking men who are busy in their deliberations; ominously, there's also a man who carries an axe.

A new Merchants' House was attached to the offices and its entrance (with large Corinthian columns) faced westwards to Garth Street. The rest of the block was completed in 1868-71 by the same architects and eventually the whole building became a courthouse, with both the council and the merchants flitting to George Square. In 1986, the work of the courthouse was taken over by the new Sheriff Court. The future use of this building is still uncertain.

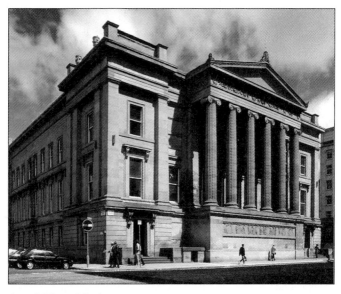

County Buildings and Courthouses

Hutchesons' Hall ㊾ (1802-05, David Hamilton) stands a little beyond the former courthouse and its clocktower is a particularly well-known Glasgow landmark. It was funded by two philanthropic brothers, George (*c*.1558-1639) and Thomas Hutcheson (1590-1641), whose statues appear on the front. They had previously supported a hospital for *aged decrepit men of the age above fifty years* and, when that was superseded by a system of providing pensions for those in need, this building was erected as offices and a meeting hall. The statues, which came from the hospital, were carved in 1649 and these are the only seventeenth-century figures left in Glasgow. Part of this building was used latterly by the school that the charity also supported. The building was remodelled in 1876 by John Baird II, who turned the first floor hall into one of the finest rooms in Glasgow. Its plasterwork is particularly impressive and it provides a fine setting for the concerts and lectures which are held here. The building is now owned by the National Trust for Scotland and used by them as offices and a shop.

Further along Ingram Street, the **Italian Centre** ㊿ is on the right just after John Street. The nicest part of this group of buildings is at 176 Ingram Street which was formerly the Bank of Scotland (*c*. 1840, William Burn). This redevelopment (1987-9, Page & Park) fronts three streets and it houses a number of shops selling expensive Italian goods. It is an interesting adaptation of traditional buildings and features rooftop statues of *Italia* (representing Italy), *Mercury* (the Roman messenger of the gods and also the god of traders) and *Mercurius* (a variant of Mercury). In good weather the centre's café spills out into the pedestrianised area in John Street and around the statue *Mercurial* which, like the rooftop sculptures, is by Alexander Stoddart.

The centre's internal courtyard is well worth a look. On the northern wall is a metalwork frieze by Jack Sloan representing Phaeton riding a chariot across the sky. Phaeton was the son of Helios the Greek sun god who was allowed to drive the sun chariot for one day. Unfortunately, he lost control of the horses and nearly set the Earth on fire. The sculpture is mounted on rails, which allows the spaces between the panels to be altered in size. Below it are two metal figures (*Cloudbusters*) who are pulling the sky earthwards. In the middle of the courtyard is a sculpture of a man and a dog – intriguingly entitled *Thinking of Bella* (Shona Kinloch) – and between them runs a little watercourse.

At 177 Ingram Street stands the former **Savings Bank of Glasgow** ㉛ (1894-1900, J. J. Burnet), now the Trustee Savings Bank. The architect's father (John Burnet) designed the bank's main office building behind it in 1866.

This is a surprisingly low building, given the important corner location it enjoys, but there is a special charm about it, especially in the huge dome which allows light to flood into the banking hall. The Glasgow coat of arms and a statue of St Mungo are above the doorway; to either side are crouched figures, obviously straining while supporting the heavy stonework. A number of smaller figures can be seen above the

The Italian Centre

front and side windows. On either side of the main door are badges with the letters *SBG* and the words *Industry* and *Frugality*. At the corner with Glassford Street is a carving showing two rather young-looking shipyard workers; behind them is an old ship whose ends are decorated with birds' heads.

Walk down Glassford Street, named after another of Glasgow's Tobacco Lords, John Glassford (see p.363). Farther down the street, at the junction of Glassford Street and Trongate, once stood the **Shawfield Mansion** (1711-12, Colin Campbell). The finest house in the city when it was built, it was the home of Daniel Campbell, Member of Parliament. After he had made himself unpopular because he favoured raising the tax on tobacco, he infuriated people by voting in favour of the malt tax, which put up the price of beer. On 23 June 1725, the first day of the tax, local people stopped the excise officers from carrying out their duties and later a huge crowd attacked the house and ransacked it. Soon troops were called in and although nine citizens were killed, the soldiers were run out of town. Two weeks later, it took a substantial force led by General Wade to quieten things down. Glaswegians take their drink seriously.

Walk a short distance down Glassford Street to the **Trades Hall** 🟢 (1791-4, Robert Adam). Palladian in style, with a raised Ionic portico and a prominent dome, this historic building is best seen from Garth Street. To the side of each pair of columns are metal plaques depicting two griffins and an urn. The sculpture at the top of the building has two female figures (one holds a trident, the other a pitcher) flanking a crest which is similar to the city's coat of arms. Unfortunately, this is Adam's only surviving building in Glasgow and it has been changed or added to over two centuries; however, it is, after the Cathedral, the second-oldest public building in the city still used for its original purpose. The front of the building was originally used for shops, with a range of meeting rooms behind and above, and today it is still used for meetings of various sorts.

The building was originally established as a meeting place for the city's fourteen incorporated trades: hammermen (engineers), tailors, cordiners (bootmakers), maltmen (brewers), weavers, bakers, skinners, wrights (metalworkers), coopers (barrelmakers), fleshers (butchers), masons (stone masons), gardeners, barbers and bonnetmakers & dyers. The men who belonged to these individual trades banded themselves together for mutual protection and were involved in setting wages and standards of work, effectively organising many aspects of small- and larger-scale manufacturing in the city. As a combined body, the trades gradually took over many aspects of local government, ranging from setting up an almshouse (for the relief of poverty) to regulating the erection of buildings. Indeed, their elected leader, the Deacon Convenor, came to be regarded as the city's second citizen after the Lord Provost.

Inside, the wooden-panelled entrance hall leads to a fine staircase which is lit by skylights in a barrel-vaulted ceiling. This leads to the large Grand Hall which is lit by electroliers from the old Grosvenor Restaurant (see p.168). The original Adam ceiling was lost long ago and the present wooden ceiling, which dates from 1955, has the building's dome set into it. Another interesting part of the room's decoration is the fascinating Belgian silk frieze (1902-3) depicting the work of the trades.

From the Trades Hall doorway, head eastwards along Garth Street and towards the former courthouse (see p.48); its Classical frieze, which depicts men with horses, elephants and lions, can be seen from here. At the end of the street turn right and at 83 Hutcheson Street is the bar and restaurant called **Rab Ha's** 🟢. Its name celebrates Rab Ha', who was known as the 'Glesca Glutton' because of his enormous appetite. He often took wagers on what he could eat and it is said he only once failed, and that was with a dish of oysters, cream and ground lump sugar! He died in 1843.

Turn left at Wilson Street and follow it past the former courthouse to **Candleriggs**. In 1652 the city suffered a great fire with many of its wooden buildings destroyed and, to lessen the chances of another catastrophe, the candle factories were moved to the 'riggs' (fields) situated here. The street was built up in the 1720s, banishing the factories but retaining the name they had given to the area.

The **City Halls** ⑤⑤ (1841, George Murray) are in the huge block in front and its main entrance is on the left. The halls, including the Great Hall, were built above the 1817 Bazaar which housed the cheese and fruit and vegetable markets. The halls became the city's main venue for concerts, dances, meetings and other events such as readings by Charles Dickens. Although the merchants moved out in 1969, the market, with its elaborate cast-iron structure, still remains at the southern end of the block. Note the sculpted basket of fruit on the roof.

Outside the halls' main entrance are a series of large slabs of red granite (from Altamira in Spain) on which are carved various poems and symbols. The four poems are by Edwin Morgan (1920–) and deal with the four elements (tree, bird, bell and fish) of the city's coat of arms, various old trades carried out in the Candleriggs area, industry and (echoing the previous use of the halls) fruit and vegetables. The two panels of carved symbols are made up of emblems of the fourteen trades and the fruit and vegetables mentioned in the poetry, together with four others representing merchants, a candlemaker, old and new music (for the concert hall) and a fruit basket (for the market). The work is by Frances Pelly (1995).

A plaque outside the main entrance is dedicated to the memory of **John Maclean** and is inscribed: *John Maclean 1879-1923 Socialist pioneer who spoke here frequently to unemployed workers was sentenced to one year's imprisonment in 1921. In his defence he declared that the only city in the world where the unemployed were organised and where there were no riots was Glasgow.* Maclean is the most famous of the city's 'Red Clydesiders' and his ideas and aspirations are still debated by socialists in Scotland. He was born in Pollokshaws, the son of Highland parents and, as a young man, he worked as a teacher in the city's Southside. He joined various local educational and political organisations and became a member of the Social Democratic Federation, a socialist group which was later involved in the founding of the Labour Party. He became a popular speaker and gave numerous lectures to large audiences in which he spoke against the scourge of unemployment and the coming war, which he condemned as a struggle between two capitalist powers. His outspoken attacks against the British Government's policies were answered quite brutally and led to Maclean and a number of his associates being jailed for sedition. He was imprisoned in 1916-18 but was released after a year and a half as a result of much public pressure.

The war in Europe led to the fall of the Russian Czar and Maclean's forthright support for the Russian Revolution again led him into prison. This time he went on hunger strike, claiming that he was being given drugged food, and the authorities' policy of force-feeding him led to a huge public outcry which eventually led to his release from Peterhead Prison and to a tremendous reception on his arrival back in Glasgow.

Huge political upheavals were taking place all around Europe at this time and Maclean's ideas and activities were well known internationally. This standing was recognised by Lenin, who appointed him Soviet Consul for Scotland. He continued his political work after the war but was never able to build an effective organisation to fight coherently for real change. He declined to join the newly formed Communist Party of Great Britain, instead espousing the theory that the national issues that existed in Scotland required an independent Scottish Workers' Party, but this idea never really gained much popular support. Finally, his ceaseless campaigning and six spells in prison took their toll and he contracted pneumonia while contesting a parliamentary election; he died upholding the Clydesiders' proud tradition of struggle against injustice. Maclean's desk is on display in the People's Palace (see p.66).

Walk southwards along Candleriggs. On the right, at 55-7 Candleriggs, is the pub **Granny Black's** ⑤⑤ (1790, James & William Carswell). It was previously the Bazaar Bar and the original Granny Black's pub (known as the city's smallest pub) was recreated here in 1970.

Trongate is now reached. On the other side of the road, at **109–15 Trongate** ⑤⑥ (1857, Thomas Gildard & R. H. M. MacFarlane), a warehouse contains within it the shell of the Britannia Music Hall, the second-oldest surviving theatre in the country. When it was built, the music hall was the city's most important venue for entertainment and many successful acts played at it. Those who weren't so good, however, were pelted with the rotten eggs and ripe tomatoes that were sold just outside the doors. Early in the twentieth century it was taken over by the showman A. E. Pickard, who changed its name to the Panopticon and included a museum, waxworks and even a zoo. (Intriguingly, a panopticon was originally an eighteenth-century prison design with a circular building containing cells which faced inwards towards a central rotunda.) Later, the building was turned into a cinema.

Each of the facade's individual storeys are based on Italian palazzi but they are very different in style, with the higher ones being much lighter than the lower ones. The date *MDCCCLVII* (1857) is engraved at the top.

Turn left to head towards Glasgow Cross. At the corner with Albion Street is **74–92 Trongate** ⑤⑦ (1854, John Thomas Rochead), an extravagant Scots Baronial structure with turrets and crow-stepped gables which was constructed for the City of Glasgow Bank to match neighbouring buildings. They must have been quite a sight!

The **Tron Steeple** ⑤⑧ is the imposing tower that straddles the pavement on the southern side of the Trongate. This clock tower was originally part of an old church but its own name comes from the 'tron' (public weighing machine) which was kept here. It was begun around 1592; its Gothic spire was added in 1630-66 and the pedestrian arches were created in 1855.

The steeple is all that remains of the collegiate church of St Mary and St Anne, founded here in 1484, after the original church was destroyed by fire in 1793 by members of the Hell-Fire Club who were out for an evening's revelry. The evening's 'entertainment' consisted of entering the church and feeding the building's fire to find out how much heat the revellers could endure, but the fire got completely out of control and the building was destroyed. Today these vandals would be branded as rich lager louts!

Behind the tower is the former **Tron Kirk** (1793-4, James Adam) which was built to replace the vandalised church. This is now the very popular **Tron Theatre** ⓳. The Tron is one of the city's smaller and more intimate theatres which hosts touring companies, contemporary and traditional plays, comedy and music.

Continue along Trongate to **Glasgow Cross** ❶ where the walk ends.

Glasgow Green and the River Clyde

A walk through the city's oldest park and along both banks of the River Clyde as it makes its way through the centre of the city.

GLASGOW CROSS TO GLASGOW GREEN

Glasgow Cross ❶ is described at the start of Walk 1. Head southwards from the Cross, down **Saltmarket**. The salt market was set up here in medieval times as many salmon fishermen worked nearby in the River Clyde and salt was needed for preserving the perishable fish. Originally, the street only went as far as Bridgegate; it then veered to the right and went down to the river crossing.

The River Clyde

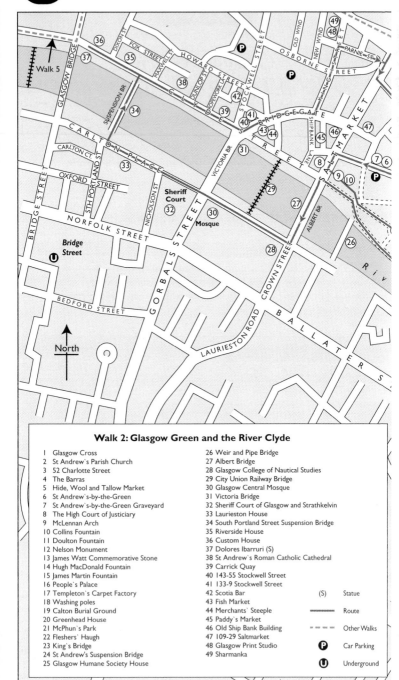

Walk 2: Glasgow Green and the River Clyde

1 Glasgow Cross
2 St Andrew's Parish Church
3 52 Charlotte Street
4 The Barras
5 Hide, Wool and Tallow Market
6 St Andrew's-by-the-Green
7 St Andrew's-by-the-Green Graveyard
8 The High Court of Justiciary
9 McLennan Arch
10 Collins Fountain
11 Doulton Fountain
12 Nelson Monument
13 James Watt Commemorative Stone
14 Hugh MacDonald Fountain
15 James Martin Fountain
16 People's Palace
17 Templeton's Carpet Factory
18 Washing poles
19 Calton Burial Ground
20 Greenhead House
21 McPhun's Park
22 Fleshers' Haugh
23 King's Bridge
24 St Andrew's Suspension Bridge
25 Glasgow Humane Society House

26 Weir and Pipe Bridge
27 Albert Bridge
28 Glasgow College of Nautical Studies
29 City Union Railway Bridge
30 Glasgow Central Mosque
31 Victoria Bridge
32 Sheriff Court of Glasgow and Strathkelvin
33 Laurieston House
34 South Portland Street Suspension Bridge
35 Riverside House
36 Custom House
37 Dolores Ibarruri (S)
38 St Andrew's Roman Catholic Cathedral
39 Carrick Quay
40 143-55 Stockwell Street
41 133-9 Stockwell Street
42 Scotia Bar
43 Fish Market
44 Merchants' Steeple
45 Paddy's Market
46 Old Ship Bank Building
47 109-29 Saltmarket
48 Glasgow Print Studio
49 Sharmanka

(S)   Statue

———   Route

– – –   Other Walks

P   Car Parking

U   Underground

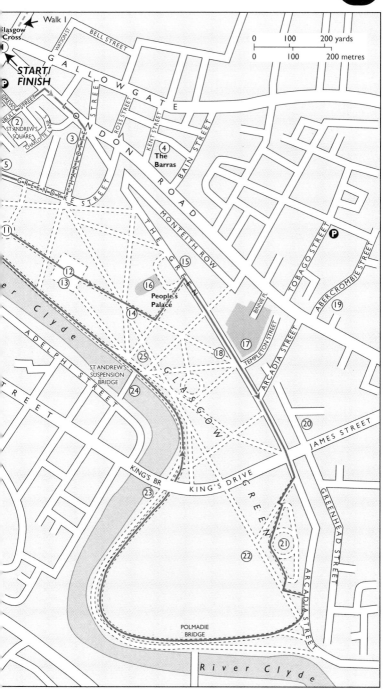

Main places of interest	St Andrew's Parish Church ❷ (former church)
	The Barras ❹ (weekend open-air market)
	St Andrew's-by-the-Green ❻ (former church)
	St Andrew's-by-the-Green Graveyard ❼
	Glasgow Green ❾ - ㉖ (park)
	People's Palace ⑯ (museum of Glasgow life)
	Calton Burial Ground ⑲
	St Andrew's Roman Catholic Cathedral ㊳
	Merchants' Steeple ㊹ (17th-century building)
	Glasgow Print Studio ㊽ (art gallery)
	Sharmanka ㊾ ('kinetic sculpture' gallery)
Circular/linear	circular
Starting point	Glasgow Cross ❶
Finishing point	Glasgow Cross ❶
Distance	7 km (4.5 miles)
Terrain	level pavements and paths
Public transport	St Enoch Underground Station
	Argyle Street Railway Station (C)
Sections	Glasgow Cross to Glasgow Green
	Glasgow Green
	Glasgow Green to Carlton Place
	Carlton Place to Glasgow Cross
Architects	–
Nearby walks	1, 3, 5
Refreshments	People's Palace
Notes	Be aware of safety advice (see p.16) as Glasgow Green can be very quiet at times. Take care with valuable belongings when in the crowds in The Barras.

As the city developed in the eighteenth century, the Saltmarket area became a fashionable place and in his novel *Rob Roy,* Sir Walter Scott placed Bailie Nicol Jarvie's home here. In the following century the street deteriorated into a squalid slum, with one guidebook of the time describing it as having *a large gathering of loafers at every* [tenement] *close mouth.* However, after 1866 the City Improvement Trust started rebuilding the district. Their work began in the Glasgow Cross area where the old and decrepit tenements were swept away, along with many buildings that could perhaps have been saved. Indeed, the Victorians' keenness to start afresh has left Glasgow with relatively few pre-nineteenth century buildings.

Turn left into St Andrew's Street, heading towards **St Andrew's Square**, named after Scotland's patron saint. In 1785, the square was used as a launching site by the Italian balloonist Vincenzo Lunardi who, watched by an enormous crowd said to be 100,000 strong, soared upwards and headed south-east towards the Borders, landing near Hawick some two-and-a-half hours later.

This was once a very prosperous area but became run-down and is now being rebuilt, with new houses round the former **St Andrew's Parish Church ❷** (1739-56, Allan Dreghorn). This Georgian church is modelled on St Martin's-in-the-Fields in London, with six tall Corinthian columns supporting a pediment bearing Glasgow's coat of arms. Above that is a clock tower with an octagonal bell chamber. When built, there was concern about the wisdom of having so heavy a portico and one story relates that its builder, Mungo Naismith, demonstrated its safety by spending a night under it; a variant of this tale maintains he spent that time anxiously looking out for signs of the structure settling! The Baroque interior has marvellous plasterwork and exceptionally fine acoustics, so good that it is to become a venue for Scottish traditional music, song and dance.

Leave the square at the north-western corner by going along James Morrison Street. Turn right at London Road and right again at Charlotte Street. On the right is **52 Charlotte Street ❸** (*c.* 1790), a two-storey villa of the type associated with the wealthy inhabitants of the Merchant City (see p.47). The decorative urns at roof level were a common exterior decoration.

The route of the walk continues down Charlotte Street but there is a short detour from here along London Road to **The Barras ❹** market which is open at weekends. To get there, follow the northern side of London Road to the Barras' arched entrance on the left at Kent Street. This is Scotland's best-known market and while some stallholders operate out of doors, most are found inside the old warehouses that still stand here. Many of the goods on sale are new, but there are great numbers of second-hand dealers offering a huge variety of items, including antiques. Take your time and savour the busy and very noisy atmosphere!

To the north of The Barras (with market stalls underneath it) is the **Barrowland Ballroom**, a dance and live music venue which was described by one Glasgow writer as 'the venue for Glasgow's unso-phisticated youth'.

From The Barras, retrace your steps back to the top of Charlotte Street and rejoin the route.

Walk down Charlotte Street and turn right at Greendyke Street. Glasgow Green is now on the left. Follow the edge of the park and on the right at 33-39 Greendyke Street is the handsome four-storey former **Hide, Wool and Tallow Market** ❺ (1890, John Keppie), also known as the Tannery Building. On either side of its entrance are plaques (dated 1856 and 1890) depicting fountains.

The building after this is the former **St Andrew's-by-the-Green** ❻ (1750-2, William Paull and Andrew Hunter), now the offices of the West of Scotland Housing Association. This is the oldest-surviving Episcopal church building in the country and was the first Episcopal church built in Scotland after the 1745 Jacobite Rebellion. The Episcopalians (known as 'Piskies'), wanted to retain bishops in the church and were often regarded with great suspicion; indeed many of their meetings in Glasgow were broken up by mobs bent on violence. However, an Act of Parliament gave them some legal protection, provided they used the English Prayer Book and prayed for the Hanoverian dynasty (against whom the Jacobites had fought).

The building is a simple but elegant structure and its design is similar in certain respects to the villa at 52 Charlotte Street. As it was the first church to be equipped with an organ (an anathema to strict Presbyterians!) it soon became known as the 'Whistlin' Kirk'.

The small **St Andrew's-by-the-Green Graveyard** ❼ is described on p.365.

Continue along Greendyke Street to the Saltmarket, on the opposite side of which stands **The High Court of Justiciary** ❽ (1809-14, William Stark). This large building was originally built as a jail, courthouse and offices to replace the old Tolbooth, but was later converted into courthouses. Its fine Greek Doric portico and entrance steps are modelled on the Athenian Theseion (the temple to Theseus, the Greek hero who killed the Minotaur in the Labyrinth). However, its imposing appearance was spoiled when the surrounding land was raised to prevent the river flooding, as it put the building's plinth below road level. The entrance, which has been described as being 'austere to the point of Calvinism', has a modern extension (1996-7) at the rear. The Justiciary Courts act as Glasgow's High Court and deal with more serious cases than those handled by the Sheriff Court (see p.71).

The area just to the north of the courts was called **Jail Square** which until 1865 was the scene of public executions. Anyone hanged here was said to have 'died facing the monument' – Nelson's Monument in Glasgow Green. The last person to suffer this fate was a Dr Pritchard, watched by a crowd of over 80,000 people. He had poisoned his wife and mother-in-law; his story was later used by James Bridie in his play *Dr Angelus*. Perhaps appropriately, the city's mortuary now occupies the small building beside the courts.

Opposite the courts stands the huge McLennan Arch, marking the entrance to Glasgow Green.

GLASGOW GREEN

Glasgow Green is the city's oldest park and its history can be traced back to at least 1450 when it was granted by James II to Bishop William Turnbull. It was used as grazing land and the Town Herd was employed to look after the burgh's animals which were kept here. This use (which carried on into the 1890s) encouraged the setting up of slaughterhouses nearby.

During the Industrial Revolution and beyond, the Green was the most important open area in the rapidly developing East End and the growing population made good use of the park's open spaces. Sports were popular, with swimming in the Clyde (until it became too polluted), golf (from the sixteenth century), athletics and football. Since it was beside the river, the area was also well-used for washing and bleaching linen and there was a local wash-house and drying green.

The park's present layout was generally established in 1815-26; as much of the land was subject to flooding this involved raising the ground level and providing good drainage. However, in the mid-nineteenth century the threat of extensive coalmining became a real possibility as a means of raising money for the council's plan to build West End Park (see p.197) in the prosperous western suburbs. The fight to save the Green was even put to verse in the poem *Airn John* (1858), addressed to Councillor John McDowall who wished to lease the mineral rights:

> *If ye maun sink a pit, John,*
> *Sink it in George's Square,*
> *Or sink it in the Crescents John,*
> *Amang the rich folk there,*
> *An' they'll be highly pleased, John,*
> *To see sic noble wark,*
> *Gaun on amang thesel's, John,*
> *To pay the west-end park.*

Other threats to the Green, including proposals to drive railways and motorways through it, have been fought against in the last hundred years or so. During one recent dispute, a decision of the council dating from 1576 was quoted in defence of the Green's integrity: *na mair pairt or portioun of the commoun muris sal be in na tymes cuming set nor gevin in few to ony persoun or persones, bot to ly still in communitie to the weill of the haill tounschip.*

The Green has many connections with the people's struggle for reforms and justice and in the 1830s, during the agitation for electoral reform, large Chartist demonstrations took place here. In many ways, the Green was similar to London's Hyde Park Corner, with religious and political speakers entertaining weekend crowds with their oratory. Temperance, trade union rights, women's rights and all manner of causes were espoused and hotly debated.

The **Glasgow Fair** has been an important public event for many centuries and many of its activities took place near the western end of the Green. It was inaugurated in the late twelfth century and traditionally began on 7 July, but in time the start was changed to Fair Monday which was fixed as the second Monday in July. The fair was originally an important market and included sales of horses and cattle and the engagement of servants. In the nineteenth century it began to attract amusements including theatres, circuses and drinking booths; later in the century it changed again and Fair Monday became the start of Fair Fortnight when many Glasgow people went on holiday, often going 'Doon the watter' (see p.146).

The Green's entrance is marked by the grand **McLennan Arch** ❾ (1792, Robert & James Adam), which was, as inscribed high up, *presented to his fellow citizens by Bailie James McLennan MP*. The arch is dated *MDCCCXCIII* (1843) and it was originally the centrepiece of Robert Adams' Assembly Rooms in Ingram Street (see p.101), which were demolished about 1890. Since then the arch has had two other resting places near Glasgow Green before it was moved here around 1990. It has four large Ionic columns and a wide central opening which originally framed a window in the Assembly Rooms. The two plaques above the smaller openings have figures which may possibly represent music and the muses.

A little further on is the **Collins Fountain** ❿ (1881, John G. Mossman), inscribed *Erected by temperance reformers in recognition of valuable services rendered to the temperance cause by Sir William Collins*. His bust is shown on the side facing the arch and the fountain is topped by a figure representing a sentimental girl with a pitcher.

The **temperance movement** in Glasgow has had a long struggle against the 'demon drink'. Glasgow used to have an enormous number of pubs, especially in the older parts of the city, while in other areas, local veto polls could be used to keep areas dry. The movement founded organisations such as the Scottish Band of Hope and the Glasgow Abstainers Union; the various bodies were involved in many activities, from running propaganda film shows to fighting local elections; one march they organised in 1842 attracted 50,000 people to Glasgow Green. Sir William Collins (1817-95) involved his huge publishing business in producing many religious and anti-drinking tracts and his zealousness in championing the temperance cause earned him the nickname 'Water Willie'.

His father (William Collins, 1789-1853) had started the publishing business, with Bibles and temperance literature being two of his most important subjects. He wrote and published *The Temperance Society Record* in 1839 and in that year the company produced an estimated half a million temperance tracts! The publishing firm of Collins (now HarperCollins) still exists and has offices in Bishopbriggs, to the north of the city.

Glaswegians' drinking habits have given the city a reputation that has travelled far. What might be less well known, however, is the claim that the Glaswegian's keenness for his *bevvy* led to the development of square-toed shoes – which allowed the drinker to get closer to the bar!

Continue straight ahead to the much larger **Doulton Fountain** **⓫** (1888, A. E. Pearce). This wonderfully elaborate fountain is 14m (46ft) tall and was made for the Glasgow International Exhibition (see p.197) before being moved here in 1890. The imperial theme is displayed here with great artistic effect, with Queen Victoria at the top holding an orb and sceptre. Below her are four female figures holding water-spouting vases and four military men (a sailor and soldiers of the Black Watch, Grenadier Guards and the Royal Irish Fusileers. Below them are larger and very intricate figures representing India, Australia, South Africa and Canada. This is a superb terracotta masterpiece from the famous Doulton workshops in England's Black Country, but sadly it has been ravaged by vandals.

The route continues to the 44m (144ft) tall **Nelson Monument** **⓬** (1806, David Hamilton). This was the first monument erected in Britain to commemorate the naval victories of Viscount Horatio Nelson (1758-1805). Around the base are the names of his famous victories: Aboukir (1798), Copenhagen (1801) and Trafalgar (1805), where he was killed. Only four years after it was built, the monument was struck by lightning, knocking 6m (20ft) off the top; the damage is still visible. It was later fitted with a lightning conductor.

To the south of the monument lies a large boulder, the **James Watt Commemorative Stone** **⓭**, which is inscribed *Near this spot in 1765 James Watt conceived the idea of the separate condenser for the steam engine; patented 1769.* Watt's life and work is described on p.86.

Head towards the People's Palace but keep to the right of its perimeter fence. On the right is the granite **Hugh MacDonald Fountain** **⓮** which was moved here from near Paisley in 1880. It has his dates (1817-60) and an inscription taken from one of his poems:

> *The bonnie wee well on the breist o' the brae*
> *Where the hare steals to drink in the gloamin' sae grey.*
> *Where the wild moorlan' birds dip their nebs and tak' wing*
> *And the lark weets his whistle ere mounting to sing.*

(For those not aquainted with 'guid Scots', the following is offered as an aid to translation: *bonnie* = 'nice'; *wee* = 'small'; *breist* = 'breast'; *brae* = 'hill'; *gloamin'* = 'the light from the dusk sky'; *sae* = 'so'; *moorlan'*= 'moorland'; *neb* = 'beak'; *tak'*= 'take'; *weets* = 'wets'; *whistle* = 'throat')

In the first chapter of *Rambles Round Glasgow* (see p.378), MacDonald describes a walk around Glasgow Green, saying, 'Few towns can boast such a spacious and beautiful public park as the Green of Glasgow, with its wide-spreading lawns, its picturesque groups of trees, its far-winding walks, its numerous delicious springs, and, above all, its rich command of scenery.'

MacDonald is buried in the Southern Necropolis (see p.378).

Keep following the fence round to the front of the People's Palace but, before going in, cross the road (The Green) that runs past it to see the **James Martin Fountain ⑮**. This elaborate cast-iron Moorish canopy was erected in 1893 to honour James Martin (1815-92), a local bailie (senior councillor). He is remembered for his opposition to the council's speculative development on Woodlands Hill. This expensive building venture was undertaken to provide homes for the rich at a time when the East End's housing was in an appalling state.

The fountain is decorated with the city's coat of arms, flowers, birds, lions and various strange-looking beasts, and was made in the Possilpark area of Glasgow in the world-famous Saracen iron foundry of Walter Macfarlane (see also p.222). This firm manufactured countless types of ironwork, from lampposts to entire buildings; indeed, their most celebrated construction was the Durbar Palace in Quatar, India (1912). Glasgow is well known for its decorative ironwork, and though much of it was removed for re-use in the wartime armaments industry, some good ironwork still exists in the older parts of the city. This fountain originally stood outside Langside Halls.

The **People's Palace ⑯** (1893-8, Alex. B. McDonald) is a tall red Locharbriggs sandstone building in French Renaissance style. The entrance is decorated with the city's coat of arms on either side of which is an angel. Tall columns and pilasters decorate the first floor. Above these are six statues (by Kellock Brown) which represent *Shipbuilding, Mathematics and Science, Painting, Sculpture, Engineering* and *Textiles*. Above

The People's Palace

them are *Science* and *Art*, and at the top is *Progress*. Outside the main entrance are a number of decorated lampstandards; one is dated *1902*, another bears the name of the ironfounder, Walter Macfarlane (see above) and another bears the insignia *G & S W R* (Glasgow & South West Railway).

The People's Palace was originally conceived as a museum for everyone in the city, rather than for the select few who frequented the public galleries in the West End, and it is no accident that it is situated here to ensure that the East End had at least one of the city's important museums on its doorstep. At the time of its construction, great changes were taking place in the city and lots of important artefacts from old buildings were rescued and put on display, though it was not until 1940 that it became the home of memorabilia from Old Glasgow. The Palace is essentially a museum of Glasgow and it traces the history and social life of the city over the last few hundred years.

The palace is a popular place for grandparents to bring their grand-children to see how previous generations lived in the city; children's interests are catered for mainly on the ground and first floors while the second floor is of more interest to adults. The museum has a wealth of material on display and there are numerous exhibits which illustrate many of the local topics dealt with in this book.

On the ground floor is **I belong to Glasgow**, an exhibition dealing with the different ethnic groups which have made their home here over the last two or more hundred years. Many came because of famine or persecution in their own country or in other parts of Scotland – in the mid-nineteenth century only one-fifth of the city's population had been born in the city, and the waves of immigrants have had an extremely important effect on Glasgow. The city has been multicultural for a very long time!

The first floor has a wide variety of displays. **The Patter** introduces the visitor to the city's dialect, with assistance from well-known masters of the language such as Rab C. Nesbit and Stanley Baxter. English translations are available for some items. **The Bevvy** traces the history of the Glaswegians' indulgence in the 'demon drink'. The exhibits include a punch bowl from the 1760s that was made by the Delftfield Pottery for the Saracen's Head Inn. There's also a 'drunks barrow' which Govan police used to carry drunks to the cells. The displays on the **World Wars** include a reconstruction of an Anderson Shelter in which people sought refuge from the air raids of 1940-3. **The Steamie** is all about the public wash-houses in which women laundered the weekly washing until the days of the launderette and the domestic washing machine. Other displays on the floor include one on **Crime**, which has reminders of the city's violent past, **Doon the Watter**, a celebration of the days of the popular steamer trips down the River Clyde, and **Dancing at the Barrowland**, about the famous ballroom nearby.

The second floor has displays dealing with the city's successes in **manufacturing and trading**. A large painting, *John Glassford and family, in the Shawfield Mansion, Trongate, c1767* (Archibald McLaughlin), represents the wealth and conspicuous consumption of the Glasgow capitalists. In complete contrast are eight paintings by Ken Currie (1960-) which are placed within the building's dome; these depict the city's labour history and were commissioned by the People's Palace to mark the 1987 bicentenery of the Calton Weavers (see p.366). Other exhibits in this area include the desk of the Glasgow socialist John Maclean (see p.52), a Spanish Civil War banner and memorabilia of the women's suffrage movement. Two quite remarkable items, both made of silver, reflect the two opposite sides of the city's wealth (albeit they are from different periods of history). These are a slave collar of 1732 and a huge yachting trophy in the shape of a galleon, won by Sir Thomas Lipton (see p.376). A neighbouring gallery deals with the city's manufacturing industries. There are various examples of locally manufactured items, including a periscope (made by Barr & Stroud), cast-iron railings (by Walter Macfarlane), pottery by the Verreville Pottery and J. & M. P. Bell & Co., carpet made by Templeton for the *Queen Mary*, books by R. & A. Foulis and paper by Edward Collins & Sons. More light-hearted exhibits include the banana boots worn by the comedian Billy Connolly (1942-) and a painting (1973) of him by John Byrne (1940-).

The last display is about the city's **housing** and life at home. Life in Glasgow's traditional tenements forms the core of the exhibition, with the main exhibit being a reconstruction of a 'single-end', the single room in which a whole family lived. There are also a number of detailed paintings of tenement life in the 1930s by Thomas McGoran (1927-). Another interesting painting on show is *The Barras* by the Glasgow painter Avril Paton (1941-).

At the back of the building are the massive **Winter Gardens**, a large steel and glass structure whose shape is said to be that of the upturned hull of the *Victory*, Lord Nelson's flagship. This conservatory has marvellous displays of plants which provide pleasant scenery for the museum's cafeteria which is located here.

After leaving the palace, walk eastwards along The Green, heading towards the extraordinary **Templeton's Carpet Factory** ⑰ (1889-92, William Leiper), now the Templeton Business Centre. Leiper used the Gothic Doge's Palace in Venice as his inspiration and a wide variety of materials were used including glazed and unglazed brick, terracotta and sandstone. The western facade has been called an 'exotic tapestry' with its four storeys of windows surrounded by a mass of detail, including mosaics, pillars, towers, roundels and shields. The figure on the top of the western wall may be St Enoch (see p.143) presenting the infant Mungo to Glasgow. Beneath her is the city's coat of arms, a balcony and five coats of arms representing England, Scotland, Wales, Ireland and Great Britain. In many ways this is the most amazing (and probably the most bizarre) building in the whole city which has been described by the architectural historian Frank Wordsall 'as the world's finest example of decorative brickwork'. It certainly shows what can be done with the humble brick, a lot of imagination and a client willing to clothe an industrial building

Templeton's Carpet Factory

in an artistic masterpiece. How many twentieth-century factories can compare with this?

During construction, the facade collapsed in a strong wind and twenty-nine people working in the neighbouring weaving sheds were killed. It was rebuilt to the same design. The wing to the east (1936, George Boswell) is a more modern rendition of the ideas used by Leiper which blends well with the earlier work.

Washing poles ⑱ will be noticed in the Green opposite the factory. Part of the site occupied by the carpet factory used to have a public wash-house (a 'steamie'), and this was where the clothes were hung out to dry. Even after the wash-house was closed, local women carried their clothes here for drying up to the 1970s and the remaining poles celebrate a centuries-old tradition. Glasgow's first public wash-house was opened in 1732 and the last closed as late as the 1990s. Cleaning the family's clothes involved hard manual work (and a lot of gossip), a part of Glasgow history celebrated in Tony Roper's hilarious and very popular play *The Steamie*.

Bear right when Arcadia Street is met and keep following the perimeter of the Green. A detour is possible here to visit the **Calton Burial Ground** ⑲ (see p.366).

Following Arcadia Street, the former **Greenhead House** ⑳ (1846, Charles Wilson) can be seen on the left. It is dominated by its large sculpture of a child studiously reading a book; a jack plane lies beside the child's foot. In 1859 the house became the Buchanan Institute for orphan boys and the figure was added in 1873. It is now Greenview School.

King's Drive is now met. The route crosses this and continues to follow the edge of the Green; however, readers wishing to take a short cut here can turn right at this junction and turn right when King's Drive meets the River Clyde in order to rejoin the route by King's Bridge **⑳**. The name King's Drive celebrates John King, a noted flesher (butcher) who sold this land to the city in 1773.

Cross King's Drive, pass the entrance to the bowling greens and a lane which goes into Glasgow Green. Go through a gate on the right and enter **McPhun's Park** **㉑**. There is a granite **war memorial** here, in the form of a Celtic Cross, dedicated to soldiers of the 7th (Blythswood) battalion of the Highland Light Infantry (see p.131) who died in *The Great War 1914-18*. Go left, round the side of the memorial and straight through **a small formal garden**. The path then bends round to the left to pass a headless statue of **James Watt** (see p.86) who is holding a pair of dividers and leaning on what is probably part of a steam condenser. This statue came from a local weaving shed called the Atlantic Mills, erected in 1864. Further on is a mysterious-looking **plinth** that is decorated with a frieze of children and animals.

Follow the path out of the garden to meet Arcadia Street again and turn right. A little after the perimeter fence of McPhun's Park has ended, turn right to join a path that curves round to the right. The open space now on the right is called **Fleshers' Haugh** **㉒**, once owned by the Incorporation of Fleshers (butchers). A haugh is a low-lying piece of ground near a river, and this particular site was sold to the city in 1792. In 1746, during the Jacobite Rebellion, Charles Edward Stewart (or Bonnie Prince Charlie as the tourist industry prefers to call him) reviewed his troops here. The army stayed for ten days (their leader living at Shawfield Mansion (see p.50)) and successfully demanded that the city provide them with 12,000 shirts, 6000 coats, 6000 pairs of shoes, 6000 pairs of stockings, 6000 waistcoats and 6000 bonnets.

Another claim to fame for the haugh is that Glasgow Rangers Football Club (see p.285) had its origins here in 1873. A group of rowers, many of whom came from Gareloch (on the Firth of Clyde), played football here after spending the earlier part of the evenings on the river. They called themselves 'Rangers', and stayed here for two years before moving to various locations, eventually ending up at the site of their present stadium in 1899. This area is still used for football.

The **River Clyde** (see p.144) soon comes into view on the left and, if wished, a lower path nearer the river can be followed. In the eighteenth century this was a popular place from which to swim in the river but there is no doubt that increasing pollution levels put many people off the pursuit. This part of the walk is a pleasant stroll among mature trees though the noise of the traffic is never far away. A little after passing the pedestrian **Polmadie Bridge** over the river, a plaque on the right commemorates the planting of trees here in 1974-5.

Rowers are often seen here as there is a long tradition of rowing on this section of the river and the Glasgow Rowing Club has its clubhouse on the other bank.

Keep close to the river and pass under **King's Bridge** **23** (1930-3, Thomas P. M. Somers), where the short cut along King's Drive rejoins the walk. A rowing club building is then passed.

The **St Andrew's Suspension Bridge** **24** (1854, Neil Robson) is now met. With its fluted cast-iron Corinthian columns, it is certainly a grand pedestrian link between the Green and Hutchesontown. This bridge seems to typify Victorian architecture in Glasgow as even a mundane pedestrian bridge is used to show off the engineering talents of the architect and builders.

On the right is the **Glasgow Humane Society House** **25** (1935-7, J. Thomson King) with the society's riverside premises just after the bridge. The society dates back to 1790 and was founded to rescue people from the river. With many ferries crossing the river, business was obviously brisk and by 1825 some 600 people had been saved from drowning. In 1859, George Geddes I (see p.378) was appointed as a full-time officer, to be succeeded by his son George Geddes II. When the younger George died Ben Parsonage took over and in fifty-one years of stalwart service he saved over one thousand people, although he also recovered over twice that number of bodies. His son, George, succeeded him in his duties.

The path then passes the clubhouse of the Clydesdale Amateur Rowing Club and then the unusual **Weir and Pipe Bridge** **26** (1945, Robert Bruce). The weir helps maintain the level of the water and the three sluice gates are designed to be raised and rotated in order to allow boats to pass along the river.

Pass to the left of the McLennan Arch to leave the Green. Turn left at the bottom of Saltmarket and head towards the river.

GLASGOW GREEN TO CARLTON PLACE

Follow the Saltmarket down to the River Clyde and cross the **Albert Bridge** **27** (1868-71, R. Bell & D. Miller). This is the fifth bridge to be built in this locality and the three-span cast-iron structure replaced the bridge built by Robert Stevenson, grandfather of the author Robert Louis Stevenson. A plaque on the bridge indicates that the foundation stone was laid in 1870; there are also large Glasgow coats of arms on the parapet. On the outer side of the bridge are various coats of arms and roundels featuring the heads of Queen Victoria and Prince Albert.

Turn right immediately after crossing the bridge in order to follow the riverside walkway along to the pedestrian suspension bridge. On the left is the **Glasgow College of Nautical Studies** ❷❽ (1962-70, Robert Matthew, Johnson-Marshall & Partners). The college's most interesting building, its dome-shaped planetarium, is to the south of the main block.

The Merchant Shipping Act of 1854 made the certification of various classes of mariners mandatory and, since that date or even before, there has been training for seafarers in Glasgow. The Royal Technical College (see p.44) ran navigators' courses from 1910 which were taken over by the Glasgow College of Nautical Studies in the 1960s. Around the same time, Stow College (see p.270) transferred its Marine Engineering Department here. Although there has been a drastic reduction in the British merchant fleet, maritime courses are still an important facet of the college's range of interests and students are trained on equipment such as a ship simulator and all the high-tech communications systems used by ocean-going vessels these days.

Pass under the **City Union Railway Bridge** ❷❾ (1897-9, William Melville). This is an ornate bridge with castellated piers and a fine cast-iron Gothic parapet.

On the left is the **Glasgow Central Mosque** ❸⓪ (1984, Coleman Ballantine Partnership) with its golden dome (illuminated from inside at night) topped by a crescent moon. A tall and graceful concrete minaret stands above the low arcade that joins the two main structures. This is the city's main Muslim building and it is used as a religious, educational and social centre.

Glasgow's links with the Asian continent, and Muslim people in particular, go back a long time as many Scots were involved in the British Empire's forays into their lands, notably the Indian subcontinent. The first recorded Indian immigrant arrived as late as around1916, but a few thousand more arrived in the next three decades and the first of the city's (and the country's) mosques was established in Oxford Street in 1944. This was just three years before separate Indian and Pakistani states were created, and the problems caused by partition led to a new wave of immigrants in the succeeding years. The majority of Glasgow's Muslim community have their roots in Pakistan and the mosque was built here as many of them live in surrounding districts. Many of the immigrants settled in the Gorbals, Govanhill and Pollokshields areas of the South-side and in Woodside in the West End.

Gorbals Street is now met and on the right is **Victoria Bridge** ❸❶ (1851-4, James Walker). This is the oldest bridge over the river in the city and it stands at the medieval crossing point. The first stone bridge was built by Bishop Rae around 1350 and, with various additions and quite a lot of rebuilding, it lasted (as Glasgow Bridge) until this fine structure took its place. Five hundred years of use! It got into a bad state of repair on many occasions, and in 1658, in order to lessen the wear and tear, the council decided that it could not 'allow ony cairtis with wheilleis go alongst the brig untill that the wheilleis be taken off and the boddie of the cairt alon harled by the hors' (*harled* = 'dragged').

The bridge was the terminus of the 'Clutha' ferries which plied between here and Whiteinch. This service lasted from 1884 to 1903 and was very popular.

The **Gorbals** district is now on the left. This area would be almost unrecognisable to someone who knew it in the 1960s as most of the tenements have disappeared, many of them replaced by massive multi-storeyed blocks.

In 1661 this became the first area to the south of the river to be 'taken over' by the expanding Glasgow. It gradually became a fairly fashionable area but the encroachment of industry and its concomitant pollution saw it decline to the point where 40,000 people were crammed together in the district at the end of the nineteenth century, and 90,000 in the 1930s. The squalor that existed for a number of generations gave rise to an unenviable reputation that travelled far and wide. The novel *No Mean City* (1935, Alexander McArthur and H. Kingsley Long) was based on life in the slums and the violence that stalked the streets. The book starts without pulling punches: 'Johnnie Stark was a product of the Gorbals. Tall, broad-chested, and with dark, sullen eyes he looked like a fighter and he was. Johnnie liked women and women liked him. For their sake, and for any other reason that seemed good to him, Johnnie was ready to fight. There were no Queensbury rules in the Gorbals, and when violence erupted, any weapon was used…' As an antidote to the fearful reputation the area once had, it is heartening that the main building of interest in the area is the Citizens' Theatre, one of Glasgow's most popular theatres.

The very large building on the left is the **Sheriff Court of Glasgow and Strathkelvin** 🕸 (1980-6, Keppie, Henderson & Partners), which replaced the 'warren' that existed inside the County Buildings and Courthouses (see p.48). It's the busiest court in Europe, and the building's austere angular design seems suited to its function; indeed, it has the air of a fortress. And with all its fine sandstone, granite and marble, to say nothing of the stainless steel cells in the basement, it's an expensively built fortress at that.

The interior has been carefully designed to withstand a substantial amount of wear and tear and, as one of the court's own publications states, the building's accommodation is 'of a more robust nature to withstand the vagaries of behaviour of some of the apprehended and this may give an atmosphere of foreboding that is not inappropriate'.

Continue on the riverside path in order to reach **Carlton Place** (1802-18, Peter Nicolson). This very elegant street was built by James and David Laurie and was the first major development of good-quality residential buildings south of the river. This new district of Laurieston was given 'prestigious' street names but it never prospered as it soon suffered from the relentless encroachment of factories (and their pollution) from further south.

The row is made up of two blocks: the eastern block was built in 1802-4 and the western in 1813-8. Nicolson designed them with end pavilions (as at number 40) but the symmetry of the row has been lost by later rebuilding. Many of the buildings are now used as offices, but numbers 51 and 52, the brothers' own houses, have many of the original features still extant. These two houses make up **Laurieston House** ㉝, and number 52, James Laurie's house, has been described as the most ornate Georgian townhouse in the United Kingdom, with its superb plasterwork believed to be the work of the Italian Francisco Bernasconi. It is hoped that the building will be renovated and opened to the public.

CARLTON PLACE TO GLASGOW CROSS

Continue along Carlton Place and cross the river by the **South Portland Street Suspension Bridge** �34 (1851-3, George Martin). This graceful and often-photographed bridge offers good views of the riverside buildings. The grand Greek Ionic pylons are in the form of a triumphal arch and the bridge has wrought-iron latticework. When first opened, pedestrians had to pay a toll of a halfpenny to cross the bridge.

Turn left at the northern side of the bridge and follow Clyde Street westwards. At 242-62 Clyde Street stands **Riverside House** �35 (1906-7, Eric A. Sutherland), a tall red sandstone building with little turrets at the top. The lack of fussy detail on this warehouse is probably what makes it so attractive. �36

Continue along to the Greek Doric **Custom House** (1840, John Taylor) at 298-306 Clyde Street. In the days when the docks were very busy this building would have been a hive of activity, with customs

South Portland Street Suspension Bridge

officers checking documents and collecting duties on cargoes going in and out of the port. The building is topped by a beautifully carved royal coat of arms featuring the emblems of the (then) four home countries, a unicorn, a lion, a crown and *Dieu et mon droit* ('God and my right'), the motto of British sovereigns, and *Honi soit qui mal y pense* ('Evil to him who evil thinks').

Opposite the Custom House, turn left and head down some steps to the riverside walkway; this part is the **Custom House Quay Gardens**. The quay used to be where ships unloaded sand and gravel as well as the stones that were used to pave the city's streets and pavements.

The tall statue here is of **Dolores Ibarruri** ㊲ ('La Pasionara') in honour of those who fought against Franco's army in the Spanish Civil War in the 1930s. Ibarruri (1895-1989) came from the Basque country and wrote for the socialist press under the name La Pasionaria ('the passion flower'). She was elected to the Spanish Cortes (parliament) in 1936, later helping to establish the Popular Front Government which was overthrown by the fascists. She then fled to the USSR, returned to Spain after Franco died, and was re-elected to the Cortes at the age of 81. The plinth bears her words *Better to die on your feet than live for ever on your knees.* Below, another plaque explains *The City of Glasgow and the British Labour Movement pay tribute to the courage of those men and women who went to Spain to fight Fascism 1936-1939. 2,100 volunteers went from Britain; 534 were killed, 65 of whom came from Glasgow.* The monument is quite a change from the statues of the 'worthies' who decorate George Square.

Either follow the walkway or Clyde Street eastwards to get to **St Andrew's Roman Catholic Cathedral** ㊳ (1814-17, James Gillespie Graham). Unlike its Church of Scotland counterpart, this cathedral is relatively modern and, considering its status, is really quite unadorned and unostentatious. It is a tall and narrow building, with two octagonal towers flanking a statue of St Andrew. Slender stone finials decorate the edges of the building. Keen photographers usually spot the cathedral's reflections on the glass-fronted Archdiocesan Offices next door.

In 1805 there were only about 450 Catholics in the city, but by 1814 this had grown to 3000 and was increasing rapidly. This building was originally erected as an ordinary church and only became a cathedral in 1889, its elevation being celebrated by its renovation by Pugin & Pugin. Inside, the church is bright and airy and the focus of attention is the group of stained-glass windows behind the altar. The ceiling is decorated with curved ribs and ornamental bosses; although much of the interior decoration may look like carved stonework, a lot of it is painted plasterwork.

The last building on Clyde Street before Stockwell Street is **Carrick Quay** ㊴ (1989-90, Davis Duncan Partnership), so-called because the sailing ship SV *Carrick* (built in 1864) was berthed here from 1949 to 1990. Sadly, the clipper has left the river in order to be refurbished at the Scottish

Maritime Museum in Irvine. The building's nautical features celebrate the ship which was still here when the flats were being constructed.

The name Stockwell Street may come from the fact that it was the site of the Stok Well, a well in which the water was raised by a stock or shaft of wood. An alternative story about it comes from the days of William Wallace (1270-1305). During one of his many exploits, his men defeated a force of English and then threw the bodies down a nearby well, with Wallace encouraging them with the words 'Stock it well, lads stock it well!' The street was originally called Fishergait as it was the main route to the river.

There are a number of interesting buildings near this junction of five roads. Many important crossroads in Glasgow are marked by imposing tenement buildings and, in this case, the tall tenement building **143-55 Stockwell Street** ④⓪ (1905, Alex. B. McDonald) is a good example of this architectural tradition. It has various carvings, including the date *1905* and, as the building was designed by the City Engineer, a Glasgow coat of arms.

The building to its left, **133-9 Stockwell Street** ④① (Alex. B. McDonald), has a number of pleasant features on it, including four central pillars which are flanked by two towers topped by decorated parapets. There are many carvings on the facade and a bell, tree, fish and bird can be seen just below the second-storey windows.

The **Scotia Bar** ④② is at 112-4 Stockwell Street. It was established in 1792 and is another claimant to the title of 'the oldest pub in Glasgow'. This is a cosy little pub with a low wooden ceiling and is famed as a 'writers' retreat'. It sponsors the Scotia Bar Writers Prize and in its first year (1990) this led to the publication of the anthology *A spiel amang us* ('A blether between us' – see the Bibliography).

Cross Stockwell Street and follow Bridgegate. On the right is the former **Fish Market** ④③ (1872-3, Clarke & Bell), usually referred to as 'The Briggait' after the road (the 'gait') to the old bridge. This contains a fine galleried market hall, vacated by the fishmerchants in 1977, but which unfortunately does not yet have a permanent use. The city's coat of arms, flanked by large fish, is above the doorways.

The market's southern side is in French Renaissance style. It has two massive cast-iron gates above which are medallions of Queen Victoria. These are flanked by pairs of winged seamonsters called hippocampuses

In the seventeenth century, Bridgegate (also called the Briggait) used to be *the* fashionable place in the city and many of the wealthiest merchants built their houses here. The Gothic **Merchants' Steeple** ④④ (1665) rises out of the buildings around the fishmarket and the tall clock tower is all that remains of the Dutch-style Merchants' House of 1659. This important building was, as a contemporary account described it, 'beautified with the gilded broads, names, designations, and sums mortified for the use of poor old members of merchant rank.' The tower

The Briggait and the Merchants' Steeple

stands high above the river and is said to have been used by merchants to see if their ships were approaching; as a link with the past, the Merchants' House emblem, a sailing ship, decorates the top. The merchants moved out of here in 1817, eventually settling in George Square (see p.88).

Continue along Bridgegate to where a railway bridge crosses overhead. At this point, the narrow Shipbank Lane on the right leads to **Paddy's Market** ㊺, where a 'flea market' is held. This old-established market has occupied many sites since it started early in the nineteenth century. As the name suggests, it was run by immigrants from Ireland who sold second-hand clothes to the large population of poor people who were living in nearby hovels; their numbers increased dramatically as a result of the 1845 Irish Potato Famine.

Follow Bridgegate to the Saltmarket. On the right at the junction stands the nineteenth-century **Old Ship Bank Building** ㊻, which was altered in 1904. This houses the Old Ship Bank pub whose windows sport an etching of the Ship Bank that was established here in 1750. This was originally founded by some of the city's wealthy merchants in order to help the financing of the tobacco trade.

On the opposite corner of this junction stands a block of tenements at **109-29 Saltmarket** ㊼ (1880, John Carrick). These were the first houses to be built by the Glasgow Improvement Trust and their design retains features of the previous buildings that stood here (notably the crow-stepped gables). Like many new buildings of that time, these houses were not built with inside toilets; however, in this case each 'landing' had two toilets – one for either sex.

The end of this walk is now just a short distance away up Saltmarket. However, the route now returns along Bridgegate and turns right after going under the railway bridge. Follow King Street to King's Court, where there is a group of shops selling second-hand furniture and various sorts of antiques.

Continue on King Street to the junction with Parnie Street. The area around here has some small galleries, together with a number of shops selling prints.

The best-known gallery in the area is the **Glasgow Print Studio** 48 at 22 King Street. The studio was founded in 1972 and it has a large gallery which is used for frequently changing exhibitions. It also has a printmaking studio which produces high-quality prints of pictures (many by Scottish artists); these are available at The Original Print Shop across the road.

The most unusual of all the city's galleries is at 14 King Street: **Sharmanka** 49 (Eduard Bersudsky's 'gallery of kinetic sculptures'). This houses a collection of mechanical sculptures which use motors, wheels, levers and all sorts of mechanical contrivances to make model figures and animals move. The models dance, spin, fly through the air and generally keep the viewer wondering what will happen next. The sculptures are works of art in themselves and their performance is bizarre, fascinating and entertaining all at the same time. The gallery was given the name *Sharmanka* (Russian for 'street organ') as the artist was first inspired to create these kinetic sculptures by a wooden model of a Russian organ-grinder.

Head eastwards along Parnie Street, another interesting street not well known by visitors (and many Glaswegians), but one which contains numerous small specialist shops, many of them for collectors of various kinds.

Saltmarket is then met. Turn left and walk up to **Glasgow Cross** 1 where the walk ends.

The City Centre

Starting at George Square in the heart of the city, this walk explores the administrative, commercial and shopping heart of Glasgow.

George Square and the City Chambers

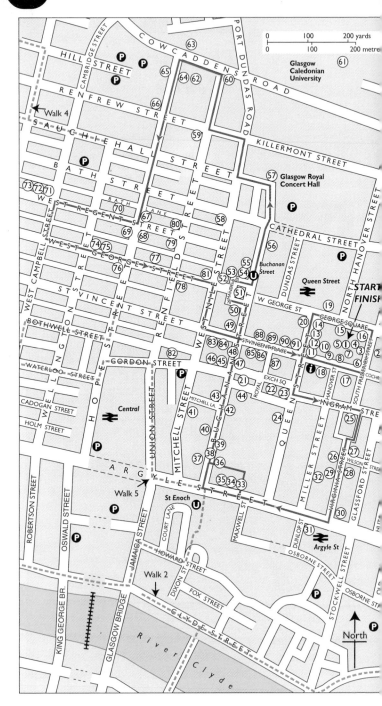

Walk 3: The City Centre

1 George Square
2 City Chambers
3 Cenotaph
4 Hiroshima Memorial Plaque
5 Sir Walter Scott (S)
6 Thomas Graham (S)
7 Thomas Campbell (S)
8 Lord Clyde (S)
9 Sir John Moore (S)
10 Robert Burns (S)
11 James Watt (S)
12 Prince Albert (S)
13 Queen Victoria (S)
14 Robert Peel (S)
15 William Ewart Gladstone (S)
16 James Oswald (S)
17 Former Post Office
18 Tourist Information Centre
19 Copthorne Hotel
20 Merchants` House Buildings
21 Royal Bank of Scotland
22 Gallery of Modern Art
23 Duke of Wellington (S)
24 South Exchange Court
25 Lanarkshire House
26 Jacobean Corsetry Building
27 Scottish Legal Buildings
28 42 Virginia Street
29 Crown Arcade
30 Robert Burns Plaque
31 Buck`s Head Building
32 The Tobacco Laird`s House
33 Argyll Arcade
34 106-14 Argyle Street
35 Morrison`s Court
36 Argyll Chambers
37 45 Buchanan Street (Frasers)
38 *Concept of Kentigern*
39 Prince of Wales Buildings (Princes Square)
40 Glasgow Herald Office
41 Glasgow Herald Building
42 North British Rubber Building
43 Clydesdale Bank Building
44 Rogano
45 Royal Bank of Scotland
46 8 Gordon Street
47 Police box
48 street plan
49 Western Club
50 Glasgow Stock Exchange
51 St George`s Tron Parish Church
52 Royal Faculty of Procurators` Hall
53 The Athenaeum
54 Liberal Club
55 The Old Athenaeum Theatre
56 Buchanan Galleries
57 Glasgow Royal Concert Hall
58 99-107 West Nile Street
59 Pavilion Theatre
60 Annan Fountain

61 Glasgow Caledonian University
62 Scottish Television
63 The Piping Centre
64 Theatre Royal
65 McConnel`s Building
66 Royal Scottish Academy of Music and Drama
67 Lion Chambers
68 Pot Still pub
69 79 West Regent Street
70 100 West Regent Street
71 Institute for the Adult Deaf and Dumb
72 John Ross Memorial Church for the Deaf
73 176-84 West Regent Street
74 198 West George Street
75 Ocean Chambers
76 157-67 Hope Street
77 James Sellars House
78 Sun, Fire and Life Building
79 Castle Chambers
80 De Quincey`s Bar
81 Commercial Bank of Scotland
82 The Horse Shoe bar
83 John Smith & Son
84 National Bank Chambers
85 Scottish Amicable Building
86 Scottish Provident Institution Building
87 The Auctioneers pub
88 Clydesdale Bank
89 Citizen Offices
90 Anchor Line Building
91 Bank of Scotland Building

(S)	Statue
▬▬▬	Route
▬ ▬ ▬	Other Walks
P	Car Parking
⇆	Rail Station
U	Underground
i	Tourist Information

Main places of interest	**George Square** ❶ (the heart of the city) **City Chambers** ❷ (elaborate municipal headquarters) **Gallery of Modern Art** ㉒ Glasgow Herald Building ㊶ (architecture and design centre; open in 1999) Glasgow Royal Concert Hall ㊗ The Piping Centre ㊳ (bagpipes)
Circular/linear	circular
Starting point	George Square ❶
Finishing point	George Square ❶
Distance	4 km (2.5 miles)
Terrain	pavements; increasing slope up Buchanan Street; slope back down to the end of the route
Public transport	Queen Street Railway Station (Q) Argyle Street Railway Station (C) St Enoch Underground Station Buchanan Street Underground Station Cowcaddens Underground Station Central Railway Station (C)
Sections	George Square George Square to Buchanan Street Buchanan Street Buchanan Street to West George Street via Cowcaddens West George Street to George Square via St Vincent Place
Architects	Thomson: Buck's Head Building ㉛ 99-107 West Nile Street ㊵ Mackintosh: former Glasgow Herald Office ㊶
Nearby walks	1, 2, 4, 5
Refreshments	Gallery of Modern Art; Princes Square; Glasgow Royal Concert Hall; many places in all sections
Notes	This walk goes through or near many of the city centre's main shopping areas and the streets will generally be crowded. Sunday morning, before the shoppers appear, is the best time to walk this route.

George Square

George Square ❶ was laid out in 1781, even though a few years later it was still being described as a 'hollow, filled with green-water, and a favourite resort for drowning puppies, while the banks of this suburban pool were the slaughtering place of horses.' Large two- and three-storey houses were built around it between 1787 and the 1820s, but only the present-day Copthorne Hotel on the square's northern side retains these early buildings. The square itself was given over to private gardens which only the privileged householders could use; this so annoyed other Glaswegians that its railings were torn down on several occasions. Later the council discovered (as an 1872 guide relates) 'that the whole enclosure belonged to the public who had been so long excluded from it.' The square was to achieve its pre-eminence when the city moved its centre westwards and the merchants and manufacturers who controlled the council wanted a lavishly decorated building and a grand civic space which reflected their position as leaders of 'The Second City'.

Although Glasgow has continued its westward expansion, George Square is still regarded as the centre of the city as it is the site of the City Chambers, Glasgow's main public building. During the Christmas period the square is ablaze with its decorations while, during the hottest part of the summer, office workers flock to the benches in a desperate bid to soak up some sunlight. The square is also used for large public gatherings, whether it is to see in the New Year or for public rallies or protests. The most famous demonstration here was on 'Black Friday' (31 January 1919) during the campaign for a forty-hour week (to prevent post-war unemployment). Some 50,000 workers were on strike that day, 10,000 of them gathering in the square. Tempers flared when a tramcar tried to make its way through the crowd and a pitched battle ensued. The government ordered troops onto the streets that evening, tanks were kept at the ready and machine-gun nests were installed in various places in the square. Emmanuel (Manny) Shinwell, one of the leaders, described how the troops 'had nothing to do but chat to the local people and drink their cups of tea', leaving the officers complaining about 'fraternisation with the "enemy"'. The authorities continued their clampdown when fifteen people were charged with 'inciting a mob of 20,000 or thereby riotous and evilly disposed persons', and three of them, Manny Shinwell, David Kirkwood and William Gallacher, were imprisoned for their roles. All three later became Members of Parliament, the first two eventually making their way into the House of Lords.

The **City Chambers** ❷ (1882-90, William Young) dominates the eastern end of the square. This is the seat of local government and is the city's most finely decorated building. It was built to reflect Glasgow's proud boast of being 'The Second City of the Empire' and the magnificent exterior and interior attests to the wealth the city possessed at the end of the nineteenth century.

The building's entrance is based on the third-century Arch of Constantine in Rome which the architect, William Young, had visited before preparing the plans. Young wrote a book about the building in which he explained that:

> here a similar display of art in stone (by Mr G. A. Lawson, who also executed the sculptured pediment) declares the peaceful victories of art, science, and commerce. Over the key-stone of the centre arch is a representation of the city coat of arms, with the motto 'Let Glasgow flourish'; and to this the sculptured subjects add for supports – By the aid of Religion, Virtue, and Knowledge.

> The figures supporting the coat of arms on both sides represent Religion, the emblems being victory and glory. The other figures in the central arch symbolize the Virtues – Faith, Hope, Truth, Charity. The sculptured band continuing to the left over the side arch represents the Art, Knowledges, Architecture, Sculpture, Painting, Music, Oratory, Literature; while on the other side are figures representing Astronomy, Geology, Chemistry, Engineering, and the Healing Art – all bringing their respective knowledge to support the central motto, 'Let Glasgow flourish'.

The second-floor windows are decorated with eleven sculptures of the city's trades and industries which can be identified by the tools, equipment and symbols included with the figures. The third floor has eight statues; the architect's description is that 'these sculptured figures on the pedestals over the columns represent Hygeia [the Greek goddess of Health], Harmony, Piety, Peace, Plenty, Prosperity, etc.' The imposing pediment at the top shows Queen Victoria, sitting on a throne and attended by lions and figures representing England, Scotland, Ireland, Wales and other countries of the British Empire. Above that is *Truth* (holding a torch) with *Riches* and *Honour* by her side. Domed cupolas are at the building's corners and also on top of the tall central tower which rises high above George Square. This central tower has figures representing the four seasons and on top of its cupola is a gilded orb and cross. Many of the sculptures on the exterior show off the talents of Glasgow's best-known sculptor, John G. Mossman.

At the bottom right-hand side of the facade are two plaques, the one on the right explaining that *Standards of Imperial linear measures placed on this wall and on the adjoining footpath by the Corporation of the City of Glasgow 1882. Standard measures of 100 feet, 1 yard, 2 feet, 1 foot, 1 inch, also of 1 chain, 1 link. Verified by the Standards Department, Board of Trade.* The other plaque has on it pins that mark measurements of 1 foot, 2 feet and 1 imperial yard; these were used by tailors to check that their tape measures measured the right length. Since these tapes were made of linen (which stretched), they also brought scissors with them to this spot so that they could cut the tape to the correct length.

Beyond the two corners of the facade, the two sides of the building have more fine detail and then, at John Street, there are elaborate triumphal arches which link the main building to an eastern extension which was added in 1914-23 by Watson, Salmond & Gray.

Inside the main door, the **Loggia** (Entrance Hall) is quite stunning and overall there is a strong Italian influence as it is in the shape of a Renaissance Roman church. The patterned vaulted ceiling, its domes and the floor are all covered in Venetian mosaic, with the ceiling and domes alone made up of one-and-a-half million individual pieces. The floor's most elaborate design is that of the city's coat of arms. In the first part of the Loggia are four statues which represent *Wisdom*, *Purity*, *Strength* and *Honour*. Red Aberdeenshire granite columns topped by Ionic capitals of green marble frame the central passageway and elaborate wrought-iron lamps light the whole space. Originally, the Loggia stretched through the building to John Street, but now there is a wall blocking the way. A reception desk is in front of this wall and doors on either side of the desk lead to the interior's most outstanding architectural features, the two main staircases.

On the southern side is the magnificent **Council Hall Staircase**, rising two floors and lit from above by an oval glass dome. Ornamental plasterwork decorates the ceilings and the marble pillars have alabaster inserts. This leads to the second floor and the **Council Hall** where full meetings of the city's council take place. This is lined with Spanish mahogany and has a highly ornamented plaster ceiling. Its windows, which look onto George Square, have their original double glazing. The councillors' seats are arranged in arcs that face the Lord Provost's chair, in front of which the Municipal Mace is placed when the council is meeting. Also on the second floor is the **Councillors' Corridor** which is decorated with elaborate ornamental glazed tiles.

On the northern side of the building is an even grander staircase, the **Marble Staircase**, which rises the full three storeys of the building. It features very fine columns and arches cut from high-quality Carrara marble from northern Italy. Blocks and panels of alabaster have also been used here.

This staircase leads to the large barrel-vaulted **Banqueting Hall** which is awash with golds, browns and reds; their combined effect is quite overwhelming. Each of the early twentieth-century paintings on the walls has a special significance for the city. On the southern wall is *Glasgow unfolding its plans for the future* by D. Forrester Wilson and on the west wall are representations of four important Scottish rivers: the Tay, Forth, Clyde and Tweed by William Findlay (1911). The northern wall features *Granting of Glasgow's charter by William the Lion* by George Henry. The long eastern wall has large mural paintings depicting Glasgow by three members of the group of artists known as 'The Glasgow Boys': *Legendary Glasgow* (Alexander Roche) shows St Mungo with the ring retrieved from the salmon; *Medieval Glasgow* (Edward Walton) shows the fifteenth-century Glasgow Fair; and *Modern Glasgow* (Sir John Lavery) shows shipbuilding and other important industries.

The third floor has a portrait gallery with paintings and photographs of the city's past Lord Provosts; the Lord Provost is the councillor who chairs the full meetings of the council and who acts as the city's 'figurehead' and ambassador.

The City Chambers

Guided tours of the City Chambers are available; enquire inside the main entrance or at the Tourist Information Office.

Directly in front of the City Chambers stands the white Kemnay granite **Cenotaph** ❸ (1921-4, Sir J. J. Burnet), the city's war memorial to those who died in two world wars. The two massive lions and the figure of St Mungo (which is on the tall granite block) were by Ernest Gillick. Lying horizontally between the two lions is a sculptured wreath and a palm frond, together with the single word *Pax* ('Peace').

Eighteen thousand men of the city died in the First World War and the inscription on the monument bears the words *Their name liveth for evermore*. This tall block also bears a sword (in the form of a cross) and four carved wreaths. Various other inscriptions are given and on the rear are the royal arms with the words *Pro patria* ('For their country').

Just in front of the cenotaph lies the small **Hiroshima Memorial Plaque** ❹, placed here in 1985 *to commemorate the 40th anniversary of the loss of civilian lives caused by the dropping of the first atomic bombs on the cities of Hiroshima 6 August 1945 and Nagasaki 9 August 1945.*

How ironic it is that just farther down the River Clyde lie some of the world's most 'important' stockpiles of nuclear weapons.

In the centre of George Square rises the tall Doric column (1837, David Rhind) on which is a stone statue of **Sir Walter Scott** ❺ (1771-1832), carved by A. Handyside Ritchie. Scott was an Edinburgh lawyer who settled in the Scottish Borders as Sheriff-Depute of Selkirkshire. He collected a great number of Border ballads and old tales and used his story-telling skills to become Scotland's best-known 'romantic' writer. Amongst his best-known works are the long poem *Lady of the Lake* (1810) and the novels *Waverley* (1814) and *The Heart of Midlothian* (1818). His best-known Glasgow character was Bailie Nicol Jarvie, a merchant who featured in the novel *Rob Roy* (1818). The statue shows Scott with a plaid carried over the right shoulder in the manner of the Border shepherds.

The other statues in the square are described below, going clockwise from the Cenotaph.

Thomas Graham ❻ (1805-69).

Graham was born in Glasgow and became Professor of Chemistry in the Andersonian University (see p.44) in 1830. He later moved to University College in London and then became Master of the Mint. An internationally known scientist, he discovered the properties of the group of unusual substances called colloids and formulated Graham's Law which dealt with the diffusion of gases. His best-known work was *Chemical and Physical Researches*, published posthumously in 1876. The statue, sculpted by William Brodie in 1871, shows him seated and clutching a scientific text.

Thomas Campbell ❼ (1777-1844)

Campbell was born in Glasgow (see p.33) and studied law in Edinburgh. However, his real interest was poetry, his best-known works being 'Pleasures of Hope' (1799) and 'Hohenlinden' (about the battle of 1800 between France and Austria). He was elected Rector of Glasgow University three times. This John G. Mossman sculpture of 1877 depicts him in Regency dress and holding a feather quill in his right hand.

Lord Clyde ❽ (1792-1863)

Field Marshall Lord Clyde (previously Sir Colin Campbell) was born in Glasgow but educated in England. He went into the army and fought in Iberia (during the Peninsular War of 1808-14), America (1814) and Jamaica (1823), where he put down a slaves' uprising. He was also involved in the Crimean War and was in command of the Highland Brigade who held back the Russian cavalry at the Battle of Balaclava (1854); an event made famous by the painting *The Thin Red Line* by Robert Gibb (1845-1932). In the Indian subcontinent he fought to put down the Indian Mutiny (see p.200). The statue (1867, J. H. Foley) shows him dressed in military uniform, leaning on a palm and with a telescope in his hand.

Sir John Moore ❾ (1761-1809)

Lieutenant General Sir John Moore was born in Glasgow and fought with the British army during the American War of Independence (1776-83). During a period at home, he became the Member of Parliament for the Lanark Burghs. In 1790 he received further promotion, this time to lieutenant colonel, by simply 'purchasing' the rank. In 1808 he was sent to Iberia to fight against the French in the Peninsular War (1808-14) but, greatly outnumbered, he was forced to retreat with his army to La Coruña where he was killed during the ensuing battle. The statue was sculpted by John Flaxman in 1819.

Robert Burns ❿ (1759-96)

Burns is, undisputedly, the country's best-known literary figure and he has inspired many hundreds of active Burns Clubs throughout the world. As well as being famous for his superb poetry, Burns as an individual has been a subject for study and debate for two hundred years. Arguments continue as to whether he should be considered as a gifted (but primitive) 'ploughman poet' or whether he was simply a superb example of how the Scottish educational system can successfully mould a poor (but very widely read) Scots boy into a celebrated literary figure. His personal life, whether it be his amorous relationships or his drinking habits, has also been the subject of much speculation and is still the topic of thousands of 'Burns night' speeches. Burns nights are held all over the world to celebrate this great poet's birthday, 25th January.

This sculpture by George Edwin Ewing (1876-7) shows him holding a daisy in his left hand as a reminder of his poem 'To a Mountain Daisy' (1786). He is dressed as a Scottish farmer and has a Kilmarnock bonnet in his right hand. The plinth has decorated plaques by J. A. Ewing showing scenes from Burns' poems; the most detailed is from the epic 'Tam O' Shanter' (*c.* 1790), with Tam looking through the window of Kirk-Alloway:

And, vow! Tam saw an unco sight!
Warlocks and witches in a dance:
Nae cotillion, brent new frae France,
But hornpipes, jigs strathspeys, and reels,
Put life and mettle in their heels.

(*unco* = 'wondrous'; cotillion = a French dance employing elaborate steps; *brent* = 'brand'; *frae* = 'from')

Others plaques represent scenes from 'The Cotter's Saturday Night' (1785-6) and 'The Vision' (1785-7).

James Watt ⓫ (1736-1819)

Watt has been described as 'the inventor who made the Industrial Revolution possible' and, as such, someone who has made an enormous contribution to Glasgow's success. He worked at Glasgow University as an instrument repairer for Joseph Black (see p.189) and while working on a Newcomen steam engine he mused over how it could be improved. Popular history has it that Watt 'discovered' the power of steam while watching a kettle of boiling water, but the reality is more mundane. The essential idea of making a separate condenser (and thus cooling the steam *outside* the cylinder) came to him while walking in Glasgow Green, an innovation which allowed the rapid development of much more powerful engines. These were used in mines, factories and, because of the weight-savings, also in ship propulsion, thus revolutionising the ship-building industry. Watt is recognised elsewhere in the city: in Glasgow Green (see p.63) and Glasgow University (see p.183).

The statue, by Sir Francis Chantrey (1832), shows Watt with a pair of dividers in his hand poring over drawings.

Prince Albert ⓬ (1819-61)

Prince Albert married his cousin Queen Victoria (see below) in 1840, becoming the Prince Consort. This equestrian statue (1866) was designed by Baron Carlo Marochetti and its pink granite plinth is decorated with scenes representing the Arts and the Sciences.

Queen Victoria ⑬ (1819-1901)

Queen Victoria was queen of the United Kingdom from 1837 to her death, a reign which coincided with the massive economic, military and political might of the British Empire. Indeed, a nineteenth-century history of George Square expresses the view that 'The whole of Her Majesty's reign has marked a wonderful and brilliant era in civilization.' Despite Glasgow being the 'The Second City' of the Empire, Victoria visited it only three times, and her visit in 1849 (*en route* to Balmoral) was the first time a British monarch had been in the city since the seventeenth century.

This equestrian statue was designed by Baron Carlo Marochetti and its pink granite plinth is decorated with two elaborate panels. This statue was originally erected in St Vincent Place in 1854 but was moved here when Prince Albert's statue was unveiled in the square. The two panels celebrate Victoria's visit to the city on 14 August 1849. Victoria and Albert arrived from Dublin and were taken to Broomielaw by the yacht *Fairy*. Lord Provost Anderson and the magistrates went on board and one of the panels shows Anderson being knighted. The queen and her entourage then proceeded to the Cathedral and the other plaque shows them being met there by the minister Duncan Macfarlan.

Robert Peel ⑭ (1788-1850)

Peel came from a rich family of English manufacturers and became a Tory Member of Parliament at the age of 21. He was Home Secretary in 1822-7 and 1828-30 and is best-remembered for founding of the modern police force, whose members were nicknamed 'Bobbies' after Peel. He later became Prime Minister (in 1834-5 and 1841-6), during which time he repealed the Corn Laws, an important blow against the strength of landowners and large arable farmers. In 1836 he was elected Lord Rector of Glasgow University. The sculpture is by John G. Mossman (1859).

William Ewart Gladstone ⑮ (1809-98)

Gladstone entered parliament as a Tory in 1833 and held offices in Peel's government. In 1846 he crossed the floor of the House of Commons and joined the Liberals, later serving four spells as Prime Minister, the last being in 1892-4. His championing of Free Trade was supported by Glasgow's industrialists and he was given the Freedom of the City in 1865 and elected Lord Rector of Glasgow University in 1877 (see p.228).

The statue, sculpted by W. Hamo Thornycroft in 1899-1902, shows Gladstone in the robes of the university's rector while the two bronze reliefs depict him in the House of Commons and felling a tree at his Welsh home.

James Oswald ⑯ (1779-1853)

Oswald was a wealthy merchant who became a Whig Member of Parliament for Glasgow in 1833. The election took place after the

Scottish Reform Act of 1832 which ended the right of councils to nominate MPs. Nevertheless, in the 1833 election only five per cent of the people had the right to vote. The Whigs could perhaps be described as 'radical liberals' who were in favour of free-trade and anti-drink legislation and against the power of the emergent trade unions. The statue (1856, Baron Carlo Marochetti) originally stood at Charing Cross but was moved here in 1875. It is said that the top hat he holds out had to be given a drainage hole when it became home to nesting sparrows. It is also a well-known target for throwing things into; Glaswegians are a sporting lot, especially on Friday and Saturday nights!

On the south-eastern side of the square stands the former **Post Office** **17** (1875-8, Robert Matheson). This large Italianate building, which replaced the Assembly Rooms (see p.101), has its entrances flanked by granite pillars. At attic level is a balustrade, a royal coat of arms with the motto *Dieu et mon droit* ('God and my right') and the inscription *Victoria Regina MDCCCLXXVIII* (1878).

The **Tourist Information Centre** **18** is situated on the square's southern side at 11 George Square. The building, erected about 1870 in the style of an Italian palace, has some nice detailed carving above the second-storey windows. The staff of the centre can supply a great deal of information about the Glasgow area and can arrange accommodation and transport. Maps and books can also be purchased.

The **Copthorne Hotel** **19** (*c.* 1807-18) is the only remnant of the Georgian square, although it has been spoiled by an ugly extension and glass conservatories. In the centre of the middle balustrade is a roundel with the initials *NBR* – the building was taken over and added to by the North British Railway in 1903 to house the North British Hotel. The nicest part of the original building are the end houses' fluted Corinthian pilasters, which give an indication of the original building's proportions.

On the western side of the square are buildings that represent the commercial interests of the city. At the north-western corner, near Queen Street Station, is the **Merchants' House Buildings** **20** (1874, John Burnet), which has its main entrance at 7 West George Street. One storey above this entrance is a sculpture featuring a pair of female figures on either side of a sailing ship which is atop a globe. The engraved phrase *Toties redeuntis eodem* ('So often returning to the same place') is the Merchants' House motto. A series of faces decorate the ground floor windows' keystones, and the first floor oriel windows are supported by pairs of straining figures, looking very much like ships' figureheads. The top two storeys, added in 1907-9 by J. J. Burnet, are topped by a domed tower on which is perched a ship on a globe, symbolising the worldwide trade in which the merchants were involved; this is similar to the sculpture on the Merchants' Steeple (see p.74). With a pair of binoculars, it is possible to see the rather alarming angle at which the Earth's axis is placed! As befits the gathering-place of the city's merchants, the interior decoration is very fine, especially in the tall and elegant Merchants' Hall.

The city's Merchants' House formed an influential body which played a pivotal role in helping Glasgow become 'The Second City'. Founded in the seventeenth century, it campaigned for the deepening of the River Clyde and helped recruit troops to quell the 'rebellion' in America (to safeguard the important tobacco trade). It also had an important role in local government as the organisation was entitled to a great number of seats on the city's council. Although most of these privileges were swept away in 1832, the last vestiges of their tenure in the City Chambers ended only in 1975.

GEORGE SQUARE TO BUCHANAN STREET

Leave George Square by its south-western corner, heading down Queen Street until **Royal Exchange Square** is met on the right. This was developed from 1827 onwards and, as with other important squares in the city, it is built around a notable building, in this case the Gallery of Modern Art. This fine example of early town planning has substantial commercial buildings on its north and south sides which were erected to complement the major building at the western end, the Royal Bank of Scotland. The original buildings were subject to strict planning regulations, including some proscribing the type of shops' signs allowed. Perhaps the proprietors of shops in Argyle Street and other busy shopping areas might do well to learn from this example.

The former **Royal Bank of Scotland** **㉑** (1827, Archibald Elliot II) is a classic Greek Ionic structure modelled on the Athenian Erechtheum, a temple on the Acropolis. It has six massive columns sitting on a raised platform and these support a large portico. The flanks of the building are joined onto the rest of the square's buildings by triumphal arches which lead to Buchanan Street, the city's most impressive shopping area.

The building's Buchanan Street frontage (see p.99) was added in 1850-1 by Charles Wilson. One of the most notable features of this large Italianate building are its large windows which are decorated with sculpted human heads and foliage. Much higher up, the cornice has more ornate carvings and there are many curious small heads.

The very grand **Gallery of Modern Art** **㉒** sits in the middle of the square. It was originally built in 1778-80 as a magnificent home for the very rich tobacco merchant William Cunninghame at the enormous cost of £10,000. The house was later purchased by the Royal Bank of Scotland who sold it in 1827 so that an Exchange (designed by David Hamilton) could be established. The massive Corinthian portico with its twelve pillars was added to the front of the house and above it rose a cupola and clock tower. The Exchange's hall, with its magnificent barrel-vaulted ceiling, was added at the back, leaving the house sandwiched in between. The hall is reckoned to be the city's best early nineteenth-century interior. Initially dealing with trade in tobacco,

Gallery of Modern Art

sugar and rum, the Exchange was later involved in more 'modern' goods such as iron, coal and shipping. In 1949 the building was taken over by the council to house Stirling's Library and in 1996 it was refurbished to accommodate the gallery.

Today, the gallery houses the city's large collection of contemporary art. It is arranged in four themed areas named after the four ancient elements: 'Earth', 'Fire', 'Water' and 'Air'.

At ground-floor level is the former Exchange which houses the **Earth Gallery**. A spacious room with numerous fluted Corinthian columns and a beautiful ceiling, it has many of the collection's larger and more spectacular works. Three well-known Scottish painters represented here are Peter Howson (1958–), Steven Campbell (1953–) and Ken Currie (1960–). Howson's *Patriots* (1991) shows three aggressive and ugly men with two equally aggressive dogs, symbolizing the senseless bigotry and violence prevalent in Britain in the 1990s. Campbell's *Painting in Defence of Migrants* (1993) represents vulnerability and Currie's *The Bathers* (1992-3) is a haunting portrayal of victims of hatred which resulted from a dream experienced by the artist. Quite different in style is the *Buka War* (1990) by Mathias Kauage (born *c.* 1944), a bold and colourful depiction of the clash between international mining interests and his people of Papua New Guinea. In addition to the paintings is Eduard Bersudsky's (1939–) kinetic sculpture *Titanic* (1994), an assortment of wheels, a butter churn, a propeller, various *objects trouvées* and some small human figures, which regularly springs into life to musical accompaniment.

The **Fire Gallery** is downstairs. In 1913 this became a restaurant and the collection of marble panels, many of which are from Italy, date from this time. This is the 'high-tech' part of the museum with computers and various types of imaging equipment.

On the first floor are the **Mansion House Galleries**. This is part of the original house and the rooms are arranged around an oval balcony above which is a domed and ornamented rooflight. The galleries contain more examples of Bersudsky's rather bizarre and fascinating sculptures which are programmed to perform at certain times of the day. Despite their novelty they carry a political statement about Russia, the artist's home country. Nearby is the three-dimensional model *Inner City* (1977-9) by Michael McMillen (1946-) – you can almost anticipate the gangsters round the next corner.

On the second floor are the **Water Galleries** in which are hung a wide variety of paintings and photographs. Some of the bold geometric paintings by Bridget Riley (1931-) such as *Arrest III* (1965), *Punjab* (1971) and *Luxor* (1982) are quite startling.

This leads to the **Air Gallery**, a top-lit open space. Of particular note are pictures by Beryl Cook (1926-) such as *Karaoke* (1992) and *By the Clyde* (1992); their inclusion in the gallery caused quite a stir but most visitors will probably consider them much less controversial than other exhibits. With *Windows in the West* (1993), Avril Paton (1941-) has shown that Glasgow's tenement life is an art form in itself. A number of colourful paintings by Scotland's Alan Davie (1920-) such as *Cornucopia* (1960) are also on show. Even more eye-catching is the three-dimensional *Jubilee* (1995) by Patrick Hughes (1939-); walk past it slowly and watch it change!

This gallery leads to the **Exhibition Galleries** which are also within the original house. Above them is the top-floor **café**, its walls and ceiling decorated by Adrian Wiszniewski (1958-) with a series of bold and bright figures. Its Tower Room, which is under the clock tower, is decorated with a pattern of flowers and bees. This work is by Timorous Beasties, a Glasgow-based textiles group.

The equestrian statue of the **Duke of Wellington** ㉓ (1769-1852) by Baron Carlo Marochetti (1844) stands outside the gallery. Wellington (the 'Iron Duke') commanded the British forces in the Peninsular War against Napoleon in 1808-14 and in his most famous victory at Waterloo in 1815. He was also involved in politics and became British Prime Minister from 1828 to 1830. The well-executed bas-relief sculptures on the plinth depict the battles of Assaye and Waterloo, *The return of the soldier* and *Peace and agriculture*. Wellington often sports a colourful traffic cone on his head, a popular Glasgow custom started many years before the inside of the building behind the statue was devoted to modern art.

Leave Royal Exchange Square and continue down Queen Street to number 77, the entrance to **South Exchange Court** ㉔ (c. 1830,

Robert Black). On the inside of the right-hand entrance pillar is a plaque in memory of the poet and essayist **Alexander Smith** (1829-67) who *worked in this building as a muslin pattern-designer from 1846 until 1853 'A sacredness of love and death dwells in thy noise and smoky breath' ('Glasgow': 1854).*

Smith wrote a number of well-known poems, such as the popular 'A Life-drama' (1851-2). In 1854 he became Secretary of Edinburgh University, possibly as an attempt at giving him more time to write. Soon a collection entitled *City poems* was published which included 'Glasgow', from which the above quote is taken. He was obviously fond of Glasgow and marvelled at the changes which were taking place in the city at the time. The rapid growth of industry, its concomitant pollution and the burgeoning population was dramatically transforming his surroundings:

> *But all these sights and sounds are strange;*
> *Then wherefore from thee should I range?*
> *Thou hast my kith and kin:*
> *My childhood, youth, and manhood brave;*
> *Thou hast that unforgotten grave*
> *Within thy central din.*
> *A sacredness of love and death*
> *Dwells in thy noise and smoky breath.*

As well as poetry, he wrote articles for *Encyclopedia Britannica* and *Chambers' Encyclopedia*, as well as for various newspapers and magazines. Indeed, his massive literary output was a major factor in the exhaustion which led to his untimely death. Smith is hardly recognised in Scotland, although his work has enjoyed a small revival in recent years. In contrast, the English philosopher Herbert Spencer is reported to have written about Smith:'I consider him unquestionably the poet of the age. Though a Scotchman (and I have no partiality for the race), I am strongly inclined to rank him as the greatest poet since Shakespeare. I know no poetry that I read over and over again with such delight.'

Return to Royal Exchange Square and cross Queen Street. Head eastwards along Ingram Street to **Lanarkshire House** **46** (1841, David Hamilton). This started as the Union Bank, but in 1876-9 the facade was rebuilt by John Burnet in an Italian style using sandstone and polished granite. There is a remarkable amount of sculpture here. Immediately above the doorway is a badge with a sheaf of cereals, a sword and an axe. Above this are eight shields which carry inscriptions relating to the Union Bank's history: *Paisley 1788, Ayr 1773, Glasgow 1809, Ship 1760, Thistle 1761, Sir W Forbes 1773, Aberdeen* and *Perth.* These are flanked by carved reliefs of men on horseback.

The large sculpture over the entrance has two female figures on either side of a coat of arms (with three towers, the elements of the city's coat of arms and a sheaf of cereals). At second-floor level are six individual statues representing *Britannia, Wealth, Justice, Peace, Industry* and *Glasgow.* To their left is *Navigation and commerce* and to their right is

Mechanics and agriculture. These are by John G. Mossman. In between the statues are badges representing Dundee, Kilmarnock, Greenock, Perth, Ayr, Paisley and Aberdeen.

Walk past Lanarkshire House and turn right at a lane called Virginia Place. This leads into **Virginia Street**. The name recalls the important tobacco trade that was developed during the eighteenth century until the American War of Independence (1776-83). After the 1707 Union with England, the Glasgow merchants were quick to build up trading links with the Americas, their special advantage being that Clyde-based vessels could make the round trip in four to six weeks less than some of their rivals. During this time, Glasgow controlled about half of Britain's tobacco trade, with nearly all of the leaf being re-exported to mainland Europe. The concentration of the trade in only a few hands made the 'Tobacco Lords' incredibly wealthy and helped to finance industries that grew up in the eighteenth century. See also p.47.

The Tobacco Lords were also involved in slave trading and there was a 'triangular trade' between Glasgow, Africa and the Americas in tobacco, slaves and other 'merchandise'. Slave trading was eventually outlawed in Britain in 1807 and in the British Empire in 1833, but Glasgow money was still involved with American slave-operated cotton plantations for a long time afterwards.

The street has some interesting buildings such as the **Jacobean Corsetry Building** ㉖ (*c.* 1817) at 51 Virginia Street. The building bears a plaque on which is written *Virginia Court. Tobacco Lords worked here from 1817*.

Just opposite, at 76-84 Virginia Street, are the **Scottish Legal Buildings** ㉗ (1884, Alexander Skirving), a large red sandstone structure originally built for the Scottish Legal Life Assurance Company. The carved detail is still very crisp and in good condition, featuring scrolls, anthemia, flowers and small grotesque faces. The corner is topped by a dome.

At **42 Virginia Street** ㉘ (1867-70, Melvin & Leiper) is a handsome Italianate building originally constructed for the Glasgow Gas Company. The imposing doorway features three carved faces that shelter under an unusual stone canopy; there are further examples of fine carving at the cornice.

The Virginia Galleries, originally the **Crown Arcade** ㉙ (*c.* 1819) are at 31-5 Virginia Street. This used to be the Tobacco Exchange, where huge volumes of tobacco were once auctioned, and later served as the Sugar Exchange. Inside, a glass-roofed arcade contains tiers of pleasant old-style timbered galleries. The premises are now occupied by some small shops.

Continue along Virginia Street until it meets Argyle Street; on the left at this junction a **plaque** ㉚ records that **Robert Burns** (see p.85) lodged at this spot in 1787 and 1788 in the Black Bull Inn. The hotel was opened in 1759 and was the finest in the city. Burns came up to Glasgow in order to do business and, while in the hotel, he wrote some of his well-known love letters to 'Clarinda' (Nancy McElhose), signing them 'Sylvander'. Burns wrote his famous 'Ae Fond Kiss' for her.

Turn right at **Argyle Street** to walk along one of the city's most important shopping streets, part of which is pedestrianised. Unfortunately, with few notable exceptions, this is a rather uninteresting street and the shops are similar to those found on other busy shopping streets all over Britain.

On the southern side of the road, at 63 Argyle Street, stands the **Buck's Head Building** ㉛ (1862-3, Alexander Thomson), named after the eighteenth-century Buck's Head Hotel which once stood here. A sculpture of a buck graces the top of the building. At first sight, the design is not in the style of Thomson's best-known work as it has exposed cast-iron stanchions which rise through two storeys as a dominant feature. However, the decorative cast-iron balcony at third-floor level is quite typical of his ironwork. Elsewhere, especially in the stumpy columns between the third-floor windows, Thomson's favoured decorations of incised Greek motifs are used to good effect. Further detail is added by the roof's plant pots! The building's windows are particularly large as the glass is fitted directly onto the framework, making the rooms very bright; as with other Thomson buildings, the heights of the windows decrease upwards.

Thomson also designed a **warehouse** (1864) beside this building and three bays of its facade remain, helping the Buck's Head Building to run round the corner into Dunlop Street. The warehouse has four giant pilasters and it has the incised detail, balcony and plant pots of its more-elaborate neighbour.

As a short detour, turn next right at Miller Street, heading towards Sir Walter Scott's monument. At 42 Miller Street stands **The Tobacco Laird's House** ㉜ (1775, John Craig), the earliest house to be found in the Merchant City and the best-surviving example of this type of house in Glasgow. It has a fairly standard design for its type, with three storeys and a plain pediment supported by fluted Corinthian pilasters. The roof is decorated with attractive sculpted urns.

Very appropriately for such an interesting building that has been saved from redevelopment, it now houses many organisations which are concerned with the preservation of the city's architectural heritage.

Return to Argyle Street and turn right. There are two possible routes to Buchanan Street. The first is to go through the Argyll Arcade (see below), the second is to continue along Argyle Street until a right turn is made at Buchanan Street.

The entrance to the L-shaped **Argyll Arcade** ㉝ (1828, John Baird I) is at 98-102 Argyle Street and it comes out at 28-32 Buchanan Street. This delightful little arcade has a cast-iron and wood hammerbeam framework supporting its glass roof and it owes something of its style to Parisian arcades. A wide variety of merchandise used to be sold here but now most of the occupants are jewellers' shops. The entrance to Sloan's Restaurant (see below) will be met on the left; it has a lovely tiled entrance beyond which is some very high-quality woodwork.

The opening of the arcade was obviously of great interest to Glaswegian ladies of leisure in 1828 as the *Glasgow Herald* reported that 'the comfort and convenience of Ladies who resort to it has been so much studied, and where amusement is combined with utility, we have little doubt but it will be found attractive. The place will form an agreeable promenade in every kind of weather. Those arriving in carriages may be set down at the one end, and the carriages be sent round to take up the company at the other.' Life was hard in those days!

It is worth noting that the name of the arcade has a different spelling from that of 'Argyle' Street, although both were originally spelled 'Argyle'.

Return to Argyle Street and turn right. The building at **106–14 Argyle Street** ❸❹ (1770) was substantially remodelled in 1897-8 by H. & D. Barclay to house Miss Cranston's Crown Lunch and Tea Rooms (see p.123) and its large eaves and sweeping gables are very unusual for Glasgow. This large structure acted as Kate Cranston's tea rooms' central stores, bakery and laundry; these facilities were located above the tea rooms which had dining areas, games rooms and smoking rooms. Charles Rennie Mackintosh designed the tea rooms' furnishing and a Dutch Kitchen (in 1906) but very little of this is visible.

Within the facade of the building at 106-14 Argyle Street is a low opening and the entrance to **Morrison's Court** ❸❺ (1798). This is an interesting courtyard, the eastern side of which has changed little in shape for a long time; in the south-eastern corner stands a circular staircase tower, once a very common feature of Glasgow's buildings. The Argyll Arcade was designed to skirt the buildings that can be seen here. In days gone by, the courtyard was sometimes used for cockfighting and it is said that bets of up to a thousand guineas were wagered on these brutal fights.

The well-known Sloan's Restaurant is on the right and, since this originated in the courtyard, it is claimed as the oldest restaurant in the city.

Return to Argyle Street and walk westwards. Turn right when Buchanan Street is met.

BUCHANAN STREET

In the 1760s Andrew Buchanan built a house at the bottom of Buchanan Street and over the next few decades substantial mansions were erected here. Gradually the street became a great thoroughfare with large shops lining it; now pedestrianised, it is Glasgow's principal shopping street. On Saturdays it is thronged with shoppers, with street entertainment often laid on by buskers ranging from classical musicians to kilted pipers. This is arguably the city's finest street with a number of very attractive commercial buildings which were built towards the end of the nineteenth century at the height of the city's prosperity.

The street's entrance to the Argyll Arcade (see p.94) is at 28-32 Buchanan Street, under the **Argyll Chambers** ㊱ (1902-4, Colin Menzies). This flamboyant Franco-Flemish building is decorated with two allegorical figures and lots of fussy detail. As with many Glasgow buildings, granite columns are included as a decorative, not structural, part of the facade. Two gold semi-domes above the entrance add an unusual touch.

Opposite this is Frasers, essentially a large collection of warehouses which have been amalgamated over decades to form one huge department store. One particular building, **45 Buchanan Street** ㊲ (1883-5, James Sellars), opposite the Argyll Arcade, is worth looking at. The facade has a lot of delicate Renaissance-style carved detail and above the entrance is a royal coat of arms (with a unicorn and lion) and two seated winged figures representing *Art* and *Industry*.

Its very grand interior has tiers of galleries under a glazed arched roof and its remarkable design caused a minor sensation when it opened. This was originally Wylie & Lochhead's store; it was probably the most famous of all the great Glasgow warehouses as it could supply the complete furnishings for a house, and export it all if necessary; in its heyday much of its fine furniture was made in the company's own local workshops. Shops of this style were also involved in the furnishing of many ships built on the River Clyde, hence the huge scale of their business and the development of so many ancillary trades in the wake of the shipbuilding industry.

In the centre of the street stands the massive bronze sculpture *Concept of Kentigern* ㊳ (1977, Neil Livingstone), which represents the bird brought back to life by St Mungo (see p.415).

The whole of the next block on the right is occupied by the Prince of Wales Buildings (1854, John Baird I), much better known today as **Princes Square** ㊴, one of the city's most attractive shopping areas. Enter by the middle of the three entrances (look out for the peacock sculpture on the roof) and take the escalator past a set of cleverly drawn faces of well-known people associated with Glasgow. Their faces are contorted and only look right when seen from a particular angle. Inside, the once-empty courtyard has been covered over with a massive glass roof which gives shelter to four levels of shops.

Inside, one curiosity worth looking at is the Foucault pendulum, named after Jean Foucault, an eighteenth-century French physicist who used a pendulum to show that the Earth rotated on its axis. Although the pendulum keeps swinging in the same direction (independent of the Earth), the Earth beneath it is rotating so that the pendulum's bob appears to be moving clockwise. This is because the Earth is rotating in the opposite (i.e. anticlockwise) direction, making one revolution every twenty-four hours. Watch it over a couple of hours!

Princes Square in Buchanan Street

The former **Glasgow Herald Office** ⓛ is at 63-9 Buchanan Street. It was originally erected in 1870 by John Baird II and then remodelled in 1879-80 by James Sellars. Its facade has four sculptured reliefs of putti (plump boys with cherub-like faces) involved in writing and printing. Above them, eight Corinthian columns rise over two storeys and there is a Glasgow coat of arms flanked by two more cherubs. Near roof level, where few passers-by will notice them, are statues of two great printers, William Caxton and Johann Gutenberg, by John G. Mossman.

The Glasgow Herald was first published as *The Advertiser* in 1783 and it is generally recognised as the oldest English-language national newspaper in the world. It was produced here (and later in Mitchell Street, see below) from 1869 to 1980, when it moved to Albion Street. In 1992 it again changed its name, this time to *The Herald*, emphasising that its readership was not confined to the Glasgow area. It is the most widely-read broadsheet newspaper in Scotland and is a sister paper to the city's tabloid, *The Evening Times*.

As a short detour, turn left at Mitchell Lane to view the back of the building in Mitchell Street. This extension to the newspaper's offices is known as the **Glasgow Herald Building** ④①, and was built by Honeyman & Keppie in 1893-5 with an important contribution by Charles Rennie Mackintosh. Its position in the narrow Mitchell Street means that it is hemmed in, but its curious bulbous octagonal water tower, at the top of the six-storey sandstone building, does its best to make the structure dominate its surroundings. The facade is divided by a bold cornice which cuts abruptly across the many vertical features, including the stone ribs, narrow windows and the nice rectangular water pipes (dated *1895*).

The building has a new role as the home of '**The Lighthouse**', which is dedicated to the study of architecture and design. The ambitious plan to turn this important (but not all that well known) building into yet another exhibition hall came about after Glasgow won the competition to become the British Art Council's choice for the title 'UK City of Architecture and Design 1999'. The architects chosen for the conversion were Page and Park. The name 'The Lighthouse' arose from a number of different ideas (including the fact that the water tower is to be illuminated), but essentially it is because the exhibition is intended to 'throw light' on how architecture and design affects our lives.

Return to Buchanan Street. At 60 Buchanan Street is the **North British Rubber Building** ④② (1889, Robert Thomson). This tall and narrow red sandstone building has lots of detail including an extravagant crow-stepped gable. Two statues of females are placed high above the street; the one on the left holds a sword and the scales of justice and the one on the right holds what may be a torch and a shackle. Between them is a highly detailed arched window above which are carvings of reclining figures.

The **Clydesdale Bank Building** ④③ (1896, George Washington Browne) at 91 Buchanan Street is a narrow sandstone building which has had a variety of uses. It was originally designed for Kate Cranston (see p.123) as one of her tea rooms and the interior decoration contained work by Charles Rennie Mackintosh. It was taken over by the Clydesdale Bank after the First World War but in recent times it has served as a shop. Its French-influenced facade tapers up to a Dutch-style, highly ornamented gable. It has a lovely arched window at ground level and oriel windows rising for two floors above the entrance. Look for the sculpted cherubs and fruit.

A little further on the right is Exchange Place and at number 11 is the **Rogano** 🅰️, the city's finest surviving Art Deco restaurant. The facade has a classic black and cream Vitrolite front decorated with a huge red lobster; this was erected when Rogano's Oyster Bar (interior: 1935-6, Weddell & Inglis) was established here. This was modelled on the Parisian Prunier fish restaurants and came complete with tanks of live fish.

The former **Royal Bank of Scotland** at 98 Buchanan Street has its grandest entrance on Royal Exchange Square. The whole building is described on p.89.

Gordon Street is to the left of Buchanan Street and the corner building at 2 Gordon Street is the former **Royal Bank of Scotland** 🅰️ (1886-8, A. Sydney Mitchell). This dominates the junction with its elaborate three-door entrance and domed tower. High above the street is a carved plaque featuring the elements of the city's coat of arms and two horns filled with fruit.

Number 2 Gordon Street was designed as an addition to the original Italianate bank at **8 Gordon Street** 🅰️ (1853-7, David Rhind), which serves as one of the main Glasgow branches of the Royal Bank of Scotland. This large and elaborate building has eleven bays with the middle five rising a storey above the two wings, its height emphasized by the Corinthian columns framing the top storey's arched windows. At ground level there are bearded heads in the windows' keystones. The facade has many interesting carvings of children by Handyside Ritchie. At ground floor level there are children minting coins and printing notes. The three pediments above the first-floor windows contain, from left to right, *Glasgow with Trade and Manufacture*, *Commerce with Navigation and Locomotion*, and *Edinburgh with Science and Art*. Inside, the banking hall is decorated with numerous twentieth-century plaques representing the country's industry and commerce.

The Royal Bank of Scotland was founded in 1727 in Edinburgh. Over a long period of time the country's banking was concentrated in the capital and it was not until 1783 that the bank established a branch in Glasgow. David Dale (see p.364) was one of the two local managing agents. In time, the growth of the city's manufacturing and trading wealth ensured that the Royal (and other banks) paid a bit more attention to this part of the country.

Just opposite Royal Bank Place stands a rather surprising addition to the streetscape, a surviving example of a two-tonne reinforced-concrete **Police box** 🅰️. They were designed in 1930 by Gilbert McKenzie-Trench and many thousands of these boxes were used in Britain, Glasgow having 323 of them strategically placed around the city. Only twelve are left in the United Kingdom and three of these are in Glasgow: the other two are on Great Western Road (see p.231) and on Wilson Street.

Before the days of police radios and the widespread appearance of ordinary telephone boxes, police boxes such as this had a telephone inside which could be used by the police or by a passer-by in the case of an emergency. They were originally red, but were later repainted blue and became well-known sights in many city streets, especially in the city centre. Gradually they were removed and almost became extinct, until local people started writing into the letters page of *The Glasgow Herald*. Most people will probably associate them with the BBC's intrepid time-traveller Dr Who. His spacecraft, the *Tardis* ('Time And Relative Dimension In Space'), looked like a police box on the outside but was enormous inside. In the very first episode of the programme, screened on television in 1963, the mechanism which allowed the craft to change its outward appearance failed, leaving it police box-shaped for eternity!

Before crossing St Vincent Street, pause to look at the three-dimensional **street plan** 48 (1990, Kathleen Chambers). As it is made of bronze, you can tell which buildings are the most talked about by the polish they have been given by visitors' fingers! The model clearly shows the city centre's gridiron street pattern and the hilly nature of the land on either side of Buchanan Street.

St Vincent Place is on the right and it is dealt with later in the walk (see p.110).

At 147 Buchanan Street stands the former **Western Club** 49 (1839-42, D. & J. Hamilton). This large building, which is based on a Genovese palace (the Palazzo Doria Pamphilii), has a large porch with square Corinthian columns. The first storey has elaborate balconies and there is further decoration at the first-storey windows and around the small windows in the attic storey. This substantial structure was built at the start of the Victorian era and as one of the first Italianate buildings in Glasgow its design influenced many later buildings.

The former **Glasgow Stock Exchange** 50 (1875-7, John Burnet) is at the corner of Buchanan Street and Nelson Mandela Place. This Venetian Gothic building is highly detailed, especially around the windows. The main doorway in Buchanan Street has an arched canopy with carved figures representing four races: European, Chinese, African and Indian. Both facades of the building have substantial columns topped by first-floor arches and in the spandrels are carved medallions representing Science, Art, Building, Engineering and Mining. The narrow second-floor windows are topped by a series of arches and above them are five medallions with flower patterns. There are also three figures which may represent *Industry*, *Commerce* and *Trade*. The building's end bays project out slightly and above the second-floor windows are six shields, including those representing England, Scotland, Ireland and Glasgow. The roof has many small and intricate details around the dormer windows.

The extension in Nelson Mandela Place was built in 1906 by John Burnet's son, J. J. Burnet. It tries to continue the masterpiece next door but the differences in floor levels and windows in the two buildings clash.

In 1986 St George's Place was renamed **Nelson Mandela Place** in honour of Nelson Mandela for his stand against the South African government's racist apartheid policy. In 1981 he was made a freeman of the city, many years before he was released from prison. Glasgow has often voiced its civic anger towards repressive regimes and this particular name change was made all the more sweet as the South African Consulate was at that time located in St George's Place!

St George's Tron Parish Church **51** (1807-9, William Stark) stands in the middle of the Place. It is an early example of a Glasgow street with a prominent building at its end and, in this case, the church breaks up the long, straight road made up of George Street and West George Street. The church is fairly squat with a tall, pointed clocktower rising high above the street. This dominating Baroque-inspired tower owes a lot to the churches of Christopher Wren but it is not as grand as Stark intended, as statues of the four Evangelists were meant to be placed where the obelisks now are.

To see the other buildings in Nelson Mandela Place, turn left at the Stock Exchange and go round the church in a clockwise direction.

The first building after crossing West George Street is the **Royal Faculty of Procurators' Hall** **52** (1854-6, Charles Wilson). This very fine Italian Renaissance library is modelled on the Venetian St Mark's Library, though it has a much smaller floor area. The faculty was founded in 1796 and today it represents solicitors who practise in the city, with this building acting as their reference library. The interior is quite magnificent, with exceptionally fine plasterwork in the Reading Room, making this one of the city's finest rooms of its period.

The building is well-known for the fourteen faces on the keystones above the ground-floor windows. These were carved by Handyside Ritchie and depict famous lawyers: Lord Erskine, the Earl of Mansfield, Lord Brougham, Robert Blair, John Erskine, Viscount Stair, Lord Kames, Lord Advocate Duncan Forbes, James Reddie, Professor John Miller, Lord Moncrieff, Lord Jeffrey, Lord Cockburn and Lord Rutherford. The second floor is decorated with pairs of fluted Corinthian columns and above these is a frieze and balustrade.

To the right of the hall stands the Beaux Arts-style building known as **The Athenaeum** **53** (1886, J. J. Burnet). The Glasgow Athenaeum was an educational body, originally set up in 1847 in the Assembly Rooms in Ingram Street; it organised classes in commercial subjects, later adding more general-interest and cultural topics. It moved to this building in 1888, offering a wide variety of subjects, including music, and in 1893 an extension (see below) was opened in Buchanan Street which included a theatre. The Athenaeum became a college in 1903 and later added a drama department. Eventually, its commercial departments were integrated into Strathclyde University and the music and drama departments became the Royal Scottish Academy of Music and Drama. The college later moved to Renfrew Street (see p.106).

The ground floor is fairly austere-looking, but above it are three large windows of the former library flanked by Ionic columns. Beyond the outer columns are figures representing teachers of Science and Literature and their pupils, and above the four columns stand statues of John Flaxman, Christopher Wren, Henry Purcell and Joshua Reynolds. The statuary is by John G. Mossman.

The next building, which stands at the junction with Buchanan Street, is the former **Liberal Club** ➎➍ (1907-9, A. N. Paterson). This grand building occupies an important corner site and its height is emphasised by the tall first-storey windows with their substantial cast-iron frames. The entrance is flanked by two carved lions and the initials *GLC* ('Glasgow Liberal Club'). The building was taken over by the Royal Scottish Academy of Music and Drama in 1928 as part of their expanding complex until it moved out in the 1980s to its new site on Renfrew Street (see p.106).

Turn left at Buchanan Street. Number 179 Buchanan Street also bears the name *Athenæum* as this was an extension to the college and it is often called **The Old Athenaeum Theatre** ➎➎ (1891-3, J. J. Burnet). This slender structure contains a theatre which has been used by many of the city's theatre companies, including the Citizens' Theatre.

The building's facade is asymmetrical and is in a wide variety of styles. The left side has decorated bay windows above which is a large semicircular window, then a gable. In contrast, the right side has long and narrow slit-like windows, above which are much smaller windows then an octagonal Tower of Winds cupola decorated with classical figures. This was one of the first buildings in Glasgow to include an elevator and the inclusion of a lift has been used as a design feature, with the cupola being built around the top of the lift shaft.

The facade has a number of statues. At the top is a classical male figure, below which is an angel standing on the prow of a boat. Below this are seated figures probably representing the *Arts* and *Music* (which holds a lyre). A couple of cherubs are above the door and elsewhere on the facade are sculpted fruit, faces and stylised 'A's.

The route now crosses Bath Street and on the right are the **Buchanan Galleries** ➎➏ (1997-9, Jenkins and Marr), a huge stone-clad shopping complex. The size of this massive structure makes this part of Buchanan Street rather like an urban canyon, especially since the erection of the building created a bridge over Cathedral Street. The shopping centre is 56,000m^2 (600,000 sq ft) in area, making it more than twice the size of the St Enoch Centre (see p.143).

At the top of Buchanan Street is the **Glasgow Royal Concert Hall** ➎➐ (1987-90, Sir Leslie Martin). The hall, which was opened during the city's reign as the 1990 European City of Culture, is Glasgow's main venue for orchestral concerts and this is where the Royal Scottish National Orchestra plays (see p.134). The hall replaced the burned-out

St Andrew's Halls (see p.135) and was partly financed by the insurance money from the fire.

The design of this massive and rather gaunt-looking building echoes a much more traditional style as it is clad in large yellowish slabs of sandstone and has tall external pillars. Its strategic position at the junction of Buchanan Street and Sauchiehall Street continues the popular Glasgow tradition of closing the end of an important street with an imposing public building. In this case, together with the neighbouring shopping centre, the building's size allows it to close two streets. To the left of the entrance is the city's coat of arms.

The interior is spacious, allowing plenty of room for milling crowds. The large main auditorium can seat over 2400 people; smaller spaces arranged around it host concerts, conferences and other events. Temporary exhibitions of art are often on display from the city's museums and there are also some notable works which form part of the hall's permanent collection. Four large murals by Glasgow artists near the main internal staircase were specially commissioned; they are *Pillows of Dreams* (1996, Steven Campbell), *Forest* (1996, Ken Currie), *Concert Hall Painting* (1996, Adrian Wiszniewski) and *My Great Heart* (1996, Peter Howson). In the Lomond Foyer (at the north side of the building) there is the large mural *Trains and Boats and Planes* (1995) by Helen McLean which reflects Glasgow's traditions in heavy engineering. The five panels, depicting railway engines, shipbuilding and military aircraft, reflect the Glaswegian's inclination to reminisce about the days when people proudly made world-class machinery which was exported all over the globe. Continuing this theme, the Clyde Foyer on the opposite side of the building has a collection of photographs and paintings of the most famous ships that were launched on the River Clyde, including the three 'Queens': *Queen Mary*, *Queen Elizabeth* and *Queen Elizabeth II* ; see also p.211.

Guided tours are available; ask in the hall or at the Tourist Information Centre.

BUCHANAN STREET TO WEST GEORGE STREET VIA COWCADDENS

Walk westwards along Sauchiehall Street (see p.119), another of the city's important shopping streets.

At West Nile Street the route goes right, but down to the left is a warehouse at **99–107 West Nile Street** 🔢 which was designed by Alexander Thomson in 1858. Probably only a few people each day give this building a second glance but it is unmistakably in the 'Greek' Thomson style. The clues are in the incised patterns that run the full width of the frontage, the use of anthemia near the top and the manner in which the second-storey windows are sunk behind a bold pilastrade.

Walk up West Nile Street. Turn left into Renfrew Street and then right at Renfield Street. To the left of this junction stands the **Pavilion Theatre**

59 (1902-4, Bertie Crewe). It is French Renaissance in style, with its yellow terracotta facade highly decorated with musical instruments (especially on the towers), clowns' faces and various animals. Inside, its decoration is rich and flamboyant and 'is executed in pure Louis XV', as its own early publicity claimed; it was built with a sliding roof 'ensuring coolness in the hottest weather'.

The building was originally called the Palace of Varieties and it became famous as an important music hall venue, with stars such as Marie Lloyd and Vesta Victoria playing here. Charlie Chaplin also trod the theatre's boards. As fashions changed, it entertained later generations with its pantomimes, plays and countless individual performers such as the stand-up comedians Lex McLean, Tommy Morgan and Billy Connolly.

Follow Renfield Street up to the granite **Annan Fountain** **60**, made more noticeable by its tall column supporting a unicorn holding a shield. A plaque records that the fountain was donated by William Annan in 1915. A metal plaque bearing the city's coat of arms is attached to the stonework.

The surrounding district is called **Cowcaddens**, so-called because cattle were once driven to rich pastures here. This rural idyll changed drastically at the end of the eighteenth century with the building of the Forth and Clyde Canal (see p.255) and the railway lines, factories and tenements which were built in the century or so after that. With few factories left, the tenements flattened and with the large Buchanan Street Railway Station gone, the area would be unrecognisable to someone who had left the area in the 1950s. However, memories of Cowcaddens' former tenement life are kept alive in the 'patter' of the much-loved 1950s stage characters Francie and Josie (played by Jack Milroy and Ricky Fulton).

To the north-east of the fountain is the city campus of **Glasgow Caledonian University** **61**. This is the city's third university and was established in 1993. It originated in the Glasgow College of Technology (1971) which subsequently became Glasgow College and then Glasgow Polytechnic. The university has three campuses, the others being in the West End (see p.219), and has important links with local colleges. This campus specialises in a range of disciplines, including many associated with health care. One interesting link with the city's written history is that the science departments are based in the Charles Oakley Laboratories which are named after the author of the well-known history of Glasgow: *The Second City*.

To the west of the fountain are the buildings housing **Scottish Television** **62** (usually known as STV). This is the country's major commercial television station which serves the highly populated central belt. The studios are used to produce many different programmes, some of which are well known in a number of parts of the world. Its most recent notable programmes include the *High Road* soap (based at Loch Lomond) and the detective series *Taggart* (see p.261).

Go left and walk round the STV building to the top of Hope Street. At the junction, the building on the opposite side of the busy Cowcaddens Road is the former Cowcaddens Parish Church (1872-3, Campbell Douglas & Sellars), now **The Piping Centre** ⑬. This handsome building, originally a church of the Free Church of Scotland, has a Greek-style portico beside which is an Italianate tower.

There can be few museums in the world devoted to one particular musical instrument, but bagpipes have been in use, in various forms, from as far back as Roman times. Indeed, related instruments have been used in numerous parts of Europe and many areas still have a rich tradition of piping including Ireland, Brittany in France, northern Spain and Northumbria in England. Bagpipes were probably played in the Scottish Highlands around the fourteenth century and they have evolved over the centuries to become what is now called the Great Pipe, or *Piob Mhor* in Gaelic. Pipers were encouraged by many of the Highland chieftains and the leading pipers of the day became important and respected custodians of Scotland's musical traditions. However, after the 1745 Jacobite Rebellion, and with the break-up of the clan system, the pipes' importance declined. Later they became fashionable amongst a section of the landed aristocracy who were keen to show off their 'Scottishness'; this encouraged various bodies to organise competitions, establish civilian bands and to revive its fortunes. However, the main boost to the pipes' popularity was their use by Scottish army regiments, who combined them with drums in order to produce a beat to which soldiers could march. This innovation developed into the pipe band as we know it today. The rise of the military bands helped standardise the design of the instrument, encouraged the writing down of the tunes and, above all, encouraged organised tuition. Today, the pipes are immensely popular, with competitions taking place at many Highland gatherings and many traditional music bands incorporating the instrument in their repertoire.

The centre's National Museum of Piping has a wonderful display of pipes, many of them on loan from the National Museums of Scotland. Elsewhere in the building are rehearsal rooms and a performance hall – all suitably soundproofed!

Walk down Hope Street and pass under the canopy of the **Theatre Royal** ⑭. The front of the building is fairly uninteresting but it does carry a royal coat of arms with the mottoes *Honi soit qui mal y pense* ('Evil be to him who evil thinks') and *Dieu et mon droit* ('God and my right').

The first theatre built here was Bayliss's Coliseum Theatre and Opera House which was erected in 1867. This came under new owners in 1869 and it changed its name to the Theatre Royal but it burned down in 1879. The replacement (1880, Charles John Phipps) lasted a little longer but, in 1895, it too went up in flames but was soon rebuilt by Phipps to the same design. It was taken over by STV in 1956, only to be badly damaged by fire in 1970. Today, the theatre is home to Scottish Opera, though it is also used by other companies including Scottish Ballet and the Royal Shakespeare Company.

Scottish Opera was started by Alexander Gibson in 1962 in the King's Theatre (see p.136) and it is the country's main opera company. It also performs in Edinburgh and other towns and cities throughout Scotland, playing to audiences in venues large and small. The company's wide repertoire includes 'classical' opera (sung in English or foreign languages) and more modern works, some of them specially commissioned.

The splendid red sandstone building on the right, at 307-33 Hope Street, is **McConnel's Building** ⓺ (1906-7, Honeyman, Keppie & Mackintosh) which must rank as one of the city's finest tenements. This was built by the City Improvement Trust and it confidently bears the city's coat of arms and the date *1907*. With a corner dome, curved pediments and chimney-stacks, which are actually part of the overall design instead of being tacked on, this building illustrates how a city tenement can be a work of art. The back, with its railed access balconies, is also worth looking at.

Next door is the enormous brick building housing the **Royal Scottish Academy of Music and Drama** ⓺ (1982-7, Sir Leslie Martin and Ivor Richards). The architect presumably (and if so, quite justifiably) thought its name rather a mouthful, so the letters *RSAMD* are also prominently displayed. The academy developed originally from the Glasgow Athenaeum (see p.101) and at long last it has a purpose-built building in which to train its students. This bold building houses various departments including the Alexander Gibson Opera School, which was erected on Cowcaddens Road in 1997-8.

The academy trains singers, musicians and actors and many of today's well-known performers on stage and television were originally students, including some (such as Tom Conti and Robert Carlyle) who have achieved international success.

At 172 Hope Street stands the eight-storey **Lion Chambers** ⓺ (1904-7, James Salmon II & John Gaff Gillespie). This is an early example of a reinforced-concrete building; this innovative technique allowed the use of thin walls, only 10cm (4in) thick, thus saving space on a very constricted site, and meant that much more wall space could be used for windows. The building was intended to house lawyers' offices (hence the two busts of judges above the fourth storey) with the tall top floor for artists' studios. There are few embellishments (save the busts and a heraldic shield lower down the facade) which allows the crispness of the building's shape to remain its most prominent feature.

Continue on Hope Street, past shops and offices of various eras. At 154 Hope Street stands the former **Pot Still** pub ⓺ (*c.* 1835), now called the Cask and Still. This became a pub as far back as 1870 and one of its most celebrated customers was Tam the coalman who, at the end of each working day, parked his horse and cart outside the pub so he could go in enjoy a couple of drams. This went on for nearly sixty years! Today it is a small but comfortable city-centre pub with a good selection of whiskies. No doubt Tam would be pleased.

Go back up Hope Street to West Regent Street and turn left. The street has a number of interesting buildings including many early nineteenth-century houses, most of which have been turned into offices.

On the left is **79 West Regent Street** **69**, which was originally built as a house in the middle of the nineteenth century but was altered in 1903-04 by James Salmon when it became offices, a tea room and a restaurant. It was then given some bay windows and exterior panels in beaten lead, a very unusual practice in Glasgow. Their Art Nouveau designs include a representation of the cty's coat of arms, the Scottish lion rampant and various masonic symbols.

At **100 West Regent Street** **70** (1895-7, J. L. Cowan) is a red sandstone building which contains a masonic hall as well as offices. The facade has a number of finely carved details, the most noticeable being the large sun (appropriately, at the top), below which are two figures representing the Good Shepherd and St Margaret. Fine details lower down include foliage, lions' heads and stylised dolphins.

At the junction with West Campbell Street is the former **Institute for the Adult Deaf and Dumb** **71** (1893-5, Robert Duncan). The lovely doorway of this red sandstone building has a sculpture *Christ healing the dumb man* above which is the word *Epiphatha* ('speech'). The building's name used to be within the delicately carved frame at the top floor. The facade is set off nicely by the two little towers and their conical roofs.

The building next door is the former **John Ross Memorial Church for the Deaf** **72** (1925, Norman A. Dick) and was erected as part of the neighbouring institute. The gable end has some unusual small details arranged around the door. They include the letters IHS (Iesus Hominum Salvator – 'Jesus, saviour of mankind'), small animals eating ears of grain, a couple of rather grotesque-looking beasts, two serpent-like creatures, a lamb ('the lamb of God') and alpha and omega (the first and last letters of the Greek alphabet).

   One very unusual design feature inside the church is the provision of two pulpits, one for the minister and the other for the interpreter who signed for deaf members of the congregation. The interior has been imaginatively converted into an architects' office.

A little further up the hill, the classical houses contained within **176–84 West Regent Street** **73** (*c.* 1830, Robert Scott) have large and very bulky Ionic porches which are very different from the slimmer styles more usually found in the city.

Return to West Campbell Street, turn right and then turn left at West George Street.

West George Street to George Square via St Vincent Place

At **198 West Street** ⑦ (*c.* 1820, probably John Brash) is an attractive example of a Glaswegian townhouse, complete with its decorated columns, cast-iron railings and an elaborate chimney-stack.

At 188-94 West George Street is **Ocean Chambers** ⑦ (1899-1900, Robert A. Bryden). This tall red sandstone office building has an ornate doorway framed by pink granite columns. Above this is a relief sculpture depicting a lighthouse flanked by sailing ships and walruses. Three storeys above this are Poseidon (the Greek god of the sea) and his wife Amphitrite (who holds a trident).

At the junction of West George Street and Hope Street is a massive office block whose main entrance is on the latter street. **157-67 Hope Street** ⑦ (1902-03, John A. Campbell) is an eight-storey building which combines the plainness of many Art Nouveau designs with some nice decorative touches. Above the main doorway are a stylized *163*, two cherubs (one with a bulging moneybag, the other with a pen and an open book) and two lions bearing shields. A two-storey arcaded gallery provides the main architectural feature of the upper part of the building. The West George Street facade is similar in overall appearance, with one of its doorways topped by a blindfolded head representing 'blind justice'. An oriel window can be seen one storey higher up and just below this are three sculpted angels.

At 144-6 West George Street is **James Sellars House** ⑦ (1877-9, James Sellars), formerly the New Club. This is very French in style and its most outstanding feature is the lovely doorway with sculptures by William Mossman. The doorway's keystone figure is Mercury (with the word *telegram* on his headband), with the reclining figure on the left holding a

West George Street

sickle and a sheaf of cereals, and the figure on the right holding a bunch of grapes and a pitcher of wine. To the left of the doorway are three unusual oval-shaped windows and above them are two sets of balconies.

At 121 West George Street (at the junction with Renfield Street) is the former **Sun, Fire and Life Building** 78 (1889-94, William Leiper). This very complex building is in French Renaissance style and obviously impressed the French judges who gave its design a medal at the 1900 Paris Exhibition. Its most obvious feature is the corner tower on top of which is a dome and finial; at the base of the dome is Aurora (the goddess of dawn), a bearded man and two horses. On the Renfield Street side, the group of figures above the third floor are copies of three of Michaelangelo's works: *Apollo* is in the centre flanked by reclining figures representing *Night* and *Day*. Above the corner's first floor are three panels inspired by Botticelli's *Primavera* with the arms of England, Scotland and Wales. William Birnie Rhind was responsible for the building's sculptures and, as well as the main figures, he also included balconies, pillars and other architectural devices. Some of the smaller details that can be seen include faces representing the planets Jupiter, Uranus, Mars, Venus, Mercury and Saturn. At ground-floor level is a nice little carving of Mithras, the Persian god of light.

Turn left at Renfield Street and walk up to the junction with West Regent Street. At this corner are the very large red sandstone **Castle Chambers** 79 (1898, James Carruthers), which were built for the distillers and brewers McLachlan and Co.

This tall building has a number of attractive pieces of sculpture including four medieval maidens at the very corner. Above these are cherubs and a shield depicting three towers of a castle with the motto *Fortis et fides* ('Bravery and fidelity'). This shield, along with sculptures of female heads and lions holding shields, are found elsewhere on the facade. Near the top of the tall octagonal corner tower is a female figure holding a spear.

Continue uphill to the attractive glazed-brick building at 71 Renfield Street. Here, **De Quincey's Bar** 80 occupies what used to be the telling room of the Prudential Buildings (1888-90, Paul Waterhouse); it is named after the author Thomas De Quincey (1785-1859) who once lived in a house on this site. He is probably best-known for his addiction to opium and his book *Confessions of an English opium eater* (1821). A plaque erected by the Pen and Pencil Club is on the building's facade which states that he lived here in 1841-3.

Inside, the bar has lots of Moorish-style arches and the walls and ceiling are clad in faience tiles. It is a remarkable place and very different from the traditional Glasgow pub.

Walk back down Renfield Street to West George Street and turn left.

At 92 West George Street stands the former **Commercial Bank of Scotland** 81 (1930-7, James Miller), a tall and elegant American-style building. The height of this white limestone structure is emphasised by the pilasters and the detailed cast-iron window frames that lead the eyes upwards. The restrained use of carved decoration adds to the elegance of the building.

Turn right at West Nile Street. Cross St Vincent Street and turn right at Drury Street. On the left at 17-21 Drury Street is **The Horse Shoe** bar **82** (*c.* 1870). This is one of the city's busiest watering holes and has been a pub since 1872. It is best known for its horseshoe-shaped bar which is 31.7m (104ft 3in) in length, making it for a long time the longest pub bar in Britain (it is now only the second longest). In 1885-7 the bar was redesigned by John Scouller, whose passion for horses resulted in the shape of the bar and all the other horseshoe motifs. There's also a statue of a farrier inside. In the 1920s the then proprietor John Y. Whyte transferred the panes of glass emblazoned with the Union Jack from his Whyte's Union Café and had the *JYW* motifs erected. Large mirrors, decorated columns, etched glass and wooden panelling all help make this a fine example of a traditional Glasgow bar and a very popular 'howf'.

Retrace the route back to St Vincent Street and turn right. On the right at 57-61 St Vincent Street is an Italian Renaissance building housing the city's most famous bookshop, **John Smith & Son** **83** (*c.* 1850, John Thomas Rochead). Having started in business in 1751, this is the country's oldest bookselling firm. It has long been associated with Scotland's literature and in 1778 it was involved in selling the first Edinburgh Edition of Robert Burns' poems (see p.85). Indeed, the fact that they only charged a modest commission rate of five per cent led Burns to write to John Smith: 'You seem a very decent sort of folk, you Glasgow booksellers; but, eh! they're sair birkies in Edinburgh.' (*sair birkies* = 'very lively lads')

The former **National Bank Chambers** **84** (1898-1906, J. M. Dick Peddie) is at 47 St Vincent Street. Above the doorway is a magnificent coat of arms featuring two unicorns and the mottoes *Nemo me impune lacessit* ('No-one provokes me with impunity') and *In defence*. This is now a Post Office and its interior still retains the very fine domed banking hall, its ceiling supported by large green marble columns.

Cross Buchanan Street into **St Vincent Place**, which has one of the city's finest concentration of commercial buildings. In the days of horse-drawn transport this was developed as the carriages' city-centre terminus, hence the exceptional width of the street.

The former **Scottish Amicable Building** **85** (1870-3, Campbell Douglas & Stevenson) is at 31-9 St Vincent Place. The bottom three storeys are Italianate in style and feature arched windows and a charming group of cherubs which are perched above the first floor's central window. The upper floors were added in 1903-6 (Burnet, Boston & Carruthers) and have oriel windows above which are pairs of carved figures sculpted by Mossman.

Next door, the **Scottish Provident Institution Building** ⓷⓺ (1904-8, J. M. Dick Peddie), looms above the street. This very large French-inspired building has a total of nine floors (including two in the tall mansard roof). While its main external features are the two end pavilions with their three-storey columns, what makes the building unusual is the use of curved astragals in a number of the floors' windows.

North Court is to the east of the Provident building and within it is **The Auctioneers** pub ⓷⓻, in a former auction hall. It is complete with cosy valuation booths, just the place for a quiet refreshment.

Numbers 30-40 St Vincent Place house the Italian Renaissance **Clydesdale Bank** ⓷⓼ (1871-4, John Burnet). This has lots of fine sculptural details, with Charles Grassby responsible for the head of *Father Clyde* at the door. Just below this is a globe and the Latin phrase *Litore ad litus* ('From shore to shore'). Also on the ground floor are roundels representing the towns (Dumfries, Ayr, Greenock and Dundee) in which the bank had branches. The first floor is decorated with graceful female figures (*Spring* and *Autumn*) and on the second floor is St Mungo and the city's coat of arms. This is flanked by *Industry* and *Commerce* by John G. Mossman. At the top of the building there is a bold stone balustrade which is decorated with sculpted urns. Inside, the magnificent banking hall rises two storeys and is lit by an elliptical glass dome. With its ornate columns, numerous carved heads (by John G. Mossman) and its splendid ceiling, this ranks as one of the city's most attractive bank interiors.

The Clydesdale Bank was founded in 1838 by James Lumsden in order to help provide the finance necessary to develop what became the city's huge manufacturing industries. A very grand building such as this helped to express the bank's confidence in itself and in its role in financing of some of the country's foremost manufacturers and traders. As is still the case today, the architectural style of the bank's headquarters was very much a public relations exercise.

The building was originally planned to be symmetrical (and even bigger) by the addition of three bays on the eastern side, but unfortunately for the bank the neighbouring *Citizen* newspaper bought the land that they needed.

The former **Citizen Offices** ⓷⓽ (1885-9, Thomas Lennox Watson and W. J. Anderson) is at 24 St Vincent Place. This asymmetrical Renaissance-style building is faced with a rich red-coloured sandstone from Mauchline in Ayrshire and its delicate carvings are by James Hendry. The ground floor has attractive arched openings and four columns, two of them spirally fluted. Above these, the words *Citizen Office* are cleverly included in the carving on the stonework. At the third floor there are four elliptical arches which abound in carved detail, including the date *1887*. Two tall and elaborate stepped gables are at roof level and to their right is an attractive octagonal clocktower.

This housed the offices and the printing press of a number of notable Glasgow newspapers. Dr James Hedderwick started the *Glasgow Citizen* in 1842 but this had its name changed to the *Weekly Citizen* when the *Evening Citizen*, the city's first evening paper, was brought out in 1864. To confuse historical matters even more, from 1914 to 1924 the evening paper was called the *Glasgow Citizen*. Publication ceased in 1974.

At 12-16 St Vincent Place is the former **Anchor Line Building** 🟥 (1905-7, James Miller). This is an unusual building for Glasgow as its facade is composed of white glazed terracotta blocks made by Doulton. It's also a very impressive structure and its height is emphasised by the tall columns which dominate the upper part of the facade. The central entrance is decorated with Ionic columns, a large keystone head and cherubs happily playing with seaweed and seashells (by H. H. Martyn). Above the ground-floor windows are sculpted heads of Mercury (the Roman messenger of the gods), complete with a winged helmet on which sits a curious little figure. A little higher, gilt badges depicting anchors can be seen above the first-floor windows and these act as reminders of the first occupants.

The Anchor Line was founded in the 1830s and became famous for its service between Glasgow and New York. By 1865 there was a sailing each week, so great were the numbers emigrating; and in 1880 the line carried 62,000 people over the Atlantic. The line had their own shipyard at Meadowside (near where the River Kelvin meets the Clyde) and this building's architect had also been responsible for designing interiors for their SS *Lusitania*. See also p.153.

At the end of St Vincent Place (and situated at the corner of George Square) is a large Italianate building, the former **Bank of Scotland Building** 🟥 (1867-70, John Thomas Rochead). Its door is surmounted by two huge Atlantes (by William Mossman) and above them is the bank's coat of arms with the phrase *Tanto uberior* ('So much the more plentiful'). The two female figures that flank this represent *Plenty* and *Justice*.

The former banking hall is now used as a bar ('The Counting House') but it fortunately still retains the magnificent interior. The hall's most notable features are the ground-floor columns and the caryatids above them; together, these support the ceiling in which is set a large circular glazed dome. The bank's safe is still in place and is set into a wall on the left hand side of the main banking hall.

The walk ends at **George Square** ❶.

Blythswood Hill, Garnethill and Charing Cross

This walk covers the western part of the city's main shopping area and the Garnethill district, within which is Charles Rennie Mackintosh's acclaimed Glasgow School of Art.

5 Blythswood Square

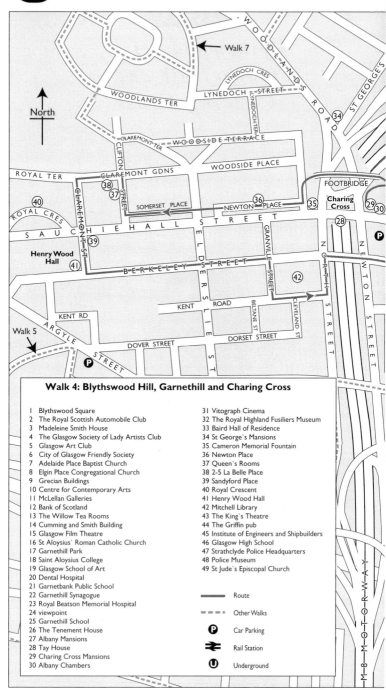

Walk 4: Blythswood Hill, Garnethill and Charing Cross

▬▬▬▬▬ Route

▬ ▬ ▬ Other Walks

🅿 Car Parking

🚉 Rail Station

Ⓤ Underground

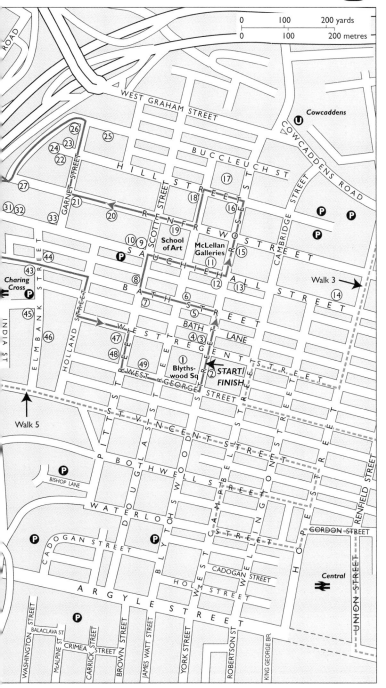

Main places of interest	Centre for Contemporary Arts **⑩** (art gallery)
	McLellan Galleries **⑪** (occasional exhibitions)
	Willow Tea Rooms **⑬**
	(Charles Rennie Mackintosh)
	Garnethill Park **⑰**
	Glasgow School of Art ⑲
	(Charles Rennie Mackintosh)
	Tenement House (museum) **㉖**
	Royal Highland Fusiliers Museum **㉜**
	(regimental museum)
	Mitchell Library **㊷** (reference library)
	Police Museum **㊸**
Circular/linear	circular
Starting point	Blythswood Square **❶**
Finishing point	Blythswood Square **❶**
Distance	4 km (2.5 miles)
Terrain	pavements; hilly near Blythswood Square; steep hills in Garnethill
Public transport	Cowcaddens Underground Station
	Charing Cross Railway Station (Q)
Sections	Blythswood Square to Sauchiehall Street
	Sauchiehall Street to Rose Street
	Rose Street to Charing Cross via Garnethill
	Charing Cross to the Mitchell Library
	Mitchell Library to Blythswood Square
Architects	Thomson: Grecian Buildings **❾**
	Mackintosh: 5 Blythswood Square **❹** (doorway)
	Willow Tea Rooms **⑬**
	Glasgow School of Art **⑲**
Nearby walks	3, 5, 7, 9
Refreshments	Centre for Contemporary Arts; many places in Sauchiehall Street; the Mitchell Library and its environs
Notes	Remember about the steep hills.

Walk 4

BLYTHSWOOD SQUARE TO SAUCHIEHALL STREET

Blythswood Square ❶ is one of the finest squares in the city, having kept its original buildings and not allowed modern intrusions to spoil the overall balance of the early nineteenth-century design. Large terraced houses, now generally turned into offices, line the four sides of the square with mature private gardens in the centre. The square was started in 1823 at a time when it was just outside Glasgow's boundary and its rectangular shape maintained the city's gridiron layout of streets to which subsequent developments adhered. Although the square is generally quiet at weekends, the peace can be shattered on occasions as it is a popular assembly place for public marches and demonstrations.

The whole of the square's eastern side is taken up by **The Royal Scottish Automobile Club** ❷ (remodelled 1923-6, James Miller). The club's entrance is the most elaborate in the square with four fluted columns supporting a first-floor balcony, above which is the club's badge incorporating a St Andrew's Cross and the motto *Gang warily* ('Go carefully'). Inside, the main entrance hall has a marble floor, fluted columns and a nicely decorated plaster ceiling. Access to the upper floors is via a splendid staircase above which is another fine ceiling.

The club was originally founded in Edinburgh in 1899 but this building was established as its home in 1909. As well as providing social amenities for its members, it still plays an important role in Scottish motor sport, including organising rallies.

The building at the north-eastern corner of the square, 6-7 Blythswood Square (1829), bears the name **Madeleine Smith House** ❸, its name celebrating an affair that rocked polite Victorian society in the middle of the nineteenth century.

In 1855 Madeleine Smith (1835-1928) and Pierre L'Angelier met for the first time and began a love affair which ended with one of the

Madeleine Smith House, Blythswood Square

country's most famous murder trials. Madeleine's father considered Pierre beneath her station in life and forbade her from seeing him; however, they continued to meet clandestinely and she wrote him a long series of love letters, some two hundred in number. Her bedroom was on the ground floor of this house and in the evenings she used to chat to him through the barred window, passing out hot cups of cocoa to keep him warm. However, Madeleine found a new (and more wealthy) suitor and asked Pierre to return her letters, which he steadfastly refused to do. Soon after the breakup of their relationship she bought quantities of arsenic and on 23 March 1857 Pierre collapsed and died of arsenic poisoning. Smith was arrested and her trial for his murder was held in Edinburgh for fear of a biased jury in Glasgow. The proceedings became what we would now call a 'media event' and were eagerly followed all over the world, particularly when many of her 'steamy' letters were read out in open court. Finally, the jury took only thirty minutes to return the peculiarly Scottish verdict of 'Not proven' and Madeleine was freed. After moving to London, she later lived in America where she refused offers to star in a film about her life. Pierre L'Angelier is buried in the Ramshorn Graveyard (see p.364).

Next door, 5 Blythswood Square (1829), is the former home of **The Glasgow Society of Lady Artists Club** ❹. Some alterations were made here in 1908 by Charles Rennie Mackintosh, the most obvious being the doorway. As with many of Mackintosh's features, the whole doorway is black, with the slim pilasters similar to those found in the Art School's boardroom. The society's name and the date *1882* are engraved beside the doorway. As well as work by Mackintosh, the building has alterations by George Walton (1867-1933) who designed an L-shaped gallery in 1896.

Leave the square by the side of Madeleine Smith House and follow Blythswood Street. This was originally called Mains Street and number 120 was once the home of Charles Rennie Mackintosh; his time there is described on p.405.

Continue to **Bath Street,** which got its name from the baths established here by William Harley early in the nineteenth century. The street still has many of its original houses extant though generally these are now used as offices, many of which have had their interiors drastically altered. Fortunately, most of the exteriors are in good condition with interesting doorways and original decorative ironwork.

Turn left at Bath Street and the premises of the **Glasgow Art Club** ❺ will be found on the left at 185 Bath Street. This private club was originally started in the mid-nineteenth century by local amateur artists in order to look at and discuss art; they also welcomed other artists (including those from other countries) in order to broaden their knowledge of artistic trends elsewhere. The success of the club at the turn of the century mirrored the achievements of the Glasgow School of artists and many well-known painters and architects of the day have been members. This building was originally two terraced houses, but in 1892-3 the architect John Keppie linked them and added a long top-lit exhibition gallery at the ends of which are splendid fireplaces. As well as being the home of many interesting paintings, the club holds private exhibitions which are staged in the gallery. Members are drawn from the ranks of professional artists and architects as well as lay members with an interest in art.

At 198-200 Bath Street stands the former **City of Glasgow Friendly Society** ❻ (remodelled 1920-1, Keppie & Henderson). There is nothing at the front to make this building stand out from its neighbours, but at its western side there is a niche in the wall in which is a statue of John Stewart (by Kelloch Brown) who founded the society in 1862. The elegant rear of this otherwise ordinary former terraced house is topped by a copper dome; this (and the statue) were added to the building in 1920-1.

Continue along Bath Street to the junction with Pitt Street where there are two interesting churches. On the left is **Adelaide Place Baptist Church** ❼ (1875-7, Thomas Lennox Watson). It stands on a platform a little back from the street which helps the church make more of an impression as the building itself is not that large compared to other city-centre churches. Above the three main doors are four sets of coupled Corinthian columns in the style of a Greek temple. The interior is bright and airy (helped by the Baptist custom of doing without fixed pews) and there are good stained-glass windows in the western wall.

Diagonally opposite is the former **Elgin Place Congregational Church** ❽ (1855-6, John Burnet), now a night club (how times have changed!). This large Greek-style temple is generally based on the Erechtheion temple (*c.* 400BC) in Athens. It has a massive Ionic portico with six fluted columns which is made all the more imposing by its base being raised above street level (thus giving more space for the basement halls). The stone decoration is fairly minimal but is complemented by that of the elaborate street-level ironwork.

Turn right at Pitt Street and follow it to Sauchiehall Street.

SAUCHIEHALL STREET TO ROSE STREET

Sauchiehall Street is one of the city's most important shopping streets and takes its name from Sauchie Haugh, meaning a low-lying area covered with willows. When the Blythswood Estate was developed for housing, this became a fashionable residential area in the early nineteenth century but the houses eventually made way for shops as the city centre moved westwards. As a shopping street it has been eclipsed by Buchanan Street but it is still busy with shoppers, often serenaded by buskers of various styles (and talents).

On the northern side, at 336-56 Sauchiehall Street, stand the **Grecian Buildings** ❾ (1865, Alexander Thomson). Unusually for one of

Thomson's commercial buildings, this building stands on a corner site, thus allowing him to continue his exterior designs into Scott Street. This is a fairly squat three-storey building, with Egyptian and Greek ideas being incorporated into the overall plan. The tall ground floor has a Greek-style central doorway leading to the upper floors. Above that are narrow windows topped by carved anthemia. At second-storey level, the dominant feature is the long row of stumpy Egyptian-style columns which carry a lot of incised detail; behind them is what is designed to look like a continuous wall of windows. Above the pillars are rows of incised patterns and these help link the central section of the building to the two substantial end pavilions which are topped by pediments incorporating many of Thomson's frequently used Classical patterns.

Within the Grecian Buildings is the **Centre for Contemporary Arts** **❿**. The CCA was opened in 1993 and has galleries for exhibitions and other activities. As its name suggests, it deals with modern art forms and features regularly changing exhibitions which originate in Scotland or further afield. Live performances also play an important part in the centre's work. There's also a café and an arts bookshop.

Follow Sauchiehall Street eastwards. After crossing Douglas Street, the very large building on the left is the **McLellan Galleries** **⓫** (1855-6, James Smith). Above the main entrance are the city's coat of arms, a statue of a crowned female and another coat of arms.

This was originally built as an art gallery to house the paintings owned by Archibald McLellan. In 1856 the city acquired both his collection and the building and this gave Glasgow the nucleus around which was built its magnificent art collection. After the paintings were transferred to the Kelvingrove galleries, this building had its end dome added and the street front was transformed into the Trerons department store. In 1912-13 the city built new exhibition halls into the rear of the building; these are used today as large display areas for 'blockbuster' exhibitions, some of which are on major international tours.

On the opposite side, at 235 Sauchiehall Street, stands the box-like **Bank of Scotland** **⓬** (1929-31, Graham Henderson), its doorway surmounted by a sculpture of the bank's coat of arms. This includes two figures representing *Plenty* (with her cornucopia of money) and *Justice* (with a set of scales), a shield, a knight's helmet and the motto *Tanto uberior* ('So much the more plentiful'); the shield carries the cross of St Andrew and the four round objects represent gold coins. Above this are carvings of a woman and a man by Benno Schotz (see p.203).

At 217 Sauchiehall Street is a gem of a building that is often missed by passers-by, **The Willow Tea Rooms** **⓭**. In 1903 this former warehouse was converted by Charles Rennie Mackintosh for one of Kate Cranston's famous tea rooms and much of the original interior still survives. The name comes from the original meaning of Sauchiehall Street (see p.119) and the tea rooms have many design features drawn from the shape of the willow tree. The tea rooms and all other rooms were designed in their entirety by Mackintosh, with his wife Margaret Macdonald being involved in some of the interior design. The tea rooms were closed in 1928 and the building was occupied by the neighbouring Daly's department store. New owners took over in the late 1970s and the reconstruction was carried out by Keppie Henderson, the descendant of the very firm in which Mackintosh had been one of the partners. After much research, the rooms have been largely recreated, with the Salon de Luxe and the Gallery again used as tea rooms (opened in 1983 and 1996 respectively).

The bold exterior (complete with stencilled patterns which separate it from its neighbours) is startlingly different from the surrounding buildings and, as if to emphasise these differences (and its brave originality), it is asymmetric with each floor having its own particular style of windows. It must be remembered that the exterior is not Mackintosh's original work but a reconstruction following his original design. The large ground-floor window is divided into two sections, with small panes in the upper half and two wrought-iron designs featuring leaves and teardrops attached to it. Above that there is a wide bow window with tall, narrow leaded panes; to each side of this are stylised wrought-iron name signs decorated with birds and bells. The top two storeys each feature three deeply recessed windows with those on the left rather larger that the other two.

Inside, Mackintosh designed two interconnecting rooms at ground-floor level and one in the mezzanine-level gallery which runs round a wide central well. The front room (now converted to a jewellers' shop) was a ladies' tea room and was coloured white; it still has a large and very distinctive white frieze composed of plaster panels on which is an abstract pattern. Light can enter from the upstairs tea room through the metalwork screen which divides the gallery from the ground floor. The ground-floor's back room (also used by the jewellers) was for lunches and its use of dark-stained oak panelling made this a more sombre space, although lots of light does come through the opening above. The decoration consisted of grey textile panels on which were stencilled female heads and roses. At the far end is a small fireplace (with a very large surround) which uses wood, plaster and ceramic tiles in black, white and purple; curved mirrors at the top add extra interest.

The **gallery** contains a tea room and it is decorated in white, black, grey and pink. The wall decoration has a bold arrangement of regularly spaced white uprights which 'support' a black trellis pattern; the stencilled pink roses at the top of this add warm splashes of colour. The trellis pattern is complemented by the tallish black chairs, the backs of which have horizontal spars. Eight tapering wooden pillars in the shape of trees rest on substantial horizontal joists which run under the gallery and are used to support a false ceiling. Sections of this ceiling have an open framework which allows light to enter from the partially glazed roof, a feature that makes this whole space very bright and airy.

The first floor houses the **Salon de Luxe** which was intended mainly for ladies. It was, as its name suggests, the most luxurious of the rooms; it was painted white and was full of leaded mirrors and leaded glass with graceful stylised flower patterns. Mackintosh also used panels of purple silk to decorate the walls. The most famous part of this interesting design is the pair of intricate entrance doors which are filled with leaded glass. (At present they are not *in situ*.) Most of its panels contain clear glass but there are splashes of colour, including green flower heads. At the side of the room is a reproduction of a gesso panel by Margaret MacDonald (entitled *O ye, all ye who walk in Willowwood*) featuring women's heads and flower patterns. On the opposite side of the room is a small fireplace above which is a leaded mirror. Three sets of silver-coloured pendant lanterns (not the originals) provide interior light while the leaded windows, which take up almost the entire width of the building, allow natural light to enter this north-facing room. The windows also give a good view of Sauchiehall Street for those who wish to sit and just watch the world go by. The (reproduction) furniture

The Willow Tea Rooms in Sauchiehall Street

consists of square wooden tables and high-backed chairs which are painted silver with pink inlays and are upholstered with purple velvet.

The second floor contained the (male) billiards room and the smoking room. In 1917 Mackintosh added a basement tea room called the Dug-Out. This had no windows at all and its walls were black, with brightly coloured geometric patterns added to relieve the starkness. Sadly, no photographs of this amazing room exist.

Kate Cranston (1849-1934) opened a number of tea rooms in Glasgow and she has been afforded an important place in the history of modern Glasgow because of her patronage of artists and architects such as George Walton (1867-1933) and Charles Rennie Mackintosh. Her brother was a tea merchant and he had the novel idea of charging people for a cup of tea and some cakes and biscuits. This caught on, particularly with middle-class women who now had a socially acceptable place in which to meet their friends – licensed premises were certainly not acceptable in those days! The tea rooms fitted in with the aim of many in the temperance movement (see p.62) who sought alternatives to pubs and other licensed premises, and in time they became the 'in places' in which to meet – and to be seen. Kate Cranston took up her brother's ideas and opened up a tea room in 1878 in Argyle Street (see p.95) and another in 1886 in Ingram Street. She opened her third in 1897 in Buchanan Street (see p.98) and commissioned Walton to design its interiors; Mackintosh contributed wall decorations. She then asked them to refurbish the expanded Argyle Street premises and in 1900 Mackintosh and his wife created the Ladies' Luncheon Room in Ingram Street; other rooms were added in later years. The Willow Tea Room was her fourth and final tea room. The unique style of her rooms put Kate Cranston in a league of her own and the collaboration between her and Mackintosh was an important chapter in the development of the city's expertise in interior design. Fortunately, the Ingram Street tea rooms still exist (they are in the city's museums' collection) and hopefully will be recreated in the near future. Mackintosh also designed interiors and furniture for Kate Cranston's home, Hous'hill at Nitshill in Glasgow (1903-09), which is now demolished.

The **Cumming and Smith Building** ⑭ (1891-5, H. & D. Barclay) stands at 128-52 Sauchiehall Street and now fronts the Savoy Centre, named after the Savoy Cinema which was entered through the main entrance. The ground floor is spoiled by new shop fronts, but the floors above have a host of detail, especially around the windows. Tall columns rise through three storeys and ten allegorical figures stand above them, an impressive piece of work by William Birnie Rhind. Above these is a row of squat Ionic columns and then four decorated urns stand on the roofline. On the building's flanks are end pediments which are decorated with faces.

Retrace the route back along Sauchiehall Street and turn right at Rose Street.

Rose Street to Charing Cross via Garnethill

Walk up Rose Street and on the right is a dark brick building housing the **Glasgow Film Theatre 🟊** . This was originally the Cosmo Cinema (1938-9, W. J. Anderson II) which was opened as an 'art cinema' which brought European films to city audiences, even during the Second World War. The original 'Cosmo' name, shortened from 'Cosmopolitan', reflected an outward-looking philosophy and the 'GFT' continues this work, showing a selection of more unusual and esoteric films from many different countries. The cinema organises other events such as discussions after films.

Rose Street leads into the district of **Garnethill** which was originally called Summerhill but took its new name after Thomas Garnet who built an observatory at the top of the hill in 1810 (see p.127). When it was being developed as a residential area the planners ignored the steep hills and maintained the city's gridiron layout. This decision probably gave architects and builders a host of problems. By the 1840s the area had become quite fashionable, and as well as a number of villas, there were many good-quality tenement buildings, including one which contains the fascinating Tenement House (see p.128). One of the local inhabitants was Catherine Carswell (1879-1946) who described life here in her book *Open the Door!* (1920).

Although the area is ringed by busy roads, there is still a quiet charm about it, particularly after the shoppers and students have departed, and there are a number of interesting buildings to look at. It is also one of the most cosmopolitan areas of the city with a sizeable Chinese population.

On the left after the Film Theatre is **St Aloysius' Roman Catholic Church 🟊** (1908-10, Charles Menart). This handsome building, with its tall, square belltower, is positioned at the top of a steep street and dominates the space around it. As well as having a small dome on top of the tower, there is a large copper-covered dome over the church's central space. Above the main door is the motto *Divo Aloysio Sacrum* ('Dedicated to St Aloysius'). Well above that are the inscriptions *IHS* (*Iesus hominum salvator* : 'Jesus, saviour of mankind') and *AMDG* (*Ad majorem dei gloriam*: 'To the greater glory of God', the motto of the Jesuits).

The Italian influence is even more apparent inside, with an extremely rich interior which features a lot of detailed work in marble and mosaic.

Turn left at Hill Street and pass the small **Garnethill Park 🟊**. This joint Scottish-German project was opened in 1991 as part of Glasgow's celebrations as the European Cultural Capital 1990; it is a peaceful little haven, complete with an urban babbling brook which runs between large blocks of stone. At the back of the park is a huge mural (dated *1978*) which is a mosaic made from 186,000 individual pieces of tile.

Turn left at Dalhousie Street. At this corner stands **Saint Aloysius College 🟊** (1882-3, Archibald Macpherson). The main building is in the form of a Venetian palace and incorporates the Doric portico of a school built here in 1866. Above this are two sets of balconies and then the inscriptions *IHS* and *AMDG* (see St Aloysius' R.C. Church above). The building is flanked by single-storey wings of 1892 and additional and more modern buildings can be seen farther along Hill Street.

Turn right at Renfrew Street to see what is now reckoned to be the city's architectural masterpiece, Charles Rennie Mackintosh's **Glasgow School of Art** ⑲.

The institution began its life in Ingram Street in 1845, later moving to the McLellan Galleries in 1869. It was originally established to teach designers the skills needed in Glasgow's important textile industry but, with the decline of that trade, the school broadened its interests. In 1896 the director Fra (Francis) Newberry and the Board of Governors invited local architects to submit plans for a new building on the steep slope above the galleries and the competition was won by Honeyman & Keppie, their designer being the young Charles Rennie Mackintosh. The building was built in two phases; in the first (1897-9) the east end and the main entrance were built, and in the second (1907-09) the west end was completed and a further storey was added to the first building.

The overall design echoes many of the traditions of Scottish architecture, with its use of good-quality sandstone and the castle-like harled south wall. It also heralded elements of the Modern Movement, particularly with its plain, relatively unadorned facade. The competition brief stressed the need for bright, airy, north-facing studios. Two blocks of these were built, one on either side of the main entrance; in addition, by positioning the building back from the road, light is allowed to enter the basement studios as well. As a foil to the rather plain facade there are elaborate wrought-iron railings, delicate ironwork at the upper windows, and a curious arch spanning the base of the entrance stairs. Just above the narrow main door are stone panels depicting two Art Nouveau female

Glasgow School of Art

figures and above these are two balconies, serving the Director's Room and the Director's Studio. A curious little tower stands to the left of the upper balcony, emphasising the asymmetry of the facade. The western extension ends at the very steep Scott Street and the three long western windows (three storeys high) emphasise the height of the building, while allowing copious amounts of light into the famous library.

Inside, the ground floor has a long east-west corridor with many massive sculptures which are used by students in drawing classes. Upstairs, the **Museum** has displays set beneath a large glass canopy which allows the light to flood in and this space is often used for temporary exhibitions. The roof's trusses are in the Arts and Crafts style and they add to the overall charm and interest of the design. In the stairwell is a Mackintosh wrought-iron sculpture representing the four elements (a fish, a bird, a tree and a bell) of the city's coat of arms. To the north of the Museum is a doorway flanked by a copy of the *Ancestors of Christ* from Chartres Cathedral; beyond it is the Director's Room with its studio directly above it.

To the east of the Museum is a corridor with more classical statues and friezes; this leads past large studios, specially designed to maximise the amount of northern light that Newberry insisted the studios should have. The corridor ends at the **Mackintosh Room** which was originally designed as the school's governors' Board Room. The fireplace and the panelling were designed for this room, the light fittings were designed for the house Windyhill (see p.405) and the carpet is a larger copy of a carpet designed for The Hill House (see p.406). There is a display of Mackintosh's furniture, some of which was originally made for houses he worked on, and altogether the room gives a fascinating glimpse of the breadth of his talents.

To the west of the Museum, another corridor leads to the **Library**, set in the extension. Despite Mackintosh's choice of dark wood, parts of the library are quite bright as it is lit by three full-length windows on the west wall. The tall wooden pillars supporting the gallery seem to grow out of the floor, dividing the room into definite spaces in the process. Steep and narrow stairs lead to the narrow Japanese-style gallery. The library is very stark in overall design but in places there are dashes of colour or small carvings. The overall effect is quite stunning — it must be impossible *not* to have an opinion about it!

The uppermost floor contains studios erected at the same time as the extension and these are not readily visible from Renfrew Street. Behind them, a glass-walled linking corridor (known as the 'hen-run') gives marvellous views over the city.

The **Furniture Gallery** is situated above the library. This was originally designed as a bookstore but is now full of pieces of Mackintosh's furniture from many places including Hous'hill, Windyhill and Kate Cranston's tea rooms (see p.123), while some of the pieces were made for his own use. Samples of his drawings and paintings are also exhibited.

This is certainly not a building to walk around with eyes fixed straight ahead; the intricate details are there to find and savour.

There are a number of other Art School buildings on Garnethill, although they are of a very different character from Mackintosh's masterpiece. One place of note is the **Newberry Gallery** (directly opposite the Mackintosh building) which is used to display students' work.

Continue along Renfrew Street, passing (on the left) the **Dental Hospital** **⑳** (1927-31, Wylie, Wright & Wylie). Its main doorway depicts the hospital's badge which incorporates parts of the city's coat of arms, the book of knowledge, its earlier name (The Incorporated Glasgow Dental Hospital) and the motto *Labore et scientia* ('By work and knowledge'). Cast-iron panels carry Art Deco zigzag patterns which are repeated on the flanking stonework.

Apart from dealing with patients needing specialist treatment, the hospital trains dentists and it has been part of Glasgow University since 1948.

The former Garnetbank Public School (1905, Thomas Lennox Watson), now **Garnetbank Primary School** **㉑**, is next door. Erected by the School Board of Glasgow, this is a variant on the standard design used for the city's schools and it has a graceful bowed Art Nouveau centrepiece.

Turn right at the very steep Garnet Street and climb it to meet Hill Street, this junction marking the spot where Thomas Garnet built his **observatory**. He was professor of Natural Philosophy at Anderson's College and was presumably attracted to this site by its altitude and relatively clean air. It was housed in one of the city's earliest Egyptian-style buildings and contained equipment suitable for both professional and amateur astronomers. In many ways it operated like a gentlemen's club and it kept its subscription deliberately high in order that (as its own literature assured prospective members) 'the subscribers are as select as possible'.

To the right, Hill Street has a number of interesting buildings, with some particularly attractive terraces of tenements and a couple of early villas.

On the left, a little down Hill Street, is **Garnethill Synagogue** **㉒** (1878-9, John McLeod), Scotland's first purpose-built synagogue. An L-shaped building, its entrance is in a very attractive stone tower which has a good deal of carved detail in a variety of styles. Decorated collonettes support a round-arched Romanesque portal and within this is a circular stained-glass window. Above the doorway is a Hebrew phrase from Deuteronomy and near the top of the building, the pediment is decorated with an incised Star of David.

There were very few Jews in Glasgow until the early nineteenth century and the first synagogue was established in 1823. Many of the immigrants came from the Netherlands or Germany, but their numbers greatly increased in the late nineteenth century as people fled from the programs in Russia and Poland. A large proportion of these settled in the Gorbals where there was a sizeable Jewish community early in the twentieth century.

On the north side of Hill Street is the former **Royal Beatson Memorial Hospital** ㉓, once the Glasgow Royal Cancer Hospital. To the left of the substantial entrance porch is a mosaic plaque bearing the letters *CCHA* ('Charing Cross Housing Association'), the date *1992*, and a phoenix rising out of flames. The 'Beatson' has been relocated to the Western Infirmary (see p.212).

Continue to the bottom of the street where there is a **viewpoint** ㉔ with a magnificent view looking westwards. The tall towers of Trinity College and Park Church (see p.221) stand on Woodlands Hill and behind them (and to their right) is the tower of Glasgow University. The Kilpatrick Hills form the north-western skyline behind the city.

Retrace the route back to Garnet Street and turn left. This descends to meet Buccleuch Street and on the right at the junction is the former **Garnethill School** ㉕ (1878, James Thomson). This large Italianate building has two storeys with a substantial tower over the Roman Doric porch. To the east is a taller extension built in 1886 by W. F. McGibbon.

The school was opened by the Glasgow School Board 'for the children of less wealthy parents', and it became so successful in fostering new educational techniques that it attracted large numbers of pupils, to the extent that it had some classes with over one hundred pupils in them! The school eventually became the Glasgow High School for Girls but moved out in 1968 to Kelvindale. The buildings were converted into houses in 1998.

Turn left at Buccleuch Street in order to reach **The Tenement House** ㉖ (1892, Clarke & Bell) at 145 Buccleuch Street. In here, the National Trust for Scotland owns a small tenement flat which was the home of Miss Agnes Toward from 1911 to 1965. The house is virtually unchanged from her time and it gives a wonderful insight into the type of accommodation lived in by many Glaswegians in the first half of the twentieth century. In many ways the house is one of the most worthwhile buildings to visit in Glasgow as the city is (or perhaps, was) the tenement city *par excellence*. Indeed, the cohesiveness of the city is partly attributed to the very sociable nature of these buildings.

Most of Glasgow's tenements were four- or five-storey buildings, often arranged in a square with a communal area in the middle. In busy working-class areas, shops were placed at street level with houses piled above them, while the more expensive (and better-made) tenements were usually found at the top of hills (away from the noise and dirt of busy thoroughfares). Tenement life was adopted all over Glasgow, from the leafy suburbs of the West End to the poorer areas of Clydeside and the south and east of the city. Sizes varied considerably, and while some flats (notably in the West End) could have seven or more rooms, some (called 'single-ends') comprised only one room which was home to a whole family, which would have included quite a few children. The example found at the Tenement House was definitely one of the better tenement flats.

For anyone not acquainted with tenements, the building is entered by going into the 'close' (passageway) – the Tenement House has a 'wally close', so-called because it has tiled walls. In this building there are only two 'flats' (individual houses) on each 'landing', though some of the poorest tenements had as many as six or seven. The open area at the back of the building is called the 'back-court' and in this was found the 'wash-house' (communal laundry), the 'drying-green' (where washing was hung up to dry) and the 'midden' (where rubbish was put).

Agnes Toward (1886-1975) came to live at 145 Buccleuch Street with her mother (who died in 1939). She then lived by herself for a further twenty-six years and in all this time she accumulated many ordinary domestic artefacts. The NTS acquired this first-floor house in 1982 and later established a small exhibition area in a ground-floor flat; this should be visited first.

Miss Toward's house has a hall and four rooms: a parlour, a kitchen, a bedroom and a bathroom. In many houses, the **parlour** was only used on special occasions but since Miss Toward's mother was a dressmaker she may have worked in this room; her sewing machine (of around 1860) is on display. Miss Toward was keen on music and was able to afford the nice rosewood piano found in the room. A small recess in the corner holds a 'box-bed'. These were banned from 1900 in order to curb overcrowding.

The **kitchen** is possibly the most fascinating room, its main feature being the large black 'range' which is heated by coal. The range was a useful multi-purpose appliance as it had a fire, an oven and a hot plate, but inevitably the whole area around the range got very dirty and it had to be meticulously cleaned until it shone. The coal bunker is also in the kitchen; handy, but obviously a source of a lot of dust and smell. The 'jawbox' (sink) and the fixed furniture are all of the original 1892 design and the wall's shelves are well stocked with kitchen implements. Miss Toward slept in the box-bed in the corner of the kitchen; this room, after all, was heated far more than any other.

The **bedroom** may have been used by Miss Toward's lodgers. Taking in paying lodgers was a common practice in the city as it allowed many people to afford a house in one of the 'better' areas. The room has a lovely cast-iron fireplace which will be the envy of many present-day Glaswegians who own flats and whose original fireplaces were stripped out in the 1960s or 1970s. The existence of a separate **bathroom** (other tenements shared a WC on the landing) marks this house as a well-appointed flat.

This house is one of the city's little gems and for many visitors it will certainly offer a trip down memory lane.

Continue on Buccleuch Street, following the pavement as it bends round to the left, and take the right fork when it splits. The path leads through a little wooded area and then meets Renfrew Street. The block of flats at 347-53 Renfrew Street is **Albany Mansions** **㉗** (1897, J. J. Burnet), a handsome block of tenement flats featuring stone balconies and intricate wrought-iron work.

A little to its left, at **341 Renfrew Street**, is a massive bust of Beethoven. This marks the back of a music shop that once stood on Sauchiehall Street.

Turn right at Renfrew Street and follow the pavement downhill as it curves round to the left to meet **Charing Cross**. This used to be a very grand junction with a number of traditional buildings but the M8 (which is underground at this point) has scythed its way through the area, leaving a great gash in the city's fabric.

At Charing Cross, the large salmon pink monstrosity that straddles the motorway is **Tay House** ⓴ (1991, Holford Associates). Of all city-centre buildings, this is probably the one most Glaswegians would wish knocked down as it blocks views of the finest buildings remaining at the cross. The bridge-like structure which carries Tay House over the motorway was originally dubbed 'the bridge that leads to nowhere' and it was left like that for years until this ghastly 'state of the art' office block was plopped on top of it.

The pavement bends round the front of **Charing Cross Mansions** ⓴ (1889-91, J. J. Burnet). This fascinating curved block of 'mansion flats' is one of the city's best-known tenement buildings, especially as its steep mansard roof gives it a distinctively French look. The most noticeable feature is the tall galleried cupola, its little balcony complete with delicate cast-iron railings. The building's centrepiece features a Baroque clock (decorated with the signs of the zodiac) around which is statuary by William Birnie Rhind. Above the clock, a female figure holds a dough paddle (for making bread) while a male holds a hammer and leans on a gearwheel. At third-floor level are two figures holding a shield and on either side of them is an attractive stone balustrade. A lion rampant on a

Charing Cross Mansions

pedestal stands above these figures. Below the clock are more figures (four females and two cherubs), together with a diminutive St Mungo perched on top of the city's coat of arms. Finally, the letters *R S & S* appear on the facade a number of times as the mansions were built for the warehousemen Robert Simpson & Sons. The building is best seen later on from the Cameron Memorial Fountain (see p.133).

From Charing Cross the walk heads westwards, but there are interesting buildings to be seen just to the east, so walk a short distance in that direction along Sauchiehall Street.

Firstly, the **Albany Chambers** ❸⓿ (1896-9) stand next door to Charing Cross Mansions; the fact that both buildings were built by the same architects for the same clients accounts for their similarities. Near the top of the building is a plaque on which are the words: *erected 1897 the 60th year of Queen Victoria's reign* and at the very top, a statue of *Britannia* is holding her traditional shield and three-pronged trident.

At 520 Sauchiehall Street is the former **Vitograph Cinema** ❸⓵ (1914-15, John Fairweather), one of the city's earliest picture houses. This has been drastically altered at ground floor level, but above are two torch-bearing statues (the one on the right holds a lyre) and at roof level there is a winged angel playing pipes. The building is very narrow and when it was used as a cinema the auditorium was only eight seats wide.

Next door is **The Royal Highland Fusiliers Museum** ❸⓶ (1903-4, Honeyman, Keppie & Mackintosh). The two statues standing high above the street are copies of Michelangelo's *The Delphic Sibyl* and *Isaiah* from the Cistine Chapel in the Vatican. Above them is a carving of the regimental badge and the regiment's colours (flags).

The regiment has been in existence under this name since 1959 and, despite what its name might suggest, it has had a long association with the city. It was formed by the amalgamation of the Glasgow-based Highland Light Infantry (the 'HLI') and the Royal Scots Fusiliers. The HLI was formed in 1881 when two separate eighteenth-century battalions were amalgamated. The battalions fought in most of the wars conducted by the British Empire as well as being involved in action at home. Indeed, in 1848, the year of enormous revolutionary upheaval in Europe, the troops were called upon to police the city because of political unrest.

The museum charts the history of the regiment and describes its role in many of the foreign wars in which it was involved. The section on music includes recordings of tunes played on the bagpipes by the regimental band.

The back of the building was originally a townhouse and the front part was added in 1903-04 for the photographers T. and R. Annan who remained here until 1959. The original lift is still in place but unfortunately it is no longer in use; it is very unusual as it was powered by water pressure. **Thomas Annan** (1830-88) is best known for the various editions of his book *The Old Closes and Streets of Glasgow* which featured between thirty and fifty photographs of Victorian Glasgow between 1868 and the end of the century. These pictures were commissioned by the City Improvement Trust (see p.33) to record the old city before wholesale demolition of its slums took place. These evocative pictures are still very popular and can even be found decorating the walls of pubs around the city. In complete contrast, he took around one hundred photographs for the book *Old Country Houses of the Old Glasgow Gentry* (1870), which is another important pictorial record of nineteenth-century Glasgow. His son James Craig Annan also worked here as a photographer and the family still maintains a gallery in the West End.

Strathclyde University's **Baird Hall of Residence** ❸❸ (1937-8, Weddell & Inglis) stands at the corner of Sauchiehall Street and Garnet Street. This tall building, its height accentuated by its drum towers and narrow ribs, was originally built as the Beresford Hotel for the 1938 Empire Exhibition in Bellahouston Park (see p.281) and it is in the same Art Deco style as the exhibition's temporary structures. It was originally decorated with red, black and mustard tiles which have since been painted over. In addition, its fins were black and scarlet and the twin towers were capped by flagpoles. It was obviously built as something to be noticed!

Inglis designed and owned cinemas, hence the similarity between this facade and those of some contemporary cinemas. This is probably the city's most interesting building of the 1930s and it has been described by the architectural historians Gomme and Walker as being 'deliberately, insistently alien, kicking all the old Glasgow manners in the teeth, a strident eye-catcher from a brash bypass world, [a] monument to an age which vanished almost as soon as it was born.'

Retrace the route back along to Charing Cross.

CHARING CROSS TO THE MITCHELL LIBRARY

The busy roads to the west of the Charing Cross Mansions must now be crossed. The easiest and safest way to do this is via the pedestrian bridge which was encountered at the bottom of Renfrew Street. Following this (higher) route also has the advantage of allowing a good view of another of the city's most imposing sandstone tenement blocks, **St George's Mansions** ❸❹ (1900-1, Burnet & Boston), situated to the north of Charing Cross. This French-style building was erected for the City Improvement Trust and is a good example of how a tenement can be used successfully at an awkward corner. While both sides of this large building are extremely fine, it is the corner section that is quite outstanding. The first floor has a stone balustrade decorated with the city's coat of arms and above that are three pairs of variously detailed bow windows. At the fourth floor is an iron railing, two attractive semi-circular windows and three pairs of sculptured angelic cherubs who hold shields depicting a bell, a tree (and the date *1902*) and a bird. Above these is a clock (inserted into a beaten metalwork plaque) and a stone balustrade which links this central feature to the two flanking ogee-topped turrets.

On the west side of Charing Cross stands the **Cameron Memorial Fountain** ㉟ (1896, Clarke and Bell). The base is constructed from pink granite from Peterhead in Aberdeenshire while the elaborate upper part is made in terracotta by Doulton. On two sides are bronze plaques of Cameron and the words *In honour of Sir Charles Cameron, BART. D.L. L.L.D. in recognition of his many services to this city and to Scotland during 21 years in parliament. 1874-1895.* Cameron was born in 1841 and during his time in parliament as a Glasgow MP he secured a number of reforms, including the ending of imprisonment for debt.

Head westwards along **Newton Place** ㊱ (1837, George Smith) which runs alongside Sauchiehall Street but is separated from the busy road by its narrow garden. This was originally built as Caledonia Place with a long row of fashionable two-storey terraced houses and three-storey pavilions in the centre and at the ends; most are now used as offices. This is an exceptionally attractive example of Glaswegian terrace design especially since the houses have kept their exterior cast-iron features such as railings, lampstandards and balconies.

Continue on Somerset Place and turn right at Clifton Street to the lovely former **Queen's Rooms** ㊲ (1857, Charles Wilson). This was originally built as a concert hall and assembly rooms for chamber concerts and dances, and in 1872 John Tweed's guidebook described it as 'such a place as the most fastidious might enjoy themselves in with comfort and satisfaction.' Since 1948 it has been used by various religious or cultural organisations. An Italian Renaissance building, it is essentially a temple without the traditional grand portico; instead the main decoration is a wonderful frieze at cornice level (by the sculptor John G. Mossman) which runs round into La Belle Place where the front door is located.

The eastern portion of the frieze depicts the development of civilisation, with prehistoric people, horse-taming, agriculture using oxen, harvesting, industry and commerce, a ship, a battle and a musician with a lyre. The seven windows on the eastern wall have their arches decorated with carvings representing the arts and sciences and above them are roundels depicting James Watt (science), Robert Burns (poetry), Joshua Reynolds (painting), David Hamilton (architecture), John Flaxman (sculpture), George Frederick Handel (music) and Robert Peel (commerce). This side's door has above it a lion and unicorn as part of a royal coat of arms which bears the motto *Honi soit qui mal y pense* ('Evil be to him who evil thinks'); above that is a lyre. At the northern end of this side is a variation of the city's coat of arms (complete with two horns of plenty) and another lyre.

The north side's three semicircular windows are decorated with sculptured lyres, the middle window also having a swan and two dolphin-like creatures. In the centre of the frieze is Minerva (the Roman goddess of intelligence, handicrafts and the arts) giving gifts to the arts and sciences. To the left of this are sculptures representing music, while on the right are the arts, including Charles Wilson himself (representing architecture) holding the plans for the building. On the extreme right is a mason in the act of chiselling a sculpted face.

The wall nearest Sauchiehall Street has engraved on it *Erected by David Bell of Blackhall merchant in Glasgow   MDCCCLVII   Charles Wilson MQR architect   Mossman sculptor   W.T. Edmiston wright   William York builder.*

Turn left at the top of Clifton Street to see **2-5 La Belle Place** 🟤 (1856-7, Charles Wilson). Wilson designed these two tenement buildings (the first in the city to have bow windows at the front) in Italian Renaissance style in order to complement his neighbouring Queen's Rooms. Decorations include shells, laurel leaves, heads, a bell and the letters *DB*; the last two features being for David Bell for whom this was also built. The street's unusual name is said to have been derived from that of Bell – since this is the West End, living in a street called 'La Belle Place' was presumably preferable to something rather common like 'Bell Street'.

Continue along La Belle Place, then turn left at North Claremont Street to reach Sauchiehall Street. The terrace on the left (on the south side of Sauchiehall Street) is **Sandyford Place** 🟤 (1842-56, Brown & Carrick); the Glasgow Eye Infirmary occupied numbers 3-6 from 1938 to 1998 (alterations by Burnet, Tait & Lorne).

Turn right at Sauchiehall Street and walk the short distance to the graceful curved **Royal Crescent** 🟤 (1839-49, Alexander Taylor), once described as a 'pretty specimen of the dwellings of the better classes of Glasgow.' The terrace, which is flanked by tall end pavilions, is composed of a series of houses the ground floors of which have substantial porches and deep curved bay windows.

Return to the junction of Sauchiehall Street and Claremont Street and turn right (onto Claremont Street) to reach the former Trinity Congregational Church (1864, John Honeyman). This is now the **Henry Wood Hall** 🟤, home since 1978 of the **Royal Scottish National Orchestra**. The church's finest feature is its tall, slim spire and, although there are no substantial decorative embellishments on the building, the exterior stonework has many small carved details including faces and foliage.

The orchestra began its life in 1891 as the Scottish Orchestra but it has only been playing full-time since 1950. Although it is based in Glasgow and gives its main series of performances here, it appears in other Scottish towns and cities and makes tours abroad. As well as performing a wide range of classical music, the orchestra also plays various other types of music, including music for film soundtracks such as *Braveheart*. The hall is named after the English composer Henry Wood (1869-1944) who started the London Promenade Concerts.

Turn left at Berkeley Street and continue along it to Granville Street. At this junction stands the huge **Mitchell Library** ⑫, the biggest public reference library in Europe. Approached from this direction, the eyes are instantly drawn to the large statues at what is now the rear of the building. This Granville Street facade was originally the front of the **St Andrew's Halls** (1873-7, James Sellars) which could hold 4500 people, well before the days of much stricter fire regulations! The Grand Hall's acoustics were reckoned to be amongst the finest in Europe and it was a great loss to the city when the building was gutted by fire in 1962. In 1972-80 the building was rebuilt to provide a library extension and the Mitchell Theatre.

Two Atlantes (by William Mossman) flank the middle door. Above, there are sixteen massive fluted Ionic columns and four groups of fine sculptures by John G. Mossman. These represent literature (Homer, Dante and Shakespeare), painting (Michelangelo, Raphael and Leonardo da Vinci), architecture (Pallas Athene, the Greek goddess of arts and crafts, with figures representing architecture and sculpture) and music (Apollo, the god of music and leader of the Muses, with two figures holding musical instruments). At the top are two sets of four female figures (called caryatids) who carry symbols associated with various giants of the arts and sciences which are named below: Raphael, Watt, Michelangelo, Newton, Flaxman, Purcell, Bach, Handel, Mozart and Beethoven.

As well as being the venue for concerts and other leisure activities, the halls were also used for large meetings and in 1914 the suffragette leader Emily Pankhurst spoke at a big gathering here. A warrant had been taken out for her arrest and a force of 120 policemen had the unenviable task of enforcing it; not surprisingly, a riot ensued. In the aftermath, an official report carried very different versions of what actually happened. A witness who was in the meeting stated that: 'The audience consisted of over three, possibly four thousand people… [and]… after Mrs Pankhurst had been speaking for a very few minutes, the platform, which please mark, was occupied solely by women, old and young, was rushed by detectives and policemen with drawn batons who laid out in all directions hitting and felling women.' In contrast, an Inspector Walker reported that: 'we were immediately assailed with chairs, flower pots, water bottles, and other missiles thrown from the platform by men and women who fought like tigers.' See also p.199.

Turn left at Kent Road and left again at North Street to get to the library's front entrance. This is the original library and was designed by William B. Whitie (1906-11). It is of white Northumberland sandstone on a base of grey Creetown granite. The facade has a tower-like entrance flanked by wings with taller end pavilions. The overall impression is one of bulkiness rather than monumentalism and the main examples of stone decoration are tall pillars and stone balustrades. The entrance is the most interesting part of the facade and above the door is a sculpted head of *Victory* and a statue of a seated man (by Johan Miller). A classical female figure with flowing robes (by Thomas J. Clapperton) poses on top of the large copper dome.

The library is named after the tobacco manufacturer Stephen Mitchell (1789-1874) who left a bequest to the city for the establishment of a public library. This started in the city centre in 1877 with a stock of about 17,000 books. The present building had its corner-stone laid by Andrew Carnegie (see p.297) and was opened in 1911. 'The Mitchell' now houses over one million items and includes especially important collections on Glasgow and Robert Burns.

Many of the rooms in the original part of the library are really too attractive to work, especially the main reading room.

Mitchell Library to Blythswood Square

After leaving the library continue on North Street to reach Berkeley Street and then turn right in order to cross North Street and the M8 motorway, the busy highway which cuts through this part of the city in a very brutal fashion.

Follow Bath Street to Elmbank Street and on the right is **The King's Theatre** **43** (1901-4, Frank Matcham). This interesting red sandstone building has a very intricate shape, with two tower-like structures, a corner dome, stone balustrades and a variety of window shapes. Also of note are the lion holding a shield (with *KT* on it), urns, some peculiar-looking lions' heads and four men's heads.

Just inside, the foyer gives a foretaste of the theatre's internal decoration. The walls are lined with marble and there is a barrel-vaulted plastered ceiling 'supported' by caryatids. Above the foyer can be seen the Picture Gallery which has a fascinating collection of pictures of well-known Scottish actors and actresses; of particular interest is *Entertainment* (June Chrisfield Chapman) featuring twenty-six Scottish entertainers. The auditorium is very spacious and is, to say the least, elaborately decorated. Fancy Baroque-style plasterwork seems to be everywhere, with gold being the predominant colour.

This 2000-seat theatre started its life showing musical comedy and it clearly aimed its productions towards the well-off West End clientele. The range of shows has changed over the years and it has featured many famous actors and actresses such as Laurence Olivier, Katharine Hepburn, John Gielgud, Fred Astaire and the legendary Harry Lauder (see p.375). It was here in 1962 that Scottish Opera (see p.106) began its life. Today it provides a wide variety of entertainment, including performances from numerous amateur societies. But perhaps its most important role in the life of the city is that it is home to Glasgow's most extravagant and over-the-top Christmas pantomime, loved by children and adults alike.

On the opposite corner of this junction is **The Griffin** pub **44**, originally the King's Arms (*c.* 1852). It was given its Art Nouveau touches, most notably the etched windows and exterior woodwork, by William Reid in 1903-4.

Turn right into Elmbank Street. On the right (at Elmbank Crescent) is the former **Institute of Engineers and Shipbuilders** ㊟ (1906-8, J. B. Wilson), now rehearsal studios for Scottish Opera (see p.106).

This is not a very well-known building as it is tucked away in a side street but it bears a host of detail connected with its original occupants. The main facade is three storeys tall, with giant pilasters (decorated with cherubs and torches) linking the upper two storeys. Between the two pilasters, a bow window is decorated with heads and a ship with its sail unfurled. Flanking the pilasters are two carvings with various engineer's tools including a protractor, a spanner, calipers and a chisel. Above these, a semi-circular stained-glass window (featuring a ship) is contained within the pediment. At street level, the tall elaborate doorway has two columns which are decorated with more cherubs and the dates *1857* and *1907*.

Inside, the marble-floored entrance hall leads to a stairway lit by stained-glass windows depicting Scottish places associated with engineering. This leads to the Rankine Hall which has a barrel-shaped roof and is lit by stained-glass windows depicting ships of the sixteenth and twentieth centuries. The hall is named after William Rankine (1820-72) who was a professor of Engineering at Glasgow University and a major contributor to the science of thermodynamics.

On the opposite side of Elmbank Street is the former **Glasgow High School** ㊤, a large group of buildings now used by various council departments. The main building (1846-7, Charles Wilson) is in Italian Renaissance style and is linked to two wings (1886 and 1897, J. L. Cowan) by imposing arches. Above the main doorway are statues (by John G. Mossman) of various important figures of the arts and sciences holding objects associated with their achievements: Homer (scroll), Galileo (globe and telescope), James Watt (governor) and Cicero (lyre).

The High School (which is now located in the north-west of the city) is Glasgow's oldest school as its history can be traced back to the times when the cathedral set up its own Grammar School. It later came under the control of the burgh and for a long time it was the only school of note in the city. In 1878 it moved from the old part of the city to this new site, taking over the buildings from Glasgow Academy (see p.225) which had relocated to Hillhead. It gradually assumed the role of a private school, though the city still had control over it, but in the 1970s the council decided that none of its schools should charge fees or have a selective intake. When the school moved out these buildings were taken over by (the now defunct) Strathclyde Regional Council and its council chamber was located here. The complex of buildings is now used by Glasgow City Council.

Head back along Elmbank Street, turn right at Bath Street, then right at Holland Street; this leads to the eastern side of the school. The large cast-iron gates feature the school's coat of arms and the motto *Sursum semper* ('Ever upwards'). Look through the gateway to the main building where the school bell can still be seen.

Walk back along Holland Street for a short distance and turn right at West Regent Street. On the right is the brick-built **Strathclyde Police Headquarters** ❼ (1931-4, James Miller), previously the Glasgow and West of Scotland Commercial College. Although Strathclyde Regional Council ceased to exist in 1996, the force still polices the vast Strathclyde area, covering Glasgow and much of western Scotland, from Mull to Girvan. Turn right at Pitt Street to pass the main door, beside which is a badge with the motto *Semper vigilo* ('Ever vigilant').

In the basement is one of Glasgow's least-known museums, the **Police Museum** ❽. It charts the history of the Strathclyde Police, from the individual burgh forces, through the formation of the regional force in 1975 and up to the present day. Displays show uniforms, badges and equipment used by the forces over the last couple of centuries. Examples of various types of crimes are shown, together with the tools of the criminals' trade, including the skilfully fashioned equipment used by forgers. Getting more gruesome, there are various nasty-looking weapons used by the city's criminal fraternity and information on some of the most infamous of the region's murders, including those that took place in the 'Square Mile of Murder'. In 1961, Jack House wrote a book of that title based on four murders that happened very close to this very building. The newspapers' accounts of the trials of Madeleine Smith (1857), Jessie McLachlan (1862), Dr Pritchard (1865) and Oscar Slater (1909) fascinated Glaswegians, and even today occasional newspaper articles delve into various aspects of one or other of these cases. The Madeleine Smith case is described on p.117. Further displays on modern police detection techniques and the application of forensic science make this a fascinating little museum to visit.

Turn left at West George Street and pass the Malmaison Hotel, formerly **St Jude's Episcopal Church** ❾ 1838-9, John Stephen). This is a very unusual Greek-style building and its tall and very austere frontage carries a Greek phrase which means 'God as head of the church'. Embellishments are kept to a minimum and are found mainly around the door, on the side porches and at roof level; a tall lantern in the style of the Choragic Monument of Lysicrates, similar to those found in the Glasgow Necropolis (see p.357), used to stand on top of the building but was removed in the 1960s. The name Malmaison comes from the French Chateau of that name in which Napoleon Bonaparte and his wife Josephine stayed.

Continue along West George Street to **Blythswood Square** ❶ where the walk ends.

North Clydeside
and Anderston

A walk which follows the River Clyde downstream from the city centre to the Scottish Exhibition and Conference Centre. The route passes various reminders of what made the Clyde one of the world's most important industrial rivers. The return route to the city goes through the western section of Glasgow's commercial area which has many fine Victorian buildings.

The Renfrew Ferry and the Clyde Navigation Trust Building

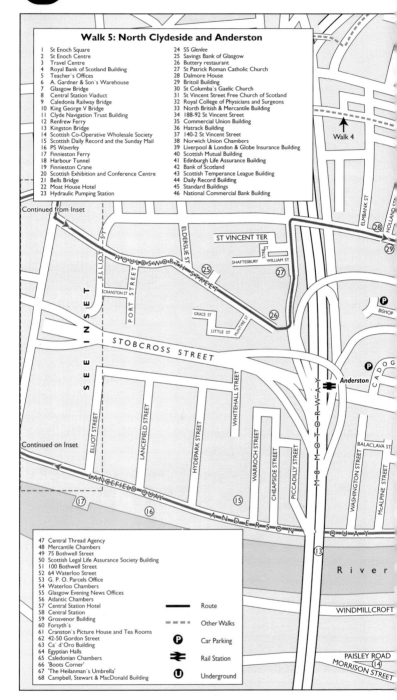

Walk 5: North Clydeside and Anderston

1 St Enoch Square
2 St Enoch Centre
3 Travel Centre
4 Royal Bank of Scotland Building
5 Teacher's Offices
6 A. Gardner & Son's Warehouse
7 Glasgow Bridge
8 Central Station Viaduct
9 Caledonia Railway Bridge
10 King George V Bridge
11 Clyde Navigation Trust Building
12 Renfrew Ferry
13 Kingston Bridge
14 Scottish Co-Operative Wholesale Society
15 Scottish Daily Record and the Sunday Mail
16 PS Waverley
17 Finnieston Ferry
18 Harbour Tunnel
19 Finnieston Crane
20 Scottish Exhibition and Conference Centre
21 Bells Bridge
22 Moat House Hotel
23 Hydraulic Pumping Station
24 SS Glenlee
25 Savings Bank of Glasgow
26 Buttery restaurant
27 St Patrick Roman Catholic Church
28 Dalmore House
29 Britoil Building
30 St Columba's Gaelic Church
31 St Vincent Street Free Church of Scotland
32 Royal College of Physicians and Surgeons
33 North British & Mercantile Building
34 188-92 St Vincent Street
35 Commercial Union Building
36 Hatrack Building
37 140-2 St Vincent Street
38 Norwich Union Chambers
39 Liverpool & London & Globe Insurance Building
40 Scottish Mutual Building
41 Edinburgh Life Assurance Building
42 Bank of Scotland
43 Scottish Temperance League Building
44 Daily Record Building
45 Standard Buildings
46 National Commercial Bank Building

47 Central Thread Agency
48 Mercantile Chambers
49 75 Bothwell Street
50 Scottish Legal Life Assurance Society Building
51 100 Bothwell Street
52 64 Waterloo Street
53 G. P. O. Parcels Office
54 Waterloo Chambers
55 Glasgow Evening News Offices
56 Atlantic Chambers
57 Central Station Hotel
58 Central Station
59 Grosvenor Building
60 Forsyth's
61 Cranston's Picture House and Tea Rooms
62 42-50 Gordon Street
63 Ca' d'Oro Building
64 Egyptian Halls
65 Caledonian Chambers
66 'Boots Corner'
67 'The Heilanman's Umbrella'
68 Campbell, Stewart & MacDonald Building

	Route
	Other Walks
P	Car Parking
	Rail Station
U	Underground

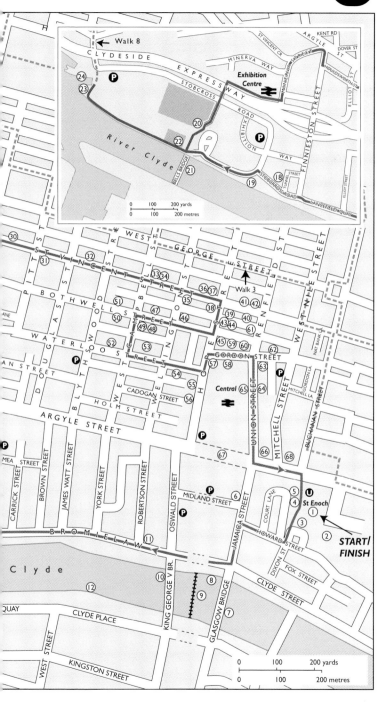

Main places of interest	Clyde Navigation Trust Building **11**
	PS *Waverley* 16
	(world's oldest sea-going paddle steamer)
	SECC **20**
	(Scottish Exhibition and Conference Centre)
	SS *Glenlee* **24** (maritime museum)
	St Vincent Street Free Church of Scotland 31
	(Alexander Thomson)
Circular/linear	circular
Starting point	St Enoch Square **1**
Finishing point	St Enoch Square **1**
Distance	7km (4.5 miles)
Terrain	pavements and paths; long hill along St Vincent Street and then downhill to the end of the route
Public transport	St Enoch Underground Station
	Exhibition Centre Railway Station (C)
	Charing Cross Railway Station (Q)
	Central Railway Station (C)
Sections	St Enoch Square to the Kingston Bridge
	Kingston Bridge to the SECC
	SECC to Hope Street
	Hope Street to St Enoch Square
Architects	Thomson: St Vincent Street Free Church
	of Scotland **31**
	Grosvenor Building **59**
	Egyptian Halls **64**
	Mackintosh: former Daily Record Office **44**
Nearby walks	2, 3, 4, 8
Refreshments	near St Enoch Square; SECC; many from western end of St Vincent Street to the end of the route
Notes	Once the river is reached, the riverside walkway can be used; it also acts as a route through an underpass below the George V Bridge However, it is worth walking along Clyde Street past the Clyde Navigation Trust Building in order to view it closely. Be aware of safety advice (see p.16) as the route beside the River Clyde can be very quiet at times.

St Enoch Square to the Kingston Bridge

St Enoch Square ❶ took its name from a corruption of St Thenew, mother of St Mungo (see p.415). It was initially laid out for housing in 1786 and ninety years later the City of Glasgow Union Railway built a large terminus on the eastern side of the square, with the lines linking the city to the south of the country and to England. St Enoch Station was very large with an enormous arched glazed roof 62m (205ft) wide and 160m (525ft) long. The Gothic St Enoch Hotel (1879) was built in front of the station and its size (it was at the time the country's largest hotel) and elevated position above the square allowed it to dominate this important open space. Sadly, the railway only lasted a hundred years and in 1977 the station and hotel were torn down in order to make way for the huge steel and glass St Enoch shopping centre which now dominates the square.

The **St Enoch Centre** ❷ (1981-9, Reiach & Hall with Gollins Melvin Ward Partnership) was, when built, the biggest glass-covered shopping mall in Europe, and its huge transparent roof is an echo of the former station's design. The massive expanse of glass gives this building its interest and keeps it very bright and pleasant to shop in. However, in case the Glasgow sunshine is too hot, there are automated motorised solar blinds to keep shopaholics cool.

Much of the square is now pedestrianised, with the only building actually in the square being the delightful little Jacobean **Travel Centre** ❸, formerly the entrance to the St Enoch Underground Station (1896, James Miller). This red sandstone building is dwarfed by the surrounding buildings but it has many points of interest. At each corner is an ogee-roofed turret and at the back of the building are sculptures featuring the city's coat of arms, urns and various small faces. Grotesque grimacing faces also surround the doorway, while other little faces are cleverly included in the detail at each corner. The subway system is described on p.210.

The square's western side is impressive, the finest building probably being the **Royal Bank of Scotland Building** ❹ (1906-7, A. N. Paterson) at 22-4 St Enoch Square. Its granite entrance is flanked by figures representing *Exchange*, *Security*, *Prudence* and *Adventure* (by Phyllis Archibald) and between each pair of figures are sculptures featuring horns of plenty, entwined serpents and a pair of wings. Above the doorway is the phrase *In patriam fidelis* ('Faith in our country') and above that is a plaque with a sheaf of grain, St Andrew (with his cross) and a ship. These symbols are also used on the doorway and on the gate's coat of arms. The building's next three storeys are relatively plain but the top two contain a lot of carved detail.

Just beside it, at number 20, are the **Teachers' Offices** ❺ (1875, James Boucher), built in Italian style for the whisky distillers. It boasts some very nice carved detail (especially around the windows) and delicate cast-iron work.

Leave the square by the south-western corner and head westwards along Howard Street to Jamaica Street. This latter street was developed in the 1750s and its name celebrates the important trade the city had with the Caribbean.

At the corner pause to look over the road to the **A. Gardner & Son's Warehouse** ❻ (1855-6, John Baird I) at 36 Jamaica Street. This very handsome four-storey building was a remarkable structure when erected as its skeleton was composed of cast-iron and wrought-iron members. The ironwork allowed the walls to be kept as thin as possible, enabling the facade to have a great expanse of glass. At first glance the three upper storeys may seem to be the same but there are subtle differences in window heights and in the shapes of the window frames.

Turn left at Jamaica Street and follow it down to the River Clyde at **Glasgow Bridge** ❼ (1895-9, Blyth & Westland), also called Jamaica Bridge. A plaque at the centre of the eastern parapet explains that this is the third bridge at this point, the first being Broomielaw Bridge (1768-72) which was only 10m (30ft) wide. It had seven arches and was obviously a handsome structure, being known as the 'Bonny Brig'. The second was built in 1833-5 by Thomas Telford (1757-1834); this was 20m (60ft) wide but in time it also proved too small. The present bridge was then planned to replace it but there was an outcry when the design showed that it would bear no resemblance to Telford's much-loved bridge. By public demand the new bridge's design was changed to make it very similar to Telford's; not only did it have the same number of arches (seven), but the original granite facings, balustrades and copestones were re-used as a marvellous gesture of admiration for the work of one the country's greatest engineers.

Turn right and head along Clyde Street. From here the route follows the River Clyde all the way to the SECC complex and then to the Hydraulic Pumping Station by going along the riverside **Clyde Walkway**, a long-distance urban footpath which runs from Strathclyde Park (near Hamilton). The walkway ends at Bells Bridge, where it joins the Glasgow to Loch Lomond Cycleway, one of the many designated cycle routes that have been established to give cyclists a safe route through the Glasgow area.

The **River Clyde** is Scotland's third longest river and it flows about 160km (100 miles) from the Lanarkshire hills to the town of Greenock, falling some 600m (2000ft) on its journey downstream; thereafter, the river turns southwards and becomes the Firth of Clyde. The river sits in a broad valley and altogether it drains an area of about 4000km² (1600 square miles) with its main tributaries in Glasgow being the River Kelvin (see p.242) and the White Cart Water (see p.304).

Glaswegians would certainly claim it to be the country's most important river as it flows through the most densely populated area of Scotland and because it has been closely connected with many of the country's industries. Glasgow is situated at an important crossing point where a busy ford and bridge (see p.70) were established long ago, but the original significance of the medieval city depended on the cathedral, not the river, and the well-known phrase *Glasgow made the Clyde and the Clyde made Glasgow* reflects the role of the river in more recent centuries.

For a long time the stretch of the river between Glasgow and Greenock was very shallow, less than 1m (3ft) in many places, and was thus quite unsuitable for navigation. Harbours in Ayrshire were used by the city's merchants and in the 1690s Port Glasgow (30km (20 miles) downstream) was established as the city's harbour. After the 1707 Union with England there were more opportunities for peaceful seaborne trade and some attempts were made to deepen the river, but it was not until 1768 that John Golborne took on the huge task of making the river navigable. Golborne narrowed the river using a series of jetties about 13km (8 miles) downstream of the city. These allowed a faster flow of water which scoured the riverbed, taking huge amounts of silt downstream into the Firth of Clyde. Until this time the river was some hundreds of feet wide in places and had a number of sandy islands (or 'inches'); Golborne arranged the dredging of these or joined them up with the riverbanks. Further deepening was undertaken in 1799 by John Rennie and in 1805 by Thomas Telford who joined up Golborne's jetties and filled the resulting enclosures with material dredged from the riverbed. As well as allowing substantial ships to reach the city, all this engineering work provided new land on which docks, shipyards, houses and farms could be established.

By this time steamboats were regularly plying the river, shipyards were further developed and huge docks were built to accommodate the massive amounts of goods brought into and taken out of the city. All this rapid development was put under the control of the Clyde Navigation Trust (see p.146) and the Clyde soon became one of the most important industrial rivers the world has ever seen. Shipbuilding (see p.153) was to be the river's most important export and the phrase 'Clyde built' became known the world over as a guarantee of first-class workmanship.

But times have changed. Most of the yards have now gone, as have most of the docks. As a consequence, few ships are seen on the river nowadays, certainly in the centre of the city, although the tradition of cruising 'Doon the watter' is kept alive by the paddleship *Waverley* (see p.149).

Just downstream of the Glasgow Bridge stand the massive Dalbeattie granite piers of the former **Central Station Viaduct** ❽ (1876-8, B. H. Blyth); the original cast-iron bracing also still remains in place. Greek and English inscriptions can still be seen on the side of the piers facing the Glasgow Bridge, with the phrase *All greatness stands firm in the storm*, the words of the poet Ian Hamilton Finlay (1925-) – possibly a comment on the city's engineering skills?

Walk under the **Caledonia Railway Bridge** ❾ (1899-1905, Donald A. Matheson) which carries ten railway tracks from Central Station to the south. Thousands of steel girders and millions of rivets have been used to construct this substantial and very complex structure.

Beyond this is the three-span **King George V Bridge** ⑩ (1924-7, Considère Constructions Ltd) which is at the southern end of Oswald Street. Although it appears to have three arches, in reality the bridge is of box girder design with grey Dalbeattie granite facings used as decoration; these and the parapets allow the bridge to be compared rather more favourably with the older Glasgow Bridge. The bridge's profile is unusual as it is only the middle part of the roadway that is arched, giving the centre quite a pronounced 'hump' for a relatively modern bridge. This shape was used to allow enough clearance for the Clyde 'puffers' which berthed just upstream of here. Although these famous west-coast supply ships are now rarely seen near Glasgow, memories of them are kept alive by Neil Munro's stories about the fictional puffer *The Vital Spark*, skippered by Para Handy; see also p.260.

The inside of the bridge's eastern parapet has a plaque inscribed: *This memorial stone was laid by his majesty King George V. 12th July, 1927.*

The **Broomielaw** lies ahead. This was one of the busiest and noisiest places in Glasgow in the nineteenth and early twentieth centuries when cargo ships would berth here and the area between here and Argyle Street was filled with huge warehouses. Changed days!

Many different types of goods were dealt with here, with grain and tea being important in the early nineteenth century. Later, many of the warehouses were used to store whisky and tobacco. A number of the remaining warehouses are being refurbished while others have been replaced by modern blocks of various styles. As a sort of compromise, some warehouses have had everything knocked down except the original facade in order to retain some continuity with the past.

The Broomielaw was also the embarkation point for countless thousands of Glaswegians who took summer trips 'Doon the watter', especially during the Glasgow Fair (see p.62), to coastal resorts such as Dunoon, Rothesay and Largs in the Firth of Clyde. These trips were so popular that on some days as many as forty or fifty steamers operated from this quay.

At the junction with Robertson Street stands the former **Clyde Navigation Trust Building** ⑪ (1882-6 and 1905-8, J. J. Burnet), now occupied by Clydeport. This is one of the city's architectural gems and was built to reflect the wealth associated with the shipping trade. The building was constructed in two stages, with the five northern bays built in the first phase and the grand cornerpiece added later. The Trust was one of the city's most important and powerful bodies and it originally planned its headquarters to be even larger, hence the unfinished look at the northern and eastern extremities. The facade's sculptures (by Albert Hodge) are based on Greek mythology and are some of the best in the city.

The main entrance is flanked by two ships' prows, complete with anchors, and above them are four columns which support a pediment. Within this is Poseidon (the Greek god of the sea) being paid homage, while on top he is shown with seahorses. To the left of the pediment is a statue of Thomas Telford (with dividers), and to the right are James Watt (with a steam condenser) and Henry Bell (with a model of his *Comet* steamboat). Above these statues are plaques and sets of 'grown-up' cherubs holding various objects. Two of the plaques feature the city's coat of arms, while the plaque above Bell has the Trust's symbol (a lighthouse) representing Glasgow's connections with the sea.

The main feature of the cornerpiece is the dome which rises above six fluted columns; look for the grotesque faces round the base of the dome. There are two superb sculptures at roof level: on the left is Europa (the daughter of the king of Tyre) leading a bull (in reality, Zeus, chief of the gods, in disguise) and on the right is Amphitrite (wife of the Poseidon), with trident in hand, driving a pair of seahorses. Below Europa is St Mungo with the city's coat of arms and a globe, which represents Glasgow's world-wide shipping interests. A similar sculpture is below Amphitrite.

The Clyde Navigation Trust Building

The Clyde Navigation Trust was established in 1858 and was involved in dredging the river and in the provision of quays, dry docks and ferries. However, with the rundown of the Clyde's shipping and shipbuilding the Trust's role diminished and in 1966 it was replaced by the Clyde Port Authority which later became Clydeport.

Continue along Clyde Street or, if preferred, walk beside the river. Reminders of the riverside's previous activity are few and these days not many ships tie up at the bollards that punctuate the cobbled walkway. On the opposite bank, the former **Renfrew Ferry** ⓬ has taken on a new life as an entertainment venue, its steel car deck now providing a very sturdy dance floor. The ship was built in 1953 by Ferguson's Shipyard (in Port Glasgow) and it plied the crossing between Renfrew and Yoker, about 9km (5 miles) downstream from here. It did this until 1984 when it was replaced by the smaller boats the *Renfrew Rose* and *Yoker Swan*, which are the river's last two ferries in Glasgow.

The huge **Kingston Bridge** ⓭ (1970, W. A. Fairhurst & Partners) comprises two parallel bridges that tower 18m (60ft) above the river, the main span being 143m (470ft) long. The substantial clearance was needed to allow dredgers to pass underneath but a number of ships, including the paddleship *Waverley* (see later), still had to have their masts reduced in height in order that they could pass upstream. The bridge carries the M8 motorway and has a 9km (3 mile) maze of approach roads and elevated ramps in a relatively compact area. It carries five lanes each way and drivers often have to make a number of lane changes during the brief journey across the Clyde – very stressful, especially during the rush hour!

When it opened it carried 31,000 vehicles a day but in 1996, 155,000 vehicles crossed it every day, making it Britain's busiest road bridge. The bridge has certainly suffered from its heavy use and in 1994 it was discovered that the 55,000 tonne structure had slipped alarmingly, the centre span had dropped by about 30cm (12in), and the supports on the northern end were 15cm (6in) off centre. The only way to remedy this situation was lifting the monster back into place!

Just as the bridge is reached, look over to the other bank to the massive warehouse blocks. The very large building nearest the bridge is a warehouse built for the **Scottish Co-Operative Wholesale Society** ⓮ (1886-95, Bruce & Hay). It is often suggested that this building's design was the runner-up in the City Chambers competition. The area around this building was a huge complex of manufacturing and retail buildings operated by the Co-Op.

Kingston Bridge to the SECC

At the junction with Warroch Street stands the office housing the *Scottish Daily Record* and the *Sunday Mail* ⓯. These papers have a long history which can be traced back to 1847 when Lord Rothermere founded the *North British Daily Mail.* This was printed in Frederick Lane but the premises moved to Renfield Lane (see p.162) at the turn of the century. The *Daily Record* was then launched as the first halfpenny morning newspaper in the United Kingdom. The paper now known as the *Sunday Mail* was launched in 1914 and in the 1920s the company moved its (then) four titles to 67 Hope Street (see p.166). After falling circulation resulted in financial losses, the company was taken over in 1955 by the *Daily Mirror* and in 1971 all editorial and production work was transferred here to Anderston Quay, though the printing presses have since moved to Cardonald on the city's Southside. Today, the *Daily Record* is a successful tabloid which is widely read in Scotland, though it has to compete with the Scottish editions of numerous London-based papers.

The next stretch of riverside is called **Lancefield Quay** and in this area were the important Lancefield Works where David and Robert Napier (see p.289) built engines for steamers. The works closed down, the quays took their place and now all that remains of the quayside buildings are a curious-looking row of former sheds now reconstructed as houses.

The next item of interest at the quayside might not be here at all (it might be at sea!) as this is the berth of the **PS *Waverley*** 🜯, the world's oldest sea-going paddle steamer. It was built in 1947 at the A. & J. Inglis shipyard at Pointhouse (see p.291) and was named after the *Waverley* novels by Sir Walter Scott. The ship is 73m (240ft) long and 18m (58ft) wide and is powered by oil-fired engines which burn about 820 litres (180 gallons) of fuel an hour. These drive two paddles 5.5m (18ft) in diameter which can propel the ship at up to 34kmph (18 knots).

The ship was built for the Craigendoran service of the LNER railway company and was latterly a Caledonian MacBrayne ferry. By 1973 she was in a poor state of repair and in 1974 she was purchased by the Paddle Steamer Preservation Society for the grand sum of £1. Since then (and after a lot of repairs) the *Waverley* has been delighting countless Scots and visitors with her cruises on the River Clyde and around the west coast.

PS *Waverley*

Her ports of call 'Doon the watter' include Dunoon, Rothesay, Helensburgh, Tighnabruaich, Brodick, Largs and Ayr (to name but a few); indeed, including the places she visits in other parts of Britain, the *Waverley* can be seen in around one hundred ports in a single summer season. On some occasions so many people crowd to one side to admire a good view that the paddle on the opposite side hardly touches the water! Once on board, passengers are encouraged to take a trip down below to see the engines, read the ship's own newspaper, listen to the band or even sing the *Waverley* song (written by shipyard worker Jim Brown).

In many ways Glaswegians view her as an important symbol of the Clyde and she provides a nostalgic link with the recent past.

On the opposite side of the river are some tall triangular-shaped blocks of flats in a very different style to any other houses found in Glasgow. Their design echoes the shape of the prow of a ship and they stand on the site of the 1988 Glasgow Garden Festival (see p.287).

After Lancefield Quay is some quayside equipment that was associated with the **Finnieston Ferry** **17**. This high-level vehicular ferry was introduced in 1890 and operated here until 1966. Close by, there is a steep stairway leading down to the river and there is a similar one on the opposite bank. These were used by passengers getting to and from the Finnieston Ferry. The passenger service lasted until 1977 but the last ferry is still afloat and is now moored on the Forth and Clyde Canal as the *Caledonian*.

Slightly further along on both sides of the river is a round brick building with an iron-framed domed roof. These are the two entrances to the former **Harbour Tunnel** **18** (1890-6, Wilson & Simpson) and are often referred to as the 'rotundas'. The rotunda on this side has six former entrances which are framed by tall cast-iron Corinthian columns. These gave access to horse-drawn vehicles. Inside, there was a 24m (80ft) diameter vertical shaft containing six hydraulic lifts as well as 138 steps (for pedestrians). These led down to the tunnels below the river which were in the form of three cast-iron tubes each 5m (16ft) in diameter. In 1947 only the single pedestrian tunnel was still used and this remained open until 1980; it was eventually closed off in 1986 although access was maintained for inspecting the important water main that still runs through it. The rotundas were then put to new use, the northern one operating as a restaurant and the southern one being used for a similar purpose during the Glasgow Garden Festival.

The enormous **Finnieston Crane** **19** (1931, Cowans, Sheldon & Co. Ltd) stands by the river, infrequently used but kept in well-maintained order. This 59m (195ft) high hammerhead crane can lift 178 tonnes at a time and was used to load railway locomotives and military tanks into cargo vessels. Newly built ships could also have their engines and boilers lifted in if this had not proved possible at the yard in which their hull had been constructed. The crane is classed as an industrial monument and, while that is one reason for its preservation, it may also be because of its possible future 'strategic' (i.e. military) importance.

Its prominent position on the skyline has made it an important symbol of the city and in 1987 a straw locomotive made by the Glasgow sculptor George Wylie (1921-) was hung there and later set ablaze, an obvious comment on the curent state of the local engineering industry.

The crane is sometimes referred to as the Stobcross Crane as this is the name of the quay on which it stands.

On the opposite bank stands a prominent brick building, made all the more noticeable by its two towers. This was Prince's Dock's **Hydraulic Pumping Station** (1894, Burnet, Son & Campbell) and it was used to supply high-pressure water to hydraulically-operated cranes and a swing bridge.

The huge **SECC** ㉑ (Scottish Exhibition and Conference Centre) (1987, James Parr & Partners) is on the right. This was purpose-built as the city's new exhibition hall to replace the smaller Kelvin Hall (see p.209), but it also hosts conferences, concerts and the annual Christmas Carnival. (Special drains have been installed for the carnival's elephants!) The centre is really a huge barn, or rather a series of barns, which can host lots of individual events simultaneously or be used for one huge gathering; indeed, it can cope with conferences with as many as 8000 delegates, concerts attended by 12,000 people or four-course meals for 3500 diners.

The 1997 riverside extension (designed by Sir Norman Foster) houses the massive Clyde Auditorium which seats up to 3000 people and which can be used for conferences and concerts. Its complex outer shape, composed of a series of large curved ribbed shells, quickly earned it the nickname the '**Armadillo**' and now even the SECC uses this name to describe the structure.

The 'Armadillo' at the Scottish Exhibition and Conference Centre

The SECC (and all its many car parks) occupies the site of the former Queen's Dock which operated from 1877 to 1969. This tidal basin was the river's main berthing area and it had 3000m (10,000ft) of quays which were used to accommodate both cargo and passenger ships plying between here and all the continents. It was eventually filled in with rubble from the demolished St Enoch Station and Hotel (see p.143) and Cathcart Castle (see p.331).

The riverside walkway now meets the gently arched **Bells Bridge** ❷❶ (1988, Crouch & Hogg). This is constructed in steel and was built specially for the Glasgow Garden Festival. Thankfully, the bridge is one lasting benefit that the city has retained from 1988 and it provides a useful link between the two banks.

It has three spans; the northern one is fixed while the other two are supported on a steel pier which also acts as the pivot around which the bridge turns. The actual opening is near the centre of the middle span. The bridge needs to be opened when tall ships such as the *Waverley* pass along the river. Its deck affords good views of the section of the river between the Kingston Bridge and the Meadowside Granaries (see below).

The tall, slim hotel that pierces the sky was originally built as the Forum Hotel (1988-9, Cobban & Lironi) but is now the **Moat House Hotel** ❷❷. It's certainly one of the most striking new buildings in the city, not just because of its height and the prominent position it commands by the river, but also for its sheer walls of highly-reflective silver-blue mirrored glass.

From the northern end of Bells Bridge, the route continues along the riverside to the Pumping Station (see below) and returns to this spot. If this detour is not followed then walk past the SECC to the covered way (see p.155).

Follow the river bank to the **heliport**. This provides emergency air services, pleasure trips and, most importantly for rush-hour drivers, up-to-date aerial reports on the locations of the worst traffic jams.

The next building is the Italian-style **Hydraulic Pumping Station** ❷❸ (1877-8, John Carrick) which was built to supply high-pressure water to hydraulically-operated machinery in Queen's Dock, notably a swing bridge and some cranes. Its campanile tower (originally used to store water) bears the date *1877*. The main structure has an engraving of a badge (which is akin to the city's coat of arms) with the words *Clyde Navigation*, accompanied by chains and an anchor; this is the badge of the Clyde Navigation Trust (see p.146). Outside the station, a fountain features three maidens and, appropriately, its base is in the form of a capstan.

Beyond the pumping station are the low sheds that stand on **Yorkhill Quay**. This area was once the site of a number of shipyards and more than three hundred ships were built here. When the quay was subsequently built it was used by the Anchor Line (see p.112) which carried emigrants to America as well as taking passengers on cruises to the west coast of Scotland and the Mediterranean Sea.

Yorkhill Quay is now the home of the three-masted ship the **SS Glenlee** ㉔, the centrepiece of a museum which is planned by the Clyde Maritime Trust. This steel-hulled sailing ship was built in 1896 by Anderson Roger & Co. (in Port Glasgow) and is 75m (245ft) long and weighs 1800 tonnes. What makes her so special is that she is one of only five nineteenth-century Clyde-built sailing ships still afloat.

The *Glenlee* started life as a cargo ship and this phase of her history lasted until 1920 during which time she spent over 5000 days at sea, circumnavigating the world five times and going round Cape Horn fifteen times. For much of this period she had been called the *Islamount*. She then served in the Italian merchant fleet as the *Clarastella*; in 1922 she was bought by the Spanish navy, renamed the *Galatea*, and used as a training vessel. The ship was decommissioned in 1969 and for many years faced an uncertain future until she was purchased by the trust in 1992. After being towed back home to the Clyde she was renamed the *Glenlee* and work was started on restoring the exterior to what it had been in 1896. This involved a lot of painstaking work and necessitated using the traditional crafts of rivetting and caulking.

To the north of Yorkhill Quay is **Yorkhill** itself. This prominent hill was once the site of a Roman outpost guarding the river and the nearby Antonine Wall (see p.180). Two large hospitals, the Royal Hospital for Sick Children and the Queen Mother's Maternity Hospital, are located here; see p.243.

Farther downstream are the massive thirteen-storey **Meadowside Granaries**. They were built with twenty million bricks and are reckoned to be the largest brick buildings in Europe. The first building was erected in 1911-13 by the Clyde Navigation Trust (extensions were added in the 1930s and 1960s) but the buildings are no longer in use as granaries. The site was once the ground of Partick Thistle Football Club, so-named as the pitch was within Partick. The club, which is a little less well known than its two 'Old Firm' rivals, Rangers and Celtic, is now located in Maryhill (see p.265).

On the southern bank, opposite the pumping station, are the Govan Graving Docks (see p.288) and farther downstream, opposite the granaries, is a forest of cranes at the Kvaerner Govan Shipyard (see p.295).

The River Clyde has long been one of the world's greatest **shipbuilding** centres and over the last two centuries over 35,000 ships have been launched from its many shipyards. Indeed, just before the First World War, Clydeside yards produced one-third of the British output of ships. Various factors allowed the river to achieve this feat, including the local presence of coal and iron ore, an advanced mechanical engineering industry, a highly skilled workforce and trading links with the Americas and the British Empire. It was an incredibly complex industry and there were many important links with other parts of the Scottish economy, from steelmakers and marine engine builders to quality carpet and furniture manufacturers. Indeed, the amount of business the shipbuilders gave these firms helped them to develop their expertise to the extent that they became large enterprises in their own right and in time many of them were exporting their own goods worldwide. Another factor which helped the yards' success was that a number of the yards were owned by shipping lines and these shipowners ensured that there was a steady stream of orders going to their own yards. There were also strong links with the government and the numerous naval orders were profitable enough to allow yards to offer relatively low prices for other ships to keep the order books full.

The history of shipbuilding on the Clyde goes back to the time when the upper reaches of the river were deepened (see p.145), allowing yards to develop on many parts of the riverbank, including upstream of the city centre. In 1811 Henry Bell built the *Comet* steamboat at Port Glasgow and in 1812 it could travel from Port Glasgow to Broomielaw in only three-and-a-half hours, thus ushering in the age of seagoing steamships. Its success encouraged yards to be built in many Clydeside towns and in 1834 Tod & MacGregor began to construct iron hulls, allowing bigger and more powerful ships to be made. Robert Napier (see p.289), who had built the boiler for the *Comet,* then opened a yard at Govan, thus establishing himself as one of the most influential shipbuilders the Clyde has ever known. He invested in companies who bought his ships (for example, the forerunner of Cunard) thus beginning the important link between shipbuilders and shipowners. The development of the compound engine (see p.295) further enhanced the reputation of the river's yards as innovative builders and, in the 1860s, an incredible eighty per cent of the British tonnage was built on the Clyde. However, the Glasgow yards soon faced competition from Clydebank firms and generally the companies were forced to specialise. Steel hulls were introduced from the late 1870s and more sophisticated machinery was needed to cope with the new technology, forcing yards to invest heavily or go bankrupt. At the turn of the century, competition from other areas, notably Tyneside and Barrow-in-Furness, began to cause serious problems on the Clyde.

In general, a wide variety of ships were made on the river, but while some yards' reliance on naval orders ensured a steady flow of orders before the First World War, the end of hostilities meant that they had to become active in seeking out new business. From then on there were periods of boom and slump, and while the prospect of war had ensured lots of naval work, periods like the Great Depression of the 1930s made the yards idle and put huge numbers of workers on the dole. The Second World War was a busy period on the Clyde but by the 1950s there was drastic contraction in the industry. There were many reasons for this, including the results of low reinvestment, the emergence of new competition from the Far East, undercutting by government-subsidised foreign yards, fewer emigrants to the Americas and also cheap air travel. The government was forced to intervene in this crisis and in 1966

Upper Clyde Shipbuilders was formed as a means of restructuring the industry. This collapsed in 1971 and led to the workforce's famous UCS 'work-in' which gained support from all over the world. This quite remarkable action involved the men taking over three shipyards and controlling who and what went in and out of the gates. Although the yards' liquidator had declared many men redundant these workers were kept on and their wages paid by the large funds which were donated from all over the world. Eventually, the government was forced to do a 'U-turn', ensuring that there was at least some viable shipbuilding left on the upper reaches of the river.

Alas, the industry is now only a shadow of its former self and the only yards of importance in the city are Kvaerner Govan (see p.295) and Yarrows (which builds naval vessels in Whiteinch).

The Transport Museum (see p.211) has a superb collection of model ships including many from the yards mentioned here. The museum's Clyde Room also has on display a large map indicating the sites of all the shipyards.

Retrace the route back to Bells Bridge.

SECC TO HOPE STREET

From the northern end of Bells Bridge, walk through the space between the Armadillo and the hotel. Bear right and follow the perimeter of the main SECC building to its main door. Opposite this is a covered walkway which goes over the busy Clydeside Expressway to the entrance to the **Exhibition Centre Railway Station**.

Turn left and follow Minerva Street up to the junction with the grand **St Vincent Crescent** (1850-5, Alexander Kirkland) which bends round to the left. When built, this long and gently curving street of tenements was hailed as a fine piece of town planning especially as it had extensive gardens situated in front of it. Sadly, these are long since built upon.

Bear to the right and continue on Minerva Street, following it to its junction with Argyle Street. Turn right into Finnieston Street and then left into Houldsworth Street, one of the older streets in the **Anderston** area. In the 1720s this was developed as the weavers' village of Anderstoun, named after James Anderson who owned the mansion of Stobcross House, which was later demolished to make way for the Queen's Dock (see p.152). The weavers produced woven linen cloth, much of which was exported to England or overseas, and this trade grew into one of Anderston's most important industries. Later, breweries and the notable potteries of Delftfield and Verreville were established nearby, and by 1794 the village had 3900 inhabitants. Examples of the potteries' products are on display at the People's Palace. As Glasgow became more industrialised and the Clyde was made more navigable, the land between here and the river soon became covered with numerous factories, engineering works, shipyards and docks, making the district one of the busiest in the Glasgow area.

Houldsworth Street was named after **Henry Houldsworth** who owned a large mill on the banks of the River Kelvin in the early part of the nineteenth century. When the cloth trade became less profitable he developed the mill's workshops into an important foundry, a good example of the flexibility of nineteenth-century Glasgow and a pointer to the next phase of the city's rise as an industrial powerhouse. As with many important manufacturers he was very influential in local politics and in 1824 he became Anderston's first provost. Elections in those days were quite undemocratic. As an example, in 1835, out of Anderston's population of nearly 15,000, only 112 of them had the right to vote!

The next stretch of the route leads past buildings representing a bewildering range of architectural styles from many different eras. In the 1960s and 1970s 'Comprehensive development' swept away huge numbers of sandstone tenements and only a couple are left.

At 752 Houldsworth Street is the Art Nouveau former **Savings Bank of Glasgow** 🕦 (1899-1900, James Salmon Jnr & J. Gaff Gillespie) which has some interesting sculpture by Albert Hodge. The main doorway of this red sandstone building is particularly fine and it has an unusual blue mosaic featuring peacocks and the date *MDCCCC* (1800). On either side of the door are sculptured figures and shields. On the left are a knight, a woman and St Andrew (holding his cross), with the shield having a lion rampant and the phrase *Nemo me impune lacessit* ('No-one provokes me with impunity'). On the right are St Mungo, a woman and a warrior, with the shield having elements of the city's coat of arms and the motto *Let Glasgow Flourish*. A little higher up are

The Savings Bank of Glasgow on Argyle Street

cherubic faces, a design incorporating stylised leaves and then an angel. Above this is Henry Duncan, the bank's founder, clutching his £10 money bag very tightly and tapping his forehead as if to pass on to passers-by a wise message about the prudent use of money. As the bank originally occupied a busy corner site it has a prominent domed turret and below this are a number of Art Nouveau motifs and two angels (wearing cloche hats!) sheltering under their wings.

The next building of note is the **Buttery** restaurant **26** (1869) at 652-6 Argyle Street. Masonic symbols and five sculpted heads decorate the lower half of this tenement building. Higher up, there is a deer's head and the phrase *Fulget virtus intaminata* ('Excellence shines untarnished'). Inside, many of the lovely wooden furnishings in the restaurant and the adjoining Belfry bar come from former churches.

Argyle Street now comes to sudden halt where the M8 motorway was built through this part of the city in the 1960s, so turn left when the road comes to an end. Follow the pavement past the red sandstone **St Patrick Roman Catholic Church** **27** (1898, P. P. Pugin) and turn right at St Vincent Street in order to cross the motorway.

St Vincent Street is named after the headland Cabo de São Vicente, which is now part of Portugal, to mark a British naval victory over the Spanish in 1797. This is one of Glasgow's most important commercial streets and it has an interesting collection of buildings. Some are grand, others a bit brash, but together they offer a wide array of different styles. The first important group of buildings are in India Street (on the left), housing departments of Glasgow City Council.

In most cities, many modern office blocks are very bland, but at 310 St Vincent Street, is the attractive **Dalmore House** **28** (1990, Miller Partnership) which soars skywards, its glass panels reflecting the surrounding offices. The exterior's shape is in the form of a series of glass towers of various heights, with those at the corner being the tallest in order to accommodate the lift shafts.

On the opposite side of the road is the former **Britoil Building** **29** (1982-8, Hugh Martin & Partners). This massive office block has its own rooftop gardens.

St Columba's Gaelic Church **30** (Gaelic: Eaglais Chaluim Chille) (1902-4, William Tennant & Frederick V. Burke) stands in stark contrast to the nearby office blocks. It has a 60m (200ft) high tower and spire but the most interesting parts of this large sandstone church are around the main doorway. The two separate doors have above them the Gaelic phrase *Tigh mo chridhe, tigh mo ghràidh* ('House of my heart, house of my love') and above this is an elaborate archway within which is a sculpted burning bush and the phrase *Nec tamen consumebatur* ('Nor was it consumed'). This refers to the Bible's Old Testament story of the burning bush (*Exodus* chapter 3) and the image of the unharmed bush is used as the emblem of the Church of Scotland. To the left of this is a figure with hands clasped and to the right is one with arms crossed. Higher up, an angel with a banner carrying the name *Columba* supports a tall statue of St Columba (521-97).

St Columba is one of Scotland's most important religious figures but he originally came from County Donegal in Ireland and he had founded a monastery in Derry. After being accused of being involved in the Battle of Cuildreimhne he was excommunicated and exiled from his home so he set sail for Scotland, landing on Iona and founding a monastery there. In time, this became an important Christian centre and today Iona Abbey (where he is buried) is regarded by many as the country's most notable place of pilgrimage.

This church was built to serve the needs of the Gaelic-speaking people who had fled the grinding poverty of the Highlands and had come to Glasgow to work in the factories and docks. By the mid 1830s it was estimated that there were around 20,000 Highlanders in the city, with 16,000 of them unable to understand English, thus creating a pressing need for ministers who could conduct services in both languages. The Highlanders were faced with many problems in the city, apart from the obvious language barrier, and they were despised by many lowlanders, as demonstrated by the *Scotsman* newspaper when it stated quite categorically: 'It is the fact that morally and intellectually the Highlanders are an inferior race to the Lowland Saxons'. Today, there are large numbers of Glaswegians with important family ties with the Highlands and Islands and as a measure of their attachment to their forebears' culture, the 1991 Census counted some 6500 Gaelic speakers in the city.

The **St Vincent Street Free Church of Scotland** ③① (1857-9, Alexander Thomson) stands at the junction with Pitt Street. This was originally built for the United Presbyterian Church and it is now recognised as one of the city's finest buildings. Ugly office blocks stand to the east and south of the church but its corner position and the steep streets beside it allow it to dominate the surrounding area.

The upper part of the church is essentially in the form of a large Greek temple with six fluted columns supporting a substantial portico; this structure is made all the more imposing by being placed on a massive podium which contains the lower part of the church and the basement. Further interest is added by the two large ground-floor entrances and Thomson's usual inscribed patterns. The side elevation is dominated by two tall Egyptian-style pylons and lower down, a side door is given more prominence by being flanked by four stumpy decorated columns which support a massive lintel. The rear also has a grand portico and it utterly dominates everything around it; or it would, if modern buildings didn't encroach on the space.

The church's tall tower is a fascinating structure which encompasses elements from a number of countries, including Egypt, India and Assyria. It seems quite separate from the temple and soars high above it. It also uses many curved elements which contrast sharply with all the rectangular shapes employed in the church. At the base of the tower is a tall pylon and about halfway up are T-shaped windows which are decorated with pairs of caryatid heads. Next comes the clock faces and then four elaborate turrets. The design gets even more flamboyant farther up, with the tower using an octagonal then a circular shape. This final part is more reminiscent of a mausoleum than anything else and it features stumpy columns and an egg-shaped dome on top of which is an urn. Inevitably, there is a lot of incised detail and lots of flower and geometric motifs.

The church's interior is as spectacular as the exterior and it was made big enough to hold a congregation of around 1500 people. Light floods in through plain windows on three levels and this illuminates the marvellous decoration. Cast-iron columns with elaborate and highly colourful flower-like capitals support the wide gallery and the clerestory above it. The tall wooden platform from which services are conducted is a wonderful example of Thomson's work: two doorways within tall pylons frame the pulpit and above these rise the organ pipes. The pulpit area is decorated with numerous patterns incorporating designs such as daisies and anthemia and this is matched by the woodwork surrounding the gallery and also by the plasterwork above the gallery. A dark timber ceiling provides a more sombre touch to the interior but it too has decorations matching those of the platform.

This is undoubtedly one of the city's most exciting buildings and both the exterior and the interior have a wealth of fascinating detail. Recently, much attention has been given to Thomson's work and this building in particular is now being appreciated by a world-wide audience.

The next stretch of the street is composed mainly of former large houses, many of them still with their original cast-iron railings; most are now used as offices. The **Royal College of Physicians and Surgeons** 🅓 is at 234-42 St Vincent Street. The college initially moved into number 242 which was altered for them by J. J. Burnet (1892-3), with the adjoining houses added later. The original three-storey building has fluted columns supporting a stone balustrade.

The college was founded in 1599 by Maister Peter Lowe (see p.361), a talented doctor who had written *The whole course of chirurgerie* (1597), the first English-language text on surgery. After working for some time in France he wanted to set up a 'faculty' which would help improve medical facilities and training in Scotland, as these were woefully inadequate. Indeed, the faculty's royal charter from James VI stated that 'the great abuses committed by ignorant, unskilled and unlearned persons who, under the colour of surgeons, abuse the people to their pleasure.'

In many cities and towns there were scant differences between the roles of surgeons and barbers and in Glasgow the latter practitioners were gradually 'weeded out' of the faculty. In 1704 Glasgow University founded a medical school and the university and the faculty contested the right to control the teaching and practice of surgery in the city, a conflict that lasted well into the nineteenth century. With the transfer of the university to Gilmorehill the university developed its expertise in training doctors while the college (its present title) has concentrated on its role as an examining body for postgraduate medicine.

The college has a fine library which, as well as possessing modern medical texts, boasts a copy of Lowe's book and non-medical books such as the acclaimed *Birds of North America* (1827) by John James Audubon.

At 200 St Vincent Street stands the former **North British & Mercantile Building** ㉝ (1926–9, Sir J. J. Burnet). This tall building is relatively plain, which adds to its charm, but it has a few items of sculpture which add interest. The lowest part of the building is decorated with arches and pillars, and on the capitals of the two central pillars are carvings of very old ships, perhaps reflecting the commercial interests of the original owners. Above these are badges representing Edinburgh and London. Two short pillars above them have strange-looking sea creatures and a young-looking figure blowing a horn. The two large sculptures above the doorway were added some time after the building was erected: on the left is a crouched woman in a cloak and on the right is a crouched man wearing a cape and holding a model ship. Above them is a statue of St Andrew (with his cross) who is standing at the prow of a boat and holding a model ship; this sculpture was by Archibald Dawson and is dated *1927*. The final sculpture is high up on the corner of the building and it has a grotesque winged beast clutching a shield with *N B & M* on it.

Next door, at **188-92 St Vincent Street** ㉞ (1897, Frank Burnet & Boston), is a narrow red sandstone building topped by a cloaked female figure carrying a sword and the scales of justice.

At 145 St Vincent Street is the former **Commercial Union Building** ㉟ (1931-2, Burnet & Boston), a large red sandstone office block. The entrance is flanked by ornate lampstandards below which are carvings of winged lions; above the doorway is a large shield with the motto *Per curam placebimus* ('We will please through care').

The very narrow **Hatrack Building** ㊱ (1899-1902, James Salmon II) is at 142a-4 St Vincent Street. This gets its popular nickname from its numerous and elaborate rooftop projections, especially the tallest pinnacle. This is a very good example of the Glasgow Style and the facade seems to be composed entirely of windows and fancy stonework which includes lots of little sculptural details worth looking for. No two storeys look the same as there are stone and iron balconies, rectangular and arched window spaces, and various ornaments around the windows. Specific items of interest include carved angels, lions' faces, suns, plaques, crowns, grotesque faces, beads and lanterns. The doorway is topped by an unusual semi-cylindrical lantern glazed with a stained-glass picture of galleons.

140-2 St Vincent Street ㊲ (1899-1900, Burnet, Boston & Carruthers) has two nice entrances, with that at 142 featuring two diminutive cherubs. Indeed, the architect seems to have been very keen on cherubs as there are more on an ornate frieze farther up and even more on the Hope Street facade. Intriguingly, of the cherubs which have wings, those on the upper floors seem to have larger wings than those on the lower floors. As befits a building positioned at a prominent junction, there is a columned tower at the corner and, inevitably, the corner's lowest window has below it a couple of winged cherub faces.

At 127 St Vincent Street are the red sandstone former **Norwich Union Chambers** ❸❽ (1897-8, John Hutchison), a six-storey Renaissance building with an enormous variety of windows. Above the doorway are winged cherubs with trumpets and above a second-floor window is an elaborate frieze which is continued on Hope Street. The various panels depict grotesque faces, mythical beasts, cherubs and a gatehouse tower. The corner is turned by an elaborate circular tower topped by a conical roof.

At the junction with Hope Street is the **Liverpool & London & Globe Insurance Building** ❸❾ (1899-1901, J. B. & W. A. Thomson). This very tall building is well decorated on both street fronts, but the Hope Street side is more ornate and is also easier to see. This facade has numerous vertical features on it, drawing the eye towards the upper storeys with their granite columns. About halfway up the facade are two male and two female figures and above them are four sets of double windows which have relief sculptures above them. These represent the original occupants and show a male angel with a liver bird (for Liverpool), a female blowing a trumpet, a man with a globe and a female angel holding a banner on which is the word *Insurance*. Readers can draw their own conclusions about the architect's decision to connect London with blowing a trumpet. The tallest group of windows have a further group of three figures. These are flanked by a lion and a unicorn and at the top is a tall finial with a gold weathercock. Else-where there's a host of small human and animal faces and other carved detail; this extravagantly designed office block is certainly very different from the modern blocks of offices which have been built in the city in recent years.

The building turns the corner with an octagonal oriel topped by an onion dome. The St Vincent Street facade is narrower than that on Hope Street, but it has similar features. From the ground floor upwards can be seen liver birds, a globe, female figures, faces, various animals, two cherubs holding a banner on which is *L & L & G* and two large lions. Quite a collection!

The former **Scottish Mutual Building** ❹⓿ (1911-12, Frank Southorn) at 105-13 St Vincent Street is a generally unexciting building but it does have four seated female figures which catch the eye of passers-by.

At 122-8 St Vincent Street is the former **Edinburgh Life Assurance Building** ❹❶ (1904-6, J. A. Campbell). The Glasgow coat of arms is on the left, above the doorway, while on the right is the Edinburgh coat of arms with its motto *Nisi Dominus frustra* ('Unless the Lord is with you, your efforts are in vain'). Farther above, giant pilasters rise up through three storeys to a three-bay balcony.

The main Glasgow office of the **Bank of Scotland** 🔵 (1924-7, James Miller) is at 110-20 St Vincent Street. This very large New York-style building has tall fluted Ionic columns in the lower part of the building; these and those in the upper half draw the eye upwards to the elaborate cornice. Look out for the carved lions' heads which appear at intervals right round the building. The building has an interesting banking history as it was once the headquarters of the Union Bank (founded 1830). In 1843 this merged with the Glasgow and Ship Bank and in 1955 the Union Bank merged with the Bank of Scotland. The British Linen Bank (see p.290) joined in 1971.

Inside, the banking hall is one of the brightest and airiest of any in the city; it also has some very massive columns which give an air of solemnity to the huge space. Some interesting artefacts can be seen, including a war memorial and a set of three tapestries celebrating the 1995 tercentenery of the bank. As a piece of banking history, there's also a beautifully made plaque that came from the Ship Bank's offices in Ingram Street; this bears the bank's coat of arms and its motto *A shield and stay*.

Return to the junction with Hope Street and turn left.

HOPE STREET TO ST ENOCH SQUARE

Hope Street, originally called Copenhagen Street, has a number of commercial buildings of interest. On the left, at 106-08 Hope Street, is the former **Scottish Temperance League Building** 🔵 (1893-4, J. Gaff Gillespie and James Salmon). It is in a Franco–Flemish style and carries some interesting pieces of sculpture. At first floor level are two roundels with female figures holding plaques dated *1844* and *1894*. Above that is a narrow balcony and four tall columns rising through two floors. These frame a frieze depicting winged cherubs and plaques on which are the Scottish lion rampant and elements of the city's coat of arms. The top of the building is in the form of a Flemish gable and it has three male figures on it. The lower two carry temperance shields bearing an urn and a flaming torch while the highest figure carries a book and a pen.

To the right of the Temperance Building is the narrow Renfield Lane and at 20-8 Renfield Lane stands the former **Daily Record Building** 🔵 (1900, Honeyman & Keppie) which was designed by Charles Rennie Mackintosh. Glasgow's city centre has many such narrow service lanes; often their buildings are faced with bricks, but here Mackintosh has used white glazed bricks, with green, blue and red bricks added to lend some brightness and colour to a narrow and ill-lit space. The bricks' tree-like pattern leads the eye upwards to the fourth-floor oriel windows and the small dormer windows above them. These latter windows are very difficult to see.

This was the *Daily Record's* printing works but it was converted into a warehouse when the newspaper moved out. See also pp.148 and 166.

The **Standard Buildings** 45 (1890, James Thomson) are at 94–104 Hope Street. This tall and good-looking office building had its upper floors added in 1909 (J. B. & W. A. Thomson), just four years after James Thomson died. This addition allowed Atlas, complete with globe on his shoulders, to be erected high above the street. There are many stories concerning Atlas, one of which has him turned to stone by Perseus. He is often portrayed holding the heavens or the terrestrial globe and this image was used by the sixteenth-century mapmaker Gerardus Mercator to illustrate his collection of maps, hence the name given to a book of maps.

Around the corner, the Gordon Street facade is similar in general appearance but it also has a pediment (supported by granite pillars) which features many figures in a Classical scene.

Turn right at Bothwell Street. This was originally laid out for housing in the 1820s and today the eastern end has one of the city's nicest collections of commercial buildings; however, many of those at the western end are not really worthy of note.

At 30 Bothwell Street is the former **National Commercial Bank Building** 46 (1934-5, James Miller). The height of this white limestone building is emphasised by its two elaborate Corinthian columns and above these are panels of Classical figures by Gilbert Bayes. The group of six panels starts in Wellington Street and represents *Justice*, *Wisdom*, *Contentment*, *Prudence*, *Industry* and *Commerce*.

The former **Central Thread Agency** 47 (1891-1901, H. & D. Barclay) is on the right and it takes up the whole length of the street from Wellington Street to West Campbell Street. It was built in three separate sections, starting from the eastern end, and there are significant differences in the facades.

The eastern building (1891) is the most highly decorated and the facade is dominated by its numerous columns, with each of the storeys treated quite differently. On the first floor there are lions' heads on the columns and also two plaques with badges. The second floor is decorated with heads and on the third floor is an Irish shamrock and a Scottish thistle. Two caryatids are above this and then the three gables at the top feature three faces: a crowned female, a turbaned man and an Egyptian man. This design is continued on the Wellington Street facade. On the first floor are two plaques; the one on the left has three horns and the one on the right has the Glasgow coat of arms. On the second floor is an English rose and a Scottish thistle. Above these there are two more caryatids and the head of a man wearing a feathered head-dress.

The central building (1892-1900) is much plainer, with its lions' heads just below the two sets of winged cherubs in the gables. These cherubs are shown with lengths of fabric, a connection with the business of the original occupant. The western block (1901) uses many of the design features of the eastern block, notably the pillars and the lions'

The Central Thread Agency, Bothwell Street

heads. The middle gable features a winged cherub with outstretched hands holding lengths of fabric.

This large and impressive building was the headquarters of Coats Paton, the cotton thread manufacturers who had mills in Paisley. These employed 10,000 people before 1914. The company also had mills abroad and it was able to control much of the world's thread trade.

The **Mercantile Chambers** ❹❽ (1897-8, James Salmon Jnr) stand opposite at 39-69 Bothwell Street. The two sharp-pointed gables, below which are nice little balconies, give this Glasgow-style building an unusual profile. The facade is relatively flat; this has allowed for the erection of a multitude of Francis Derwent Wood's statues and other sculptures, making this one of the city's most interesting office buildings.

The entrance is fairly narrow and is flanked by windows, four of which have carved heads as keystones. Beside the windows are lots of little carvings which have features such as grotesque faces and a horn of plenty. Above the main door small 'putti' support a cage-like structure in which sits Mercury, the Roman messenger of the gods. This intricate 'baldacchino' is inscribed with *The Mercantile Chambers Ltd*. and below the words are intricately carved ships, complete with sails. Flanking this are four plaques with crowns placed above a Scottish thistle, an English rose, an Irish shamrock and a Welsh daffodil; the inclusion of the Welsh emblem is quite unusual in the city. Linking these sculptures are the words *Trees grow, birds fly, fish swim, bells ring*, a reference to the four elements of the city's coat of arms. To the left of this is a lion and a bird (with outstretched wings) and to the right are stylised forms of a reptile and a fish.

The four second-storey statues of females represent *Prosperity* (holding a moneybag), *Prudence* (holding an hourglass), *Industry* (holding a flaming torch) and *Fortune* (holding a ship). Then, above the third storey are two faces depicting a turbaned man (ringed by serpents) and a crowned woman (ringed by birds). Finally, the gables have statues of a lion and St Mungo.

Number **75 Bothwell Street** ㊾ (*c.* 1875, Clarke & Bell) has a very elaborately carved doorway. It features a turbaned man's head on the keystone, horns of plenty and a ship's prow which is flanked by serpents.

The massive **Scottish Legal Life Assurance Society Building** ㊿ (1927-31, E. G. Wylie) fills the block from West Campbell Street to Blythswood Street. This is the city's largest American-style building and it has many distinctive features. Its height is emphasised by the three two-storey entrance arches, within which are bronze doors, and by the giant pillars which rise up through four storeys. The pillars' capitals have small carvings on them, including one with a human hand strangling a serpent and another with a bee and beehive. Between the pillars, the windows have elaborate cast-iron frames which feature lions, horses and zigzag motifs. Above the main entrance is a large coat of arms which has lions, horses, flowers representing Scotland, Ireland and England and the motto *Prudence and thrift*. The first floor is decorated with four reliefs by Archibald Dawson representing *Industry*, *Prudence*, *Thrift* and *Courage*. At the very top, lions' faces can be seen along the cornice. Finally, two corner clocks jut out over the heads of passers-by.

At **100 Bothwell Street** (51) (1980-8, Holmes Partnership) stands a very large modern office block, big enough to balance the more ornate building across the road. Red granite has been used for facing the tall colonnade in the lower part of the building and for the tall lift towers. Sheer walls of mirrored glass provide extra interest by reflecting the neighbouring buildings.

This building replaced the remarkable Christian Institute, built in 1879 and demolished in 1980, which was decorated with copious numbers of towers, turrets, gable and lots of other eye-catching details.

Return along Bothwell Street and turn right at West Campbell Street. Turn right at Waterloo Street, named after the battle in Belgium where the Duke of Wellington defeated Napoleon Boneparte in 1815. Number **64 Waterloo Street** (52) (1898-1900, James Chalmers) was originally built for Wright and Greig, wine and spirit merchants, for their offices, blending rooms and cellars. Their best-known blend was the Rhoderick Dhu Old Highland Whisky, named after a character in 'The lady of the lake', a poem by Sir Walter Scott which was set in the Trossachs. The firm established the Dallus Dhu Distillery near Forres in order to produce the fine malt whisky that was the main constituent of this blend; this distillery is still in existence and is owned by Historic Scotland.

As a novel means of advertising the whisky, statues of Rhoderick Dhu ('Black Rhoderick') and Fitzjames, both of whom wooed Ellen (the 'lady'), are above the door. To their left is a sheaf of barley, a vital ingredient in the manufacture of whisky; curiously it is being eaten by two winged beasts. The statue on the extreme right of the facade is the Lady of the Lake represented as a Highland woman holding a malting shovel which is used to turn the barley. Beneath her is a vine bearing grapes, representing the wine interests of the original occupants.

This dark red sandstone building has an unusual octagonal tower on the eastern side which was originally capped by a copper dome. The tower was meant to have statues of the seasons but the elaborate niches created for them were never filled.

Walk eastwards along Waterloo Street. The whole of the north side between West Campbell Street and Wellington Street is taken up by the massive former **G.P.O. Parcels Office** **53** (1903-05, W. T. Oldrieve). This white sandstone building has very elaborate capitals on its many columns and a nice cornice, above which is a balustrade. As with many buildings in this area, lions' heads are featured, but while some of them are particularly fierce looking, others have large rings in their mouths, perhaps to stop them from baring their teeth. As a reminder of its previous role as part of the Royal Mail, a doorway on the building's Wellington Street side has a royal coat of arms and the letters *ER* ('Elizabeth Regina').

At 15-23 Waterloo Street are the red sandstone **Waterloo Chambers** **54** (1898-1900, J. J. Burnet). The doorway has the building's name and the date *1899* above it. There are also two female figures, one whose cloak is caught by the wind, the other studiously reading from a scroll. Beyond this, tall fluted columns support an eaves balcony which runs across three bays.

Waterloo Street ends at the very large former Central Station Hotel, behind which is Central Station. Turn right at Hope Street.

The first red sandstone building on the right is the former **Glasgow Evening News Offices** **55** (1899-1900, Robert Thomson & Andrew Wilson). One doorway is decorated with two winged cherubs reading from a book while two wise owls look on. Above this are five lions' heads and then, much higher up, are statues of two females holding shields.

In the 1920s, the *Daily Record* (see p.148) moved here from Renfield Lane (see p.162) and published their own papers and the *Evening News* from here. The printing works located in the next-door building were erected in 1933-7.

At 43-7 Hope Street stand the **Atlantic Chambers** **56** (1899-1900, J. J. Burnet). At first-floor level are two statues of females, the one on the left holding a shield; the statue on the right is Boudicca (the leader of the Iceni who fought the Romans in the first century AD) who holds a shield and a sword. Above the door is a ship and an angel wearing armour. The upper part of the building is equally fine, with balconies and two eaves galleries, distinctive features of a building which is probably completely ignored by the hordes of commuters who pass by it each day.

Walk back up Hope Street and turn right at Gordon Street.

The former **Central Station Hotel** ❺❼ (1882-4, Robert Rowan Anderson), now the Quality Central Hotel, is an integral part of the Central Station complex (see below) and was originally built as the Caledonian Railway Company's headquarters offices. The premises at 91-115 Hope Street were planned to be the station's hotel but the directors wanted to challenge the rival St Enoch Hotel (see p.143) so this building was converted into a hotel, a task which took Anderson three years to complete.

Its most important feature is the tall Swedish-style corner tower (with its pyramidal roof and clock faces), although many other parts of the building use styles from various European countries. The nicest parts are at the corner, with its cast-iron detail at the entrance, the curved wall of windows above it and the oriel just at the start of the Hope Street facade. The building was farther extended in Union Street (see below) and Hope Street (1905-7). Above one of the rooftop windows on the Gordon Street side is a badge on which is Scotland's lion rampant and the motto *Nemo me impune lacessit* ('No one provokes me with impunity') above which are two letter Cs for the railway company.

As well as providing luxury accommodation for its visitors, it was built with a state of the art communications system and in 1883 *The Illustrated London News* reported 'that from the various parts of the house 1200 electric bells communicate with 600 indicators; the speaking-tubes extend to fully 5000 feet, weighing 4½ tons, and the wires in connection with the bells measure 29 miles and weigh 2½ tons.'

Central Station ❺❽ (1876-9, Blythe & Cunningham) was built by the Caledonian Railway as the Glasgow terminus for their southern services. As the big railway companies of the day were in direct competition, the city once had four important termini but since they were not directly connected to each other there has never been a continuous north-south mainline route through the city. The station was later extended in 1899-1906 to accommodate thirteen platforms and today it is one of only two remaining mainline stations in the city; this serves the southern routes while Queen Street Station serves the northern routes. Below this station is the low-level Argyle Line, which links Motherwell in the east to Helensburgh in the west, making this a very busy interchange, especially during the rush hours.

The entrance still has its detailed cast-iron canopy and large gates. Walk through the gates and on the right are polished limestone panels containing numerous marine fossils. Inside, the spacious concourse is flanked by the original wooden-fronted station offices (most of which are now converted into retail outlets) and at the back of the concourse is the domed lounge of the hotel. Above all this is a complex three-dimensional maze of girders which support a large glazed roof. The girders also support a large clock, the area below which is one of Glasgow's best-known rendezvous points.

The **Grosvenor Building** ❺❾ (1859-61, Alexander Thomson) stands opposite the entrance to Central Station. This was originally a four-storey warehouse built by Thomson as one of his speculative ventures. Unfortunately, it was burned down in 1864 but was rebuilt to virtually the same design in 1865-6. The upper portion was added in 1902-07 (J. H. Craigie); this part features three sets of four fluted Ionic columns and, at the top, two large domes. These alterations were made to house the luxury Baroque-style Grosvenor Restaurant which, in turn, burned down in 1967. The building's name comes from that period of its life.

Unfortunately, the ground floor's modern design is an affront to the wonderful architecture above. The next three floors are by Thomson and they carry many of his buildings' usual hallmarks – carved anthemia, incised geometric patterns, square pilasters, consoles and storeys of decreasing height. Since this was built to his own specifications, and not to those of a client, Thomson was able to give full rein to his ideas and two particular details are worth looking at: the manner in which the second storey's pilasters seem to 'grow' out of the stonework below them and also the false cornice above the second storey.

Gordon Street now meets a major junction. On the left is Renfield Street and on the right is Union Street. At the corner with Renfield Street stands the former **Forsyth's** ⑥⓪ which was originally built in 1858 as a warehouse (Boucher & Cousland) but converted into a shop for Forsyth's around fifty years later by J. J. Burnet.

Both sides of the building have lots of little details including grotesque heads on keystones and below the balustrade; lions' heads appear above the balustrade. The most interesting part of the building is the curved corner which is topped by a dome and finial. Above the main doorway, Boudicca drives a horse-drawn chariot. Higher up, there are statues of females; the one on the left carries fruit while the other is enshrouded by a cloak. Above them are cherubs representing Britain and India. Sculptures representing Canada, Australia and Africa can be seen on the Renfield Street side.

Turn left in order to see 13-17 Renfield Street which is the large Beaux Arts building just after Renfield Lane. This is the former **Cranston's Picture House and Tea Rooms** ⑥① (1914-8, James Miller) which were owned by Stuart Cranston, brother of Kate Cranston (see p.123). He opened a tea room here in 1897 and business was so good that he was able to buy the building. When James Miller was given the job of rebuilding the tea rooms their facilities were greatly expanded and the new building even included a picture house. A builders' journal of the day reported that 'The picture house will be contained on the first floor, while the other floors will be fitted up in a luxurious manner as high class tea rooms, a special attraction being the tea garden on the roof of the building.' The interior (by John Ednie) was in the style of Louis XVI and was unfortunately destroyed by fire in 1981.

When originally built, the facade was composed of white faience tiles but the present facade (1935, John McKissack) is a replica which uses concrete. Since much of the elaborate decoration is at the top, many of the facade's nicest details will be missed by most passers-by.

Walk back down to the junction of Renfield Street and Gordon Street and turn left. At **42–50 Gordon Street** ㊷ (1886, Clarke & Bell) is a four-storey sandstone building with an elaborate doorway featuring *Britannia* (plus a serpent and an owl). Above the first floor is a winged cherub holding a plaque on which is the date *1886* and this is flanked by pillars supporting sculpted urns.

Return to the junction with Union Street. At the corner stands the remarkable Venetian-style **Ca' d'Oro Building** ㊿ (1872, John Honeyman), which many people consider to be one of the city's finest pieces of architecture. This was built as a warehouse but takes its name from a restaurant established here in 1927. The structure of the lower part has a series of stone pillars and arches, above which is the cast–iron facade which gives the building its real charm. The windows are variously arched, rectangular or circular in shape, and the glass seems to form a continuous wall behind the external ironwork. Further fine detail is included at the intricate cornice.

During refurbishment in 1987 the building caught fire and the whole structure was in great danger of being destroyed but fortunately the exterior walls were saved. The facade was subsequently extended by replacing the two southernmost bays in Union Street (a 1920 extension constructed in stone) with replicas of the cast-iron design.

Turn left at Union Street.

The **Egyptian Halls** ㊽ (1871–3, Alexander Thomson) stand at 84-100 Union Street. The four storeys of this cast-iron framed building are all different, allowing Thomson to demonstrate different architectural styles; as with many of his other buildings, the storeys decrease in height farther up. The tall ground floor has been greatly altered by modern shopfronts but it originally had a central doorway with two shops on either side of it; Thomson even provided street lamps on the pavement outside but these are long since gone. Both the first and second storeys have double pilasters (but with different details) and the capitals on the lower floor feature exceptionally elaborate Assyrian scrolls. In contrast, the third floor has a series of squat Egyptian fluted columns behind which is a continuous series of windows, a design similar to that used in the earlier Grecian Buildings (see p.119). Finally, there is a heavy and fancy cornice which is decorated with carved anthemia.

The Union Street pedestrian entrance to Central Station is contained within the large **Caledonian Chambers** ㊺ (1901-3, James Miller). The two flanks of the building have tall towers, each of which carries a series of pillars leading up to an eaves gallery. Each tower has a pair of crouched figures at first-storey level with the southern pair the more elaborate of the two, as they also have ships' prows on which are animal figureheads. Both end towers also have a large plaque with a lion which represents the Caledonian Railway as this building was used as their offices.

The chambers' central doorway is decorated with the building's name and at the level of the third-storey balcony is an elaborate shield featuring the royal arms of Scotland. This depicts a lion (above which is a knight's helmet) a horse and unicorn (both of which bear standards) and the phrases *In defence* and *Nemo me impune lacessit* ('No one provokes me with impunity').

Continue on Union Street to its junction with Argyle Street. The building on the left stands at what is popularly called **'Boots Corner'** (66) as it replaced the large Boots the Chemist shop. The phrase 'Meet you at Boots' was well-used in Glasgow as this corner was for long a popular meeting place for Saturday night 'dates'.

The new building was erected in 1992 and is in the style of Charles Rennie Mackintosh; it was built when his work was being 'rediscovered' by many people, including a new generation of architects.

Look to the right (along Argyle Street) to what is called **'The Hielanman's Umbrella'** (67) (reconstructed 1899-1906, McDowell, Steven & Co. Ltd). This is the bridge which carries the railway lines out of Central Station and over Argyle Street; the space underneath it was a traditional meeting point for Highland people who had recently come to Glasgow to find work, hence the name. Tall decorated cast-iron pillars carry the large canopy which shelters the station's platforms.

Turn left at Argyle Street and walk along to the junction with Buchanan Street where the **Campbell, Stewart & MacDonald Building** (68) (1900-3, Horatio Broomhead) stands. This is now part of the Frasers department store (see p.96). At the entrance, two huge Atlantes support a first-floor balcony on their broad shoulders; the tynpanum high above the street has a Classical frieze with men, women and a large bull's head. At the corner is a domed tower with tall pillars and a number of small semi-circular balconies.

Turn right when Buchanan Street is met. Cross Argyle Street and enter **St Enoch Square** ❶ where the walk ends.

Glasgow University and Kelvingrove Park

A walk around Glasgow University, which has the best single collection of public buildings in the city as well as some interesting museums. After this, the route goes through Kelvingrove Park, which has numerous statues and monuments, and this leads to the Kelvingrove Art Gallery and Museum and the Transport Museum.

Glasgow University

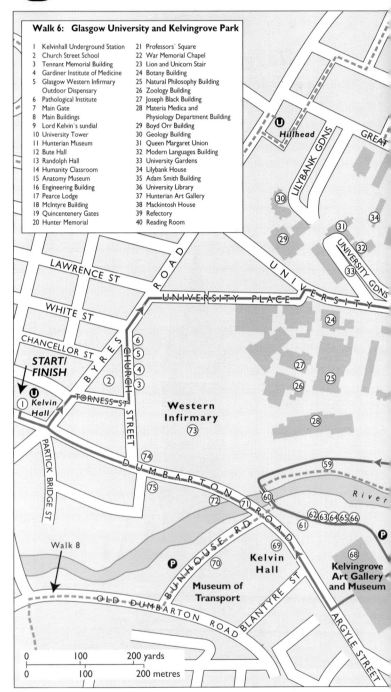

Walk 6: Glasgow University and Kelvingrove Park

1 Kelvinhall Underground Station
2 Church Street School
3 Tennant Memorial Building
4 Gardiner Institute of Medicine
5 Glasgow Western Infirmary
   Outdoor Dispensary
6 Pathological Institute
7 Main Gate
8 Main Buildings
9 Lord Kelvin's sundial
10 University Tower
11 Hunterian Museum
12 Bute Hall
13 Randolph Hall
14 Humanity Classroom
15 Anatomy Museum
16 Engineering Building
17 Pearce Lodge
18 McIntyre Building
19 Quincentenery Gates
20 Hunter Memorial

21 Professors' Square
22 War Memorial Chapel
23 Lion and Unicorn Stair
24 Botany Building
25 Natural Philosophy Building
26 Zoology Building
27 Joseph Black Building
28 Materia Medica and
   Physiology Department Building
29 Boyd Orr Building
30 Geology Building
31 Queen Margaret Union
32 Modern Languages Building
33 University Gardens
34 Lilybank House
35 Adam Smith Building
36 University Library
37 Hunterian Art Gallery
38 Mackintosh House
39 Refectory
40 Reading Room

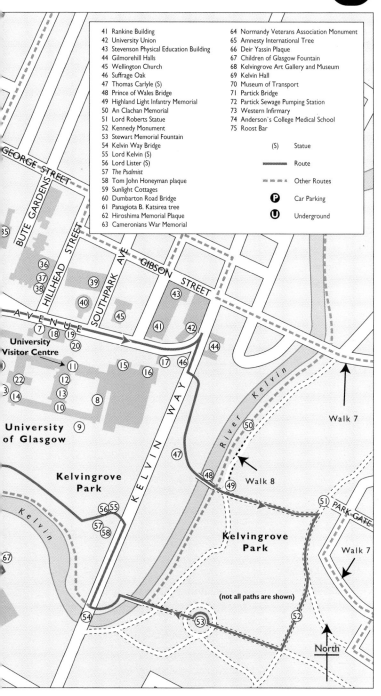

41 Rankine Building
42 University Union
43 Stevenson Physical Education Building
44 Gilmorehill Halls
45 Wellington Church
46 Suffrage Oak
47 Thomas Carlyle (S)
48 Prince of Wales Bridge
49 Highland Light Infantry Memorial
50 An Clachan Memorial
51 Lord Roberts Statue
52 Kennedy Monument
53 Stewart Memorial Fountain
54 Kelvin Way Bridge
55 Lord Kelvin (S)
56 Lord Lister (S)
57 The Psalmist
58 Tom John Honeyman plaque
59 Sunlight Cottages
60 Dumbarton Road Bridge
61 Panagiota B. Katsirea tree
62 Hiroshima Memorial Plaque
63 Cameronians War Memorial

64 Normandy Veterans Association Monument
65 Amnesty International Tree
66 Deir Yassin Plaque
67 Children of Glasgow Fountain
68 Kelvingrove Art Gallery and Museum
69 Kelvin Hall
70 Museum of Transport
71 Partick Bridge
72 Partick Sewage Pumping Station
73 Western Infirmary
74 Anderson's College Medical School
75 Roost Bar

(S)   Statue

━━━━   Route

- - - -   Other Routes

P   Car Parking

U   Underground

GEORGE STREET

BUTE GARDENS

HILLHEAD STREET

GIBSON STREET

SOUTHPARK AVE

AVENUE

University Visitor Centre

University of Glasgow

Kelvingrove Park

Kelvin

River Kelvin

Walk 7

Walk 8

Kelvingrove Park

Walk 7

PARK GATE

(not all paths are shown)

North

Main places of interest	**Glasgow University** ⑧–㊹ **Hunterian Museum** ⑪ (Glasgow University) War Memorial Chapel ㉒ (Glasgow University) Zoology Museum ㉖ (Glasgow University) **Hunterian Art Gallery** ㊲ (Glasgow University) **Mackintosh House** ㊳ (part of the Hunterian Art Gallery) **Kelvingrove Park** ㊻–(67) **Kelvingrove Art Gallery and Museum** (68) (the city's principal museum) **Museum of Transport** (70)
Circular/linear	circular
Starting point	Kelvinhall Underground Station ①
Finishing point	Kelvinhall Underground Station ①
Distance	4 km (2.5 miles)
Terrain	pavements and paths; an incline up Byres Road and up and down University Avenue; steep paths in parts of Kelvingrove Park (these can be avoided)
Public transport	Kelvinhall Underground Station Hillhead Underground Station
Sections	Kelvinhall Underground Station to Glasgow University Glasgow University University Avenue to Argyle Street via Kelvingrove Park Argyle Street to Kelvinhall Underground Station
Architects	Thomson: Lilybank House ㉞ Kelvingrove Art Gallery and Museum (68) (exhibit) Mackintosh: Mackintosh House ㊳ Kelvingrove Art Gallery and Museum (68) (exhibits)
Nearby walks	7, 8
Refreshments	many in Dumbarton Road and Byres Road; Glasgow University: Refectory (during term time) and the Visitors' Centre; Kelvingrove Art Gallery and Museum; Museum of Transport
Notes	Be aware of safety advice (see p.16) as Kelvingrove Park can be very quiet at times.

KELVINHALL UNDERGROUND STATION TO GLASGOW UNIVERSITY

Leave **Kelvinhall Underground Station** ❶ and turn right to follow a passageway which leads to Dumbarton Road, the busy thoroughfare which runs through **Partick**. The ancient village of Partick (which originally lay to the south of Dumbarton Road) was first mentioned in 1136 when King David I granted 'Perdeyc' to the bishops of Glasgow who subsequently built a castle here. The village became important because of its mills which utilised the fast-running River Kelvin (see p.242) and the bishops' meal mill was a valuable source of income. In later centuries, the village developed as a stopping point between Glasgow and Dumbarton, as a milling and weaving centre, and later as a shipbuilding area.

Partick was an independent burgh only from 1852 to 1912 when it was swallowed up by the encroaching city but great changes took place during its short period of municipal independence. in 1852 Hugh Macdonald (see p.378) could write that 'Partick altogether has a pleasant half-rural aspect, while the reputed salubrity of its air and its vicinity to the city have rendered it a favourite place of resort on holidays, and on the long summer evening, with certain classes of our citizens... the inhabitants generally have an appearance of robust health, which contrasts favourably with that of our urban population.' By 1912, only sixty years later, Partick's population had grown to almost 70,000!

The growth of the shipyards attracted many people to Partick and led to the erection of the district's tenements; many of these substantial buildings still stand, allowing local people more continuity with the past than those whose communities have suffered wholesale 'redevelopment'.

Turn left at Dumbarton Road and follow it to the busy junction of Partick Cross. Turn left and climb Byres Road. Turn first right (Torness Street) just before the former **Church Street School** ❷, originally Partick Academy (1903, Bruce & Hay). On it is engraved *Govan Parish School Board*, a reminder that the influence of Govan (see p.287) once spread quite far over the city. The school stands on the site of the ancient byres where the bishops' cattle were housed, hence the name Byres Road.

Turn left at Church Street. On the other side of the road is the complex of buildings that comprise the Western Infirmary, which is described on p.212. This is a major teaching hospital and many of the university's medical departments are based here.

The first building of note is the **Tennant Memorial Building** ❸ (1933-6, Norman A. Dick). This is named after Dr Gavin Tennant, a 'visiting physician' in the late nineteenth century, who left a bequest to found an eye department and an accompanying university chair of ophthalmology. The sculpture is by Archibald Dawson and features two carved figures above the door representing *Light* and *Darkness*. Above them is a carving of two serpents (symbols of renovation) entwined around a staff; this is the emblem of Aesculapius, the Greek god of medicine who was highly skilled in the arts of healing and restoring the dead.

On either side of the doorway are spiral columns, topped by carved owls, while rather fiercer-looking birds are featured on relief carvings at the ends of the building's facade.

The next building is the **Gardiner Institute of Medicine** ❹ (1937-8, Norman A. Dick). This is large and rather plain, though just above the main vehicular entrance is another emblem of Aesculapius (see above) together with the word *Chirurgia* ('Surgery').

When built, the hospital used the institute as a medical department while the university staff had beds available for patients who were of 'special scientific interest'.

Next door is the former Out-patient Department, intriguingly named the **Glasgow Western Infirmary Outdoor Dispensary** ❺ (1902-5, J. J. Burnet). Its two crow-stepped gables carry the words *Medicine* and *Surgery* and above the right-hand doorway are a couple of carved fish.

At the end of the street is the much-extended **Pathological Institute** ❻ (1894-6, J. J. Burnet). The Church Street side features a crow-stepped gable and a large window surrounded by elaborately-carved details. Plaques beside the window carry *PI* and *1895*, while above the window is yet another emblem of Aesculapius (see above).

Church Street joins Byres Road, which is now followed. Turn right at University Place and follow the perimeter of the infirmary and then the university. The road then joins University Avenue, which should be followed up to the university's Main Gate, found on the right at the brow of the hill.

All the university's buildings are described in the next section.

GLASGOW UNIVERSITY

After passing through the **Main Gate** ❼, turn left and follow the rear of the main building until signs for the **Visitor Centre** are seen. This can give information about the university and details of which buildings can be visited. The centre organises tours around the main building which are the only opportunity visitors have of seeing places such as the Bute Hall.

Instead of providing a walking route, the rest of this section gives general notes on many of the places of interest, leaving readers to choose their own route around the campus. Over the last few decades the university has bought many houses in the Hillhead area (which is on the hill to the north); these are not detailed here but information on them can be obtained at the Visitor Centre.

The university actively encourages visitors to learn more about its buildings and what goes on inside them and it also has some of the best museums and galleries in Glasgow. Indeed, the university area has the biggest collection of good public buildings in the whole city. The description that follows gives information not only on the main buildings of the campus but also on many of the everyday teaching buildings that are part of this 500-year-old institution.

In addition to the buildings mentioned here, a few other university buildings are described during Walk 7 on p.218. The next section of this walk resumes from the university's Main Gate (see p.197).

Glasgow University was established in 1451 when Pope Nicholas V granted a papal bull to Glasgow's Bishop William Turnbull. The university was initially accommodated in the cathedral but it soon outgrew those cramped conditions and moved to High Street (see p.32). New purpose-built buildings were erected there in the mid-seventeenth century – these are often referred to as the 'Old College' – and many famous academics taught there, including Adam Smith and Joseph Black (see pp.191 and 189 respectively).

Although these were some of the finest and most interesting buildings in the city, they were in a poor state of repair by the mid-nineteenth century. This, together with the increasing pollution in the East End, made the idea of a move to the more salubrious West End a welcome proposition. In 1846 there were plans to place it on Woodlands Hill but negotiations with the railway company which had offered to pay for the removal broke down. In 1864 there was another offer, this time from the City of Glasgow Union Railway Company, to buy the site (it eventually became the College Goods Yard) and this allowed the university to move westwards. This time, Gilmorehill was chosen and the main buildings were erected on the southern edge of this prominent hill, just across the River Kelvin from the Woodlands Hill site.

Today there are around 17,000 students and 4500 staff in the university grouped in eight faculties. The university is run by the Court, made up of members representing various interests, and the Senate, which looks after academic and educational matters. The largest university body is the General Council which includes all the university's graduates (currently numbering around 100,000) and it is responsible for, amongst other things, the election of the Chancellor (see below). The Principal is the administrative head of the university, the Chancellor is the honorary 'figurehead' and the Rector is the elected representative of the students. The choice of Rector (who is elected every three years) is a fascinating barometer of student politics and attitudes; previous rectors have included Robert Peel (see p.87), William Ewart Gladstone (see p.87) and Jimmy Reid.

Main Buildings ❽ (1864–70, Sir George Gilbert Scott)
The main building is built in Gothic style and was erected in stages as

finances permitted. It is constructed of local white sandstone and its roof has a wide variety of towers, turrets and other embellishments which lend an air of Scots Baronial to the overall design. The windows must be a window cleaner's nightmare as they are comprised of small panes of glass set in large metal frames. The overall design is of a figure of eight, with the buildings arranged around two large quadrangles separated by the Bute Hall. The quadrangles are most conveniently entered via the Visitor Centre or by entering the main door beneath the University Tower.

There is a flagpole at the front of the building and the grassy area beside it has some great views over a large part of the city.

At the front of the Main Building, and in a little grassy area to the east of the tower, is **Lord Kelvin's sundial** ❾. This large carved stone terrestrial globe has a number of sundials and it was possibly made by Lord Kelvin (see p.203).

University Tower ❿ (1864-70, Sir George Gilbert Scott; 1887, J. Oldrid Scott)

Sir George Gilbert Scott had planned a lead-covered spire for the tower but he died before it was completed. His son then took over the work and he designed this more open structure which has an observation platform giving superb views. One of Glasgow's most important landmarks, it is 85m (278ft) high and is easily spotted from most parts of the city. Above the main doorway (which is decorated with carved thistles) are two shields: one has a bull for Bishop Turnbull and the date 1451; the other has three shells (for the Marquis of Montrose, who was the Chancellor in 1870) and the date 1870. Farther above, a plaque carries the university's badge (which is essentially the elements of the city's coat of arms with a mace, an open book and the university's motto *Via, Veritas, Vita* ('The Way, the Truth, the Life'). It is possible to climb the tower, weather permitting – contact the Visitor Centre for details.

Inside the tower's main door is a passageway with a wonderful series of Gothic archways which give this space the feel of an extremely ancient institution. On the right is a marble plaque (from the Blackfriars' churchyard in the High Street) dedicated to Thomas Reid (1720-96), Professor of Moral Philosophy in the Old College from 1764 to 1796. On the other side of the passageway is a sandstone plaque on which is the university's badge and the words *University of Glasgow Founded 1451*. This was brought here from High Street where the Old College was sited. After the university moved from there to Gilmorehill this plaque was erected on the old site and in the 1990s it was saved when the land became a huge car park. The passageway narrows at the end (where there is a doorway) and at the base of the pillars on either side are brass plaques commemorating the laying of two foundation stones on 8 October 1868. That on the left was laid by Alexandra, Princess of Wales and that on the right by Edward, Prince of Wales.

The passageway leads to one of the university's finest pieces of architecture, the dramatic **vaulted undercroft** which supports Bute Hall (see below). To the right of this is the East Quadrangle and to the left is the West Quadrangle. The latter has within it a large mobile sculpture entitled *Three Squares Gyratory* by George Rickey (1972).

Hunterian Museum ⓫

This is Scotland's oldest public museum and it is based on the wide-ranging collections of **William Hunter** (1718-83). Hunter was a student here from 1731 to 1736, then attended medical classes in Edinburgh. After that, he moved to London and began a distinguished (and exceptionally lucrative) career in medicine, specialising in anatomy, surgery and midwifery. During this time he gathered together a large and wide-ranging collection of medical specimens, books, coins, paintings and other artefacts which he later bequeathed to the university, together with money to build a museum at the Old College.

The museum is entered by a very grand stone staircase which can be reached from the north end of the undercroft or from the East Quadrangle. (The Concert Hall is on the right at the bottom of the staircase.) The stairwell has a splendid wooden ceiling and on the wall is hung *Hector's Farewell to Andromache* (*c*. 1776-7) by a former student, **Gavin Hamilton** (1723-98), an important neoclassical painter who developed the technique of history painting. He spent most of his working life in Rome and amongst his work are some large canvases depicting ancient Greece as described by Homer. The museum's entrance is opposite the door into the Bute Hall.

The museum's first room (which overlooks University Avenue) has a wide variety of exhibits, many of them associated with work undertaken at the university. One example is a 'pitch glacier' experiment – originally set up by Lord Kelvin in 1887 – and still flowing (slowly!). Some medical equipment used by Hunter is also on display – so, too, is his death mask. Two marble statues near the windows are of James Watt (1823, Francis Chantry) and Adam Smith (1867, Hanns Gasser); these two are described on pp.86 and 191 respectively. Before leaving the hall, don't forget to look upwards to admire the ceiling.

The design of the main gallery is itself a masterpiece, with tall decorated cast-iron pillars supporting a gallery and a fine barrel-vaulted ceiling. The museum has a wide collection of artefacts to draw on and these are used as museum exhibits, for teaching and for research. The sections of the main gallery are arranged chronologically, using the massive expanse of time from early geological time to the (comparatively recent) Roman occupation. Once in the main gallery, bear to the left to see the **geological collection**. This starts with an extremely old meteorite (composed of rock 4,570,000,000 years old) which landed in Mexico in 1969. Rocks from the Earth's crust are also exhibited and they range from large chunks of granite, obsidian and basalt to beautiful crystalline minerals from many parts of the world. Earth's fossil record is traced from the Precambrian period through to relatively modern times, with exhibits of early plants and animals. The outstanding local fossil is the Bearsden Shark, a rather bizarre animal with a 'toothed' fin which lived in the district about 333 million years ago. Inevitably, there is a dinosaur exhibit and even a cast of a dinosaur track, a useful piece of evidence which is used to calculate the speed at which the animal moved. One very fascinating exhibit is a collection of unhatched dinosaur eggs embedded in sandstone which was found in China. These 80-million-year-old eggs are thought to be of a Saurischan dinosaur.

The museum's **ethnographic and historic collections** are used to illustrate the rest of the displays. The early development of the human race is traced, with its most interesting exhibit being 'Lucy', a partially complete skeleton of a twenty-five- to thirty-year-old female who died over three million years ago in Ethiopia and who belongs to the species *Australopithecus afarensis*. Many other skulls of hominids are used to trace how our ancestors evolved over a long period of time.

The life of hunter-gatherers, particularly those in the Americas, is then shown, and this leads on to displays about the first settled farmers, with examples from the Middle East, Australasia and Africa. The subsequent development of villages, towns and then cities is explored by more exhibits, including a group from Egypt. The age of expansion and exploration has material from Africa and from Captain James Cook's eighteenth-century exploration of the Pacific Ocean.

The final exhibit deals with some local history – artefacts from the Roman occupation. After conquering England, the Roman army headed northwards but finding they could not subdue Scotland they established their northern frontier along the Antonine Wall which they built around AD142; this stretched across Central Scotland from the Firth of Clyde to the Firth of Forth. Altars, distance slabs and gravestones are the largest exhibits on display but there are also remains from a bath-house, some funerary items and tools of various sorts.

The museum's **archaeology collection** is found upstairs and it parallels the chronology of the ethnographic displays downstairs. This traces the story of the human race's activities in various parts of the world and illustrates the evidence we have of the first inhabitants of Scotland, around 7000 years BC. The exhibits show the development of metal-working, food making and changes in daily activities up to the time of the Vikings (800-1250). The exhibits also deal with the arguments put forward by various antagonists – the creationists, catastrophists and the uniformitarians – who had radically different interpretations of the history of our planet. Indeed, the debate still continues!

The exhibition of **coins and medals** is based on Hunter's impressive collection. It starts with early forms of money, such as shells, and then shows examples of early coins from ancient Egypt, Greece and

Rome. The issuing of coins is obviously tied up with trade and politics and the collection traces the ups and downs of various states over the last 2500 years. One particularly interesting coin is the '5 Europinos', made in Hamburg in 1952 as an attempt at a 'European single currency'. The history of Scottish coins is also represented and the exhibits range from a penny of around 1150 to coins issued in 1707, the year in which Scotland and England were joined by the (still-debated) Act of Union. Medals of various types are displayed including Papal medals, medals minted in various European countries and also some produced for the university itself. One particular exhibit which has an association with the university is the Nobel Peace Prize medal awarded to Lord John Boyd Orr in 1949 (see p.189). There are also many examples of medals bearing the image of Robert Burns (see p.85), a number of which were made to raise money for statues to the national poet.

Bute Hall ⑫ (1878-84, J. Oldrid Scott and Edwin Morgan)

Bute Hall is reached by following the route to the Hunterian Museum (see above). The hall is named after the third Marquess of Bute who donated money for its construction and his coat of arms can be seen above the door into the hall. It is an extremely grand hall which is used for examinations, graduations and other gatherings; it is also very tall, which allows large amounts of space for its magnificent stained-glass windows. Its decorated cast-iron columns support a viewing gallery and a fine arched timber ceiling. On one end of the hall is a huge organ and at the other is the ceremonial platform where graduands are 'capped'. Beyond that is the smaller Randolph Hall (see below). It is really too interesting a building to use as an examination hall as there are too many nice things to look at instead of writing!

There are five sets of stained-glass windows: two on the east (left) wall and three on the west (right) wall. The description that follows deals with the windows in a clockwise order, starting with the first window on the left after the main door.

On the eastern side, the top of the first window (1900, Henry Dearle) depicts four philosophers: Plato (477-347 BC), Aristotle (384-322 BC), Benedict Spinoza (1632-77) and Georg Hegel (1770-1831). Below these are St Athanasius (298-373), John of Chrysostom (347-407), St Augustine (354-430) and St Thomas Aquinas (1225-74). Below the gallery, the window (1900, Edward Burne-Jones) has four female figures representing *Philosophy*, *Medicine*, *Jurisprudence* and *Theology*.

The next set of windows (by Alfred Webster) show various founders and benefactors of the university: Queen Margaret, Bishop Turnbull (see p.177), King James II, Queen Victoria (see p.87), Andrew Melville, John Knox (see p.358), George Buchanan (1506-82) and William Carstares (1649-1715). Below the gallery are four Scottish saints: St Ninian (*c.* 360-432), St Kentigern (St Mungo: see p.415), St Columba (see p.158) and St Modan (sixth century).

On the eastern wall, the top left-hand window (by Edward Burne-Jones) shows four physicists: Nicolaus Copernicus (1473-1543), Galileo Galilei (1564-1642), Johann Kepler (1571-1630) and Isaac Newton (1642-1727). Below these are four literary figures: Francis Bacon (1561-1626), Robert Burns (see p.85), Lord Byron (1788-1824) and Thomas Carlyle (see p.199). Below the gallery, the window (by Henry Holiday) shows four females representing the theological virtues of *Motherhood*, *Charity*, *Patience* and *Faith*.

The top of the middle window (1893, Edward Burne-Jones) has four scholars of the Classical world: Homer (*c*. eighth century), Æschylus (*c*. 526-456 BC), Virgil (*c*. 70-19 BC) and Horace(*c*. 65-8 BC). Below these are four writers: Dante Alighieri (1265-1321), Geoffrey Chaucer (1334-1400), William Shakespeare (1564-1616) and John Milton (1608-74). Below the gallery are the four patron saints of the British Isles: St George (sixth century), St Andrew (see p.236), St Patrick (389-*c*. 461) and St David (fifth to sixth centuries).

The right hand window (by Douglas Strachan) deals with the entry of women into the university and, in particular, with the achievements of women in education. It is dedicated to Jeanette Galloway who was honorary secretary of Queen Margaret College (see p.236). The top window has four female virtues: *Fidelity*, *Perseverance*, *Courage* and *Teaching*. Below the gallery are windows showing the House of Learning, the House of Fame, the House of Holiness and House Beautiful.

The hall is lit by lanterns which were made for the university's quincentenary in 1951 and their design is based on the head of the university's mace which dates back to the 1460s.

Randolph Hall ⑬ (1878-84, J. Oldrid Scott and Edwin Morgan)
Randolph Hall is reached via Bute Hall. It is rather smaller than Bute Hall but it contains a stencilled barrel roof and some fine stained-glass work. The very large window is by Gordon Webster and it shows numerous crests of chancellors and benefactors. At either end of the hall are marble fireplaces (surely never enough to heat such a room!) and on the main wall are portraits of people associated with the university. The hall is named after Charles Randolph (see p.295) who provided money for its construction.

Humanity Classroom ⑭
This nineteenth-century classroom still retains its original interior, with long wooden desks, a raised platform and timbered ceiling. Along the wall is a collection of plaques which celebrate the recipients of the Cowan medal which is awarded for excellence in the Humanities (Latin and Greek). The oral examination for this is conducted in Latin with the students sitting on the Blackstone Chair, which is on display in the Hunterian Museum. On the wall are hung portraits of Professors of Humanities.

Anatomy Museum ⓯ (1900–1, J. J. Burnet)

This fascinating museum is based on the huge number of anatomical specimens collected by William Hunter (see p.179). These were originally collected to help Hunter illustrate his lectures and the collection is still used for teaching purposes. The museum is not normally open to the public. Above one of the doorways, a carved plaque records that the building was erected by the trustees of James B. Thomson in 1901.

Engineering Building ⓰ (1901, J. J. Burnet and J. Oldrid Scott)

As befits a city which led the world in shipbuilding and railway locomotive engineering, the university has had engineering departments since 1840 and students come here from all over the world to learn their skills. High up on the eastern side of the building is an elaborate plaque decorated with a royal coat of arms and its motto *Honi soit qui mal y pense* ('Evil be to him who evil thinks'). Beneath it is carved *James Watt engineering laboratories 1901*. In the pediment above this is a carved centrifugal governor, one of Watt's many inventions (see p.86). Above the pediment are two plaques, one with *VR* ('Victoria Regina' for Queen Victoria) and the other with Ǝ*R* ('Edward Rex' for King Edward VII).

An archway links this building to Pearce Lodge (see later) and above this is a badge showing St Mungo, the university's motto *Via, Veritas, Vita* ('The Way, the Truth, the Life') and the dates *1451* and *1901*.

To the south, the **James Watt Engineering Building** (1957–58, Keppie, Henderson & Partners) is in a very different style and devoid of fussy detail. A large bas-relief (1957, Eric Kennington) on its southern end depicts engineering through the ages.

Pearce Lodge ⓱ (1885–8, Alexander George Thomson)

This building is of great historic importance to the university as parts of it came from the seventeenth-century Old College. The original sections include the gateway facing University Avenue, the prominent cornice and the coats of arms. The lodge is composed of two main elements (the gateway and a circular stair turret which has a conical roof) and was erected here through the generosity of Sir William Pearce (see p.291), hence the name. When built, the lodge was used as the naval architecture classroom.

Above the bulky archway are the words *Hae ae des extrvctae svnt anno dom* CƆ ƆCLVI; this refers to the original erection of the gateway in 1656 and the two reversed 'C's in the date are due to a medieval system of writing Roman numerals. Above that is Charles II's royal coat of arms bearing the phrases *Hony soit qui mal y pense* ('Evil be to him who evil thinks') and *Dieu et mon droit* ('God and my right'). Beyond that is a sculpture showing a sword crossed with a mace together with *CR2* ('Charles Rex II' (King Charles II)). Two carved urns flank the coat of arms, and near the roof is a plaque whose Latin inscription pays tribute to Pearce for bringing the gateway here. Other sculpted designs, including faces and crowns, appear over the windows.

The very prominent cornice also appears on the south side. There is also more sculpture here, including the university's badge on the crow-stepped gable. At the back is a rather worn plaque bearing the university's arms and a Latin inscription which came from an archway in the Old College. Above the windows are sculpted faces just as on the main facade.

McIntyre Building ⓲ (1886, 1893 and 1908, J. J. Burnet)

This building initially housed the men's union (founded 1885) and later the women's union – it took nearly a century to form a mixed union! It now houses the Students Representative Council and a bookshop. Above the main entrance are badges that represent the four 'nations' of the university to which staff and students belong according to their place of birth. They are: Glottiana: the county of Lanark, which included Glasgow (double headed eagle, hammer and paddle); Rothseiana: the counties of Bute, Renfrew and Ayr (sailing ship); Transforthana: the west of Scotland and north of the River Forth (sword, axe and horn of plenty); and Loudoniana: east and south of Scotland; everywhere outside Scotland (anchor, spade and a shepherd's crook).

Above this are two intricate window frames and between them is a plaque explaining why the building is so-named: *Per ardua* ('Through hardships') and *This building erected for the use and benefit of the students of Glasgow by John McIntyre M.D. Odiham Hampshire a former student of this university is dedicated to the memory of his beloved wife Anne daughter of the late Francis Tweddell esquire of Threepwood Northumberland 1887.*

Well to the left of this, a gable end features St Mungo with his alternative name *St Kentgernus* (St Kentigern).

Quincentenary Gates ⓳ (1954)

In 1951 the university celebrated its five hundredth birthday (it is the fourth oldest university in Britain) and these gates were erected by the General Council to mark that occasion. The gates' piers have the dates *1451* and *1951*, and are topped by a lion and a unicorn, echoing the design of the old staircase (see later). The gates feature the university's mace and the names of twenty-eight well-known people associated with the university. The names are ordered chronologically from the base up, the five levels representing the five particular centuries (fifteenth to nineteenth) to which these people belonged.

They are (starting from the lowest level): King James II (1430-60), Archbishop William Turnbull (*c.* 1400-54, see p.177), James Douglas Morton (*c.* 1516-81, Regent of Scotland), Zachary Boyd (1585?-1653, benefactor), Andrew Melville (1545-1622, Principal), Lord James Hamilton I (d.1479), Patrick Gillespie (1617-75, Principal), Viscount Stair I (1619-95, Regent of Scotland), Sir John Maxwell (1648-1732, Rector), Robert Baillie (1599-1662, Principal), Duke of Montrose (1682-1742, Chancellor), Gilbert Burnet (1643-1715, Professor of Divinity), William Hunter (see p.179), William Cullen (1710-90,

Professor of Medicine), John Millar (1735-1801, Professor of Civil Law), James Watt (see p.86), Adam Smith (see p.191), Thomas Campbell (see p.85), Thomas Reid (see p.178), Robert Foulis (see p.363), Marquis of Bute (1847-1900, see p.181), Sir William MacEwan (1848-1924, Professor of Surgery), John Caird (1820-98, Principal), Lord Kelvin (see p.203), Lord Joseph Lister (see p.203), Andrew Cecil Bradley (1851-1935, Professor of English Literature), Edmund Law Lushington (1811-93, Professor of Greek) and Isabella Elder (see p.297).

The two side gates contain panels showing the university's four nations (see p.184). The walls which flank these smaller gates bear the words *Universitas Glasguens's* and the university's motto *Via Veritas Vita* ('The Way, the Truth, the Life').

Hunter Memorial ⑳ (1925, Sir J. J. Burnet)

This substantial stone monument was erected to celebrate the brothers William (see p.179) and John Hunter who are depicted on large medallions. The sculpture is by George Henry Paulin.

In the centre of the memorial is the university's badge featuring St Mungo, an open book and a salmon with a ring in its mouth. Below this is a Latin inscription lauding the two brothers. At the eastern end is the coat of arms of the Royal College of Surgeons of England and the motto *Qua prosunt omnibus artes* ('Where the arts benefit all'). At the western end is the coat of arms of the Royal Faculty of Physicians and Surgeons of Glasgow (see p.159) and the mottoes *Conjurat amice* ('Binds together in kindness') and *Non vivere sed valere* ('Not just to live but to be strong').

John Hunter (1723-93) worked for his brother between 1748 and 1759 then studied medicine, later lecturing in anatomy. His medical interests were broad and his book *Natural history of human teeth* (1771-8) was very influential. Like his brother, he was a keen collector and his collection (containing over ten thousand items) was bought by the government and given to the Royal College of Surgeons in London. Unfortunately, his material was destroyed in an air raid during the Second World War.

Professors' Square ㉑ (1860s, Sir G. G. Scott)

The tall terraced villas in this square were originally built to house some of the professors but gradually they moved out and various university departments have taken over. The Principal's Residence is at the southern end of the square.

Number 11 was occupied by Lord Kelvin (see also p.203) and his clock is still there and keeping time. This is not a small time-piece – the clock is on one floor and the pendulum goes down into the basement! Kelvin was a great inventor this is reputed to be one of the first houses in the world to be lit by electricity. A plaque beside the door notes that *In this house lived William Thomson, Lord Kelvin. Physicist 1824-1907. He matriculated in the university at the age of 10, was its professor of natural philosophy from 1846-1899, and died as its chancellor. He is buried beside Isaac Newton in Westminster Abbey.*

War Memorial Chapel 🟐 (1923, Sir J. J. Burnet)

This tall and slender Scots Gothic building filled the gap in the western side of the Main Building and was erected in memory of the 755 men associated with the university who died in the First World War. Burnet's building fits neatly between Scott's western pavilions and there are interesting differences between the two buildings, for example in the treatment of the windows. Many pieces of the exterior's carvings are by Archibald Dawson.

Burnet's building contains not only the chapel, but classrooms and other rooms on either side of it. The outside walls of these rooms have a series of very small sculptures (six on either side of the chapel) which are of interest, though binoculars are needed to study them. The three low down on the left are a man fighting a serpent, a man singing from a book and St George and the dragon. The three high up on the left are a woman holding a model of a church, two lions fighting and a medieval bricklayer. The three low down on the right are a fisherman, a monk reading a book and a helmeted man carrying a sword (which is being consumed by flames) and a shield (with the scales of justice). The three high up on the right are a medieval carpenter, two animals and a stonemason.

The exterior of the chapel has a sculpture based on the 1453 seal of the university and in the centre of this is St Mungo. Around the figure are the words *Versitatis Glasgvensis Sigillvm Commvne* ('The seal of the community of the University of Glasgow'). Above this is a small carving of a female and below it are two angels; the angel on the left carries a fish and the one on the right holds a book. At the same level as the angels are four small winged carvings associated with the four evangelists: a man (St Matthew), a lion (St Mark), a calf (St Luke) and an eagle (St John). Below this are four tall lancet windows (see later). The prominent stone balcony is in the form of an external pulpit and the memorial stone placed there is in the shape of a lectern; it carries the inscription *In remembrance 1914-1918 1939-1945*. Above the balcony is a sculpture of a pelican feeding her young, a medieval symbol for Christ's sacrifice at the crucifixion. At the top of the chapel is an elaborate flèche, complete with winged medieval-style gargoyles.

Two flights of stairs lead to the entrance porches and above these are the symbols of Glottiana and Rothseiana, two of the university's four nations (see p.184). Beyond the porches are vaulted corridors which lead into the chapel. The interior of the chapel is tall and quite narrow; it has a lot of interesting features, especially the stained-glass windows (many of them by Douglas Strachan), the stone carvings and the woodwork (the most important pieces of which are by Archibald Dawson).

The western end has a rose window with the virtues of civic life and various coats of arms. Below this are four lancet windows showing St Andrew, St Columba, St Kentigern (St Mungo) and St Ninian, which also incorporate scenes from Glasgow's history. The three big eastern windows (by Lawrence Lee) have a Benedictine theme dealing with knowledge and wisdom. There are three small windows at the top of the eastern end and these represent the theological virtues of Charity, Faith and Hope. The main side windows represent the work of the university; on the north are Applied Science, Medicine, Law and Theology and on the south are Science, Philosophy, History and Literature. The upper parts of these eight windows, together with the two smaller windows, contain the twelve signs of the zodiac. Near the western end, the choir gallery's window shows the figure of Alma Mater as well as the Tree of Knowledge spreading to the four quarters of the earth.

The main stone carvings are at the east end of the church, where there is the communion table and the war memorial; the carvings have a lot of intricate detail. Above this is the seal of the university, featuring St Mungo, and to each side is an angel with crossed hands. Two other nice carvings in the chapel are the representations of St Andrew and St Christopher which can be seen above the entrance doors.

The three tiers of richly carved wooden stalls are particularly good and the back rows of the stalls have 'poppy-heads', some of which represent incidents in St Mungo's life (see p.415). Two of the stalls are especially ornate; on the north side is the Principal's which is decorated with St Matthew, St Mark and (above) St Columba, while on the south side is the Chancellor's which has St Luke, St John and (above) Bishop Turnbull. The coats of arms at the back of the stalls are of the university's chancellors, many of them bishops or archbishops. The pulpit is another fine piece of woodcarving and it has figures depicting St Margaret, St Columba, St Bride and St Oran. Above all this, the hammerbeam roof has carvings of the ten virgins of the Biblical parable and from these are suspended the chapel's electroliers.

Detailed and annotated drawings of the chapel (which were prepared by the architects) can be seen near the entrance doors.

Lion and Unicorn Stair ㉓ (1690, William Riddell; re-erected 1872)
This originally came from the Old College in High Street (see p.32) and in its present location it was used to link Professors' Square with the main building. However, with the building of the War Memorial Chapel the staircase's upper level was turned through 180 degrees. The staircase is guarded by stone sculptures of the two beasts, hence the name. The door at the top of the stairs leads into the Fore Hall.

Botany Building ㉔ (1900, J. Oldrid Scott and J. J. Burnet)
This is now called the Bower Building (named after Frederick Bower, a previous botany professor) and it houses Botany, Biochemistry and Molecular Biology. The doorway is decorated with the elements of the university's badge and the top of the building has elements of the city's coat of arms.

Natural Philosophy Building ㉕ (1906, James Miller)
This would be called the Physics Building in most universities but the older name is often used. There is nothing old-fashioned about the

The Lion and Unicorn Staircase, Glasgow University

research, however, as work is presently being carried out on ways to detect the gravitational waves which pass through our wee bit of the universe! This is now the Kelvin Building, named after Lord Kelvin (see p.203), and it houses astronomy as well as physics. Its Jacobean-style main entrance is decorated with the university's badge.

Zoology Building ㉖ (1923, Sir J. J. Burnet)
This is now known as the Graham Kerr Building after Professor John Graham Kerr who taught here early in the twentieth century. It contains the relatively small **Zoology Museum** which is possibly the least well known of the city's museums. It has fascinating displays of skeletons, stuffed animals, fossils and even a few live creatures from many parts of the world. Some of the artefacts were originally collected by William Hunter (see p.179) and have subsequently been added to, providing a rich teaching source as well as a fine exhibition for the general public.

Joseph Black Building ㉗ (1936-9, T. Harold Hughes and D. S. R. Waugh; 1950-4, Alexander Wright & Kay)
This sprawl of brick buildings contains the Chemistry Department and its style belongs to a very different age from that of the buildings to the east. A frieze on the wall next to the Zoology Building depicts fish,

dinosaurs, birds and mammals. This particular building is also decorated with a plaque to the chemist Joseph Priestley (1733-1804) who is best remembered for his discovery of oxygen in 1774.

Rather farther away, a plaque on the building which faces University Avenue commemorates the work of Joseph Black (1728-99) who taught chemistry *and* anatomy *and* medicine at the university. Obviously a busy chap. In 1754 he identified the gas carbon dioxide, and later he worked on the new branch of science which we now call thermodynamics; this led to James Watt's improvements to the steam engine (see pp.63 and 86).

Materia Medica and Physiology Department Building 🟠28
(1903-7, James Miller)

This is now known as the West Medical Building and is one of the important links which the university has with the various fields of medicine. 'Materia Medica' is an old Latin name for the study of medicine. This group of buildings has a number of sculptured designs, including the university's badge but its main interest are all the towers, turrets, balustrades and (at the western end) a domed cupola.

Boyd Orr Building 🟠29 (1972, Dorward, Matheson, Gleave & Partners)

It is quite appropriate that this building houses Basic Science as its design is quite basic with no real embellishments at all; an example of Brutalist architecture. John Boyd Orr (1880-71) was a doctor who became one of the world's first influential nutritionists. He helped found the Rowett Research Institute near Aberdeen and later became head of the United Nations' Food and Agriculture Organisation. His outstanding contribution to the understanding of the planet's food problems resulted in him being awarded the Nobel Peace Prize in 1961.

Geology Building 🟠30 (1980, Dorward, Matheson, Gleave & Partners)

Scotland has had a proud tradition in geology and many of the science's important ideas were worked out in this country. With the discovery of North Sea Oil, the training of geologists is even more important to the Scottish economy. Outside the building are two large shaped stones made of Ballachulish granite which were once part of a railway bridge.

The building is now known as the Gregory Building, after John Gregory who was the first professor of geology.

Queen Margaret Union 🟠31 (1968, Walter Underwood & Partners)

This is the students' main union building. The 'QM' was originally founded in 1906 in the Queen Margaret College (see p.236) as the women's union but it became mixed in 1979, eventually forcing the (men's) University Union (see p.196) to become mixed as well.

The university's observatory (see p.234) previously stood on this site.

Modern Languages Building 🟠32 (1958-9, W. N. W. Ramsay)

As one of the smaller nations within Europe, Scotland has to ensure that it produces many graduates with a command of the main European languages. Scotland has a long history of commercial and political ties with continental Europe, for example the 'Auld Alliance' with France dates back to a treaty signed in 1295.

The building's facade is quite plain but is enlivened by a bronze sculpture (by Walter Pritchard) depicting two figures. The upper figure is of a woman holding what may be a dove of peace; the lower one is of a man reading a script.

University Gardens ㉝ (1882-1904)

This delightful group of former houses has gradually been taken over by the university and are now all used by various departments. Many of them have fine wooden doors and still possess very impressive interiors. On the northern side, all except numbers 1, 12 and 14 were designed by J. J. Burnet in 1882-4. Number 1 (1902, Robert Ewan) is a large corner house which has the date *1903* on it and a weather vane on the roof. Numbers 2 to 8 have an almost continuous balcony just above the ground floor windows. Between the doors of numbers 3 and 4 are four plaques representing the university's 'nations' (see p.184). Number 7 has the date *1896* on it, together with two coats of arms; the one on the left has the motto *Be mindfu* and the one on the right has the motto *Keep tryst*. This is Hepburn House and the letters *CH* under the plaques stand for Dr Charles Hepburn (1890-1971) who lived here and who donated the house to the university. He also donated the main window in the Randolph Hall (see p.182) and was greatly involved in the published history of the local area, *A Hillhead Album*.

Numbers 12 and 14 were later additions to the terrace and are notably different from the earlier houses. Number 12 (1900, J. Gaff Gillespie) has its doorway within a turret which rises up beyond the roofline of the other houses. Number 14 (1900, J. J. Burnet) is rather more ornate than the others, with delicate carved details in the stonework and some good cast-ironwork.

On the southern side, only numbers 11 and 13 remain. They have substantial porches but the real architectural treat is the complexity of the side which faces University Avenue. At the corner of number 13 is a plaque which states that *At a dinner party held in this house in 1913 Frederick Soddy (1817-1956) introduced the concept of 'isotopes'. He was awarded the Nobel Prize in 1921 for his work on radioactivity.*

Lilybank House ㉞

This 'country villa' was originally built in two phases around the 1840s and 1850s and its southern extension was designed by Alexander Thomson in 1863-5. The front is dominated by a handsome Greek ionic portico (with four fluted columns) which leads to a tall and narrow main door. Although there are many classical features in the overall style of Thomson's exterior, there are none of the incised patterns or other geometric features which are so common on his other buildings. The university's Queen Margaret Hall once occupied the building but it is now used by the Sociology Department.

Adam Smith Building ㉟ (1967, David Harvey, Alex Scott & Associates)
Named after **Adam Smith** (1723-90), this now houses various Social Science departments. Smith was both a philosopher and economist and he held the chairs of both Logic and Moral Philosophy at the university. His best-known work is *Inquiry into the Nature and Causes of the Wealth of Nations* (1776) which, contrary to what many of his modern followers may think, did not espouse 'laissez faire' economics but rather combined economic ideas with the importance of morality. Smith wrote much else on what we would now call social sciences and he even penned a history of the study of astronomy!

University Library ㊱ (1968, William Whitfield)
This exceptionally tall building acts as a foil to the much more ornate university tower, but it is now almost as important a landmark in the city as its older partner. The building has twelve levels and it has large expanses of glass which give its 2200 readers superb views of the city –

Glasgow University Library with the Quincentenary Gates in the foreground

quite a distraction from studying! A rooftop addition was built in 1996 to house the Special Collections Department where the university's most valuable books are kept.

As well as having 1.75 million books in stock, the library has subscriptions to 7500 current journals and access to databases around the world.

Hunterian Art Gallery ❸❼ (1971–81, William Whitfield)
The university has a very impressive art collection, part of which is on display here. A number of the paintings came from William Hunter's bequest (see p.179) and since then the collection has grown to become one of country's most important. The gallery is housed in this low building which has a copious amount of light coming in through the specially-designed roof. To the left of the main entrance is the exterior of the Mackintosh House (see below) and outside the gallery's entrance stands the bronze sculpture *Diagram of an object* (1990, Dhruva Mistry) which is a modern representation of a seated mother and child.

Inside, the four large but relatively light internal doors (1976–80) which lead into the main gallery were made of cast aluminum by Eduardo Paolozzi (1924–). Various schools are represented in the gallery and they are generally arranged in chronological order and divided by large screens. In the section dealing with **sixteenth- and seventeenth-century painting**, one of the best-known works is the small and unfinished *The entombment of Christ* (c. 1633–35) by Rembrandt Harmensz Van Rijn . The large *The martyrdom of St Catherine* (1647) by Jean Cossiers is of historical interest to Glasgow as it was used as a teaching aid in the Foulis Academy (the Academy of Fine Arts, see p.363) and must have been studied by many budding artists of the day. **British and French Painting 1700–1840** has a wide variety of subjects, but pride of place here must go to the portrait of Dr William Hunter (c. 1764–5) by the well-known Scottish portrait painter Allan Ramsay (1718–84). The other paintings vary from animal portraits by George Stubbs to the historical *The abdication of Mary Queen of Scots, resigning her crown* (1765–73) by Gavin Hamilton (1723–98). This picture is rather different from the 'popular' paintings of the lady's execution which took place in 1587 (see p.321). **French and Scots Painting 1850–1900** includes works by William Taggart (1835–1910), who painted many seaside scenes, such as *The fishers' landing* (1875–7).

The gallery's most famous group of paintings is the **Whistler Collection**, dedicated to the work of James Abbot McNeill Whistler (1834–1903). Whistler was born in Massachusetts in the United States of America and studied art in Paris in the 1850s. Much of his artistic life was spent in London although he also painted elsewhere, including a period in Venice, but he did not return to America. He was greatly admired by 'The Glasgow Boys' (see p.209) and this led to the university giving him an honorary degree. Many years later, this public recognition was repaid when the artist's sister-in-law gave the university a large number of his works. Many of his portraits are very dark, with faces peering out of the background gloom – you either like them or you don't! Of particular interest are *Red and black: the fan* (1891-4) and *Harmony in blue and violet* (c. 1886). The display also includes the artist's own painting equipment as well as furniture and a collection of silverware he designed himself. Other paintings in this section are by artists who were influenced by Whistler's work.

The work of **'The Glasgow Boys** (see p.209) includes *Children at play* (1905) by John Quinton Pringle (1864-1925) and *Gathering primroses* (1901) by Edward A. Hornel (1864-1933). A little further into the twentieth century is the group of artists called the **Scottish Colourists** (see p.209) and the most notable pictures in this section are the haunting *Girl with a pewter jug* (1921) by Stanley Cursiter (1887-1976) and the dynamic *Les eus* (c. 1910-13) by John Duncan Fergusson (1874-1971).

The gallery's collection of modern art is divided into two periods. In **Scottish Art 1940–1980** the development from the colourists can clearly be seen and includes images as different as *Red Ballet* (c. 1938-40) by John Maxwell (1905-62) and *Sea devil's watchtower* (1960) by the celebrated Alan Davie (1920-). The most recent works, in the **Contemporary Art** section, continue this progression, with various media being on display. Some of the items are quite abstract, such as the colourful *Gunwale* (1994) by John McLean (1939-) and *Monumorphosis II* (1980) by John Mooney (1948-).

The **print gallery** is reached via a spiral staircase opposite the information desk. The university has a collection of around 20,000 prints and a number are always on show. The collection covers a wide spectrum of Western artists, with works such as *Adam and Eve* (1504, Albrecht Dürer) and *The frugal meal* (1904, Pablo Picasso). The displays are particularly interesting because, as well as showing prints, there are exhibits with explanations of how the various types of print are made.

The outdoor **sculpture courtyard** is reached by a door to the right of the gallery's reception desk. The exhibits are made in a variety of materials, with a number of them constructed in iron, possibly reflecting the previous importance of the city's heavy engineering industry. Certainly, the bronze *Rio* (1964-5, Sir Eduardo Paolozzi) owes much to engineering design. The sculptures are almost all modern, but pride of place goes to the (relatively old) *Lantern and finial* (1899-1900, Charles Rennie Mackintosh). This originally sat on top of a dome crowning Pettigrew and Stephen's large department store in Sauchiehall Street and it was rescued on its demolition in 1973. Now it can be seen clearly without undue craning of the neck.

The Mackintosh House (see below) is entered via the gallery but because of its importance it is dealt with separately.

Mackintosh House 🕒

Charles Rennie Mackintosh (see p.402) and his wife Margaret Macdonald lived nearby (at 78 Southpark Avenue, see p.218) and this building contains reconstructed interiors of their house, as re-modelled by Mackintosh in 1906. They lived in Southpark Avenue until 1914 and in 1920 the house (and nearly all of its furniture) was sold to William Davidson (see p.405). His sons later presented the furnishings to the university, thus allowing this unique house to be preserved. As with much of Mackintosh's work, the style is stark and austere – and very distinctive. The rooms re-created here are the hall, dining room, studio-drawing room and bedroom; Mackintosh's original furniture, which was designed by him, is also shown *in situ*. The orientation of the house is the same as the original (the front door faces east) so the lighting conditions are similar; indeed, a remarkable amount of research and care has gone into this stunning set of rooms. Prepare to be taken aback!

Even a space as 'mundane' as the **hall** was given special treatment. As a start, the front doors were changed and the inner door taken out, thus removing the small porch. The side window was altered from a vertical to a horizontal orientation and the increase in light was accentuated by placing a mirror opposite the new window. This vanity mirror (1896), with a beaten-lead frame, was made by the Macdonald sisters and Herbert MacNair (see p.403). Other interesting features include the hat, coat and umbrella stand (*c.* 1900) which is based on a design for the Argyle Street Tea Rooms (see p.95) and the colourful light fittings (*c.* 1901) which had been exhibited in Turin in 1902. Overall, this is the 'warmest' of the four rooms.

The overall design of the **dining room** was altered by removing the cornice, inserting a taller door and by adding a picture rail. The painted pine fireplace (1900) came from their previous house and is radically different from those that are seen in the likes of the Tenement House (see p.128); its tall metal finials reach up to the picture rail, echoing the vertical lines of the sideboard opposite. The sideboard (1896) is the house's earliest piece of furniture and it was originally used to hold books and drawings. The wall decoration is divided by the picture rail; the upper region and the ceiling are white, while below is a stencilled wallpaper which employs lines, dots and flower motifs. The stained oak table (1900) is matched with Mackintosh's first high-backed chairs (1900) and both table and chairs are the type used in the Argyle Street Tea Rooms (two of the chairs are not originals). The light fittings (1900) are of silver-plated brass with coloured glass inserts and the photograph on the wall is a copy of his watercolour *Reflections* (1898).

The **studio-drawing room** was made out of two existing rooms, creating an L-shaped space and allowing more light to reach the north-facing studio. In addition, the window in the southern wall was enlarged and this helped flood the room with light. A screen runs down to the picture rail, blocking the view of the top of the tall eastern window and also decreasing the amount of direct light entering the room. The original dividing wall also acts as an additional screen as it too goes down to the level of the picture rail. With muslin curtains at the windows, the light is generally diffuse, but at the same time is maximised by the overall white decoration. Even much of the furniture is painted white. The most stylish chair is the white-painted oak chair with the stencilled canvas back (1902). This, the pair of white armchairs and their oval table (1902), were all exhibited in Turin in 1902. Another unusual chair is the low stained-oak lug chair (1900) with its very high upholstered back and sides. The drawing room's fireplace (1900) came from their previous house. The two matching cabinets (1902) on either side of it have the insides of their doors painted silver and inlaid with glass in the shape of a tall female with a flower motif. These were exhibited in Moscow in 1903. The white-painted desk (1900) contains silvered copper panels which were probably the work of Margaret Macdonald.

The studio part of the room also has a new fireplace (1906) and above it is a fine gesso panel (*The white rose and the red rose*, 1902) by Margaret Macdonald. Opposite it is a bookcase (1900) made of painted oak, with leaded glass windows featuring a plant motif. The much-acclaimed writing cabinet at the window (1904) is made of mahogany and sycamore and has an inlaid mother-of-pearl pattern on the insides of the doors. Its central metal insert incorporates leaded glass which bears a flower motif. The armchair (1897) was based on a design for the Argyle Street Tea Rooms' smoking and billiards room and the tall oak chair was designed in 1904.

The **bedroom** was also enlarged by knocking two rooms into one, giving much more space for the main items of furniture. The four-poster bed (1900) is made of white-painted oak and has sinuous carved features; a dash of colour is added by the glass inserts and the stencilled hangings. The wardrobe (1900) has many similarities to the bed, with the gentle curves near the top of the facade's design making the shape of a bird. The tall mirror with its sweeping uprights (and very small drawers) was designed in 1900 and was exhibited in Vienna that year. The fireplace (1900) also came from the previous house and has a steel surround, its plainness offset by the beaten metal panel above, which is signed *Margaret Macdonald 1899*. This panel was exhibited in Vienna in 1900 and was later displayed in the drawing room of the house the couple occupied before moving to Southpark Avenue. The overall effect of the room's white decoration is, again, stark.

The next part of the gallery has a wide selection of exhibits, showing the breadth of talent exercised by Mackintosh, the other three members of 'The Four' (see p.403) and George Walton. A remarkable array is on display: furniture, stencilled fabrics, leaded glass, metalwork, paintings and drawings. The last exhibit in the gallery is the remarkable guest bedroom designed in 1919 for 78 Derngate in Northampton. In complete contrast to the warm brown of the wooden furniture there are blue and white stripes on the bedcovers, curtains, walls – and even on the ceiling!

Refectory ㊴ (1965-6, Frank Fielden & Associates)
This squat, unattractive building provides eating facilities for the university's community. The two tall concrete blocks outside it are often understood by students to be places where posters are plastered, but they are in fact sculptures: *Sections extending (two cast in-situ)* by Zeyad Dajani and Robin Lee (1996).

Reading Room ㊵ (1939-40, T. Harold Hughes & D. S. R. Waugh)
This circular building acts as a central point where students can study. Although notices inside extol students to be silent, the interior's shape and its hard walls mean that sounds rebound very easily. Many a student has been awakened by the sound of a window suddenly opening!

St Mungo stands above the entrance and he is given his alternative name of St Kentigernus (St Kentigern). A plaque beside the door explains that *This library is built within the grounds of Hillhead House which was presented to the university in 1917.*

Rankine Building ㊶ (1969, Keppie, Henderson & Partners)
The city's previous reliance on heavy engineering has given way to new technologies and this building is involved in modern electronic and communications systems. Its all-too utilitarian looks are relieved on one wall by a stainless steel sculpture (*1840-1990*) by Lucy Aird (1990) which celebrates the 150th anniversary of the founding of the Regius Chair of Civil Engineering and Mechanics.

University Union ㊷ (1929-31, A. McNaughton)
This adaptation of the Scots Baronial style was designed for the men's union which was originally formed in 1885; membership has been mixed for some time. The infamous basement Beer Bar has seen many a raucous scene, especially in the old men-only days. The union has had a long tradition of debating, with the debates run Westminster-style (and very noisy!) and this has given many students so much good practice that they have moved on to the southern chamber to continue the haranguing. The Union debates' 'Question Time' has generally been far more entertaining than the Westminster version, and at times exceptionally boisterous.

The union is also well-known for its snooker hall where too many students have spent too much time. Activity of this sort has been frowned on for centuries and an early example was in 1681 when the Town Council decided 'to caus remove all bulliart tables neir the colledge, at least to discharge theis who hes them to permitt any studentt's in the colledge to play therat, being the desyre of the maister's therof.'

The union's doorway, which is dwarfed by the twin drum towers, is decorated with a relief sculpture of St Mungo and badges of the university's nations (see p.184). The university's badge is placed high up on the gable.

Stevenson Physical Education Building ㊸

(1960, A. Graham Henderson)

This houses the gymnasia, pool and other sports facilities.

Gilmorehill Halls ㊹ (1876-8, James Sellars)

This was originally Gilmorehill Church and then served as a university examination hall for a long time; now it houses the Department of Theatre, Film and Television Studies. Internally the building has been gutted, allowing the upper half of the church to be converted into a theatre; happily this has allowed the retention of some fine windows which have stained-glass and painted glass panels. A cinema is on the ground floor.

UNIVERSITY AVENUE TO ARGYLE STREET VIA KELVINGROVE PARK

Leave the university from the Main Gate and turn right, heading down University Avenue.

On the left is **Wellington Church** ㊺ (1882-4, Thomas Lennox Watson). This large and impressive church is made all the more imposing by being placed on top of a podium and set back from the street. It is in the style of an ancient temple and has similarities with the Church of the Madeleine in Paris. It has a very grand portico and, as an interesting adaptation to the classic design, the Corinthian columns are continued round the sides of the building.

Inside, the plain glass windows allow in copious amounts of light and this can be augmented by the elaborate 'metal bowl electroliers' (1902) which hang from the ceiling. Other interesting features are the galleries which run round three walls and the fine plasterwork on the ceiling and in the organ recess.

Continue walking down University Avenue and turn right at Kelvin Way, the road which runs through **Kelvingrove Park.** In 1852 the Town Council purchased land on the eastern side of the River Kelvin and laid out what was originally called West End Park. (Additional land was bought on the western bank of the river when the university was established two decades later.) Sir Joseph Paxton was asked to produce plans and these were exhibited in public, but Charles Wilson and Thomas Kyle became the park's principal designers. The hilly northern parts were the original Pleasure Grounds and these were planted with trees and shrubs; the paths in these parts offer pleasant walks and good views. A later development was the use of the flatter areas at the park's southern end for sports facilities.

Kelvingrove has played an important part in the recent history of the city as it was the site of three of Glasgow's great exhibitions. The first was the **1888 International Exhibition** which was staged for two main reasons: firstly, to show off the city's great achievements and to emphasise its position as 'The Second City'; and secondly, to raise finance for what is now Kelvingrove Art Gallery and Museum (see p.205). The city's art collection had outgrown the McLellan Galleries (see p.120) and a large prestigious home was now needed; Kelvingrove House was already housing some artefacts but a purpose-built building was sought. The Glasgow architect James Sellars was responsible for choosing an oriental style for the exhibition's buildings and the temporary structures sported flamboyant domes and minarets. The exhibition halls had collections of paintings, sculpture (2700 exhibits in total) and all manner of industrial equipment. There was also a reconstruction of the city's Bishops' Castle and a Dutch Cocoa House. Outdoor exhibits included an electrically illuminated Fairy Fountain and the magnificent Doulton Fountain (see p.63). The exhibition lasted from May to November and nearly 6 million people visited it.

The **1901 International Exhibition** (whose architect was James Miller) built on the 1888 theme of manufacturing and the colossal Industrial Hall was the exhibition's main bulding. This sat on the southern side of the River Kelvin alongside the newly completed Art Galleries. The art exhibitions were particularly noteworthy but there were relatively few examples of the Glasgow-style designs which artists such as Charles Rennie Mackintosh were noted for; perhaps they were too different. There were a number of foreign pavilions and, while some of these were from parts of the British Empire, others were from places like Japan, Persia and Russia. All of these structures were temporary buildings but the two Sunlight Cottages (see p.204) were designed to be permanent and they still stand in their original place in the park. As well as being educational in many ways, the exhibition also had lots of amusements, ranging from musical events to the Canadian Water Chute. There were also gondolas plying the River Kelvin. The exhibition ran from May to November and proved even more popular with visitors (and Glaswegians); the total attendance was nearly 11½ million. The profits were used to purchase more works for the Art Galleries.

The **1911 Scottish National Exhibition** was held in order to endow the chair of Scottish History and Literature at the university, so the industrial themes of the previous events gave way to history. The exhibition came at a time when the city's industrial might was in a less than secure position as it was facing competition from other great cities. This was a Scottish event rather than an international one and it was strong on national image. The main architect was R. J. Walker and Scots Baronial architecture abounded, though there were numerous foreign pavilions, including one for Canadian Pacific whose facade included sculpted engine fronts with enormous cowcatchers. The history exhibits included all the charters of the Scottish kings and there were features on Mary, Queen of Scots, Charles Edward Stewart, Robert Burns and Sir Walter Scott; even Flora MacDonald's slippers were displayed. An Auld Toon was assembled (complete with its keep and the Olde Toffee

Shoppe) and An Clachan (a highland village) was built on the banks of Caol Abhain (in reality, the River Kelvin) – all the people working in it were Gaelic-speaking Highlanders and its site is still marked (see p.200). This exhibition also ran from May to November and nearly 9½ million people visited it.

On the right-hand side of Kelvin Way there is a sloping grassy area and within this is the tall **Suffrage Oak** **46**. A 1995 plaque beside it informs that *This oak tree was planted by Womens Suffrage organisations in Glasgow on 20 April 1918 to commemorate the granting of votes to women.*

The British suffrage movement was launched by Emily Pankhurst (see p.135) in 1906; a limited franchise was won in 1918 and full voting rights came in 1928. In many places the campaign involved violence; in Glasgow there was an attempted arson on a house on Woodlands Hill and in Shields Road Station, and bombs were placed in the City Chambers, the Kibble Palace and in Belmont Church.

The struggle to gain votes for women involved many British women in politics for the first time, but in Glasgow many working-class women had taken firm action during the First World War, when many men were away fighting and landlords took advantage of the housing shortage to increase rents. At this time nearly all the houses in the city were rented and the women (from Govan and Partick in particular) very quickly mobilised nearly 20,000 households in a successful fight to have the rent increases withdrawn.

Cross Kelvin Way and go though the park's gate. Walk down the driveway and at the bottom of the slope, a granite sculpture (*c.* 1883) of **Thomas Carlyle** **47** is on the right. Carlyle (1795-1881) was born in Dumfriesshire and studied at Edinburgh University. After some work as a teacher, he started to make his name as a translator of the German language (including Goethe's *Wilhelm Meister*) as well as from writing articles and books. In 1834 he moved to London and wrote, amongst other things *The French Revolution* (1837). Much of the first volume's manuscript was accidentally burned by John Stuart Mill's maid (using it to light a fire!) and Carlyle had to painstakingly rewrite a lot of material.

Bear left and cross the River Kelvin by the **Prince of Wales Bridge** **48** (1894-5, Alex. B. McDonald). In 1868 a temporary bridge was erected here as part of the processional route to be followed by the Prince of Wales who had been invited to lay the university's foundation stone. However, the bridge (made of wood but painted to resemble granite!) was popular with local people and it lasted until the present structure was built. The present bridge uses real granite (from Peterhead) for the balustrade. The bulk of the bridge is of sandstone and carries the city's coat of arms in its decorated spandrels.

The **River Kelvin** rises in the Kilsyth Hills (to the north-east of the city) and flows some 30km (21 miles) to meet the River Clyde near

Partick. This is one of the Clyde's main tributaries and it has played an important role in the city's history with many mills and factories built on its banks. Fortunately, the river seems to have greatly recovered from the huge amounts of pollution produced by these enterprises.

The path that is crossed immediately after the bridge is part of the Kelvin Walkway, which is described in Walk 8 (see p.242).

At the end of the bridge is the **Highland Light Infantry Memorial** 🔢 (1906, William Birnie Rhind) dedicated to men who perished in the South African Wars (1899-1902). As with many such monuments, the inscription puts all those who died into three distinct classes: 'officers, non-commissioned officers and men'. The sculpture shows a seated soldier guarding a bridge.

The low-lying patch of ground to the north of the memorial was used in the 1911 exhibition as the site of the Highland village (see p.198) and its name is inscribed on the **An Clachan Memorial** 🔢, a very ordinary-looking rounded boulder which lies beside the riverside path.

Readers not wishing to climb the next hilly part of the route can turn to the right at the Highland Light Infantry Memorial and follow the broad driveway which leads to the duck pond (see below) where the route can be rejoined. Keep to the left of the pond and cross the pedestrian bridge over the river. (Note that the Kennedy monument and the Stewart Memorial Fountain will both be seen on the left. Details of these are given later in the walk.)

From directly behind the war memorial, follow a path uphill, go ahead at a crossroads, bear left at a junction and take the second path on the left. This continues uphill to the **Lord Roberts Statue** 🔢 (1916, Harry Bates). Field Marshal Lord Roberts (1832-1914) was born into a military family and served in many of the British Empire's overseas possessions. He is best known for his role in what the British call the 'Indian Mutiny'; Indians call it 'The Great Revolt'. It is also known as the 'Sepoy Mutiny' after the sepoys (the Indian soldiers) in one of the British East India Company's three armies who took part in a military revolt in 1857-8. It was brutally put down.

This very fine bronze monument shows Lord Roberts mounted on a horse and below it there are relief carvings of soldiers and horse-drawn wagons. The very fierce-looking man at the rear of the monument is *War*, the female figure at the front is *Victory* and the motto *Virtute et valore* means 'By virtue and courage'. The main inscription is quite typical of its time – art and politics often go hand in hand – and it is all about fighting for an empire and putting down rebellions. This is actually a copy of the monument erected in Calcutta in 1898, though the Indian version does not have the same inscription.

The exploits of Lord Roberts have also been commemorated by the Dundee poet William McGonagall (1830-1902) who, in his poem *General Roberts in Afghanistan*, summed up the soldier's achievements with the words:

> *Success to Lord Roberts; he's a very brave man,*
> *For he conquered the Afghans in Afghanistan,*
> *With an army about seven thousand strong,*
> *He spread death and desolation all along.*

There is a very fine view from here except when the summer foliage of the trees obscures the view to the Art Galleries and the university. Behind the statue is the Park Circus area (see p.221).

From behind the monument, turn right and follow the wide driveway. Take a path on the right that goes down to a lower-level driveway and then go over a crossroads in order to reach the **Kennedy Monument** ❺❷, which is on the left. This unusual bronze sculpture shows a Royal Bengal tigress taking a meal (a peacock) to her hungry cubs. It is by

Stewart Memorial Fountain, Kelvingrove Park

Auguste-Nicolas Cain (1867) after a drawing by Rosa Bonheur and the granite pedestal is by Mossman. This was presented to the city by a former Glaswegian John S. Kennedy of New York in 1867 and there is a replica in Central Park, New York.

Head downhill to the large and ornate **Stewart Memorial Fountain** 🔢 (1871-72, James Sellars). This magnificent fountain, sculpted by John G. Mossman, is named after Robert Stewart (1811-66), the Glasgow Lord Provost who was the driving force behind the ambitious plan to bring clean water to the city from Loch Katrine, some 64km (40 miles) away (see also p.357). The fountain is topped by a tall bronze statue of The Lady of the Lake, the subject of the poem by Sir Walter Scott (see p.84); Scott's poem and his other romantic works set in the Trossachs area helped put the lake and the surrounding district firmly on the tourist trail. Below the statue are lions and unicorns holding shields and there are roundels featuring the signs of the zodiac. Various plaques and coats of arms form the other main decorations.

A plaque declares: *To commemorate the public services of Robert Stewart of Murdostoun Lord Provost of the City of Glasgow from November 1851 till November 1854 to whose unwearied exertions the citizens are mainly indebted for the abundant water supply from Loch Katrine. This fountain was erected 1872.*

This great undertaking was done in the typically confident Victorian style, and the substantial waterworks at Milngavie (to the north of Glasgow) are still in very good condition. This bold scheme had many detractors, however, including a very prophetic warning from Frederick Penny, Professor of Chemistry at the Andersonian University, who claimed that the very pure 'soft' water which was being supplied to the city in lead pipes would result in widespread lead poisoning; it took well over a century for this danger to be fully recognised and dealt with by replacing the lead with more inert materials.

The university tower can be seen from the fountain. Head towards it to reach the **duck pond**. Pass to its left and cross the River Kelvin by a **footbridge** (1964, Ronald Walker & Co.). Once across, the park's **bandstand** (1924) is on the right. Turn left immediately after the bridge and follow the path up to Kelvin Way. Turn left.

Kelvin Way Bridge 🔢 (1913-14, Alex. B. McDonald) is now met. This single-arch sandstone bridge is adorned by four pairs of large statues designed by Paul Raphael Montford; these were commissioned in 1914 but not erected until the 1920s. The statues on the left (nearest first) are *Peace* and *War*, and *Navigation* and *Shipbuilding* ; those on the other side of the road are (nearest first) *Philosophy* and *Inspiration*, and *Commerce* and *Industry.* Each pair of figures sits aside a carved pillar topped by dolphin heads and a lampstandard.

This bold group of eight statues is one of the finest set of sculptures in the city and is well worth studying. *Peace* sits by a spinning wheel and has a child by her side. *War* is a fierce-looking character and was perhaps carved in this manner to 'celebrate' the outcome of the recently ended First World War. *Navigation*, with tiller in hand, stares out to the horizon. *Shipbuilding* holds a wooden hull in one hand and a mallet in the other. *Philosophy* poses thoughtfully while looking at a human skull. *Inspiration* holds a lute. *Commerce* is carefully looking after a bag of money. *Industry* holds a heavy sledge-hammer.

Unfortunately the bridge was hit by a bomb during the Second World War and the statue most damaged was the one representing *War*! The statue was repaired by Benno Schotz (see below).

Readers wishing a short cut to the Art Galleries should cross the bridge and take the first turn on the right.

The walk heads back up Kelvin Way towards the university. Turn left after a grassy area and enter the western side of the park. A large sculpture of **Lord Kelvin** 🟤 (1913, Archibald Macfarlane Shannon) sits in a little garden below the university tower. Kelvin (1824-1907) was born William Thomson and was the son of Glasgow University's Professor of Mathematics. He entered the university at the age of ten and became the Professor of Natural Philosophy (i.e. Physics) at the age of twenty-two. His great talent was in combining theoretical and practical science and his achievements spanned many branches of the physical sciences. He proposed the Kelvin (Absolute) temperature scale, propounded the Second Law of Thermodynamics, was a consultant on the first submarine Atlantic telegraph cable and invented many types of electrical equipment. He patented over fifty inventions and published over six hundred scientific papers, making him one of the most important and prolific scientists of his day. (See also pp.185 and 359).

Continue on the path to a sculpture of **Lord Lister** 🟤 (1924, G. H. Parkin). Lister became Professor of Surgery at Glasgow University in 1860 and later combined this with clinical work at the Royal Infirmary (see p.41). At this time, being a hospital patient could be a risky matter and *The Glasgow Herald* bemoaned the fact that 'blood poisoning and hospital gangrene were of frequent occurrence.' In Paris, Louis Pasteur had been conducting experiments on micro-organisms in wine and Lister used this important work in developing germicides to counter the sources of infections in the hospital. This led him to the use of carbolic acid in keeping wounds free of germs and his pioneering work was described by the same newspaper as heralding the science of *modern surgery* as it allowed operations to be performed far more safely.

Go ahead at the crossroads and on the left is a sculpture *The Psalmist* 🟤 by the Estonian-born Benno Schotz (1891-1986). He was a shipyard worker in Clydebank who learned sculpture in evening classes and who eventually became one of Scotland's best-known sculptors.

To the left is a little planted area and in it is a plaque to **Tom John Honeyman** 🔢 (1891–1971), best remembered in Glasgow as Director of the Art Gallery and Museum from 1939 to 1954.

Bear right and walk beside the River Kelvin, then bear right at the next junction. (This next hill can be avoided; if doing so, re-join the route just before the Dumbarton Road Bridge.) The path climbs and nears the university buildings. On the left a **weir** in the river can be seen; this provided water to drive the waterwheel at Bunhouse Mill, a little farther downstream (see p.244).

Bear left at a driveway to reach the two red-brick **Sunlight Cottages** 🔢 (1901, James Miller). A plaque explains: *These buildings are facsimiles of two cottages at Port Sunlight* [near Liverpool], *occupied by the employees of Lever Bros Limited and were presented by that company to the corporation of the city of Glasgow after the exhibition in 1901.* These charming and very English looking buildings, with their red bricks and carved timbers, are remarkably different to anything else in the area.

Bear left at the next junction and cross **Dumbarton Road Bridge** 🔢 (1800), from which there is a fine view of the university tower. It has three arches over the river and another which crosses the lade that carried water to the Bunhouse Mills. In its time this was an important crossing but it was closed in 1878 and superseded by the more modern structure alongside (this is described on p.211). The bridge's railings are rather unusual as they have gates which could be opened to allow snow cleared off the roads to be dropped into the river.

Argyle Street is now met. Kelvin Hall and the Museum of Transport (see pp. 209 and 210 respectively) are on the opposite side of the road; the route, however, bears left on a wide driveway in order to reach the rear entrance of the Art Galleries.

There are a number of monuments in this section of the park. On the right of the drive is a tree dedicated to a Greek lady **Panagiota B. Katsirea** 🔢 (1911–89) and is inscribed *to her memory and out of her love to the people of Glasgow.*

On the left is a remembrance tree below which is the **Hiroshima Memorial Plaque** 🔢 inscribed *Glasgow remembers Hiroshima. 1945-84. Planted 6th August 1984.* This commemorates the dropping of an American atomic bomb on the city of Hiroshima on 6 August 1945; nearly 80,000 died as an immediate result of the bomb while countless others died from the longer-term effects of the resulting radiation.

The **Cameronians War Memorial** 🔢 (1924, P. Lindsey Clark) is close by. This striking monument of soldiers going 'over the top' commemorates the men who died in two world wars. The battles in which they were involved are recorded on the back of the monument. The Cameronians Regiment, eventually disbanded in 1959, was named after the Covenanter supporters of Richard Cameron and were recruited from the Lanarkshire area.

The next monument is the **Normandy Veterans Association Monument** ❻❹ and was erected in 1994 *To the eternal memory of our comrades who laid down their lives in the Battle of Normandy 6th June to 20th August 1944*. On 6 June 1944 ('D Day') a huge Allied sea and airborne invasion of German-occupied France began on the beaches of Normandy; this led to the recapture of Paris on 25 August and, ultimately, to the end of the Second World War.

Just beyond the Normandy monument is the **Amnesty International Tree** ❻❺, planted in 1986 *to commemorate 25 years working for human rights*. Amnesty International is a human-rights organisation which was formed in Britain in 1961. It is now a world-wide body and won the Nobel Peace Prize in 1977.

Beyond that is the **Deir Yassin Plaque** ❻❻, unveiled in 1988 to those who died at Deir Yassin in Palestine on 9 April 1948, just five days before the state of Israel was proclaimed. Deir Yassin was an Arab village which was attacked by the Jewish Irgun organisation and the massacre of the villagers prompted a mass exodus of Arabs from the area.

Continue on the driveway in order to reach the back of the Art Galleries. To the left of the car park is the *Children of Glasgow* **Fountain** ❻❼ (1991, Michael Snowdon). This celebrates two events in Glasgow: the 1988 National Garden Festival (see p.287) and the 1990 European Year of Culture. Readers will probably have noticed squirrels in Kelvingrove Park – even this sculpture has them!

The **Kelvingrove Art Gallery and Museum** ❻❽ (1891-1901, J. W. Simpson & E. J. Milner Allen) is almost certainly the Glasgwegians' favourite building. Architects may have their views on this massive Locharbriggs sandstone building, but the locals love it, with all its flamboyant towers, turrets, spires and statues. And with its marvellous exhibits, it's a popular day out – especially on wet weekends! In better weather, the light of the setting sun lends a wonderful glow to the rich red colour of the sandstone.

In order to appreciate the exterior, walk right round the building and enter it at the northern entrance. The construction of the building was financed by the proceeds of the 1888 Exhibition (see p.197) and it allowed the city's collections to be brought together in one place. Its style has been called Hispanic Baroque but there is a mixture of influences and its design got a poor reception from the Scottish architectural profession; the fact that the winners of the prestigious architectural competition were English didn't help. Early reactions to the building included 'far too much a casino… sadly wanting in sobriety'.

It's an oft-repeated story (and for the sake of completeness, it is re-told here) that the museum was built back to front in error and that the architect committed suicide when he realised what had happened – the tale is always strenuously denied of course, but it's part of Glasgow folklore. What is true, however, is that when the building was the centrepiece of the 1901 Exhibition (see p.198), the other (temporary) buildings were erected facing the museum's rear entrance so this side assumed the role of the main entrance.

The museum has a large, tall hall in the centre with wings on either side; in both wings, the ground floor has large windows for lighting exhibits and the first floor has no windows as the upper galleries are top-lit. The southern facade has two towers and a massive porch over the broad flight of steps to the main entrance.

The building's northern side has two tall towers and a smaller central tower over the porch. The porch is the most important feature of this side and it shelters the building's main statue, the bronze sculpture *St Mungo as the Patron of Art and Music* (George Frampton). The city's patron saint (with crozier in his hand) is flanked by female figures representing *Art* (with a book) and *Music* (with an organ). Above this group is a relief sculpture *The British colonies saluting the arms of Glasgow* and the porch's two sides are decorated with *Industries of Glasgow at the court of Mercury* (east side) and *Love teaching harmony to the arts* (west side); these three reliefs are also by George Frampton. Higher up, there are carvings representing three great Greek artists: Pheidias (sculptor), Ictinus (architect) and Apelles (painter). A smaller tower on the left has sculptures entitled *Music* (with a violin) and *Architecture* (with a tapered column) while the tower on the right has *Sculpture* (with a mason's hammer) and *Painting* (with brushes, palette and a painting). These four (by Francis Derwent Wood) are part of a collection of eight similar sculptures around the building. On the north-east corner is *Religion* (by Johan Keller); she holds a model of a ship and points heavenward. On the south-east corner is *Literature* (by Edward George Bramwell); she wears a wreath and holds an open book and a quill. On the south-west corner is *Science* (by William Birnie Rhind); he is resting his elbows on the arms of a chair and nearby are books and a globe. On the north-west corner is *Commerce* (by Aristide Fabbricci); she wears a helmet and holds a model of a ship's hull.

In addition, the building's sides are engraved with the names of various great artists (in chronological order) below which are the coats of arms of the Scottish counties (in alphabetical order). Apart from all these sculptures, there are many other sculptural details which are quite delightful.

The gardens in front of the gallery's main entrance has within it a marvellously detailed three-dimensional **bronze model** of the West End. This clearly shows the glacial drumlins (hills) upon which the area is built and many prominent buildings can easily be identified. This is by Kathie Chambers and it was specifically designed for people who are visually impaired or wheelchair bound.

Inside, the three-storey main hall is cavernous, with huge lights hanging from the lavishly decorated barrel-vaulted ceiling. The hall's

Kelvingrove Art Gallery and Museum

pillars are decorated with the names and badges of Glasgow's fourteen trades (see p.51); the balcony's arches have the names of thirty-six composers on them. At the hall's northern end is a large organ which was used in the Concert Hall of the 1901 Exhibition and is still in use for regular recitals. On either side of the hall are the museum's wings which have galleries arranged around their respective open display areas. Upstairs, the first-floor galleries are linked together by corridors which lead off the central balcony that goes round three sides of the main hall.

The museum's collections were originally based on the paintings left to the city by Archibald McLellan (see p.120). Subsequently, many new items came from the foreign expeditions of well-known explorers such as Captain James Cook, Charles Darwin and David Livingstone (see p.37). In addition, with all sorts of Scottish traders, soldiers and missionaries involved in the buccaneering days of British imperial expansion, many of them avidly collected (or plundered) pieces from the colonies and later donated or sold their collections to the museum. Only a fraction of the collection can be shown at any time and so only a brief outline of the main displays can be given; indeed, some of the displays described here may vary. In addition, there are frequent temporary exhibitions, often on the ground floor or in the corridors.

The ground floor's western wing has a spectacular collection of **arms and armour**; the most important pieces are a fine example of Gothic Milanese field armour (*c.* 1450) and the imposing Greenwich field armour for a man and horse (*c.* 1550-8). While these display superb workmanship they must have been incredibly uncomfortable to wear – presumably the price to be paid for being fashion conscious. While walking through this area, look up at the first-floor arches which are decorated with the names of many famous Scots. A neighbouring gallery shows archaeological finds from Egypt (to which the museum helped finance expeditions) which includes household utensils, ornaments, various funerary items and a large granite sarcophagus of the seventh century BC. This area also has many items from Scotland. There are various prehistoric exhibits from the Stone Age and the Bronze Age, including a reconstructed burial site (of *c.* 1500-1000 BC) which was discovered in Glasgow. One very mysterious object is a large boulder decorated with cup and ring marks, a good example of an art form that was practised in many parts of Scotland over many centuries BC. Of the more recent periods represented here, there are remains of the Roman occupation (see p.180) and the Vikings.

On the ground floor's eastern wing, the main display is of **natural history**, with many examples of plants and animals from Scotland's diverse environments, as well as animals which have become extinct since the Middle Ages, usually through human activity. This is probably the best part of the museum for keeping children amused as there are lots of stuffed animals, ranging from an Indian elephant to numerous birds. The **geology** gallery is beside this and has examples of plant and animal fossils as well as samples of rocks and minerals, many of them from Scotland. The displays highlight the development of life on Earth, demonstrating how living organisms have evolved over long periods of time. These days, no museum could be complete without a few fierce-looking dinosaurs and, although Scotland never had many of these intriguing animals, a number are prominently displayed here. The wide-ranging **ethnographic collection** is nearby and many of these artefacts were collected by explorers before western influences radically changed the local people's lives. This gallery contains material from such varied places as the Pacific islands, Africa, Asia, the American plains and the Arctic. The costumes, including those used in ceremonies, are particularly good and the waterproof Eskimo suit made from seal intestines might be of interest to those visitors sheltering from the rain.

The upstairs galleries are generally devoted to art of various forms, with the collection of **paintings** being quite outstanding as many European schools of art are represented here, especially sixteenth-century Italian, seventeenth-century Dutch and nineteenth-century French, as well as numerous works by Scottish artists. There are a number of works by world-famous artists such as Rembrandt Harmensz van Rijn (*Man in armour*, 1655), Joseph M. W. Turner (*Modern Italy – the Pifferari*, 1838) and Pablo Picasso (*The flower seller*, 1901). The Scottish collection contains many interesting works from various schools. There are the dreamy landscapes of the Scottish countryside by Romantic painters such as *View of Loch Lomond* by John Knox (1778-1845), *Loch Katrine* by Alexander Nasmyth (1758-1840) and *Glencoe* by Horatio McCulloch (1805-67). In stark contrast, *The Last of the Clan* by Thomas Faed (1826-1900) has as its subject the sad and very brutal Highland Clearances of the nineteenth century when landowners moved people off the land to make way for (more profitable) sheep. There are numerous works by 'The Glasgow Boys', a group of artists who painted realistic / unromantic rural scenes and landscapes, including some by Edward A. Walton (1860-1922), Sir John Lavery (1856-1941) and Edward A. Hornel (1864-1933), amongst others. The Scottish Colourists, Francis C. B. Cadell (1883-1937), John D. Fergusson (1874-1961), Leslie Hunter (1877-1931) and Samuel J. Peploe (1871-1935) are also featured. Their collective name springs from their paintings' great splashes of colour, for example in Cadell's *Interior: the orange blind*. Some Scottish Modern Art is kept in the museum but the city's main collection is now housed in the Gallery of Modern Art (see p.89).

The **Glasgow 1900** gallery has many items in the 'Glasgow Style', particularly furniture and paintings. The furniture collection has many pieces in this very recognisable (and uncomfortable?) style, with examples by artists such as George Walton (1867-1933) and Talwin Morris (1865-1911). The best-known pieces are those by Charles Rennie Mackintosh which he designed for Kate Cranston's tea rooms (see p.123), though this is really only a very small part of the museum's holding of his furniture, especially from the tea rooms.

Other items of furniture are found elsewhere in the museum and perhaps the most interesting is a very tall wooden cabinet (*c.* 1860-5) by Alexander Thomson which he designed for his own house at 1 Moray Place (see p.323). Like his buildings, it is quite 'monumental' and it is decorated by Classical motifs similar to those used in the facades of his buildings.

The sailing trophies of Sir Thomas Lipton (see p.376) are here, including one given to him in 1930 after he had just lost the Americas Cup challenge for the fifth time, hence the amusing inscription on it: *to the gamest loser in the world of sport* ! The collection of sculpture contains many busts of well-known Scots, including one of Alexander Thomson.

ARGYLE STREET TO KELVINHALL UNDERGROUND STATION

Leave the front of the Art Galleries and cross Argyle Street to the **Kelvin Hall** ⑲. This whole block was built in 1926-7 by Thomas P. M. Somers as a massive exhibition hall and for six decades this was the venue for countless large exhibitions, conferences and the annual Christmas Carnival. During the Second World War the hall's huge floor area was put to use by the government as the country's chief factory for barrage balloons. With the opening of the SECC (see p.151) in 1985, the rear part was converted into the Museum of Transport (see p.210) and the front part of the building was converted into the **Kelvin Hall International Sports Arena**. As its name suggests, the hall can host large sporting events, including indoor athletics, as well as providing various facilities for general public use.

The hall's very grand frontage complements the Art Galleries across the road and its most imposing feature is the very long covered entrance. On either side are towers with lanterns and bronze globes; the building's wings have towers with obelisks.

Walk westwards from the Kelvin Hall and turn left at Bunhouse Road, just before Partick Bridge. This leads to the entrance of the marvellous **Museum of Transport** **⑩** .

Once inside, a turn to the left leads to a trip down memory lane as '**Kelvin Street**' has been constructed as it might have been on 9 December 1938. A Regal Cinema (still working), a Lipton grocers shop (see p.376), a chemist and a number of other shops are all here, their window displays a reminder of the goods (and their prices!) of those days. Since this is a museum of transport, it's fitting that there is also a **subway station**, complete with 'caurs' ('carriages' to non-Glaswegians) of various eras. The noise, the warm damp air and the smell of Archangel Tar (which was used to grease the cables) are missing, but this display lends real authenticity to this fascinating little street. The city's subway system (or 'Underground' as it was renamed in the 1930s) was originally constructed in the 1890s with two side-by-side tunnels 10½km (6½ miles) long which linked fifteen stations. The cars gripped a continuous cable which pulled them along at 21kph (13mph), allowing the trains to make a complete circuit in forty minutes. In 1922 Glasgow Corporation took over the (then bankrupt) privately owned system and in 1935 it was electrified. Nothing major happened until the 1970s – by which time the original carriages were well past their best – and in 1980 the present system, with its 'Clockwork Orange' carriages, was inaugurated. When originally built, the route was very convenient for a big proportion of the city's population, but demographic changes since then have meant that it now serves a relatively small part of the city.

The ground floor's main exhibition area features many massive **railway locomotives** together with trams, trolleybuses, buses, fire engines, farm vehicles, horse-drawn carriages and numerous commercial vehicles. A number of the locomotives date from the nineteenth century and are resplendent in their colourful liveries. Glasgow's locomotive industry started in 1831 but it was not until 1861, when Neilson & Co. moved to Springburn (see p.346), that that area was established as the hub of the industry. With ready supplies of coal and iron, the city was well-placed to dominate this specialist industry; in addition, steam engines had already been used for pumping out coal mines for a long time, allowing local manufacturers to gain expertise in the new technologies. After various changes in the industry, the North British Locomotive Co. was formed in 1903 and was soon to become the largest locomotive manufacturer in Europe, producing about four hundred locomotives a year, exporting many of them all over the world. Up to its demise in 1962 the firm built an astonishing total of over

28,000 locomotives, including some of Britain's most famous, such as the beautifully streamlined Gresley A1 Pacifics, the trainspotter's dream. The collection is a great testament to the skills of the engineers who designed and built these wonderful locomotives. Much nicer than today's rather characterless machines!

Beside this is the display of **motor cars**, ranging from very early examples to modern family cars and 'exotic' vehicles. Although no cars are made in Scotland now, there was once an important car industry and there are gleaming examples of cars made by the Scottish firms of Arrol-Johnston, Argyll, Beardmore and Albion, the last two being from Glasgow.

Upstairs, there is a large collection of **motorbikes and cycles**. The latter include very early examples, including an 1845 copy of the world's first pedal cycle, invented by the Scot Kirkpatrick Macmillan in 1839-40.

The Clyde Room houses a wonderful collection of **model ships**, most of them scale representations of ships built in local shipyards (see p.153). There are lots of fascinating craft, including many paddle-steamers, some of which were used for trips 'Doon the watter' (see p.146); one of them, PS *Waverley* (1946, A. & J. Inglis of Glasgow) is still based in Glasgow (see p.149). One strange craft worth looking at is the flat-bottomed *Livadia*, which is described on p.295. Massive naval ships are on display such as the battle-cruiser *Hood* (1920, John Brown), at the time the world's largest warship. On a more peaceful note is the well-known tea-clipper *Cutty Sark* (1869, Scott & Linton of Dumbarton), now berthed at Greenwich near London. The most famous ships here are the three 'Queens'; these three passenger ships are famous throughout the world and were built by John Brown's shipyard in nearby Clydebank. They are *Queen Mary* (1936), now berthed in Long Beach, California, *Queen Elizabeth* (1940), sadly sunk in Hong Kong harbour in 1972 and *Queen Elizabeth II* (1967), better known as the *QE2* and still an occasional visitor to the Clyde.

After leaving the museum, turn right and walk back up to Argyle Street. Turn left in order to cross the River Kelvin by means of the **Partick Bridge** **71** (1876-8, R. Bell & D. Miller). This important bridge has a wide cast-iron arch and a small tunnel to cope with occasional flood water. Although it is more of a functional bridge than a highly decorated one, it does have the coats of arms of Glasgow and Partick in its spandrels as it was built during the time of the independent burgh of Partick (see p.175). The river was an old boundary between Glasgow and Partick so the road on the western side of the bridge is called Dumbarton Road as this is the modern route to that town.

The stretch of river downstream of the bridge used to support many mills and the history of some of them is given on pp.243 and 244.

The building on the left after the bridge is the **Partick Sewage Pumping Station** **72** (1904, Alex. B. McDonald) which raises foul water so that it can flow downwards to the sewage works. Glasgow has always been proud of its waterworks and this neat building fits well into the idea of making the most utilitarian of buildings look interesting. The Victorian architects and engineers took great pride in their achievements and the councils of those days spent money on showing off the well-designed artefacts of municipal enterprise.

On the northern side of the road is an ornate gatehouse and an arched gateway which leads to the university. The next opening is the main entrance to the **Western Infirmary** ⑦ . With the establishment of the university at Gilmorehill, it was decided to build a new teaching hospital which could also serve the new and rapidly growing western suburbs. John Burnet Snr designed the original (1871) buildings but few parts of these remain. It was planned to have 350 beds, but patient numbers were limited to 300 so that, according to the *Glasgow News* in 1874, 'different parts of the house may periodically be vacated in succession and undergo suitable purification'. The present main building (1965-74, Keppie, Henderson & Partners) has around it a bewildering variety of smaller buildings, with the most notable ones being on Dumbarton Road (see below) and Church Street (see p.175).

The hospital has had close ties with medical education since its establishment and much important work has been done here by many eminent doctors. For example, the hospital's cancer unit is named after one of them, Sir George Beatson (1848-1933), in recognition of his pioneering work on the disease at the beginning of the twentieth century. The unit was previously based in Garnethill (see p.128).

The interesting Victorian building a short distance to the left of the hospital entrance is the former **Anderson's College Medical School** ⑦ (1888-9, James Sellars (completed by John Keppie)). The college's history can be traced back to 1799 when it was a faculty of Anderson's University (see p.44) and a rival of the more prestigious medical school in Glasgow University. By the middle of the nineteenth century it was so successful that it had more medical students than the older school. It left the Andersonian in 1887 and became an independent college based in this building; in 1947 it became part of Glasgow University.

This Italian Renaissance building has a large and intricate carving which is the work of Pittendrigh MacGillivray. It depicts a patient having his pulse taken by a man whilst nine others look on. The present hospital isn't so well staffed these days. Another carving gives the name of the building and the date *1889*.

On the left side of the road stands the former **Roost Bar** ⑦ (1899-1900, James Hoey Craigie), now the Fitter & Firkin. This has an exceptionally attractive Art Nouveau wooden frontage.

Follow Dumbarton Road past Partick Cross. **Kelvin Hall Underground Station** ❶ is on the right and this marks the end of the walk.

The West End and the Botanic Gardens

A walk which skirts the university area, goes through a part of the residential West End and then the famous Botanic Gardens.

Trinity College on Woodlands Hill

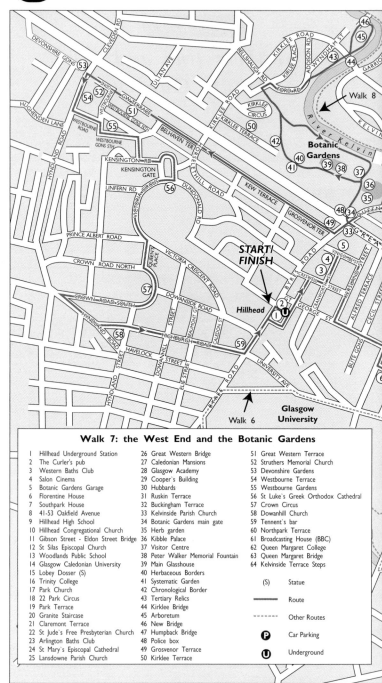

Walk 7: the West End and the Botanic Gardens

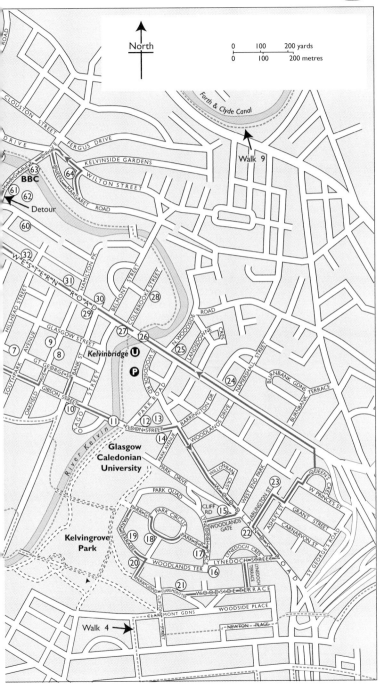

North

| 0 | 100 | 200 yards |
| 0 | 100 | 200 metres |

Forth & Clyde Canal

Walk 9

CLOUSTON STREET

ROAD

DRIVE

FERGUS DRIVE

KELVINSIDE GARDENS

MARGARET DRIVE

63

64

QUEEN MARGARET ROAD

WILTON STREET

BBC

61

62

← Detour

60

W·E·S·T·E·R·N

32

ROAD

31

30

HAMILTON PK

BELMONT STREET

COLEBROOK STREET

28

29

ROAD

27

26

N. WOODSIDE

LANSDOWNE CRES

MARSHALL STREET

HILLHEAD STREET

GLASGOW STREET

25

7

PARK AVENUE

9

8

BANK STREET

OTAGO STREET

Kelvinbridge Ⓤ

Ⓟ

24

BURNBANK GDNS TERRACE

SOUTHPARK AVE

OAKFIELD AVE

GT GEORGE ST

GIBSON STREET

WOODSIDE RD

PARK RD

BARRINGTON DR

BURNBANK TERRACE

10

ELDON STREET

11

12 13

14

WOODLANDS DRIVE

River Kelvin

Glasgow Caledonian University

BANK AVENUE

PARK DRIVE

WILLOWBANK CRES

WEST END PARK

23

QUEEN'S CRES

W. PRINCES ST

PARK QUAD

PARK CIRCUS

CLIFF RD

15

WOODLANDS GATE

ARLINGTON ST

GRANT STREET

ASHLEY ST

CARNARVON ST

ST GEORGE'S ROAD

Kelvingrove Park

PARK CIRCUS PL

PARK TERRACE

19

18

PARK CIRCUS

PARK GATE

17

22

LYNEDOCH CRES

LYNEDOCH STREET

LYNEDOCH TERRACE

20

WOODLANDS TER

16

PARK GDNS

21

WOODSIDE TERRACE

WOODSIDE PLACE

CLIFTON STREET

CLAREMONT GDNS

Walk 4 →

NEWTON PLACE

Main places of interest	St Mary's Episcopal Cathedral **24**
	Botanic Gardens 34 - 47 (park)
	Great Western Terrace 51
	(by Alexander Thomson)
	Dowanhill Church **58**
	(former church; interior by Daniel Cottier)
Circular/linear	circular
Starting point	Hillhead Underground Station **1**
Finishing point	Hillhead Underground Station **1**
Distance	12 km (7.5 miles)
Terrain	level pavements and paths; steep slopes on Woodlands Hill; slopes of varying steepness in the Botanic Gardens (the steepest can be avoided)
Public transport	Hillhead Underground Station St George's Cross Underground Station Kelvinbridge Underground Station
Sections	Byres Road to Woodlands Hill Woodlands Hill Woodlands Hill to the Botanic Gardens Botanic Gardens Botanic Gardens to Byres Road via Hyndland Detour: Kelvinside Parish Church to Kelvinside Terrace Steps
Architects	Thomson: 41-53 Oakfield Avenue **8** Great Western Terrace **51** Westbourne Terrace **54** Northpark Terrace **60** Kelvinside Terrace Steps **64** Mackintosh: former Queen Margaret College **62**
Nearby walks	4, 6, 8
Refreshments	Byres Road; Gibson Street; Great Western Road (before the Botanic Gardens); Botanic Gardens; Cottier Theatre (former Downhill Church)
Notes	Take care not to get lost when negotiating all the turns in the route between Westbourne Terrace and Hyndland Road. Be aware of safety advice (see p.16) as the Botanic Gardens can be very quiet at times.

BYRES ROAD TO WOODLANDS HILL

Hillhead Underground Station ❶ is on **Byres Road**, the hub of what might be called Glasgow's 'Latin Quarter' because of the university's influence. This is also the West End's main shopping street and has many interesting shops along it and in the side streets.

Coming out of the Underground station, turn right and walk to the nearby eighteenth-century building which houses **The Curler's** pub ❷. It takes its name from the curling pond that was once sited across the road and is one of the contenders for the title of 'oldest pub in Glasgow'. Tradition has it that one day King Charles II (1630-85) came riding by and stopped at the original inn; although it was closed the landlord was sought out and called upon to entertain the king's party. His hospitality was obviously superb as the inn was rewarded with a Royal Charter enabling it to be open day and night, seven days a week – in perpetuity!

The upstairs bar is called 'Jock Tamson's'. The phrase 'we are all 'Jock Tamson's Bairns" is an expression of our common humanity and is often used to bring a haughty person back down to earth. A mural in this bar depicts many of the pub's notable clientele, including the poet Hugh MacDiarmid who stayed in Glasgow in the 1930s and 40s. **Hugh MacDiarmid** was the pen-name of Christopher Murray Grieve (1892-1978), one of the most influential Scottish writers of the twentieth century. His complex life spanned many activities and his work as a teacher, journalist and ship's engineer gave him some of the insights he used in his poetry. While his work analysed the Scottish psyche and reflected his nationalist and socialist philosophies, he was also a political activist; as well as being a founder member of the Scottish National Party he also stood as a Communist Party candidate in 1963.

Since his portrait appears in a pub, it may be appropriate to quote from his essay 'The dour drinkers of Glasgow' (1952): 'The majority of Glasgow pubs are for connoisseurs of the morose, for those who relish the element of degradation in all boozing and do not wish to have it eliminated by the introduction of music, modernistic fitments, arty effects, or other extraneous devices whatsoever.' Fortunately, they're a lot cheerier now.

The mural was the work of the artist Alasdair Gray (1934–) who, with the success of novels such as *Lanark* (1981), is also one of the country's best-known authors.

Walk back down Byres Road and go past the Underground entrance. Turn left at the narrow **Ashton Lane** which leads into a cobbled area which has a number of bars and restaurants. This is very West End.

Turn left and follow Great George Lane. Cross Great George Street and follow Creswell Lane, along which is De Courcey's Arcade (on the right), in which there is an interesting collection of small shops. Turn right at Creswell Street and then left at Cranworth Street. The long building on the left is the **Western Baths Club** ❸ (1876–81, Clarke & Bell). The exterior of the oldest part is Gothic in style and the main entrance has three arches with carved female heads in the spandrels. The southern extension (the W. M. Mann Building) is designed to match the cinema at the end of the street.

The former **Salon Cinema** ❹, originally the Hillhead Picture House (1913, Brand & Lithgow), has its entrance on Vinicombe Street. There is a large dome over the entrance and above the door is a 'swagged' plaster decoration flanked by lions' heads. The building is an early example of a reinforced concrete structure and the cinema's interior is generally regarded as a 'classic' of its age. Unfortunately it is now closed.

Opposite the cinema entrance is the former **Botanic Gardens Garage** ❺ (1912, D.V. Wylie). This is Art Deco in style with large windows and a green and white facade made of faience (glazed terracotta blocks).

From the cinema climb Vinicombe Street, walking past a variety of tenements, four or five storeys high. Turn right at Kersland Street and then left in order to climb the steep Great George Street. Turn right at Hillhead Street, heading towards the university tower (see p.178). This is the summit of the **Hillhead** district, which was originally developed from the 1820s onwards, and has a remarkably well-preserved mixture of villas, terraces and tenements. When many of these were built, Hillhead was well outside Glasgow's boundary but, with the establishment of the university here in the 1860s, it soon became an integral part of the city. Although it became an independent burgh in 1869, this status lasted only until 1891. Now, many of the buildings in this part of Hillhead have been taken over by the university and the names of the various departments are displayed on the doors.

The handsome four-storey tenements on the right were built around 1890, well after the villa at the junction with Gibson Street, **Florentine House** ❻ (c. 1828). This was one of the earliest buildings in the Hillhead development and is presently used by the university's Psychology Department.

Turn left at Gibson Street and carry on to Southpark Avenue. The large building on the left is **Southpark House** ❼ (c. 1850), a double villa with a central Doric portico. This is now the university's Media Services Department.

Charles Rennie Mackintosh lived at 78 Southpark Avenue (to the right of this junction) from 1906 to 1914. The building was demolished in the 1960s but its interiors have been recreated in the Mackintosh House at the Hunterian Art Gallery (see p.194).

Continue on Gibson Street and turn next left in order to see **41–53 Oakfield Avenue** ❽ (1865, Alexander Thomson). This is a fairly short terrace (called Eton Terrace), with pavilions at either end which have been likened to temples. The six central houses are linked in pairs by pilastered porches and at the first-storey level the niches between the windows are filled with carved anthemia. Thomson included many of his well-known classical motifs in this building and used a Greek key pattern below the first-storey windows to link the whole terrace together.

Opposite this is **Hillhead High School** ❾ (1928-31, E. G. Wylie), a red-brick building laid out in the shape of a butterfly. It was built with its corridors open to the elements – even those which face south-west, from where most of Glasgow's weather comes!

Head back along Oakfield Avenue, turn left at Great George Street and right at Bank Street to reach the busy junction with Gibson Street. The last shop on the right was a bookshop in the late 1960s; one day a young student, presumably wanting to write an essay on Thomas More's great work, rather loudly enquired of one of the staff 'Excuse me, but has *Utopia* arrived?'.

Turn left and walk down Gibson Street. On the southern side of the street is the French Gothic former **Hillhead Congregational Church** ❿ (1895, H. & D. Barclay).

Continue downhill and across the **Gibson Street – Eldon Street Bridge** ⓫ (1895, Formans & McCall) over the River Kelvin (see p.242). This cast-iron arched bridge carries the Glasgow coat of arms in both sets of spandrels.

An entrance to Kelvingrove Park (see p.197) is soon passed on the right as the road becomes Eldon Street. Pass to the right of **St Silas Episcopal Church** ⓬ (1864, John Honeyman) which has a large rose window above the doorway.

Beyond that is the former **Woodlands Public School** ⓭ (1882, Robert Dalglish), a blond sandstone building in Jacobean style with an interesting tower. To its left is an 1896 red sandstone Italianate addition, the exterior of which is less elaborate than that of the earlier building; however, its interior has the 'classic' Glasgow school design of having its first-floor classrooms arranged around a wide central balcony lit by a massive skylight.

On the right hand side of the road is the Park campus of the **Glasgow Caledonian University** ⓮ (see p.104). The main building is at the back of this complex and was originally the Queen's College (*c.* 1905, Cowan & Watson), the College of Domestic Science, popularly known as the 'Dough School'.

Go ahead at the busy junction, following Woodlands Road. On the right hand side of the road (at the far end of a grassy area) is a very unusual sculpture – of the cartoon character *Lobey Dosser* ⓯ (Tony Morrow

Lobey Dosser — the world's only two-legged equestrian statue

and Nick Gillon). The inscription reads: *Statue erected by public subscription on May 1, 1992, to the memory of Bud Neil 1911-1970 cartoonist and poet Creator of Lobey Dosser, Sheriff of Calton Creek, his trusty steed El Fideldo, resident villain Rank Bajin, and many other characters.* This is typical Glaswegian humour and the name of this hero can be translated as someone who sleeps on a tenement close landing (although a lot is lost in the translation!) The statue shows the handcuffed villain being brought to justice by the sheriff.

The cartoon first appeared in the Glasgow *Evening Times* in 1949 and twenty adventures were printed. It developed something of a cult following, hence the erection of what is claimed to be the only two-legged equestrian statue in the world. Readers requiring more information might care to retire to the statue's 'visitors' centre' – the Halt Bar across the road – for 'a wee refreshment'.

Turn right at Woodlands Gate and climb Woodlands Hill.

WOODLANDS HILL

The **Park** area on Woodlands Hill is well known as a spectacular example of Victorian town planning on a grand scale; indeed, many architects consider it to be one of Britain's finest areas of Victorian architecture. It was designed in the mid-nineteenth century by Charles Wilson, whose intention was to have a central circus at the top of the hill surrounded by a series of outward-facing terraces, not all of which were eventually built. Wilson designed the general plan of the area as well as the exteriors of a number of the houses. These were all exceptionally high-quality mansions built for the rich, many of whom were fleeing westwards to escape the noise of the city centre. The finest part of the district is the central Park Circus which is at the crown of the hill – the best view of this is from Kelvin Way Bridge (see p.202). Not many people live here now as most of the buildings have been taken over as offices and consequently the streets are jam-packed with cars during weekdays. In contrast, it is wonderfully quiet in the evenings and at the weekends and this is the best time to savour the grand architecture.

Walk up Woodlands Gate and go left at Lynedoch Place, heading towards the tall and elegant tower which stands above the former **Trinity College** ⓰ (1856-7, Charles Wilson). Originally built as a college for the Free Church of Scotland, its three towers are so prominent on the Glasgow skyline that the building has often been described as the city's equivalent of Tuscany's San Gimignano. The main tower has a balcony which must have one of the city's most marvellous views. The original entrance to the church is marked by two side towers, their height emphasised by the slope of the road and the four pairs of tall Corinthian columns. The church suffered a disastrous fire in 1903 and was later rebuilt as a library. The bulk of the two-storey college is well lit by its many windows, with those of the upper storey being well ornamented. The building has now been converted into houses and offices.

The painted tower of the former **Park Church** ⓱ (1856-8, John Thomas Rochead) stands to the north-west of Trinity. The rest of the church was demolished in 1968 and replaced by a very ugly office block.

Pass to the right of the church and follow Park Circus Place up to Park Circus. Turn left and follow the curve of the circus.

The beautifully designed Italian Renaissance **Park Circus** (1857-8, Charles Wilson), with its central garden, is generally unspoiled – save for the myriad of cars parked here during the day. The three-storey houses were decorated to their owners' liking (and means) and many of the houses still have their original features intact, including some very fine plasterwork. The plan is oval, not circular, with the northern side composed of a long unbroken terrace, curved at the ends and straight in the centre. As with many the buildings in the Park area, the circus' cast-iron railings are particularly fine.

The most celebrated interior in the circus is at **22 Park Circus** ⑱ (1872-4, Charles Wilson and James Boucher), now used by Glasgow City Council as a Marriage Suite. It is often easy to spot this building by the confetti on the pavement outside. It was originally built for Walter Macfarlane (see p.64) and no expense was spared in creating a truly extravagant interior. Walk to the back of the building to see the cast-iron canopy in order to get some idea of the quality of work produced by Macfarlane's ironworks.

Inside, the decoration is, to put it mildly, sumptuous, with magnificent plasterwork (especially the ceilings and cornices) and woodwork (notably around the fireplaces). Indeed, many would argue that this is the most amazing house interior in the whole of the city. The ground floor is Italianate in style and consists of a long arcade with saucer-shaped domes supported on highly decorated columns; ornate plasterwork fills all the spaces available. The upstairs landing has a forest of fluted Corinthian columns supporting galleries and above them is a cast-iron framed dome decorated with painted glass panels.

Continue walking round Park Circus and turn left at Park Gate. The equestrian statue of Lord Roberts will be seen straight ahead (see p.200) and from it there is a good view over Kelvingrove Park to the university.

Turn left at **Park Terrace** ⑲ (1855, Charles Wilson) to pass along another curved terrace of big houses, these being French Renaissance in style. This was the first use of this style in the city, and the double-storeyed bay windows, the steep mansard roof and dormer windows were later used in many other Glasgow buildings. To add a bit more interest to the individual houses, every third house juts out a little and is a bit taller than its neighbours.

One interior of note is number 3, the former home of Sir James Bain of Crofthead (1817-98), a one-time Lord Provost. Its drawing room is particularly well decorated and features a remarkable amount of gold leaf. The Youth Hostel is at numbers 7-8.

Turn right at Park Street South and descend the **Granite Staircase** ⑳ (1854, Charles Wilson) to the edge of Kelvingrove Park. This steep staircase has three flights of steps and was designed as a grand entrance from the park into the circus. The tall flat-topped piers were intended as plinths for statues but these were never made.

Turn left to follow Park Gardens and turn left again at Clifton Street in order to see the mews buildings in Park Gardens Lane, just behind Park Gardens. Retrace your steps to Park Gardens and turn left to continue on the terraces, the next one being **Claremont Terrace** ㉑ (1842-7, John Baird I). Number 6 is Beresford House, originally called Claremont

Cottage; this was the first building on this street and the others were added later. These were built on a slightly less grand scale but with similar doorways flanked by Ionic columns above which are very attractive first-floor cast-iron balconies.

Walk along Woodside Terrace and turn left at Lynedoch Terrace. Then turn right at Lynedoch Street in order to reach Woodlands Road.

WOODLANDS HILL TO THE BOTANIC GARDENS

Turn left at Woodlands Road and follow it to **St Jude's Free Presbyterian Church** 22 (1874-5, John Burnet). This is an attractive church, in the northern French Gothic style, with lots of carvings clearly visible from the pavement. Look for the medieval-style water spouts, carved dogs, plants, and an angel and some small animals above the north door. High above the street, four apostles shelter beneath canopies at the base of the spire.

As with many important buildings, an architectural competition was established for the church's design. Burnet served as an assessor but as none of the entries were deemed suitable, he took on the job himself, using ideas from the competition's entries!

Turn right at Arlington Street, heading into the **Woodlands** district. At the bottom of the road is the **Arlington Baths Club** 23 (1869-71, John Burnet), one of Britain's first swimming clubs. This was originally a single-storey building and was extended in 1893 and 1902.

Turn right at Grant Street, left at Ashley Street, right at West Princes Street and left at Queen's Crescent. On the right is a little park with many mature trees and an ornamental fountain. Turn left at Melrose Street. This leads to **Great Western Road** where a left turn should be made; this long and important road is followed to the busy junction with Byres Road. The city's most impressive major thoroughfare, it started as a toll route authorised by a special Act of Parliament in 1836. Its construction allowed the important suburbs of the West End to be developed as well as providing a new route from Glasgow to Dumbarton, Loch Lomond and the western Highlands. In this particular area the road has a number of interesting small shops, many of which reflect Woodlands' cosmopolitan nature and its proximity to the university. One novel sight at this end of the road is that some of the side streets have been blocked off using concrete bollards which have been decorated with colourful mosaics. The names of the designers (some of whom are five or six years old) are engraved on individual brass plaques.

The first building of note on Great Western Road is on the right, **St Mary's Episcopal Cathedral** 24 (1871-4, Sir George Gilbert Scott), originally built in Early English style as a parish church. The spire was completed by Scott's son, John Oldrid Scott, in 1893. The position of the tower is rather unusual, being in the angle between the transept and the chancel, and it is decorated with two sets of statues.

The lower set comprises four bishops of Glasgow: Trower (who built this church), Leighton (who fulfilled his frequently stated wish to die in an inn), Turnbull (who founded Glasgow University) and Jocelyn (who built Glasgow Cathedral and who can be seen holding a model of it). The upper set, just at the base of the spire, is of four saints: St Mungo (see p.415), St Andrew (see p.41), St Margaret (*c.* 1046-93, the wife of the Scottish king Malcolm Canmore) and St George (who is standing over a rather diminutive dragon).

The bright interior has many features unusual for a cathedral, especially the painted sky (full of stars) on the roof at the crossing. The chancel, which is reached through a delicate wrought-iron screen, has a triptych by Phoebe Traquair (1852-1936), one of the country's best-known Arts and Crafts artists. To the side of the chancel is St Anne's Chapel which has some colourful modern murals by Gwyneth Leech. The church's timber roof and stained-glass windows are also worthy of note.

Lansdowne Parish Church ㉕ (1862-3, John Honeyman) is the next church on the right. This has been described by the architectural historians Gomme and Walker as 'one of the best Gothic Revival churches in Glasgow', and was built for a wealthy congregation who could afford such a splendid building. It has the most slender church spire in Glasgow, which makes for a wonderful addition to the West End skyline. The porch, which faces the River Kelvin, is flanked by medallions sculpted by William Mossman while the rest of the porch was carved by James Shanks. Look out for the winged beast on either side of the porch.

The church has a cruciform-shaped interior with fine woodwork and splendid stained-glass windows. One of its most unusual features are the boxed-in pews which are reached, not from the central aisle, but from side aisles and by way of numbered private doors; a form of segregation.

Great Western Road now passes Kelvinbridge Underground Station (on the left) and crosses **Great Western Bridge** ㉖ (1889-91, R. Bell & D. Miller), below which flows the River Kelvin (see p.242) on its way to the River Clyde. There's been a river crossing here for centuries as this was the route taken by the bishops on their way from the Cathedral to their country retreat in Partick. The present bridge, the third on this site, is large and impressive and has large cast-iron arches over the river. A plaque on the bridge indicates it was opened on 29 September 1891. Of particular interest are the three badges decorating the bridge's inside parapets. On the upstream side are the arms of Glasgow and Lanarkshire (which has a double-headed eagle, a knight's helmet, a coat of arms and the motto *Vigilantia* ('Watchfulness'). On the downstream side is the crest of Hillhead with a red lion and the motto *Je maintiendrai* ('I shall maintain').

The River Kelvin and Great Western Bridge

The bridge is seen to best advantage from beside the river. To get there, cross the bridge and descend the steps on the downstream (i.e. left) side; from here it can be seen that the outside of the bridge has the same three badges as the inside parapets. The bridge also carries the huge pipes which bring water from Loch Katrine (see p.202) and these can be seen slung below the bridge's deck.

The flat area on the downstream side of Great Western Bridge was the site of Kelvinbridge Railway Station (see p.246). This was on a route between the West End and the city centre, and the entrance to the former railway tunnel can still be seen going below the next building of interest, the charming **Caledonian Mansions** ㉗ (1895, James Miller) which was also built for the Caledonian Railway Company. This symmetrical building is in the Arts and Crafts style and its two end turrets (with their ogee domes) and the variation in window styles make this a very distinctive building. Many Glasgow buildings limit their decoration to the main facade, but here the interest continues round both sides and is particularly impressive at the rear, with an attractive first-floor access balcony.

On the opposite side of the road stands one of the city's few private schools, **Glasgow Academy** ㉘ (1878, H. & D. Barclay). These architects designed many schools in Glasgow but this is rather more elaborate than their usual style. Its main block is set some distance back from the road so to get a better view go first right after the bridge at Colebrook Street, on the way passing the school's war memorial (1924, A. N. Paterson). The main building has some interesting features, including the tall first-floor colonnades with their recessed windows, above which are finely carved faces. The school was originally set up in

1848 in Elmbank Street (see p.137) and its motto (*Serva fidem*) means 'Keep the faith'.

Continue on Great Western Road. The junction with Bank Street is dominated by the **Cooper's Building** ㉙ (1886, R. Duncan), so-called because it was built as a 'high class' grocers' shop of that name. This very individual building is in French Renaissance style and is topped by a corner circular clock tower, flamboyantly sporting an observation platform with a cast-iron balustrade and a tall cupola. It is now a pub.

In stark contrast, on the opposite side of Great Western Road is the Art Deco **Hubbards** ㉚ (frontage: 1929, James Lindsay). This is also now a pub, but it was originally built for Walter Hubbard, *family baker and confectioner*, as a shop and restaurant. Its fascia is in glazed terracotta and further decoration is provided by the first-floor's leaded windows and the unusual rooftop railing. This area has many old and (uncharted!) mineworkings, and when originally constructed in 1893, the architect was presumably not confident that the site could support the weight of a heavier building, hence the fact that it is only two storeys high.

The style of housing on either side of the road soon changes. Instead of fairly plain (but well-built) tenements, the architecture becomes a bit more grand, with terraces separated from the main road by a raised driveway, originally built for horse carriages. The first of these terraces on the right is **Ruskin Terrace** ㉛ (*c.* 1855-8). The overall design changes along the terrace, with the nicest part being the eastern end, the flank of which (in Hamilton Park Avenue) is four storeys high and has an elaborate staircase.

Buckingham Terrace ㉜ (1852-8, John Thomas Rochead) is the next terrace on the right. The long eastern end is three storeyed and contains tenement flats. This section of the terrace is flanked by projecting pavilions and is decorated with a first-floor cast-iron balcony.

At the junction with Byres Road the elaborate gateway to the Botanic Gardens can be seen at the north-west corner of the crossroads. Important junctions like this deserve substantial buildings and on the left hand side of Great Western Road stands the former **Kelvinside Parish Church** ㉝ (1862, J. J. Stevenson), now the Glasgow Bible College. It has a number of interesting features, including a tall corner tower with a pyramidal spire. The tower is joined onto the western end of the church the apse of which is decorated with windows of various shapes.

A detour starts from here (see p.235). If the detour is not being followed then cross the junction of Great Western Road and Byres Road and enter the Botanic Gardens.

Botanic Gardens

There has been a long history of botanic gardens in the city, with the first being the Physic Garden (1705) in the Old College (see p.32). In 1817 gardens were established near Sauchiehall Street by the Royal Botanic Institution of Glasgow which had strong links with the university; indeed, much of their success was due to Sir William Hooker (1785-1865), the Professor of Botany. However, the rapid industrial-isation of that area made the site unsuitable and in 1839 this plot of land in the West End was purchased and the glasshouses and plants were transferred. It soon became a popular place with West Enders and in 1854 Hugh Macdonald (see p.378) noted that 'During the season, these spacious and well-conducted gardens are generally largely attended by the rank and fashion of our city.' The Institution was a private body and the gardens were for the benefit of the members, but the general public were allowed in on Saturdays for one shilling and on occasions the gardens were 'thrown open to the Working Classes on the payment of one penny each.'

In the 1870s the Kibble Palace (see below) was brought here but by the 1880s the Institution was very short of money and in 1887 Glasgow Corporation took the gardens over, even though they were outside the city's boundary. It was opened as a park in 1891 and since then the essential purposes of the gardens have been maintained, the links with the university are strong and they still act as an important reference collection (all the plants are tagged with their Latin names).

The **main gate** ❸❹ has very fine cast-iron gates bearing the city's coat of arms, beyond which are two brick houses erected in 1904. Bear to the right, heading towards the domed glasshouse called the Kibble Palace.

Turn right immediately before the palace and a small **pond** will be seen on the right. This has some lovely water lilies floating on it during the summer months.

Between the pond and the palace is a **herb garden** ❸❺ in which various herbs and plants used as medicines are grown. Many of the plants in old remedies have been used for hundreds of years and several still form the basis of some modern drugs. A number of the plants have remarkable properties ascribed to them, for example, a plaque informs that the humble lavender *relaxes spasms, helps the digestion and peripheral circulation, lowers fevers, has anti-depressant effects and is antiseptic.* And it smells nice too!

The cast-iron sundial in this area was made in the early nineteenth century and stands on a millstone taken from a flint mill that once worked nearby.

Return to the main drive, turn right and head into the **Kibble Palace** ❸❻ (James Boucher and James Cousland), a wonderful glasshouse which was originally built in 1865 at the Coulport home of John Kibble (1818-94). It was re-erected here in 1873 and is slightly bigger that the original

Coulport structure; the main dome is 45m (146ft) in diameter and 13m (43ft) high and this is connected by a glazed passageway to a smaller dome 15m (50ft) in diameter and 10m (34ft) high. For a few years it was used for promenade concerts – the advert for the first concert proclaimed that it could hold *upwards of 6,000 persons* – and events such as the university's rectorial addresses by Benjamin Disraeli and William Ewart Gladstone. In 1881 it was converted from being 'The Kibble Crystal Art Palace and Royal Conservatory' into a Plant House and is now one of the few remaining world-class nineteenth-century glasshouses. The palace now houses a collection of plants from the Temperate areas of the world and further interest comes from eight marble statues. The building houses the National Collection of Tree Ferns.

Inside the entrance, the first open area has a pond below a glass dome and to the left is the warm and humid Tropicarium. The statues here are *King Robert of Sicily* by G. H. Paulin (left) and *Cain* (Roscoe Mullins) (right). A broad passageway leads past plants from Southern Africa to *Eve* (Scipio Todalini) and the main dome. All the plants are labelled and their country of origin is given. The eye is soon drawn to the mass of ferns and tall palms which gives the whole space a jungle-like appearance. Heading clockwise round the dome, the plants are from the Canaries (left), North America (left) and the Mediterranean (right). The *Sisters of Bethany* (Warrington Wood) is then found on the right. The plants at this point are from South America (left) and Temperate Asia (right). *Stepping Stones* (W. Thornycroft) and *The Elf* (Sir Goscombe John) are then both met on the left. Both sides of the path now feature plants from New Zealand. The *Nubian Slave* (A. Rossetti) and *Ruth* (Giovanne Ciniselli) are then on the right. Finally, all the plants from here to *Eve* are from Australia.

The Kibble Palace in the Botanic Gardens

Leave the palace, turn right and follow the perimeter of the building until the **Visitor Centre** ㊲, which is in a large sandstone building, is seen on the left. This has exhibition areas which provide a lot of information about the gardens.

Leave the Visitor Centre, turn right and pass the Kibble Palace. Take the second carriageway on the right. On the left is a large grassy area which is usually mobbed by sunworshipping locals on hot summer days. Head towards the main glasshouse, passing (on the right) the pink granite **Peter Walker Memorial Fountain** ㊳, erected by 'ZMW' (his widow Zoe McNaught Walker) in 1906. It even has drinking vessels for dogs!

The **Main Glasshouse** ㊴ is next on the right. The glasshouse's first door leads into the Conservatory which has seasonal displays of plants. Go straight ahead and loop round the much-acclaimed Orchid Collection. Many of these interesting plants live on decaying vegetation and some have aerial roots to absorb atmospheric moisture. Back in the Conservatory, turn right and go through a series of glasshouses which hold wide-ranging collections. The first is for Temperate Plants and includes some fascinating carnivorous plants. Next is the Succulent House, featuring plants from hot, dry regions. These range from the small and aptly named Stone Plants to some large cacti which almost reach roof level. This leads to the large and densely packed Palm House. And yes, it *is* possible to grow bananas in Glasgow! Farther on is the Tropical Economic House which has examples of plants used for food, dyes, medicine, timber and clothes. The next area is for the non-flowering Tropical Ferns, many of them ground-hugging plants from hot, moist regions. The last glasshouse in this row contains the large and widely recognized National Collection of Begonias which contains examples from many different countries. Turn right to enter the Tropical Flowering House, containing many plants which are popular with local gardeners. Beyond that is the last glasshouse, the Tropical Pond House which contains floating plants including very large water lilies.

Leave the Main Glasshouse, turn right and head uphill. This wide path runs between the two **Herbaceous Borders** ㊵ which feature plants which die back each year but whose roots survive in the soil.

Bear left just before the start of the left hand herbaceous border and enter the **Systematic Garden** ㊶ which is on the right. This section contains many families of herbaceous and annual plants that are hardy in Scotland. Common garden vegetables are also included here as well as wild species used in breeding new varieties.

Turn right after walking through the Systematic Garden. On the left is the **Chronological Border** ㊷ in which the plants are arranged according to the centuries in which they were introduced into British gardens. Honesty has been with us since 1595.

Walk between the children's play area and the flagpole. Head downhill, keeping to the left. Turn left at a crossroads (this crossroads is met again after visiting the Arboretum) and leave the gardens at the Kirklee Gate. Turn sharp right, walk down Ford Road and pass the remains of a disused railway bridge. Re-enter the gardens by the Arboretum Gate which is on the right. The River Kelvin (see p.242) is now on the right and Kirklee Bridge is ahead. On the right, just before the bridge, is a riverside viewpoint.

On the left of the path are the **Tertiary Relics** ❹❸, a group of plants which lived in Scotland during what is known to geologists as the Tertiary Period, which started about 65 million years ago. These particular plants died away during the last Ice Age, which ended about 10,000 years ago, but as they managed to survive in warmer climates they have been reintroduced to Scotland. They include trees such as Dawn Redwood and the Date Plum.

Pass under the arch of the **Kirklee Bridge** ❹❹ (1899-1901, Charles Formans). This very grand bridge carries a road high above the river and is one of the city's finest bridges. The bulk of it is made of good-quality red sandstone, with polished pink granite used for the Ionic columns and the balustrades. The city's coat of arms decorate the spandrels. The bridge's foundation stone is on the other side of the river and is described on p.247.

Follow the river to the New Bridge which links the gardens with the Kelvin Walkway (see p.242). On the left is the **Arboretum** ❹❺, a 'new' part of the gardens opened only in 1975. This contains many plants collected by **David Douglas** (1798-1843) who trained at the gardens. He played an important part in bringing various North American plants to Britain, including the Sitka Spruce, now the most common conifer in the country. He also introduced the Douglas Fir which was originally called the Oregon Pine until it was renamed after him. Plants to be found here include Red Alder and Corsican Pine.

Turn sharp left just when the **New Bridge** ❹❻ is met and climb through the highest part of the Arboretum. Descend a flight of steps on the left, turn right at the riverside path and walk through the arch of the Kirklee Bridge again.

Retrace the route through the Kirklee Gate and back to the crossroads mentioned earlier (see above). Cross the crossroads. Turn next left and then left again to descend a long flight of steps which leads to the river. Follow the River Walk downstream to the graceful **Humpback Bridge** ❹❼ (c. 1890) which is also called the Botanic Gardens Footbridge. Its deck is made of plate girders and it has unusual cast-iron railings.

Turn right just before the bridge is met and climb a flight of steps which leads to the back of the Kibble Palace. Turn right, go round the palace and leave the gardens at the main gate.

BOTANIC GARDENS TO BYRES ROAD VIA HYNDLAND

From the Botanic Gardens' main gate, turn right and meet the junction of Great Western Road and Byres Road. A **Police box** ④⑧ (see p.99) stands on the right at the junction.

Cross Great Western Road and turn right. Do not walk alongside the busy road, but go through a gateway in order to reach the elevated carriageway in front of the Stakis Hotel. Continue westwards, following the line of terraces all the way to Hyndland Road.

The hotel occupies part of one of the city's finest Victorian buildings, **Grosvenor Terrace** ④⑨ (1855, John Thomas Rochead). This Venetian-style terrace has a total of 85 bays and the whole facade seems to be taken up by windows and their attendant columns; even the doors seem to merge into the continuous wall of windows. A decorative balcony and carvings at the eaves also serve to accentuate the length and repetitive nature of the whole design. Only the slight projection of the end pavilions breaks up the monumental monotony of this elaborate wall. Unlike many other terraces composed of three-storey houses, each of the storeys is of the same height and their columns are (from the ground floor up) Doric, Ionic and Corinthian in style. One reason for the preponderance of glass is that the large windows are better able to take advantage of the poor light in this north-facing building as well as allowing splendid views over the Botanic Gardens.

After a disastrous fire in 1978 the facade of the hotel was so badly damaged that it was demolished but it has been successfully recreated in glass-reinforced concrete. It is quite a remarkable piece of important conservation work. It is now the Stakis Glasgow Grosvenor Hotel.

Continue along Kew Terrace. The residential district on the opposite side of Great Western Road is **Kelvinside**, reckoned by many to be the city's most 'posh' area, though with many of its large houses now subdivided and lots of students living in a large hall of residence right in the middle of the district, its character has changed a lot in the last one hundred and fifty years. The Kelvinside accent is said to be very different from any other in the city: when two cars have a collision, it is called a 'crèche' rather than a 'crash', and back in the days when coal was used in houses it was supplied in 'sex' instead of 'sacks'. It's the way that you say it!

During the late Victorian era this section of the road was the 'in place' to 'perambulate' on a Sunday afternoon and the 'Great Western Road Parade' was an occasion when families dressed up in their finery to meet their friends and to be seen.

The first terrace on the right (immediately after the Botanic Gardens) is the imposing Italianate **Kirklee Terrace** ⑤⓿ (1845-64, Charles Wilson), its situation made all that more grand by its elevated position above what the first occupants probably called a 'boulevard' rather than an ordinary 'road'. This was the first terrace to be built in Kelvinside but it took twenty years for it to be completed, perhaps reflecting the reluctance of potential purchasers to stray out of the city into what was then the countryside; it may also be that there were so many substantial mansions being erected elsewhere in the city at the same time. It is essentially a two-storey terrace, with three-storey pavilions at the ends and in the middle. This is one of the city's finest terraces with good quality stonework and ornamental ironwork. The façade's main feature is at first-floor level, with ornamented stone balconies below the windows and carved cornices above them.

Cross Horslethill Road at a busy crossroads and follow Belhaven Terrace West. Cross Westbourne Gardens South and climb a short flight of steps to meet the city's greatest terrace, **Great Western Terrace** **51** (1869, Alexander Thomson). Originally it had two large flights of steps leading directly to Great Western Road, but when the road was widened these steps and the roadside gardens were altered; however, its elevated platform and wide carriageway still allows it to dominate its surroundings. The terrace was built as a series of grand mansions for the rich, including Sir William Burrell (see p.308) who lived at number 8 from 1902-27, and the varied interiors were very ornate and featured fine plasterwork. It is much longer than many other West End terraces and the structural monotony of the row of two-storey buildings is punctuated by two three-storey pavilions placed six bays in from either end. Thomson's usual incised decorations are missing in this design; instead, the main exterior decorative work is at the entrances where the very wide porches have four Ionic columns. Even the windows are recessed and quite plain, as if to emphasize the severity of the whole façade. Apart from the general monumental appearance of the terrace, its most notable feature is its splendid cast-iron work, with anthemia-decorated railings and tall, slender lamp-posts.

The western end was completed by J. J. Burnet after Thomson's death in 1875.

Westbourne Gardens West is now crossed, and on the left the Struthers Memorial Church, originally the **Westbourne Free Church** **52** (1880-1, John Honeyman) can be seen. This lovely Italian Renaissance church looks very different from most other Glasgow churches. It has a relatively plain pedimented portico supported by two tiers of paired columns (Corinthian above Ionic) and behind these are the entrance and large arched windows. It has no tower or spire, but instead two ogee-domed bellcotes are set just a little behind the façade, thus not detracting too much attention from the portico.

The route continues alongside Great Western Road, this time following Lancaster Terrace, its houses' doorways flanked by pilasters in the form of female heads. Straight ahead at the busy junction with Hyndland Road is

Devonshire Gardens  (*c.* 1870), an interesting terrace of French-influenced houses. The first part of the terrace is occupied by the One Devonshire Gardens hotel.

Turn left and follow Hyndland Road. The first terrace on the left is **Westbourne Terrace** ❺❹ (1871, Alexander Thomson). Like his Great Western Terrace, this is sitting on a large platform, emphasizing the massiveness of the structure; the decorative ironwork is also the same as on the larger terrace. The doors are flanked by Ionic columns and, very unusually for Thomson, there are canted bay windows on the first floor, above which are quite small second-storey windows. There are projecting end bays, with the southern bays' windows being continued round the corner to give the building a more interesting perspective.

Turn left at Westbourne Road and head towards the peace and quiet of **Westbourne Gardens** ❺❺, a pleasant park around which are terraces of around 1880. Turn right at Westbourne Gardens West and left at Westbourne Gardens South. Some of the doorways are flanked by small stone carvings of plants and human heads. Turn right at Lorraine Road and left at Kensington Road to meet a small park. Skirt the park by turning left at Kensington Gate and then right at Victoria Circus.

On the left is **St Luke's Greek Orthodox Cathedral** ❺❻, formerly Belhaven Church (1876-7, James Sellars). Its position, high above the road, helps to emphasise this Normandy Gothic building's tall facade and its two buttress turrets. Many of the people who formed the new congregation in 1960 were Greek-Cypriots who came to Glasgow after the Second World War. The church was elevated to the status of a cathedral in 1970.

Westbourne Gardens on Hyndland Road

Continue uphill on Victoria Circus and then descend into the heart of the Dowanhill district, which was developed from the 1850s with a mixture of terraces and numerous large mansions. The rising ground on the left was once topped by an **observatory.** This started off in 1838 as a private venture, but was taken over by the university in 1845. When the land was acquired it was bought on the basis that no structures would be built which would obscure the observatory's view to the south, but eventually new buildings were erected and the site became unsuitable. The university's observatory moved to University Gardens and then to Garscube which is in the north of the city.

An oblique crossroads is now met. Go over the crossroads and walk along Queen's Place. Cross Crown Road North in order to meet the graceful **Crown Circus** **⑤⑦** (1858, James Thomson) which curves away to the south. This highly regarded terrace is the curved central part of a large U-shaped structure which sits on top of the hill, allowing it to command fine views over the surrounding area. Roman Doric columns flank the doors and a balustrade is added as a bold decoration below the first-floor windows.

Follow Crown Circus and turn right at Crown Terrace, which was built between 1873 and 1880. Turn right at Crown Road South and head downhill to the busy Hyndland Road. The **Hyndland** district (to the right) has many of the city's finest complete streets of good quality tenements.

Turn left, heading westwards on what soon becomes Highburgh Road. On the right is a small park dedicated to soldiers from Dowanhill Church who died in the First World War. Behind it is the former **Dowanhill Church** **⑤⑧** (1865-6, William Leiper). While this might appear to be a fairly standard church, albeit with a very fine spire, it is the interior which makes it so noteworthy. This was the work of Daniel Cottier (1838-91), an artist who gained great fame with his stained-glass windows. The original interior is striking with hand-painted stencilled designs including gold stars on a dark green background – not what you would expect in a Presbyterian church! There are many other surprises, for example, the semicircular stone pulpit which is set into the north wall and is quite separate from the congregation; it has an interesting painted wooden canopy and its importance is accentuated by the arches above it. A beautiful stained glass window is also set in this wall which features the faces of various Old Testament Bible characters surrounded by intricate geometric designs. The two side walls also have fine stained-glass windows, most of them with geometrical patterns; however, two of them have full-length portraits of two more Old Testament figures, David and Miriam.

The church's tower is also worth a look. It gradually tapers to a fine spire the height (60m (195ft)) of which dominates the sloping street below.

The building now houses the **Cottier Theatre** and the income this generates is helping the Four Acres Charitable Trust to fund the restoration of this unique building.

Continue along Highburgh Road, passing Dowanhill Park, and meet Byres Road. On the left at the junction stands the well-known **Tennent's** bar ㊾. When the original landlord Hugh Tennent applied for a licence in the 1880s he was opposed by various local people who claimed 'that the people in Hillhead were of such a class as could lay in a stock [of wine] without going to a public house'. The university also voiced their fears about the possible effects on the morals of the students. They claimed that as it was close to the gymnasium 'it might be a temptation to the students when going home fatigued in the evening after their exercises... [and that there were] ... always some who were light minded and easily led astray'. As we say in Glasgow: that's true, by the way.

Cross Byres Road and turn left in order to reach **Hillhead Underground Station** ❶ where the walk ends.

DETOUR: KELVINSIDE PARISH CHURCH TO KELVINSIDE TERRACE STEPS

This detour starts at the former Kelvinside Parish Church (see p.226) and leads to a number of places of interest, including Northpark Terrace and the BBC's Broadcasting House. The detour can also be followed as part of a walk to Queen's Cross Church and Ruchill Parish Church Halls (see pp.264 and 262 respectively).

Cross Great Western Road and follow Queen Margaret Drive northwards. This section is also called Hamilton Drive and should be followed round to the right. (The BBC is on the left.) Just along Hamilton Drive (as it heads eastwards) is an entrance to **Northpark Terrace** ㉖ (1866, Alexander Thomson). This three-storey elevated terrace filled a gap between the two neighbouring terraces and is of a rather more restrained design than that in Oakfield Avenue (see p.218) which was built a year earlier. At first glance the facade seems repetitive, with double porches projecting slightly and breaking the line of the building but, curiously, the eastern porches are doubled up, thus breaking the stucture's rhythm and symmetry. The first-floor windows are linked by a series of carvings between and above the windows, while the top floor's windows are encased in a long series of pilasters.

Retrace the route back to Queen Margaret Drive and turn right. The very large (and much extended) building on the right is **Broadcasting House** ㉗, the Scottish headquarters of the British Broadcasting Corporation. This is one of the most important cultural institutions in the country as the Scots are especially keen on ensuring that much of what we see on the 'box' is produced in Scotland and not squeezed out by London programming. With the huge developments in radio and television, this complex has grown and grown to the extent that it now sprawls over a very large site on the bank of the River Kelvin. The BBC opened its first Scottish office in Glasgow in 1923 but moved its HQ to Edinburgh in 1929. In 1935 the BBC bought this site and made it their chief Scottish base for both television and radio. Many well-known programmes are produced here, including news, documentaries, educational programmes and dramas. *Rab C. Nesbit* is also made here and viewers who are using that programme to learn more about the city may find useful the dialogue's 'translation' on Ceefax.

The building nearest Queen Margaret Drive was originally built as **Northpark House** (1869, John Thomas Rochead) for two Glasgow brothers, John and Matthew Bell. Its elaborate doorway has double Doric columns which support a first-storey balcony. Further exterior embellishment to this massive Italianate house is added by the carved heads above the ground-floor windows and the rounded pediments above the first-storey windows. The brothers founded the Glasgow Pottery, the city's biggest pottery business, and the BBC has a collection of the types of pottery they sold all over the world; there are also examples in the People's Palace. They were also keen art collectors and the house acted as their private art gallery for a collection which was said to have included ten Titians, eleven Rembrandts and twenty Rubens! They had intended to leave the collection to the city but they died without heirs and everything had to be sold off, with the result that the city got nothing. A number of the pictures were declared fakes and the sale realised far less than expected.

The house stood empty from 1880 to 1884, when it was taken over by Queen Margaret College, the first women's college in the country. The purchase of the building was made possible by the generosity of Isabella Elder (see p.297). In 1893 this became part of the university, allowing women to become university students for the first time. In 1895, the Medical Building was added (by John Keppie and Charles Rennie Mackintosh) and this particular building is now often better-known simply as **Queen Margaret College** 🚸. This has been greatly altered but it still exists, much extended and hidden in the midst of the complex of buildings on this site. It is an L-shaped structure with the attractive doorway in the angle. Above this are shields ornamented with the date *1895*, the letters *QMC* and St Mungo, all contained within the words *Universitas Glasguensis*. An ornate lamp standard stands beside the door and an ornate little porch with a stone balustrade is above it. To the right of the entrance is the stairtower which is lit by tall narrow windows. At the top is an arched belfry and a metal-clad bell-shaped roof.

Follow Queen Margaret Drive northwards to cross **Queen Margaret Bridge** ⑥⑨ (1926-9, Thomas P. M. Somers) over the River Kelvin (see p.242). This tall bridge has a simple concrete arch but it is made a little grander by having a well-built parapet of highly polished red granite from Peterhead. This is a relatively modern bridge and the previous route across the river was over the Old Queen Margaret Bridge which was farther downstream (see below).

Downstream of the present bridge is a weir and a mill lade which served a flint mill, which is described on p.246. There is also a view towards the BBC and it is possible to see the bell-shaped roof of the Queen Margaret College; it can be spotted by its weather vane. On the other side of the Queen Margaret Drive is a good view of the river as it flows past the Botanic Gardens.

Turn right after the bridge and follow Queen Margaret Road. After about 100m (*c.* 100 yards) or so, **Kelvinside Terrace Steps** ⑥⑨ (1872, Alexander Thomson) will be seen on the left; they are sometimes referred to as The Sixty Steps. The massive retaining wall beside the steps is best viewed from a wide open area which will be seen on the right. This was linked to the Old Queen Margaret Bridge of 1870 but the crossing was partly demolished in 1970, leaving the piers in the river bed. Plaques on the bridge can be seen from the path below the road and they are described on p.247.

The mass of the retaining wall is broken up by a number of typical Thomson details such as the blind colonnade above the steps, the high-level archway with its two stumpy columns and the false doorway (farther along the road).

Climb the flight of steps (checking that there are 60!). At the top, turn left at Kelvinside Terrace West and left at Wilton Street which then meets Queen Margaret Drive.

To return to the start of the detour, turn left and follow Queen Margaret Drive to its junction with Great Western Road.

The Kelvin Walkway

This urban walkway follows the River Kelvin from Clydeside up to Maryhill. *En route*, it goes through Kelvingrove Park, skirts the Botanic Gardens and passes under the Forth and Clyde Canal. It offers an interesting mix of parkland and former industrial sites and is also an important 'wildlife corridor' with many different kinds of birds and plants.

Glasgow coat of arms on Partick Bridge

Main places of interest	Museum of Transport **11**
	Kelvingrove Art Gallery and Museum **14**
	Botanic Gardens **39**–**42**
	Kelvin Aqueduct **47** (Forth and Clyde Canal)
	Maryhill Locks **48** (Forth and Clyde Canal)
Circular/linear	linear
Starting point	Exhibition Centre Railway Station **1**
Finishing point	Maryhill Railway Station **52**
Distance	8.5 km (5 miles)
Terrain	steps up and down a bridge over the Clydeside Expressway, paths (perhaps muddy); steep hills and more steps.
Public transport	Exhibition Centre Railway Station (C)
	Kelvinbridge Underground Station
	Maryhill Railway Station (Q)
Sections	The River Kelvin
	Exhibition Centre Railway Station to Argyle Street via Yorkhill
	Argyle Street to New Bridge
	New Bridge to Maryhill Railway Station via Dalsholm Road Bridge
Architects	Thomson: Kelvingrove Art Gallery and Museum **14** (exhibit)
	Mackintosh: Kelvingrove Art Gallery and Museum **14** (exhibits)
Nearby walks	5, 6, 7, 9
Refreshments	SECC; Museum of Transport; Kelvingrove Art Gallery and Museum; Gibson Street; Great Western Road
Notes	Much of the first half of the route visits places that are described in Walks 6 and 7 so there are many references to the text of these walks.
	Be aware of safety advice (see p.16) as the Walkway can be very quiet at times. This is especially important if you are alone.

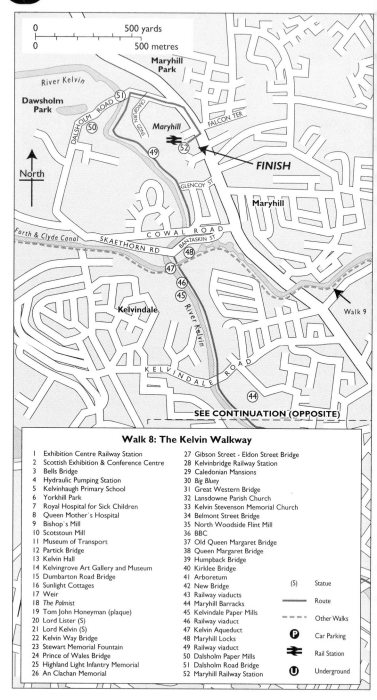

Walk 8: The Kelvin Walkway

1 Exhibition Centre Railway Station	27 Gibson Street - Eldon Street Bridge
2 Scottish Exhibition & Conference Centre	28 Kelvinbridge Railway Station
3 Bells Bridge	29 Caledonian Mansions
4 Hydraulic Pumping Station	30 *Big Bluey*
5 Kelvinhaugh Primary School	31 Great Western Bridge
6 Yorkhill Park	32 Lansdowne Parish Church
7 Royal Hospital for Sick Children	33 Kelvin Stevenson Memorial Church
8 Queen Mother's Hospital	34 Belmont Street Bridge
9 Bishop's Mill	35 North Woodside Flint Mill
10 Scotstoun Mill	36 BBC
11 Museum of Transport	37 Old Queen Margaret Bridge
12 Partick Bridge	38 Queen Margaret Bridge
13 Kelvin Hall	39 Humpback Bridge
14 Kelvingrove Art Gallery and Museum	40 Kirklee Bridge
15 Dumbarton Road Bridge	41 Arboretum
16 Sunlight Cottages	42 New Bridge
17 Weir	43 Railway viaducts
18 *The Palmist*	44 Maryhill Barracks
19 Tom John Honeyman (plaque)	45 Kelvindale Paper Mills
20 Lord Lister (S)	46 Railway viaduct
21 Lord Kelvin (S)	47 Kelvin Aqueduct
22 Kelvin Way Bridge	48 Maryhill Locks
23 Stewart Memorial Fountain	49 Railway viaduct
24 Prince of Wales Bridge	50 Dalsholm Paper Mills
25 Highland Light Infantry Memorial	51 Dalsholm Road Bridge
26 An Clachan Memorial	52 Maryhill Railway Station

(S) Statue
——— Route
- - - Other Walks
P Car Parking
⇌ Rail Station
U Underground

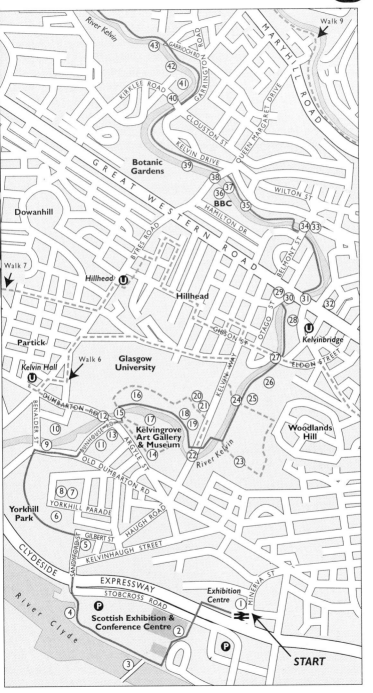

THE RIVER KELVIN

The Kelvin is the River Clyde's most important tributary inside Glasgow and runs for about 34km (21 miles) from the Kilsyth Hills (which are to the north of the city) to Partick, in the city's West End. At one time it supported numerous factories, including papermills, bleachworks and other chemical plants and, as a result, became an extremely polluted watercourse. With the demise of these industries the water is now much cleaner, to the extent that even the occasional angler can be seen in search of fish. Indeed, fish-eating birds such as cormorants can also be seen along the river and, in many ways, the Walkway acts as a 'wildlife corridor' giving shelter to many animals and a remarkable variety of plants.

Over recent years the **Kelvin Walkway** has been developed as a pleasant walking and cycling route through the west of the city; it runs from the River Clyde through the West End and Maryhill to the suburb of Milngavie which is just outside Glasgow. It then joins the West Highland Way, the long-distance footpath that runs northwards to Fort William.

The part of the Walkway described in this route is signposted by a series of wooden waymarkers on which are badges showing the outline of a bird in flight.

EXHIBITION CENTRE RAILWAY STATION TO ARGYLE STREET VIA YORKHILL

Leave the **Exhibition Centre Railway Station** ❶ and turn right. Enter the covered walkway on the right which leads to the main entrance of the **SECC** ❷. Walk past the SECC until the river is met at **Bells Bridge** ❸. Follow the route described on p.152 that goes from Bells Bridge to the **Hydraulic Pumping Station** ❹.

Cross Stobhouse Road and go over the steel pedestrian bridge over the busy Clydeside Expressway. This runs along the old Pointhouse Road which led to the shipyards at Pointhouse (see p.291). The bridge allows good views of the River Clyde and the Yorkhill hospitals (see p.243).

Go under the railway bridge and walk up Sandyford Road, at the top of which is **Kelvinhaugh Primary School** ❺ (1886, Frank Burnet). This is really quite a massive building considering the size of the young pupils who are educated here and it must intimidate some of the children. Perhaps that's the idea! The two side doors, one marked *Boys*, the other, *Girls,* might be considered even more ' oppressive' in their size and it is interesting to compare them with Mackintosh's entrances at the Scotland Street School (see p.277). A plaque on the western wall carries the date *1887* and the inscription *Jubilee of the reign of Queen Victoria*, while on the northern side are the inscriptions *School Board of Glasgow* and the original name, *Kelvinhaugh Public School.*

Turn left at Gilbert Street and follow a path which is to the left of a tall stone wall. This leads into the small **Yorkhill Park** ❻ from which there are good views over much of the western side of the city.

The prominent hill of Yorkhill was once the site of a Roman outpost guarding the River Clyde and the Antonine Wall (see p.180). A mansion was built here in the early nineteenth century and in 1813 it was bought by Andrew Gilbert, who then named the estate Yorkhill. Tenements were built nearby later in the century and when the mansion was demolished a hospital was built on its site in 1916. This has since been replaced by a large hospital complex comprising the Royal Hospital for Sick Children and the Queen Mother's Maternity Hospital.

The **Royal Hospital for Sick Children** ❼ (1968–71, Baxter, Clark & Paul) was founded in 1883 in Scott Street, Garnethill and moved to this site's first hospital in 1916. This building collapsed in 1965, forcing the hospital to move away until a replacement could be erected. Affectionately known as 'The Sick Kids", it serves a very wide area including the West of Scotland and the Highlands and Islands. It is a large complex of buildings and the main structure is quite striking in appearance with horizontal bands of white mosaic cladding and coloured glass.

The **Queen Mother's Hospital** ❽ (1964, J. L. Gleave & Partners) is a maternity hospital which has the distinct advantage of having a specialist paediatric unit next door so that sick babies can have the most up-to-date treatment with the minimum delay.

Turn right at the second path on the right and follow this uphill. Descend a flight of steps to meet Old Dumbarton Road where a right turn should be made. As its name suggests, this road is an old route between Glasgow and Dumbarton which crossed the River Kelvin fairly near its confluence with the Clyde.

The River Kelvin lies just beyond the opposite side of the road. This district used to be a very important area for mills of various types as the river's level dropped substantially in this stretch, allowing the mills to use the fast-flowing water to power their waterwheels.

Cross the road to the former **Bishop's Mill** ❾ (1839), a handsome four-storey building with two decorative stone wheatsheaves on the roof. This was converted into houses in 1987 and an old millstone lies in front of the building as a reminder of its previous use. The mill lade and waterwheel were positioned in front of the building.

As the name suggests, this is on the site of the original mill of Glasgow's bishops and their castle was situated just across the river from it. The first mill established here was possibly erected in the twelfth century and local farmers were 'obliged' to use it, thus ensuring a steady income to the Church. It was owned by the town council from 1608 to 1836 (when it was burned down) and was known during this time as the

Bishop's Mill

Old Mill of Partick. The mill was then replaced by this structure and given its historic name.

The **Scotstoun Mill** ⑩ stands on the opposite bank. This dates back to 1507 when a waulk mill (which was involved in processing woollen cloth) was established on the site. The present mill produces flour and is now the only mill on this stretch of the river. Considering how few mills are now left in the country, this remarkable survivor is an important link with a centuries-old industrial tradition.

Cross an old railway bridge and turn left at Bunhouse Road. The **Museum of Transport** ⑪ (see p.210) is on the right. The museum's car park on the left stands on the site of the very historic **Regent Mill**. This was built here by the Incorporation of Bakers of Glasgow after the land was given to them by Regent Moray in return for having provided his army with bread around the time of the Battle of Langside (see p.320). Its other name, the Bunhouse Mill, came from a nearby hostelry called the Bun and Yill House.

Turn right when Bunhouse Road meets Argyle Street. The bridge on the left is **Partick Bridge** ⑫ (see p.211) and the large building on the right is the **Kelvin Hall** ⑬ (see p.209). The **Kelvingrove Art Gallery and Museum** ⑭ (see p.205) stands on the other side of Argyle Street.

ARGYLE STREET TO NEW BRIDGE

Cross Argyle Street. Turn left and cross **Dumbarton Road Bridge** ⑮ (see p.204) which is the smaller of the two bridges that stand side by side here. This old bridge leads into **Kelvingrove Park** (see p.197). Turn right after crossing the river and go first right at a path which follows the riverbank. High up on the left are the **Sunlight Cottages**  (see p.204) and behind them are the buildings of **Glasgow University** (see p.177).

Soon a **weir** ⑰ (see p.204) can be seen in the river and on the other bank is the very large Kelvingrove Art Gallery and Museum. The land on the other side of the river has a long history as a mill site. The New Waulk Mill was here in the sixteenth century and was altered in 1554 to become a wheat mill. In 1588, by which time it was known as Clayslaps Mill, it was bought by the Town Council. They subsequently sold it to the Glasgow bakers in 1771 but bought it back in 1874 when the city needed the land in order to lay out the new Kelvingrove Park.

A little farther on will be seen the statue *The Palmist* ⑱ (see p.203), a plaque to **Tom John Honeyman** ⑲ (see p.204), and statues of **Lord Lister** ⑳ (see p.203) and **Lord Kelvin** ㉑ (see p.203). Kelvin Way is now met and on the right is **Kelvin Way Bridge** ㉒ (see p.202) which has some very fine sculptures on it.

Go straight across Kelvin Way and re-enter the park. Follow the riverside path and cross the river by a pedestrian bridge. Turn first left at the other side; the **Stewart Memorial Fountain** ㉓ (see p.202) can be seen straight ahead just before this turn is made.

Follow the river to the **Prince of Wales Bridge** ㉔ (see p.199); when this is met, the **Highland Light Infantry Memorial** ㉕ (see p.200) is on the right. Follow the river again and look out for the low-lying **An Clachan Memorial** ㉖ (see p.200) which is on the right. The path now climbs a little and the Walkway bears left and goes under the **Gibson Street – Eldon Street Bridge** ㉗ (see p.219).

Kelvin Way Bridge

After the bridge, there is a large flat area which used to be the site of **Kelvinbridge Railway Station** ㉘. This was built around 1894 by James Miller for the Caledonian Railway Company and to give the station more space, some of its buildings were erected on a plate-girder bridge over the river. Part of the open ground was also used as a goods and mineral yard. This was the site of the South Woodside Cotton Mill (1784), the only water-powered cotton mill in Glasgow; it later became a paper mill.

Cross the river by means of the old railway bridge; on the left is the blocked-off tunnel which took the railway line underground. Above the tunnel are the attractive **Caledonian Mansions** ㉙ (see p.225) which were also built for the railway company.

On the right is the unusual sculpture *Big Bluey* ㉚ (1995, Philip Benson), made from an old tree carved into the shape of a dolphin.

Walk under **Great Western Bridge** ㉛ (see p.224). The river can be fast flowing here as the water is forced into the narrow channels between the bridge's piers and the substantial walls at each side of the river. After the bridge, the tall spire on the right belongs to **Lansdowne Parish Church** ㉜ (see p.224).

There are now some cliffs on the right, at the base of which are horizontally bedded rocks. High above the bank is the red sandstone **Kelvin Stevenson Memorial Church** ㉝ which was originally built as the Nathaniel Stevenson Memorial Free Church (1898, J. J. Stevenson). Its most notable feature, especially when viewed from the Walkway, is the large open stone crown that sits atop the tower; this is similar in design to the crown on King's College in Aberdeen.

Pass under the grand **Belmont Street Bridge** ㉞ (1870), its single elliptical arch towering above the river. The bridge was originally built for the City of Glasgow Bank, which owned the land to the north of here, to allow them to develop their land for housing.

A modern bridge takes the Walkway to the northern bank where there is an open grassy area. On the left are the remains of the **North Woodside Flint Mill** ㉟ which was built in 1846 for Kidson, Cochran & Co. The mill's raw material was flint from France which it turned into powder to be used for glaze in the city's pottery industry; one of its customers was the Verreville Pottery (see p.155). A number of the mill's most important structures are still visible, including the entrance gateposts, the lade, the waterwheel pit (in which there was an undershot wheel) and the weir (which is further upstream). The tallest remaining structure is the kiln in which the flint was roasted, during which process its colour was changed from grey to white, making it suitable for sanitary ware and other types of ceramics. The grinding wheels lying nearby came from a grist mill and were never used here.

The mill is such an important link with the city's industrial past that it has been scheduled as an Ancient Monument.

The large buildings on the left belong to the **BBC** ㊱ (see p.235). The route now passes the remains of the **Old Queen Margaret Bridge** ㊲ (see p.237) the parapets of which are decorated with large round metal plaques. These feature the four elements of the city's coat of arms and the words *Erected by John E Walker Esq   Ritchie Rodger Esq   C E McElroy & Sons builders*. The bridge was often referred to locally as Walker's Bridge after 'Hookey Walker', a coach operator who built the bridge in order to link some land he owned on the north side of the river to Great Western Road.

Walk through the pedestrian tunnel which pierces the new **Queen Margaret Bridge** ㊳ (see p.236). The **Botanic Gardens** (see p.227) are now on the left and can be reached by means of the next bridge, the **Humpback Bridge** ㊴ (see p.230).

The Walkway now goes under the grand **Kirklee Bridge** ㊵ (see p.230); below one of the decorative granite pillars is a large block of sandstone which carries the inscription *Corporation of Glasgow   Kirklee Bridge Memorial Stone   Laid by Councillor John McFarlane J.P. Chairman of the Statute Labour Committee   17th January 1900   Hon Samuel Chisholm Lord Provost of this city*. Another face of the block has the words *William Wilson contractor* on it.

There are now more cliffs on the right, while on the left is the Botanic Gardens' **Arboretum** ㊶ (see p.230). The path climbs above the river then descends to pass the **New Bridge** ㊷ (see p.230) which provides another link with the Botanic Gardens.

NEW BRIDGE TO MARYHILL RAILWAY STATION VIA DALSHOLM ROAD BRIDGE

Having passed through the leafy West End, the route now skirts the more industrialised area of Maryhill (see p.261), where there are lots of reminders of this district's previous connections with industry and transportation. In particular, there are many old railway viaducts as the area was criss-crossed by a network of lines serving local industries.

Two **railway viaducts** ㊸ are soon met and a pedestrian tunnel runs under both of them. The eastern viaduct was part of the line that ran through Kelvinbridge Railway Station (see p.246) and has three semicircular main arches and two smaller arches. The western viaduct was built for the Lanarkshire & Dumbartonshire Railway and is constructed with plate girders which rest on substantial masonry piers.

The Walkway is now well above the river and there are some extremely high flats on the right. This housing scheme is built on what used to be the site of **Maryhill Barracks** ⓪, which were established here in 1876. The previous infantry barracks were in Calton, close to the city centre, but in the middle of the nineteenth century the council felt that a new and bigger site was needed for troops. These soldiers, they believed, were needed 'on those occasions of Riot and Tumult which too frequently occur in the manufacturing and populous districts of the Country ... [and which were caused] ... by stagnation in trade and want of employment among the Labouring Classes.' About nine hundred men (and about two hundred horses) were stationed here and latterly the barracks were used by the Highland Light Infantry (see p.131). The barracks were demolished in 1960 but some of the substantial perimeter walls remain and the parade ground was turned into the open children's play area which is near the Walkway.

Farther along, there are more remains of old railway bridges in the river, including some well-built masonry piers which seem set to last for a long time yet. The Walkway now bears left (and goes downhill) to meet Kelvindale Road; cross it and continue on the path though a park.

This is **Dalsholm Park** which was acquired by the city in 1921. It was originally part of Garscube Estate (see p.250), the main section of which is on the opposite side of the river. There was once a small village nearby and Hugh Macdonald (see p.378) noted that 'the farm of Dalsholm is remarkable for an ancient tumulus, which was long known by the appellation of the 'Courthill', and was supposed to have formed in bygone times the judgment-seat of some feudal potentate.' He also described an archaeological excavation there which uncovered 'a narrow flight of steps leading towards the interior of the eminence ... [and] ... a small cell or chamber was discovered underneath, lined with stone, and containing a number of curious relics.'

Walk along the wide path which runs between the river and the modern houses. Some cliffs will be seen on the right. Later on, a number of paths go off to the right; ignore these and follow the Walkway down to the riverside. Yet another set of disused bridge piers stands on the left.

The next item of interest is a V-shaped weir. This supplied water to the lade which ran to the industrial site on the opposite bank where the **Kelvindale Paper Mills** ⓭ operated until 1976. These started in the eighteenth century as the Balgray Snuff and Paper Mill and were taken over in the 1740s by Edward Collins. He built a mansion here and changed the mill's name to Kelvindale, a name that lives on in the district to the west. Unfortunately, he found the river's flow too unpredictable and moved his business to Dalmuir.

Collins was a member of the famous publishing family (see p.62) who printed Bibles and other religious books as well as being active in the temperance movement. Collins campaigned alongside local (but absentee) landlord John Dunlop, who was horrified at the inebriated state of many Maryhill people; he probably had good cause to be concerned as in the 1830s there was one licensed house to every fifty-nine people in the district!

In 1840 the firm of Edward Collins & Sons restarted work here and built a new mill on the same site. The mill made various products over time, including handmade paper from linen rags as well as paper for books and stationery. The main raw material used in the modern high-quality writing papers was esparto grass which was imported from Spain and North Africa. There are examples of the mill's products in the People's Palace.

The next **railway viaduct** 46 which is met was built around 1896 for the Lanarkshire & Dumbartonshire Railway. The line was closed in 1966 and the bridge's steel girders were removed but the tall piers are still extant.

The next structure which crosses the river is the massive **Kelvin Aqueduct** 47 (see p.259) which carries the Forth and Clyde Canal. The canal can be reached from here (there are steps on the right) affording an opportunity to see the **Maryhill Locks** 48 (see p.259).

After going under the aqueduct, follow the path on the left which goes under a small road bridge. The river is met again and the remains of yet another old bridge are on the left. The Walkway now goes under the modern **Cowal Road Bridge.**

The land on both sides of this stretch of the river is now used for housing and parkland but it was previously heavily industrialised. The land on the right was the site of the Kelvindale Mills (originally a printworks) and the land on the other bank was used for Dawsholm Gasworks from 1871 to around 1968. ('Dawsholm' is an alternative spelling for 'Dalsholm'.)

The next **railway viaduct** 49 is still in use and was built around 1858 to carry two lines over the river for the Glasgow, Dumbarton & Helensburgh Railway. The river valley is quite broad at this point and the bridge uses seven arches to carry the lines high above this large natural obstacle.

Keep to the riverside when the path divides; on the opposite bank are some substantial sandstone cliffs. The land on the other side of the river was once the site of the **Dalsholm Paper Mills** 50 which were founded around 1783 by William Macarthur and which produced handmade paper from rags. Various types of paper were produced over the years; latterly, the main product was wrapping paper, made from waste paper and wood pulp. The mills were closed in 1970.

Hugh MacDonald visited here and wrote that 'a paper-mill on the margin of the stream, and several cottages on the rising grounds, some of them half-concealed by trees through which the blue smoke is ever curling, lend a human interest to the spot, without detracting materially from its natural loveliness.'

More cliffs will be seen on the right before Dalsholm Road is met at **Dalsholm Road Bridge** 🖲. This was built around 1790 and has four arches over the river. It is a very low and narrow bridge and used to be a bad traffic bottleneck until it was closed to vehicles. The design of the bridge certainly adds to the generally rural look of this part of the river, especially when compared to the more industrialised stretches farther downstream.

Beyond this point, the river flows through **Garscube Estate** which is part of Glasgow University. The estate was owned by the Campbells of Succoth from 1687 and the large Garscube House was erected in 1827 by Sir Archibald Campbell. The land was taken over in 1921 with part of it becoming Dalsholm Park (see p.248) and part being used by the university for the Veterinary School, Wolfson Hall of Residence and, more recently, sports facilities. The house was demolished in 1954.

Unfortunately, the Walkway does not follow the river through the estate, so there is a detour through Maryhill Park.

Turn right at Dalsholm Road and follow it up to a factory service road. Turn left, walk up to the busy Maryhill Road and turn right. **Maryhill Park** is on the left and the Walkway goes through the park gates which are just across the road. However, this route continues on Maryhill Road to **Maryhill Railway Station** 🖳 (which will be found on the right), where the walk ends.

The Forth and Clyde Canal

A walk which follows the towpath of the Forth and Clyde Canal for much of its route through Glasgow. The canal is scheduled as an Ancient Monument and there are lots of interesting industrial relics to see as well as panoramic views of many parts of the city.
The walk is also good for birdwatching.

Hamiltonhill Basin

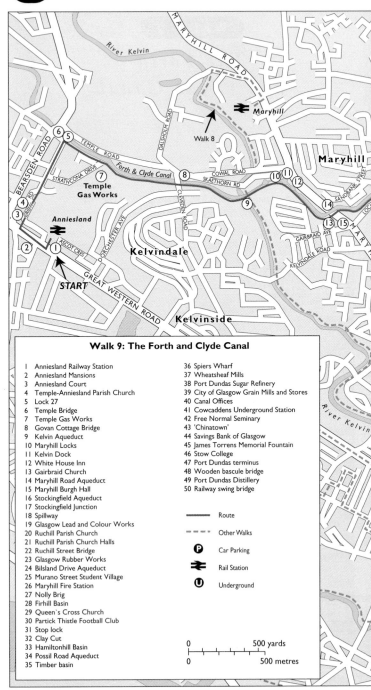

START

Walk 9: The Forth and Clyde Canal

———————— Route

- - - - - - - Other Walks

P Car Parking

⇌ Rail Station

U Underground

0					500 yards
0					500 metres

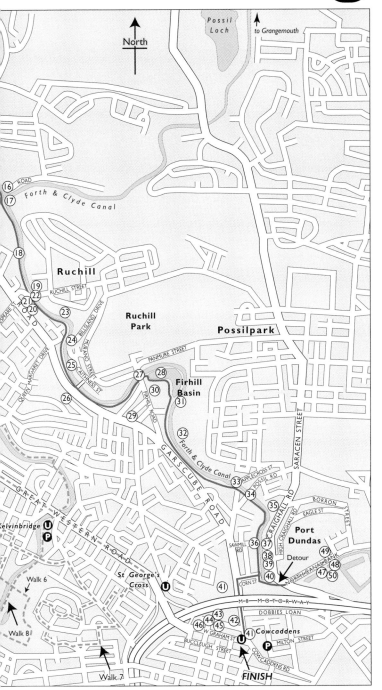

Main places of interest	Kelvin Aqueduct **9**
	Maryhill Locks **10**
	Queen's Cross Church **29**
	    (Charles Rennie Mackintosh)
	Spiers Wharf **36**
	    (former warehouses beside the canal)

Circular/linear	linear
Starting point	Anniesland Railway Station **1**
Finishing point	Cowcaddens Underground Station **41**
Distance	8.5 km (5.5 miles)
Terrain	Generally level along the towpath but there are slopes at Maryhill Locks, before Port Dundas and after Spiers Wharf.
Public transport	Anniesland Railway Station (C, Q) Cowcaddens Underground Station
Sections	The Forth and Clyde Canal Anniesland Railway Station to Temple Locks Temple Locks to Maryhill Road Aqueduct Maryhill Road Aqueduct to Firhill Firhill to Spiers Wharf Spiers Wharf to Cowcaddens Underground Station Detour: Spiers Wharf to Port Dundas
Architects	Mackintosh: Ruchill Parish Church Halls **21** Queen's Cross Church **29**
Nearby walks	4, 8
Refreshments	Anniesland; Crow Road; Queen's Cross Church
Notes	There is very little shelter on the route so keep a watch on the weather. Be aware of safety advice (see p.16) as the canal towpath can be very quiet at times.

The Forth and Clyde Canal

At one time this was the country's most important canal as it linked the Firths of Clyde and Forth and thus allowed passage for boats right across Scotland. As a result factories set up along its banks, thereby helping to develop the industrial might of the Central Belt. Its inception was fraught with difficulties, to say nothing of political in-fighting, and it was fully open from coast to coast in 1790, over two decades after it was started. It finally closed to commercial traffic in 1963 and parts of it have since been culverted. However, many canal enthusiasts have maintained boats on the waterway and their campaigning efforts over the years have kept alive the prospect of reopening the canal. Ambitious development plans have been drawn up and it is hoped that a large injection of funds will allow the canal to become once more a lively and important route through the middle of the country.

Possible routes for the canal were surveyed in 1726 by Alexander Gordon and in 1762 by Robert Mackell and James Murray. These provided the basis for John Smeaton's plan of 1764 and he suggested two possible routes, one of which was from the Yoker Burn at Glasgow to the River Carron on the Forth. He estimated the 1.5m (5ft) deep, 43km (27 mile) long canal would cost around £79,000. The political intrigue started: Glasgow tobacco merchants were angry at it bypassing the city, the influential Carron Iron Company supported it because its eastern terminus was handy for them, and various landowners along the route sought to use the canal to increase their own wealth. There were also battles between various interests in Glasgow and Edinburgh and the language used in today's 'boisterous' rivalry between the two cities pales into insignificance compared to one letter to the press which stated that 'Edinburgh, Sir, is the metropolis of this ancient kingdom, the seat of Law, the rendezvous of Politeness, the abode of Taste, and the winter quarters of all our nobility who cannot afford to live in London; and for these and other reasons equally cogent Edinburgh ought to have the lead upon all occasions. The fools of the west must wait for the Wise Men of the East.' To complicate matters even further, there was also great disquiet over the power held by London-based financial interests. Some things never change!

After gaining parliamentary approval, the 2m (7ft) deep canal was started in 1768 at the eastern end, a site which later became the busy port of Grangemouth. As work progressed, there were numerous proposed changes to the route, especially from the Carron Iron Company who were now unhappy at being unable to link their factory to the canal. By the end of 1771 the canal workings which lay to the east of the summit had been finished and Kirkintilloch was reached in August 1773. Stockingfield (see p.262) was reached in January 1775 but work stopped in July because of a shortage of money. Work restarted, but instead of heading west towards the Clyde, the canal swung southwards and headed towards Glasgow. In November 1777 the canal reached the Hamiltonhill Basin (see p.266). Work stopped again, this time until 1784. In June 1785 Robert Whitworth took over from John Smeaton as Chief Engineer and two years later work began on the huge Kelvin Aqueduct (see p.259). Great progress was now made and the canal headed for the western sea lock at Bowling on the Clyde. The last section of the canal's Glasgow branch, from Hamiltonhill to Port Dundas (see p.270), was built in 1786-90. The canal was officially opened in July 1790 and the occasion was marked by a company boat travelling the 19km (12 miles) from Glasgow to Bowling in four hours. The canal's total cost was around £330,000, quite a bit above Smeaton's estimate!

The canal was now 62km (39 miles) long, with a width of 9m (30ft) at the bottom and 18m (60ft) at the surface; it was 3m (9½ft) deep. There were thirty-nine locks, nineteen to the west and twenty to the east of the summit (see p.260), each of which was about 21m (70ft) long and 6m (20ft) wide. Traffic was able to use the canal from 1773 onwards and it readily became busy with various types of vessels carrying cargoes such as timber, grain, sugar, textiles and coal; on some occasions west-coast fishing boats used it as they headed eastwards to take advantage of the arrival of the herring shoals. The canal was very profitable at times and in 1816 the dividend was an enormous twenty-five per cent. However, its success was challenged by many factors, including competition from the railways and the deepening of the River Clyde which allowed large vessels directly into the city. A variety of vessels were used on the canal over the years, including horse-drawn boats, paddleboats, propeller-driven craft and even locomotive-hauled boats; although the introduction of these newer 'high-tech' types of boats greatly increased the speeds at which cargoes could be moved they also caused more erosion of the banks and consequently increased maintenance costs.

Railway companies were seen by many people as deadly rivals to the canals but, to the landed interests who could make money out of both forms of transport, the amalgamation of railways and canals made profitable sense. As a result, in the late 1860s the Caledonian Railway Company joined with the Forth and Clyde Canal, the Monkland Canal and some smaller railway companies. However, by that time Scotland's trading patterns were changing; factories were being sited beside railway lines and the canal could not be deepened or widened in order to help it compete. The closure of Grangemouth docks to civilian shipping during the First World War dealt another cruel blow. In 1923 the company was taken over by the London, Midland & Scottish Railway and in 1948 the country's railways and canals were taken into public ownership. By then the canal was unable to compete against road and rail transport and it was closed on 1 January 1963. It is now operated by the publicly owned British Waterways.

The canal has always been an attractive home to many species of plants and animals and this has been especially true since the canal's closure.

With few boats on the waterway, there is little scouring of the bank with only the slow movement of water from the reservoirs down to the sea locks, and this has allowed many plants to establish themselves by the banks. In particular, the bank opposite the towpath often has a very rich plant and animal diversity as it suffers little from human interference. The gradual silting up of the canal has helped many reeds and other aquatic plants establish themselves in the shallows and these give valuable shelter to other plant species as well as many varieties of water birds. Binoculars should be carried while walking along the towpath as there are many birds; the most common in the Glasgow area include mallard, coot, tufted duck and mute swans. Kestrels may also be spotted hovering over potential prey and the occasional cormorant can be seen diving for fish.

The canal is also a favourite haunt of many watersports enthusiasts and canoes are often used, especially in the basins. However, for those who want a less strenuous passage along the water, a number of organisations arrange boat trips and information on these can be obtained from the Tourist Information Centre. In addition, many anglers frequent the canal and the fish they seek include perch, eel, roach and pike. Joggers also use the towpath as it provides a rather safer and more pleasant route than the city's busy streets. Hopefully, all these aspects of community use will increase substantially in the next few years as the canal gains a new lease of life.

ANNIESLAND RAILWAY STATION TO TEMPLE LOCKS

The walk starts from **Anniesland Railway Station ❶**, the exit of which is on Great Western Road (see p.223). Turn right at this road, walk under the railway bridge and head towards Anniesland Cross. **Anniesland** is a busy district which is close to the city's boundary and this is its main shopping area. The name may possibly come from a local inn known as 'Sheep Annies' which was frequented by sheep drovers.

This was a fairly rural area in the middle of the nineteenth century, with small farms and small-scale industry in the vicinity. Great Western Road reached the toll at Anniesland Cross in 1850 but it was not until 1886, when the railway line was established here by the North British Railway, that the area came within commuting distance of Glasgow.

There are some tall red sandstone tenement blocks on the main road, and on the southern side are **Anniesland Mansions ❷** (1907-13, H. Campbell). These tenement buildings are quite unusual in that they have flat roofs and cast-iron parapets decorating the top. In recent years, many of the city's buildings which have flat roofs have had apex roofs added to them because of frequent water penetration; while many of those buildings were built in the second half of the twentieth century this example belongs to an earlier time. The centre of this facade has a pair of polished granite columns which were part of what was the grand entrance to the Anniesland Hall, a local mission hall. The most interesting part of the building is the domed corner at the western end which is topped by a decorated finial. The inscriptions *Anniesland Mansions, 1910* and the letters *MH* can be seen at this corner.

Turn right at Crow Road, just a short distance before Anniesland Cross is met. This used to be the main road northwards from the cross until Bearsden Road (which is further west) was built in the 1920s. On the left is the massive **Anniesland Court** ❸ (1966-8, Jack Holmes & Partners) which is twenty-two storeys high and incredibly out of keeping with the scale of the rest of the district. However, it is presumably highly regarded in some circles as it is a 'listed building'.

Foulis Street is passed on the right. This is named after the Foulis brothers (see p.363) and it used to be the site of the Glasgow University Press.

Temple-Anniesland Parish Church ❹ (1904-5, Badenoch and Bruce) is on the left. This is a red sandstone building with lancet windows in the front of the main part of the building and around the two flanking staircase towers. To its left is a white sandstone hall which was originally the United Free Church (1898-9, Alexander Petrie).

Follow Crow Road northwards (and through the supermarket car park) until the canal is met at Temple.

TEMPLE LOCKS TO MARYHILL ROAD AQUEDUCT

A plaque beside the canal indicates that this is **Lock 27** ❺ and that this point is 7¾ miles from Bowling and 1½ miles from Stockingfield Junction (see p.262). The lock was built around 1790 and was originally spanned by a bascule bridge, evidence of which can still be seen. However, the realignment of Bearsden Road meant that the bridge was dismantled and Temple Bridge (see below) was built to replace it. A narrow pedestrian bridge has been erected to allow access to the other side.

Lock 27 pub is on the right and stands on the site of the lock-keeper's house.

Temple Bridge ❻ (1931-2, T. Somers) is to the west of Lock 27. It was built as an electrically operated bascule bridge but was fixed in position in 1963 when the canal was closed. It carries the busy Bearsden Road over the canal.

The route now follows the towpath eastwards until it ends at Speirs Wharf (see p.267). The canal passes over the railway line which runs through Anniesland Railway Station and then **Lock 26** is met. On the other side of the canal is the West Highland Railway Line which runs from Glasow to Fort William and then on to Mallaig.

A disused railway cutting is crossed, after which **Temple Gas Works** ❼ are on the right. This was established in 1871 for the Partick, Hillhead &

Maryhill Gas Company but was taken over by the city council in 1891. The two massive gasholders are of three-lift design and were built in 1893 and 1900; they hold 140,000m³ (5 million cubic feet) and 110,000m³ (4 million cubic feet) of gas respectively.

The small **Govan Cottage Bridge** ❽ is a fixed bridge and was built around 1968 when the canal was culverted under Cleveden Road. There's not much room for craft to pass under it. A lock-keeper's house will be seen on the left, just a short distance above the bridge; this is constructed in typical railway company style as the canal was once owned by the Caledonian Railway Company. Cross Cleveden Road and on the right can be seen a plaque on which is written *Maryhill Locks 1km Clydebank 7km*. The plaques have now gone metric.

The canal heads towards Maryhill (see p.261) and is carried over the valley of the River Kelvin by the **Kelvin Aqueduct** ❾ (1787-90, Robert Whitworth). This remarkable structure may not seem very grand from the level of the canal itself, but it is worthwhile going under it to get a better view of a very impressive piece of engineering.

Four 15m (50ft) arches carry the huge weight of this substantial structure 21m (70ft) above the river and when it was built the aqueduct attracted admirers from far and wide. At 122m (400ft) long it was the largest structure of its type in Britain and at the time a Glasgow minister described it as 'one of the most stupendous works of the kind perhaps in the world'. Hugh Macdonald (see p.378) was also highly impressed by the aqueduct and the surrounding scenery and noted that 'the view of the Kelvin from the summit of the bridge is of the most lovely description, the banks on each side being thickly covered with stately trees, which, bending over the water, here smooth and unruffled, are reflected as in a mirror.' Not to be left out from the singing of praises of this new 'tourist attraction', in 1789 the *Scots Magazine* told its readers that the aqueduct was 'placed in a situation truly romantic'. As a mark of its importance to the country's industrial history, the aqueduct was one of the first parts of the canal to be scheduled as an Ancient Monument.

Looking down the river, there are views of a railway viaduct and a V-shaped weir (see pp.249 and 248 respectively). At the end of the aqueduct there is a path that gives access to the Kelvin Walkway (see p.249) from which there is a good view of the aqueduct. The river is described on p.242.

Carrying along the towpath, a small incline leads up to another fine piece of engineering, the five **Maryhill Locks** ❿ (1787-90, Robert Whitworth). These are locks 25 to 21 which raise the canal's level by about 12m (40ft) and there are large oval holding basins between the locks. Mooring rings and other reminders of past activity can be seen.

After the third lock (that is, between locks 23 and 22) there are the remains of the **Kelvin Dock** ⓫ (1789) which was one of the canal's

Maryhill Locks

earliest boatyards. Its main feature is the dry dock which was separated from the canal by lock gates. The dock is 44m (145ft) long and its width increases from 9m (30ft) at the bottom to 12m (40ft) at the top by means of stone steps, allowing the craftsmen to work on a hull at different heights. A slipway can be seen beside the dock.

The Swan family operated the yard from 1837 to 1893 and they began the practice of building iron ships in sections which were then assembled at Bowling where the canal meets the River Clyde. They also built a cargo vessel called the *Glasgow* which was the first of the well-known 'puffers' (see p.146) and around sixty puffers were constructed here. Many different types of craft were built, both for work on the canal and on the sea and, because the space in front of the boatyard is quite small, some of the launches took place broadside on. The yard continued working until 1949.

There is a pedestrian bridge over the canal just below Lock 21 and on the right is a plaque indicating that this is the western limit of the summit pond, 156 feet (48m) above sea level. Having crossed the Kelvin Valley, the canal now continues at this height for 26km (16 miles) until lock 20 at Wyndford.

All the canal's sources of water feed into this summit pond with the principal reservoirs being near the town of Kilsyth which is to the north of the canal. Water is also fed from south of the canal via some remaining parts of the Monkland Canal.

On the other side of Lock 21 is the **White House Inn 13** on Maryhill Road. This is one of the original canal inns.

Gairbraid Church 🔞 (1871) is passed on the right. This was built for the United Presbyterians and is a fairly undistinguished-looking white sandstone building with the manse (1871) standing beside it.

The canal now crosses the **Maryhill Road Aqueduct 🔞** (1881) which replaced an earlier smaller structure situated just to the north.

Maryhill Road is a busy commuter route into the city. The junction which can be seen about 200m (200 yards) away used to be a very important place when the burgh of Maryhill existed and the former **Maryhill Burgh Hall 🔞** (1876-8, Duncan McNaughtan) stands to its right. The high flats beyond the junction are on the site of the old Maryhill Barracks (see p.248) and on the opposite side of the road from them, but just out of sight, is Maryhill Police Station, where the fictional television detective Jim Taggart (see p.104) was based.

Most place names with the suffix '-hill' in them come from the name of a nearby eminence, but **Maryhill** has to be different! In the late-eighteenth century the owner of the local Gairbraid Estate was Mary Hill and she feued out parcels of her land with one of the conditions being the use of the name 'Maryhill'. This happened just after the canal had been built and she, and no doubt many other landowners, made large profits as sites beside the canal became more valuable. Locally, many plots of land were utilised for factories and yards, and also for tenement blocks for the incomers who were to create the new village of Maryhill. With the development of local industries, the population increased steadily (it was 2552 in 1841) and a burgh was formed in 1856, though this status only lasted until 1912 when Maryhill became a part of Glasgow. In many ways, Maryhill's fortunes have mirrored those of the canal. Although a number of mills had already been established along the banks of the River Kelvin (see pp.248 and 249), it was its proximity to both Glasgow and the River Clyde (via the canal) that greatly enhanced Maryhill's role as a manufacturing site. This was good news as long as the canal was viable, but once the canal's *raison d'étre* has ceased, so too had Maryhill's attractiveness as a conveniently situated industrial district. As manufacturing output declined in the mid-twentieth century, so too did the quality of the houses, so much so that 'comprehensive redevelop-ment' took decades to replace much of the substandard housing. While some of the earlier attempts to rehouse large numbers of people involved building extremely tall 'high flats' (or 'villages in the sky'), more recent developments have been 'low rise' and more in keeping with the scale of the tenement buildings which still exist.

Maryhill Road Aqueduct to Firhill

Many new houses have been built beside the next stretch of the canal, a contrast to all the industrial premises which used to be here. The canal bends to the left then sharply round to the right to the **Stockingfield**

Aqueduct ⓰ (1784–90, Robert Whitworth) where the canal crosses Lochburn Road. This is the oldest of the canal's aqueducts which still exists within the city. There are paths beside the aqueduct which allow access below the structure in order to get a better look at it.

A plaque on the aqueduct's parapet indicates that this is **Stockingfield Junction** ⓱.

This junction is where the main canal heads eastwards. The towpath, however, continues along the Glasgow branch of the canal and in the days when boats were hauled by horses, the beasts had to be led down a ramp, under the canal, and then back up another ramp in order that they could continue their work. The towpath continues on the left (that is, north) side of the main canal. It may seem odd that the main canal's towpath is discontinuous, but this is because the canal was originally constructed from Grangemouth to Glasgow; only later was the canal continued westwards from here.

There is some open space on the left before the towpath crosses a bridge over a **spillway** ⓲ which allows surplus water to escape down a stone-lined channel to a drain. A sluice can be seen beside the canal (and below the towpath) and this is used to control the water level.

Ruchill Street is on the right while the industrial buildings on the left were the **Glasgow Lead and Colour Works** ⓳, erected in 1874 and 1904. The complex is continued to the east of Ruchill Street Bridge. This is a good example of a large industrial firm which was established here in order to take advantage of the proximity of the canal, and the remains of the factory's wharves can still be seen. Varnish, paint and lead products were made here.

On the factory wall is a large and very colourful **mural** which was painted in 1996 by local schoolchildren. It carries the words *Glasgow our canal our future* and depicts a canal bridge which has been opened to allow a boat to pass. To represent the types of places the canal passes through, the mural shows high-rise buildings to represent the city and animals and wild flowers to represent the countryside.

At this point, it is worth crossing Ruchill Street to see **Ruchill Parish Church** ⓴ (1903-5, Neil C. Duff). This was originally built as the Ruchill United Presbyterian Church and was constructed with attractive Locharbriggs sandstone. It has a substantial square tower, intricate stonework at the main window and a Gothic porch which gives access to the church and the halls.

While the church building is not particularly well known, to its right is the more-famous **Ruchill Parish Church Halls** ㉑ (1898-1900, Charles Rennie Mackintosh). These were erected before the church was built as a mission hall for Westbourne Free Church. This white sandstone Art Nouveau structure is two storeys high and the facade has numerous delicately curved stone features to add interest around the rather small windows. The doorway, in particular, has sweeping curves in its decorative stonework. A caretaker's house, which has a stairtower, can be seen through the church's porch.

Mackintosh worked for John Honeyman, the architect of Westbourne Free Church (see p.232), hence Mackintosh's connection with this building. However, for some reason, he didn't get the contract for the church – perhaps this building was too avant-garde for the church members' tastes.

The canal now passes under the **Ruchill Street Bridge** ㉒ (1990) the design of which includes decorative features in the concrete facings and in the metal railings which are in the style of Mackintosh.

More industrial premises and wharves are seen on the left. The canal curves round to the left and on the left are the very large red-brick **Glasgow Rubber Works** ㉓ which were established here in the 1870s. The factory produced india-rubber, asbestos and waterproof materials.

Ruchill Park is now on the left and its summit is marked by an artificial mound topped by a flagpole. The park was opened in 1892 and the mound was made up of 24,000 cart-loads of material dumped here from Ruchill Hospital which was erected nearby in the 1890s.

The **Bilsland Drive Aqueduct** ㉔ (1879) is now crossed but unfortunately there is no access to the street below to look at the aqueduct from a lower level. A plaque on its parapet bears the inscription *Speirs Wharf Port Dundas 2 miles Stockinfield* [spelled without a 'g'] *Junction ½ mile*.

A bridge across the canal leads to the **Murano Street Student Village** ㉕ (1992-4, Ian Burke Associates), a large complex of self-catering accommodation for 1112 students who attend Glasgow University. This reclaimed land was previously occupied by a glass factory hence the three roads within the village are named after varieties of manufactured glass: Caithness Street, Monart Street and Vasart Place; the last two places are Venetian islands.

Maryhill Fire Station ㉖ is on the right (across Maryhill Road) and to the left of its main building is a tower used by firefighters to practise rescuing people from tall buildings. The station is built to a very high standard and this has resulted in it being dubbed the 'Maryhilton'!

The canal now goes under the **Nolly Brig** ㉗ (1990) which carries the inclined Firhill Road. This fixed bridge has decorative features similar to those seen on Ruchill Street Bridge. It is sometimes called the Firhill Road Bridge. When the bridge was rebuilt in 1990 the opportunity was taken to give it a substantial clearance above the canal in preparation for the eventual reopening of the waterway.

The towpath now arrives at the large **Firhill Basin** ㉘. This is situated at a wide bend in the canal where two timber basins were established: one was at the far side of the canal from the towpath and the other forms a loop on the inside of the bend. This latter basin could be shut off from the canal by inserting planks into the grooved stonework which can be seen on the left, at the end of the 'island' which separates the two basins. The basin was originally constructed in 1788 (and enlarged in 1849) for seasoning timber, and big logs were left floating in the water to keep them moist while they aged. Many timber-based industries developed in the area and the large Western Sawmills were established here. There used to be bridges joining the towpath to the island but these have been removed, allowing the island to become a haven for wildlife.

Just before the distance plaque found here, look southwest and about 500m (550 yards) away can be seen the red sandstone tower of Charles Rennie Mackintosh's **Queen's Cross Church** ㉙ (1897-9). The church can be reached by turning right at the plaque and following the perimeter of the football stadium. Turn left at Firhill Road and then right at Springbank Street. The church is on the left, just at the junction with Garscube Road.

This is the only one of Mackintosh's church designs which was actually built and it is fitting that since 1977 it has been the home of the Charles Rennie Mackintosh Society and that it now serves as a working memorial to his talents. There is a substantial collection of Mackintosh books on display in the society's shop and any visitor wanting detailed information on the architect should make a visit.

In 1897 the church's site was even more cramped than it is now as it was hemmed in by neighbouring buildings. The overall style has been described as Art Nouveau Late Gothic and there are various important influences in the design. For example, the inspiration for the corner tapering tower came from the medieval Merriot Church in Somerset which Mackintosh had studied in 1895. The building's buttress and its relatively steep roof are important in their effect on the interior's design, as they permit a large floor area devoid of substantial supporting pillars. Indeed, the main surprising features inside the church are the horizontal steel girders across the broad nave which are used to strengthen the whole structure. Above the girders is a barrel-vaulted timbered roof which is reminiscent of the hull of an upturned ship.

The main source of light is the large expanse of plain glass which helps to illuminate the darkest recesses of the building. Very little coloured glass is used but there is some in the west window and in the back wall. The splendid dark woodwork has many carved details, for example in the pulpit, on the rederos (at the back of the dais) and on the front panels of the two galleries.

The church hall's main features are the wooden roof trusses, which are very similar to those found in the Glasgow School of Art (see p.125).

The canal now skirts Firhill, home of **Partick Thistle Football Club** ❸⓪, but unfortunately there's not much of a view of the pitch from the towpath. This team is not as well known as the two members of the 'Old Firm' (see p.285) but in 1998 an article in *The Herald* described the 'Jags' as 'the football club some regard as the thinking man's alternative to Celtic and Rangers'.

The club was formed in Partick in 1876 and over the years it has had many homes, finally coming to rest at Firhill in 1909. The team are well known for their inconsistency over the years and for the fervent supporters who have followed Thistle rather than going for the 'easy' option of Rangers or Celtic. Their achievements include winning the Scottish Cup in 1921 (1-0 against Rangers) and the Scottish League Cup in 1971 (4-1 against Celtic). They have also won a place in European Championships twice, although they have yet to win a European cup. Their fans are often quite bewildered by the team's ups and downs, so much so that an official history notes, with great seriousness, that 'being a Thistle fan is, to say the least, difficult and beyond the capabilities of the average person… Jags fans may be thin on the ground but they are resilient, durable, even if by nature a little masochistic.' Still, it's only a game. Although crowds these days may not be huge, in 1922 a match against Rangers at Firhill attracted 49,838 people.

The stand nearest the canal was erected in 1994 and is named the Jackie Husband Stand after a well-known pre-Second World War player who was famed for the length of his throw-ins.

About 700m (750 yards) away to the north will be seen an ornate red sandstone tower (which looks like a Flemish bell tower) which belongs to **Ruchill Hospital** (Alex. B. McDonald). The hospital was built on a very elevated site and this is its water tower which was needed for storing water. The hospital was built at the end of the nineteenth century as the City of Glasgow Hospital for Infectious Diseases.

Pass the eastern end of the timber basin. Just beyond the basin a **stop lock** ❸① can be seen which was added during the Second World War. A number of these locks were installed and they were closed during air raids so that, if the canal's bank was breached and water poured out, the lock would prevent too much water escaping. Fortunately, the canal was never hit.

FIRHILL TO SPIERS WHARF

There is now more open land on the left. On the right is an extensive view over the west of the city and the most notable tall buildings are (from left to right) the three square towers of Trinity College (see p.221), the spires of St Mary's Episcopal Cathedral (see p.223) and Lansdowne Parish Church (see p.224), Glasgow University's tower (see p.178) and Glasgow University Library (see p.191).

An inlet, known as the **Clay Cut** ㉜, is on the left. This was made to provide access to a quarry in Hamiltonhill from which clay was extracted to 'puddle' the canal. 'Puddling' is the pressing of the clay into the bed and banks of the canal in order to make them watertight. Hamiltonhill is one of Glasgow's many drumlins, the great mounds of glacial debris that were dumped by receding glaciers at the end of the last Ice Age. In some places a lot of this debris is in the form of clay, as the city's gardeners know only too well!

The modern **Canal Offices** are found at the **Hamiltonhill Basin** ㉝ which is also known as the Old Basin. The canal reached here in 1777 and this was its Glasgow terminus until 1790. Today there is a complex of buildings here including the Scottish Office of British Waterways (1984, Ian Burke & Associates) who operate the canal. The old buildings beside the canal are the original workshops of around 1790 and the longer of the two structures has a clock at its eastern end. This is where the canal's maintenance staff are based.

Other features of interest near the basin are the mooring rings, the original stone setts that make up the towpath and the stop lock at the western end of the basin. A number of boats are moored here, including working craft used for maintaining the canal, boats that are laid up, pleasure cruisers and some houseboats. A small (modified) bascule bridge (called Rockvilla Bridge) is at the eastern end of the basin and goes across the canal to Applecross Street.

The canal now crosses the **Possil Road Aqueduct** ㉞. This was constructed around 1880 and replaced an earlier aqueduct (*c.* 1790, Robert Whitworth) which is immediately before the newer structure; the older aqueduct can be recognised by its curved parapet.

Spiers Wharf

The canal now bends round to the right and the remains of a large **timber basin** ㉟ can be seen on the opposite bank. Beside this were the City Sawmills which were founded in 1849.

A stop lock is passed and beyond it is **Spiers Wharf** ㊱. There is one isolated building at the start of Speirs Wharf North and then one enormous row of substantial white sandstone warehouses which vary from five to seven storeys in height. The wharves are still cobbled and a number of mooring rings are still extant. This was once a very busy place on the canal but it gradually became run down after the canal closed. Many of the massive warehouses were latterly used as bonded warehouses by Scottish Grain Distillers but in 1988-9 they were converted into offices and houses by Nicholas Groves-Raines; this is a marvellous piece of conservation work on a prominent site which can be seen from many parts of the city. There is a good view over Glasgow as the basin is on a prominent platform, 48m (156ft) above sea level.

The first building is the narrow former **Wheatsheaf Mills** ㊲ which were originally part of a sugar mill but in 1931 it was reconstructed as a individual five-storey structure.

The next building is the seven-storey former **Port Dundas Sugar Refinery** ㊳ (1865-6) which has the date *1866* at the top. This was built for the sugar refiners Murdoch & Dodrell.

The next four buildings comprise the former **City of Glasgow Grain Mills and Stores** ㊴ and the first has the date *1851* on it. These were built for John Currie & Co., with the initial six-storey building erected in 1851 and the others in 1869-70.

At the very eastern end of the row of warehouses is a colourful plaque dated *MCMXC* (1990) showing the *Shamrock* outside the Canal Offices.

Beyond the warehouses stand the former **Canal Offices** ㊵ (*c.* 1812). This is an ornate and beautifully proportioned two-storey Georgian building with a Doric porch above which is a pediment decorated by a clock. This was where the canal's business was carried out and opposite it was the departure point of the passenger boats (the *Swifts*, see p.271) which plied between here and the eastern end of the canal.

At the end of Spiers Wharf South is a plaque on which is written the canal's construction date (1768-90) and the wharf's distance (2½ miles) from Stockinfield (again spelled without a 'g') Junction.

The canal is closed off at this point but just a short walk away is the once-important Port Dundas which was constructed as the canal's main city terminus. (See the detour on p.270)

The Canal Offices at Spiers Wharf

SPIERS WHARF TO COWCADDENS UNDERGROUND STATION

From the eastern end of Spiers Wharf South, turn right and follow a flight of steps downhill. Turn right then bear left to pass to the left of Phoenix Park Nursery School. Garscube Road is now met. Turn left and go under the M8 motorway in order to reach **Cowcaddens** (see p.104). Keep beside the blocks of flats which are on the left to reach **Cowcaddens Underground Station** ④ on the right. The walk can be ended here at the station or a short detour on the other side of Garscube Road can be followed.

If following the detour, turn right immediately before the Underground station and go through the pedestrian underpass to reach the western side of Garscube Road. The underpass leads to New City Road and the first building on the right is the former **Free Normal Seminary** ㊷ (1836-7, David Hamilton). The building is in Italian Renaissance style and forms three sides of a square, allowing space for a playground behind the central block. The elaborate Roman Doric porch has coupled columns which support a balcony, and a tall and fairly elaborate clock tower (which is topped by a vase-shaped finial) rises above the main section of the building.

This institution was originally established by **David Stow** (1793-1864) as the 'Normal School', Britain's first teacher-training institution, and it incorporated both a school and facilities for training teachers. In many ways, Stow led educational thinking in Scotland and he advocated a number of 'revolutionary' ideas such as boys and girls being educated together, and the abolition of school prizes and corporal punishment. His ideas were outlined in his *Moral training for large cities* (1834) which was influential both in Britain and in parts of the British Empire. The book was based on his experience in setting up an infant school in the Drygate (near the Trongate) in 1826, at a time when two-thirds of all the children in the Tron Parish were receiving no education at all.

Sadly, the Normal School had recurring financial problems and in order to keep it open a grant was accepted from the Church of Scotland; however, this was arranged on the basis that the Church controlled the school's administration. Stow had previously maintained that the Church should not be involved in educational provision and this was a great blow. This situation was made even worse in 1843, during the time of the Disruption, when Stow and his staff left the Church of Scotland to join the Free Church of Scotland; this meant that they eventually had to leave the school. This they did in 1845 and Stow then established the Free Church Normal College which was later called Stow College. In 1906 the two institutions merged to form Jordanhill College of Education which is now part of Strathclyde University (see p.45).

In later years this building ceased to be a school and it operated as Dundas Vale Teachers Centre. It is now used as offices.

Continue on New City Road. The large warehouse on the right at the end of the block is **'Chinatown'** ❹, which has a number of Chinese shops inside it which are worth looking at. Follow New City Road as it bends round to the right and leads to the tall Chinese-style entrance. This has a couple of lions carved from granite and the tiled roof of the entrance is decorated with ceramic dragons.

To the left of the bend in New City Road stands the former **Savings Bank of Glasgow** ❹ (1909-10, Neil C. Duff). This is an extremely narrow building which occupies the narrow gushet between New City Road and Shamrock Street and must have occupied a prominent place at a busy junction in the days before the motorway scythed through Cowcaddens. This red sandstone Edwardian Baroque building has lots of detail around its doorway including a royal coat of arms. This has well-executed sculptures of a unicorn and a lion and bears the phrases *Nemo me impune lacessit* ('No-one provokes me with impunity') and *Dieu et mon droit* ('God and my right'). A diminutive St Andrew (holding his cross) is there too, and just below him is an even smaller carving of a man on horseback. Other features near the door include polished granite pillars, carved fruit and flowers, and four cherubs. There are lots of smaller carvings on both sides of the building, especially on the keystones of the ground-floor windows (a horn of plenty, keys on a chain and serpents intertwined round a winged torch). Sculpted faces are also included above the first-floor windows. On the northern side of the building is the date *1910* and the letters *GSB*. At the top of this side is a large sculpture showing two female figures (one of whom is holding a ship's hull) and two cherubs. The building is topped by a dome which is pierced by circular windows and topped by a weather vane.

The Savings Bank of Glasgow was founded in 1835 and became the biggest savings bank in Britain, with nearly 700,000 accounts in 1955. Savings banks were established to encourage poorer people to save and the money lodged with the bank was loaned to borrowers such as the government and local authorities. The bank eventually became part of the Trustee Savings Bank.

Opposite the bank's entrance is the **James Torrens Memorial Fountain** **45** which is dedicated to this man who was *one of the representatives of the tenth ward in the town council in 1869-1884*. It is very appropriate that this Glasgow councillor is remembered by a fountain dispensing clean water as he is best known for his adherence to the ideals of temperance. Indeed, he must have had extremely forthright views on the matter for in 1873 the Glasgow magazine *The Bailie* wrote a long article about him and in one passage the writer informs that

> *The man is no doubt well meaning, honest, and sincere, but teetotalism in its most offensive form is his hobby, and he rides it rough-shod over everybody with whom he comes in contact. There are people whose religion seems to be the worship of cold water, and Councillor TORRENS is one of them. One would imagine that water drinkers should be calm of temperament and moderate in opinion, their blood not being inflamed by either wine or strong drink. But the reverse is the case.*

Walk westwards along Shamrock Street to see **Stow College** **46** (1929-32, Whyte & Galloway). This is a tall red brick and glass building with stone features (including a carved Glasgow coat of arms) above the entrance. The college was opened in 1934 and named after David Stow (see above). This was the city's first purpose-built further education college and it trained apprentices from many of Glasgow engineering industries, especially the shipyards. With the rundown of the city's mechanical engineering factories, new courses in subjects such as electronics and computing have been introduced to keep pace with modern needs.

Retrace the route back to **Cowcaddens Underground Station** **41** where the walk ends.

DETOUR: SPIERS WHARF TO PORT DUNDAS

The **Port Dundas** terminus **47** of the canal was established here at One Hundred Acre Hill between 1786 and 1790 and was named after Sir Lawrence Dundas who had been governor of the Forth and Clyde Navigation Company. As well as becoming the canal's main Glasgow terminus its construction also allowed a link to be made with the Monkland Canal and this gave it access to a large supply of water. The Monkland Canal (which was taken over by the Forth and Clyde Canal in 1846) was closed to commercial traffic in 1935 and its route was subsequently covered by the M8 motorway; however, the extra supply of water is still available to the Forth and Clyde Canal.

Port Dundas became Glasgow's most important port until the River Clyde was deepened (see p.145) and industries such as engineering, distilling and chemicals were established in the district. This area was outside the city boundary when the canal arrived here but it was annexed by Glasgow in 1843 and it rapidly developed as an industrial centre. In 1849, James Pagan was impressed by what he saw and wrote that 'on these few acres have been established factories, colour works, chemical works, dye works, grinding works, mills for logwood, dye and bread stuffs, foundries, machine shops, potteries and soap works – presenting a view of manufacturing and curious industry which must be unparalleled in any other city in the world.' One benefit of the site's elevated position was that all the airborne pollution produced by these factories would have been blown away!

As well as carrying goods of various descriptions, the canal was also used for passenger services and the journey from here to Edinburgh would have been a lot less bumpier than by the stagecoach. In 1801 William Symington's famous steamboat *Charlotte Dundas* (named after Lord Dundas' daughter) was introduced and in 1828 the *Cyclops* was used; unfortunately, both these boats' paddles produced substantial wakes which damaged the banks of the canal. The twin-hulled *Swift* was brought into service in 1828 but this wooden boat was superseded by the iron-hulled *Rapid*, the design of which was much more suitable. By this time the journey along the canal was regarded as being on the 'tourist trail' and an 1823 guidebook for passengers proclaimed the virtues of 'the rural scenery and the lofty mountain grandeur which are so finely blended in those of the land between the Forth and Clyde.' The number of passengers reached about 200,000 a year by the 1830s but the linking of Glasgow and Edinburgh by railway in 1842 dealt a great blow to passenger traffic. A number of services were maintained and later boats included pleasure steamers such as the *Rockvilla Castle*, the *Fairy Queen* (which could carry 200 passengers), the *May Queen*, the *Fairy Queen II* and the *Gypsy Queen* (which was a floating dance venue in the 1930s). Sadly, cruising effectively ended around the time of the Second World War but today some passenger boats occasionally ply the canal; hopefully the regeneration of the canal will encourage more passenger services. But not to Port Dundas!

From the eastern end of Speirs Wharf North, walk through the gates that are near the former Canal Offices. Cross Craighall Road and turn right. Follow the pavement as it curves round to the left into North Canalbank Street. Dundashill is on the left and there is a **basin** on the right. Walk beside the basin and on the right will be found a **wooden bascule bridge 48**. This original bridge is the canal's 'standard design' and is in very good condition, with the hand-cranking gearing mechanism still intact.

On the northern side of North Canalbank Street is the extremely large **Port Dundas Distillery** ㊾, now owned by Diageo. Robert Macfarlane set up a distillery here in 1810 and this was amalgamated with another nearby distillery in the 1860s to form what eventually became a massive plant for the production of grain whisky. By 1885 this was the largest distillery in the British Isles, making 11,400,000 litres (2,500,000 gallons) a year. By-products included bakers' yeast (for making bread) and animal feed for the four hundred pigs which were kept on the premises. But a large distillery such as this can have major problems and terrible fires broke out here in 1903 and 1916. The *Glasgow Herald* reported that during the latter fire 'the whisky casks… began to burst with loud explosions, and each new crash was followed immediately afterwards by a stream of blazing whisky which rapidly found its way to the streets and thence to the canal.' What a waste!

Today, the grain distillery uses mainly wheat (from the Scottish Borders) to produce whisky which is used in the blending of well-known brands such as Johnnie Walker, Dewar's, White Horse and Bell's. One new by-product of the distillery is electrical energy. The plant has its own power station and surplus electricity is fed into the National Grid, hence the cables and tall pylons seen at Spiers Wharf.

Cross the pedestrian bridge and on the right is the **railway swing bridge** ㊿. This is made from plate girders and was opened and closed by hand. The gear mechanism for turning the bridge is still in place.

Turn left at Payne Street. This leads to other **basins**, the extent of which give a good idea of how important and busy this area must have been during the canal's heyday.

Return to the eastern end of Spiers Wharf South (see p.267).

Pollokshields, Bellahouston Park and Govan

A walk through a variety of districts not normally on the tourist routes: residential Pollokshields, the open spaces of Bellahouston Park and the industrial district of Govan, famed for its shipyards and its early Christian monuments.

Pearce Institute, Govan

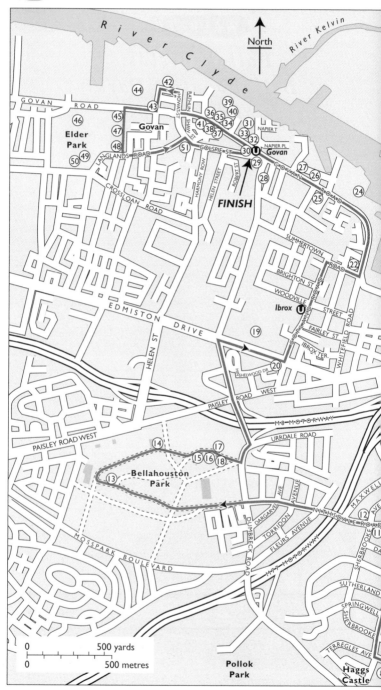

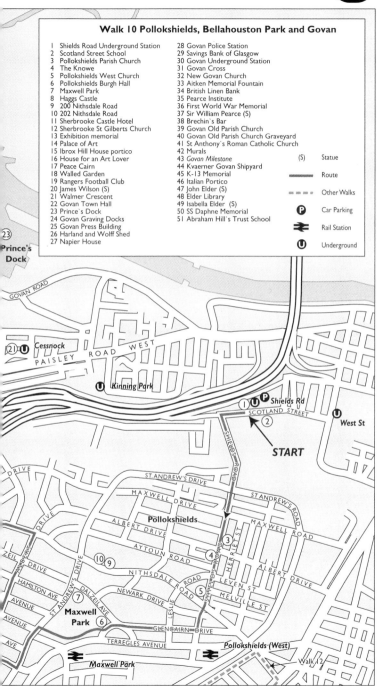

Walk 10 Pollokshields, Bellahouston Park and Govan

1 Shields Road Underground Station
2 Scotland Street School
3 Pollokshields Parish Church
4 The Knowe
5 Pollokshields West Church
6 Pollokshields Burgh Hall
7 Maxwell Park
8 Haggs Castle
9 200 Nithsdale Road
10 202 Nithsdale Road
11 Sherbrooke Castle Hotel
12 Sherbrooke St Gilberts Church
13 Exhibition memorial
14 Palace of Art
15 Ibrox Hill House portico
16 House for an Art Lover
17 Peace Cairn
18 Walled Garden
19 Rangers Football Club
20 James Wilson (S)
21 Walmer Crescent
22 Govan Town Hall
23 Prince`s Dock
24 Govan Graving Docks
25 Govan Press Building
26 Harland and Wolff Shed
27 Napier House

28 Govan Police Station
29 Savings Bank of Glasgow
30 Govan Underground Station
31 Govan Cross
32 New Govan Church
33 Aitken Memorial Fountain
34 British Linen Bank
35 Pearce Institute
36 First World War Memorial
37 Sir William Pearce (S)
38 Brechin`s Bar
39 Govan Old Parish Church
40 Govan Old Parish Church Graveyard
41 St Anthony`s Roman Catholic Church
42 Murals
43 *Govan Milestone*
44 Kvaerner Govan Shipyard
45 K-13 Memorial
46 Italian Portico
47 John Elder (S)
48 Elder Library
49 Isabella Elder (S)
50 SS Daphne Memorial
51 Abraham Hill`s Trust School

(S)　Statue

━━━━　Route

－ － －　Other Walks

P　Car Parking

⇌　Rail Station

U　Underground

GOVAN ROAD

㉓
**Prince's
Dock**

Cessnock
㉑ⓊＵ
PAISLEY ROAD WEST

Ⓤ Kinning Park

ⓊＵ**P** Shields Rd
SCOTLAND STREET
② Ⓤ West St
START

ST. ANDREW'S DRIVE
MAXWELL DRIVE
ST ANDREW'S ROAD
Pollokshields
ALBERT DRIVE
AYTOUN ROAD
③
④
HERRIET ST
MAXWELL ROAD
DRIVE
DRIVE
NITHSDALE ROAD
⑩ ⑨
LEVEN ST
ALBERT DRIVE
NEWARK DRIVE
⑤
MELVILLE ST
ZEIL DRIVE
HAMILTON AVE
⑦
ST ANDREW'S AVE
DALZEIL AVE
LESLIE RD
AVENUE
**Maxwell
Park** ⑥
GLENCAIRN DRIVE
AVENUE
TERREGLES AVENUE
Pollokshields (West)
AVE
⇌ ⇌ Walk 12
Maxwell Park

Main places of interest	**Scotland Street School 2** (Museum of Education; Charles Rennie Mackintosh)
	Maxwell Park **7**
	Haggs Castle **8** (16th-century castle)
	Bellahouston Park **13–18**
	House for an Art Lover **16** (Charles Rennie Mackintosh)
	Rangers Football Club **19**
	Govan Old Parish Church **39** (sculptured stones)
	Govan Old Parish Church Graveyard **40**
	Elder Park **45–50**
Circular/linear	linear
Starting point	Shields Road Underground Station **1**
Finishing point	Govan Underground Station **29**
Distance	11.5 km (7.5 miles)
Terrain	generally level pavements and paths; (generally) gentle hills in Pollokshields; steep hill in Bellahouston Park (this can be walked round)
Public transport	Shields Road Underground Station
	Pollokshields West Railway Station (C)
	Maxwell Park Railway Station (C)
	Dumbreck Railway Station (C)
	Ibrox Underground Station
	Govan Underground Station
Sections	Shields Road Underground Station to Bellahouston Park
	Bellahouston Park
	Bellahouston Park to Govan Cross
	Govan Cross to Govan Underground Station via Elder Park
Architects	Thomson: The Knowe **3**
	200 Nithsdale Road **9**
	202 Nithsdale Road **10**
	Walmer Crescent **21**
	Mackintosh: Scotland Street School **2**
	House for an Art Lover **15**
Nearby walks	11, 12
Refreshments	Scotland Street School; House for an Art Lover
Notes	Readers can shorten the walk by taking the Underground stations along the route. Be aware of safety advice (see p.16) as the parks, graveyards (and some of the streets) can be very quiet at times.

SHIELDS ROAD UNDERGROUND STATION TO BELLAHOUSTON PARK

Leave **Shields Road Underground Station** ❶ and cross Scotland Street.

Head eastwards to **Scotland Street School** ❷ (1904-6, Charles Rennie Mackintosh), now the city's Museum of Education. This outstanding building's most noticeable features are the two glazed curved stairtowers which rise through three storeys and are capped by conical roofs. As was the custom, there are separate front entrances for boys and girls and also separate playgrounds (with outside toilets) at the back of the school. And, as a nice touch intended to avoid the large three-storey building intimidating the 'weans', there's an especially small entrance for infants. The rear of the building is relatively plain, with Art Nouveau decorations around the central and end windows.

Each of the twenty-one standard-sized classrooms were designed to accommodate between sixty and sixty-five children, giving the school the enormous capacity of 1250 pupils! When it finally closed as a school in 1979 the roll had fallen to just 89, a reflection on the rapid depopulation of the area with the dramatic decline of local manufacturing industry. However, in 1990 it was opened as a fascinating museum.

The Infants' door leads into the bright and airy **Drill Hall** where pupils were taught what is now called physical education, its original name implying more than a little in the way of military overtones. The walls are covered in white tiles, giving it a rather clinical look. The Temporary Exhibition Gallery, café and Audio-visual Theatre are also on this floor. Stairwells on either side of the hall lead to the upper floors. One interesting feature of the staircases is that the half-landings are set back from the curved windows, making the stairs much better lit a and also giving more opportunities for pupils to drop things on others below! The first floor has more exhibition spaces and a display about Charles Rennie Mackintosh.

The second floor has a number of rooms laid out to show teaching 'regimes' in various eras. Start with Room 16 which has been restored to show a **Victorian/Edwardian Classroom**, with its tiers of extremely uncomfortable double seats, presumably designed to keep pupils awake, facing the teacher's desk. It's all very formal, highly regimented and extremely austere. Pupils weren't meant to *enjoy* education.

Room 17 is the **World War Two Classroom** which is in fact not all that different from the previous room. Slates, inkwells and a map of the world emphasising the extent of the British Empire will bring back floods of memories for many visitors. Poignantly, there are boxes for the pupils' gas masks on the desks. Since the nearby shipyards were a prime target for enemy warplanes, everyone had to keep their masks by them at all times.

Rooms 18 and 19 hold the **School Days Exhibition**; it is best to enter by Room 18. The fascinating exhibition deals with the good and not-so-good aspects of school life over a century of Scottish education with pictures, equipment and all sorts of memorabilia to remind visitors of all ages of what were always called (by our elders) 'the happiest days of our life'. Artefacts from many schools in the Glasgow area are on show. In one display there's the dreaded tawse (a thonged leather strap) which was used to administer corporal punishment up until the 1980s; intriguingly, it sits atop a Bible.

Room 20 is a **1950s/60s Classroom**; a rather less-daunting place in comparison to the other rooms, but still far removed from the much cosier carpeted rooms in which today's children are taught. The inkwells are still there, but at least the slates have gone.

On the opposite side of the corridor is the restored **Cookery Room**, a cavernous barrel-vaulted room with few 'mod cons' to take the drudgery out of cooking. A rather small black 'range' acted as a cooker and hot plate. The dressers for holding crockery and utensils have open shelves for easy access and their robust design ensured that they withstood the rough use which thousands of pupils gave them over the years.

During term time, groups of school children visit the museum and take lessons in one of the rooms with everyone (including teachers) dressed up according to the era they are re-enacting. Rooms 16, 17 and 20 are used for this and the lessons in Rooms 17 and 20 can be observed from the windowed galleries in the exhibition area.

The school also houses the **Open Museum** which lends items from the city's collections to community groups and local venues in Glasgow.

After leaving the school, walk westwards along Scotland Street and turn left at Shields Road. Cross the railway line and St Andrew's Road then climb the hill into the district of **Pollokshields**. There's a wide variety of housing types here – modern flats, tenements, terraced houses and larger villas.

Pollokshields Parish Church ❸, formerly Pollokshields Established Church (1877-8, Robert Baldie) is situated at the junction of Shields Road with Albert Drive. This Gothic-style building possesses a fine collection of stained-glass windows, reflecting the wealth of the Pollokshields area when the church was erected. Just beside the pavement is a beautifully carved First World War memorial (1921) based on the Ruthwell and Bewcastle crosses.

Diagonally across the junction from the church is a driveway at 301 Albert Road leading to **The Knowe ❹** (1852-3, Alexander Thomson). Originally Knowe Cottage, this is one of Thomson's earliest houses and is unusual in that it has rounded arches in the porch. The bulky porch and the squat tower dominate the house which was built in the

Picturesque Italian style, although there are Egyptian- and Greek-inspired features inside. The right hand portion of the house was added in 1855-8.

Continue on Shields Road, past well-built terraces and tenements to the junction with Nithsdale Road where the tall and very imposing former **Pollokshields West Church** ❺ stands. This was initially a Free Church of Scotland (1875-9, McKissack & Rowan); its Grecian style, including the campanile, is perhaps based on the work of Alexander Thomson. It is now a nursing home.

Continue on Shields Road and turn right at Glencairn Drive. This road becomes Dalziel Avenue as Glencairn Drive swings away to the left. Keep following Glencairn Drive (by keeping to the south side of the road) to get to the former **Pollokshields Burgh Hall** ❻ (1888-90, H. E. Clifford) which stands on the right at the edge of Maxwell Park.

The hall is built of dark red sandstone from Ballochmyle in Ayrshire, which contrasts quite starkly with the white sandstone used to build many of the surrounding villas. Constructed in seventeenth-century Scottish Domestic style, this was opened in 1890 but served the independent burgh only until 1891 when the rapidly expanding city swallowed up the area. The hall contained various council offices and a courtroom. There was also a masonic meeting place, hence the numerous masonic symbols in the carvings (especially at the back of the building) and in the stained-glass windows.

Above the main doorway is a shield depicting the burgh's coat of arms and the date *1890*. Above that, the entrance is guarded by two lions holding shields bearing the initials *PBH* and to the left of the doorway is the burgh's motto: *Aye ready*. The tall Scots Baronial tower standing behind the entrance has a number of interesting details including a little stone balcony. To the left of the hall is the former park keeper's lodge.

Pollokshields was once part of the huge Pollok estate which was owned by the Maxwell family (see p.302) and until the mid-nineteenth century this area was farmland. With an increasing number of rich Glaswegians wanting to build spacious mansions, part of the estate was given over to a luxury housing development upwind of the city's factories. What is now St Andrew's Drive was constructed from 1851 onwards and gradually the area's population increased, attaining burgh status in 1876.

Go through the gates at the side of the hall and enter **Maxwell Park** ❼. Land for the park was gifted by Sir John Stirling Maxwell and it was opened to the public in 1890. The ground was quite low lying and marshy so an extensive drainage system was built, allowing the water to gather in the pond on the western side of the park.

Go through the park's gates and take the second path on the left. On the right is the site of the former Hamilton Fountain; this no longer exists but the old basin of the fountain has been retained as the edging for a circular flower bed. The path now heads towards the southern edge of the park and Maxwell Park Railway Station will be seen on the left. Cross an avenue of trees and walk to the left of a large open grassy area. Follow the left-hand edge of the **boating pond** then go up a little slope on the left to reach the junction of St Andrew's Drive and Springkell Avenue.

Follow St Andrew's Drive southwards to Terregles Avenue and turn right. On the left is **Haggs Castle** ❽, but unfortunately not a great deal of it can be seen from the roadside. This was originally a three-storey L-shaped castle, erected in 1585 by Sir John Maxwell of Pollok. It was built to replace the Maxwells' laighe castle (see p.302) and was the family's main house until 1595 when they moved to Pollok House (see p.306). It was abandoned in 1753 and slowly became 'a picturesque ruin', described by Hugh Macdonald (see p.378) as having walls which 'are in some places upwards of five feet in thickness, while the durability of the material of which they are composed is obvious from the excellent state of preservation in which the carvings on their exterior surface still exist.' It was restored in the 1850s by John Baird II and in 1899-1900 the north wing (with its crow-stepped gables) was added and the staircase tower at the front of the building was enlarged. Since then it has had a variety of uses, and from the 1970s to the 1990s it housed Glasgow's Museum of Childhood. At present it is in private hands and not open to the public.

Inside, the ground floor has three vaulted rooms while the first floor contains the hall. Although it was restored as a house rather than a proper castle, it has gun loops and shot holes as reminders of its original defensive role.

Continue on Terregles Avenue then turn right at Albert Drive. This runs through a large estate of handsome sandstone villas, no two of them the same.

At Nithsdale Road, the route goes left towards Bellahouston Park. However, some distance to the right are **200 Nithsdale Road** ❾ and **202 Nithsdale Road** ❿, designed by Alexander Thomson in 1871 and 1870 respectively. They are described on p.398.

Turn left at Nithsdale Road. As the road descends there are two buildings of interest at the junction with Sherbrooke Avenue. On the left is the **Sherbrooke Castle Hotel** ⓫ (1896, Thomson & Sandilands), an extravagantly decorated building in Scots Baronial style built by John Morrison as his home; he was one of the chief contractors in the construction of the City Chambers.

On the right is **Sherbrooke St Gilberts Church** ⓬ (1900, W. F. McGibbon), based on a thirteenth-century French style. At the sides of the porch are figures of John Knox (see p.358) and John Calvin, two important Protestant leaders.

Continue on Nithsdale Road, crossing over the busy M77. The road eventually ends at Dumbreck Road on the opposite side of which are the gates of Bellahouston Park.

BELLAHOUSTON PARK

Enter **Bellahouston Park** through the ornate cast-iron entrance gates; the gates' piers contain panels depicting the four elements of the city's coat of arms. This land was purchased for the city in 1896 and is centred around the steep-sided Bellahouston Hill, with the flatter parts used for gardens and sports facilities. There are also large open areas, so important in a busy and noisy city.

The park is big enough to hold very large events, the most important of which was the **1938 Empire Exhibition**. This was held fifty years after the first great exhibition (see p.197); however, instead of being held when the city's prospects looked promising, this exhibition took place just after the 1930s Depression and with the real possibility of war uppermost in people's minds. Although there was great concern about what was happening at home, the exhibition was outward-looking and the British Empire as a body of nations was a recurrent theme. This event covered at least twice the area of the previous exhibitions and was too big for Kelvingrove Park. There were numerous pavilions, the two largest being the Palaces of Engineering and Industry, and many from the individual countries of the Empire. One of these was with the popular South African pavilion which was in Dutch Colonial style, quite out of tune with the very 'modernistic' style of all the other buildings. The shadow of rearmament was visible in the pavilions occupied by the armed forces but as a counterbalance there was a Peace Pavilion (see p.284), although it was tucked away in one of the quieter areas. Other interesting exhibits included the Palace of Art (see p.282) and a Highland village, complete with chief's castle. The eating facilities included one of the first Indian restaurants in Scotland.

The exhibition's architect was Thomas S. Tait and his name is still well-remembered in Glasgow because of the 91m (300ft) high 'Tait's Tower' (officially the 'Tower of Empire') which stood on the summit of Bellahouston Hill. Since the hill itself is 52m (170ft) high, the tower (complete with viewing platform) dominated the whole district and could be seen from 160km (100 miles) away. This was meant to be a permanent structure but in 1939 it was demolished as it would have been an obvious landmark for enemy warplanes; however, its foundations are still extant. The exhibition ran from May to October and attracted over 12½ million visitors, despite the appalling weather that summer.

From the entrance, follow the broad double avenue of trees, to the right of which is the park's large nursery. Pass to the right of a granite fountain and follow the wide driveway, all the time climbing **Bellahouston Hill**. Those who wish to avoid the hill (and the later flight of steps) should

bear left at the fountain and follow the base of the hill. This leads to the bottom of the flight of stairs below the granite Exhibition memorial (see below).

At the western end of the hill is the tall granite **Exhibition memorial** ⓭ which was unveiled in 1937 by King George VI (1895-1952). There is a wonderfully wide view from here. To the south is the wooded Pollok Country Park (see p.302). To the north can be seen two ranges of hills, both volcanic in origin: the Kilpatrick Hills on the left and the Campsie Hills on the right. The most obvious individual hill is Dumgoyne (427m (1401ft)), marking the position of an ancient volcanic vent which erupted some three hundred million years ago (during the Early Carboniferous Period). The hill is at the western end of the Campsie Hills and Glaswegians often describe the profile of this range as 'the sleeping warrior', with Dumgoyne as his head and his body stretching out to the east. The Campsies' dramatic south-facing escarpment marks the line of the Campsie Fault where the land to the south of it dropped by 900m (3000ft) during the Late Carboniferous.

Descend the flight of steps below the monument, heading towards the **Bellahouston Sports Centre**. Take two right turns and walk along to the **Palace of Art** ⓮ (1937-8, Launcelot Ross) which is now used as an indoor sports hall. This is the only building left from the 1938 exhibition but it has been altered since then. It originally had galleries around a central sculpture courtyard which were used to display works of art, with Scottish painting given special pride of place.

Pass to the right of the Palace of Art and cross a junction of paths. On the right is the outdoor **Glasgow Ski Centre**. Turn left at a crossroads and on the right is the tall stone **Ibrox Hill House portico** ⓯; this is all that remains of the house (see below). Follow the railings on the right to the main door of the House for an Art Lover. The access to the house is at the rear of the building.

The **House for an Art Lover** ⓰ was built in 1989-96 with the assistance of Glasgow City Council to a 1901 design of Charles Rennie Mackintosh. His original drawings were his entry to an international competition held by the German magazine *Zeitschrift fur Innendekoration* for a grand 'House for an Art Lover' (*Haus eines Kunstfreundes*) and the brief specified that it should be 'in a thoroughly modern style'. Various parts of the submission were the work of his wife, Margaret Macdonald, and it is fascinating to see how her interior decorations are matched to the overall design of the house. The entry (submitted under the pseudonym Der Vögel ('The bird') was disqualified as various views were not delivered in time, nor were the drawings complete, but on resubmission he received a special prize because his ideas were so startlingly original. The designs were published in 1902 and exhibited at the International Exposition in Turin where they further established

Mackintosh's reputation as one of the most innovative architects of the day.

The house is built on the foundations of Ibrox Hill House (demolished 1913) but since the drawings were never completed, nor were they intended as technical plans, much research work and inspired imagination has gone into the building's final design and it must be viewed in that context. A few rooms of this outstanding building were constructed to the original designs but there was no attempt to construct the first-floor bedrooms or what must have been an enormous attic playroom. The rooms described below are open to the public while the upper two storeys are used by the Glasgow School of Art (see p.125). The house also has displays of the architectural and perspective drawings that Mackintosh submitted for the competition; these are works of art in themselves.

The house is very large indeed and is essentially rectangular in shape. The exterior is harled and painted white and the two long walls are decorated with a few Art Nouveau relief sculptures of female figures worked in sandstone. Other symbols include the tree of life. Overall, it has a gaunt and very austere appearance, enhanced by the addition of the drum tower at the entrance.

The main door leads into the grand double-height **Main Hall.** Typically Mackintosh, this space is stark black and white, with the dark-stained wood relieved by plain walls and metalworked plaques. The overall design (which includes a gallery) is similar to the library in the Art School including the use of the vertical lines of the pillars, tall narrow windows and vertical beading on the wooden panelling. To the side of the hall is a long dark-panelled corridor which features two pairs of wooden window seats, similar to those found in the Art School.

House for an Art Lover

A flight of stairs off the hall goes up to the **Gallery**. The staircase rises through the drum tower and is lit by a tall leaded window and a large lantern in which are set pieces of coloured glass.

The panelled **Dining Room** is off the hall. This is a bit cosier and has a low barrel-vaulted ceiling and a set of gesso panels after Margaret Macdonald. The often-used rose motif (above the sandstone fireplace) and the pendant lights add further interest. In the centre, a long, low dining table is accompanied by tall straight-backed chairs.

The startling **Music Room** is also off the hall. This is very bright: not only does it have six curved glazed doors leading onto a balcony terrace, but also a white ceiling, white walls and white furniture – even the piano is encased in a white framework. Pendant lights and a few other small decorations add splashes of colour to this most intriguing of rooms.

Beside the music room is the **Oval Room**, originally designed as the Ladies Room. Its many curved features are abruptly interrupted by two box-like window seats.

The **Peace Cairn** **⑰** is sited in front of the house. The 1938 exhibition's Peace Pavilion was only a temporary structure but this cairn was erected in 1938 as a lasting reminder of people's hopes and fears. It has numerous shaped blocks of stone within it, on which are engraved the names of organisations which were deeply concerned with the very real possibility of war. These include groups such as the Airdrie Branch of the Communist Party, the Scottish Co-operative Women's Guild, Dundee Liberal Association and individuals such as the Lord Mayor of Belfast and the 'Greenock Peace Queen'. It is a poignant memorial.

Continue on the main drive. Follow it as it bends to the right, down to a park gate at Dumbreck Road. Turn right just before this exit, then take the second turn on the right to get to the **Walled Garden** **⑱**. (The garden can also be reached from behind the Mackintosh building.) This was originally the kitchen garden of Ibrox Hill House and it has fine displays of flowers and shrubs. There is a riot of colour here in the summer and it is particularly well known for its displays of sweet peas.

After visiting the garden, turn left and leave the park at the gate at Dumbreck Road. Turn left.

BELLAHOUSTON PARK TO GOVAN CROSS

Follow Dumbreck Road as it goes over the M8 and then crosses Paisley Road West. Dumbreck Road becomes Broomloan Road and should be followed down to the major junction with Edmiston Drive. Turn right and walk past the huge red-brick stadium of Ibrox Park, home of **Rangers Football Club** **⑲**. At each end of the main stand (1927-9, Archiebald Leitch) is the club's badge with the motto *Ready;* the western badge has the dates *1873* and *1928*, while the eastern one has *1873* and *1981*. The dates refer to the founding of the club (1873), the building of this stand (1928) and the completion of rebuilding the three other stands (1981). These newer stands were designed by T. M. Miller & Partners in 1978-81.

Rangers was founded in 1873 by a group of men who played football together on Glasgow Green and the club soon took an interest in helping to establish a Scottish League in order that clubs could play against one another. Even by the end of the century, Rangers was becoming one of the country's most important clubs and the rivalry with Celtic (see p.342) had taken root. The fact that Rangers' support was predominantly Protestant and Celtic's Catholic, intensified the antagonism between the opposing fans and for a very long time '**Old Firm**' games have been more than simply a football game. It is an inescapable fact of Glasgow 'culture' (if that is the right word) that clashes between the teams inevitably lead to clashes between the 'fans'; indeed, commentators have described the rivalry (or in some cases, the hatred) between groups of opposing supporters as tribal warfare. Although the two clubs have made attempts to distance themselves from the religious bigotry that follows them, it hardly helped that Rangers took so long to sign a Catholic player (1989) and so help to diminish the destructive hatred that exists between sections of the fans.

The two teams have often dominated Scotland's footballing honours over the last century, with the 'Gers winning the Scottish Cup six times and the Scottish League Championship fifteen times during the 1920s and 1930s. Rangers were also the first Scottish team to win the country's three main trophies (in 1948-9) and they were also the first to reach the final of a European championship (1961). They improved on that defeat when they won the European Cup Winners' Cup (1971-2), beating Moscow Dynamo. More recently, the club has had substantial success at home by winning the Scottish League Championship nine times in a row (1988-9 to 1996-7). But Rangers are increasingly looking abroad, for as well as signing numerous foreign footballers they are consistently setting their sights on European championships.

The main place of interest inside the stadium is the Trophy Room which is crammed full of all sorts of football memorabilia, including trophies, prizes and gifts made to the club. The trophies include replicas of some that the club has won over the years, as well as any trophies that the club has won in the most recent season. As well as momentoes from games played against Scottish teams there are others associated with championships or tours played abroad. Nearby, the Blue Room which, like nearly the whole of the stadium is blue in colour, is a reception room decorated with various paintings. At either end of the room is a mural by Senga Murray (1988), with one depicting scenes from the club's history and the other portraying the club's chairmen. The stadium's pitch is, of course, well-known to the thousands of fans who regularly visit Ibrox and it is interesting to see it from ground level. The stadium has four very large stands which have a combined seating capacity of around 50,000. This is substantially less than the ground's record attendance, set in 1939 when Rangers played Celtic in front of 118,567 people! For any fans who can't get a good view of the pitch, there's always the possibility of watching the two giant screens; these can also be used by fans who come here to watch Rangers when the team is playing away from home.

Tours of the stadium are available and generally involve visits to the Trophy Room, the Blue Room, the pitch and (possibly) the dressing rooms.

From Ibrox, walk along Edmiston Drive to the junction with Copland Road. On the right at this junction is a pink granite fountain to the memory of **James Wilson** ㉟ (1852-1906), for 21 years a doctor in Govan. It is topped with a bust of Wilson wearing academic dress.

As a detour, **Walmer Crescent** ⓭ (1857-62, Alexander Thomson) can be reached from this junction. The crescent is described on p.399.

Turn left at Copland Road. This goes northwards towards Govan, passing Ibrox Underground Station. Turn right at Summertown Road to reach the impressive Govan Town Hall, which is on the left.

Govan Town Hall ㉒ (1897-1901, Thomson & Sandilands) was built to express the wealth and aspirations of the burgh it served. Sandilands was trained in Paris and his elaborate Beaux Arts design celebrates the success of the local shipbuilding industry. On the Summertown Road side is an elaborate frieze depicting garlanded children pulling a chariot, above which are engraved the words *music* and *drama*. Higher up, two small turrets with decorative urns emphasise the shape of the tower-like structures on either side of the doorway.

Follow Summertown Road to Govan Road and turn left. The grand Greek portico over the entrance, the large central dome and the steep-roofed pavilions dominate the Govan Road facade. Above the main entrance is the Govan burgh arms (a ship on the stocks flanked by two shipyard workers) with the motto *Nihil sine labore* ('Nothing without work'). The two roundels are of Provost James Kirkwood and Baillie John Marr; a third face, on the northern wall, is of Councillor Richard Russell.

Govan is one of Glasgow's oldest districts and can trace its history back to the sixth century (see p.291). In 1134 David I gave the lands of Govan to the church in Glasgow and the village developed around the important religious site now occupied by Govan Old Parish Church. It later prospered as an agricultural centre serving the needs of Glasgow, and its important trading links were assisted by the fact that the Clyde could be forded here. By the sixteenth century, Bishop Leslie was impressed enough by Govan to describe it as 'a gret and ane large village upon the water of Clyd named Govan whare ale is wondrous guid'.

In 1793 there were 224 families in Govan, with many of them involved in handloom weaving; thirty years later the local mines were producing enough coal to fill three hundred trading vessels a year. But the big changes were just around the corner as the first shipyards were built around the 1840s and by 1864 the population had risen to 9000. That year Govan gained the status of a burgh but by 1912, when its population had dramatically increased to 91,000, it lost its autonomy as it was swallowed up by Glasgow. Shipbuilding and its associated industries dominated Govan and the local area was hit hard by the twentieth century decline of the yards (see p.154).

From Govan Town Hall follow Govan Road northwards. The River Clyde is just beyond the other side of the road and on the right, at Canting Way, there is a view to **Prince's Dock** ❸ (1893-7, Clyde Navigation Trust). This was originally opened as the Cessnock Dock and its three basins had over 3km (2 miles) of quays. It was used for general cargoes and for loading heavy engines and boilers into recently launched ships. The hydraulically powered cranes and capstans were powered from the still-existing red brick Hydraulic Power Station (see p.151). The docks were closed in the 1970s and partially filled to provide the site of the 1988 Glasgow Garden Festival (see below). The Canting Basin (originally, the place where ships could turn round) at the western end was used as a marina during the exhibition. Great debate still exists over the future use of this area.

The **1988 Glasgow Garden Festival** was one of a series of large-scale national garden events which was designed to turn derelict areas around Britain into more useful places. There were no large and ostentatious pavilions featuring industry or engineering as in the previous exhibitions (a sign of the times!) but the riverside location was put to good use by using the canting basin and encouraging interesting ships to berth at the quayside; there were even water taxis to take people to and from the city centre. The festival included horticultural exhibits and six themed areas which covered science and technology, health and well-being, plants and food, landscape and scenery, water and maritime, and recreation and sport. There were also small pavilions from a number of countries and, to take people around the extensive site, a tramway and a narrow-gauge railway.

The most notable structure was the 64m (240ft) tall Clydesdale Tower which had a passenger lift that went to the top then slowly turned round, allowing marvellous views of the whole Glasgow area. The main 'amusement' was a loop-the-loop Thrill Ride which kept thousands of screaming visitors happy while they hurtled along, upside down, at great speed. Some existing structures, such as the South Rotunda (see p.150) and the Hydraulic Power Station were refurbished and used for eating and entertainment, but the only new public amenities that have lasted are Bells Bridge (see p.152) and a small park on the southern side of the site. The festival ran from April to September and was hailed a great success, with an attendance of 4 million visitors.

Govan Road bends round to the left and the land on the right is taken up by the three enormous **Govan Graving Docks** ㉔ (1869-98, Clyde Navigation Trust). The dry dock farthest away is 168m (551ft) long, the middle one is 175m (575ft) long and the nearest is a massive 268m (880ft) long; when opened in 1898 it could take the world's largest vessels. The docks were used for fitting out ships and for ship repairs but were finally closed in 1988. Their future is still uncertain and numerous derelict dockside buildings still stand around the docks, waiting for something useful to happen.

The **Govan Press Building** ㉕ (1889-90, Frank Stirrat) stands at 577 Govan Road. This was originally the Cossar Building where *The Govan Chronicle* and later *The Govan Press* were printed. Above the first storey are roundels with the heads of Johann Gutenberg (German printer), Sir Walter Scott (see p.84), Robert Burns (see p.85) and William Caxton (English printer). The middle two heads are of John Cossar and his wife.

On the right is the huge **Harland and Wolff Shed** ㉖. In 1912 the Belfast-based shipbuilders bought over three existing Govan yards, including Napier's (see below), and developed an integrated site covering many branches of marine engineering; the new yard became one of the greatest on the river and produced many fine ships, including large tankers and cargo vessels. Other local yards were taken over and the enterprise became even bigger; but with the contraction of the industry in the middle of the twentieth century, Harland and Wolff retreated back to Ireland and all the associated yards on the Clyde closed in 1962.

Many of the yard's workers came from Northern Ireland and lived nearby, giving the Rangers Football Club (see p.284) its core of Protestant support. Since the closure, this shed has had occasional use as a theatre, with Bill Bryden's productions of *The Ship* and *The Big Picnic* being staged here.

On the eastern end of the shed is a huge mural painted on large sheets of steel depicting welders at work in the yard.

At 638-46 Govan Road is the interesting Art Nouveau/Glasgow Style **Napier House** ㉗ (1898-9, Wm. J. Anderson). It was originally built as a lodging house for seamen and was named after Robert Napier (1791-1876) whose shipyard once stood here. The building was one of the earliest reinforced concrete constructions in the city and part of it collapsed during construction, killing some of the workers.

Napier initially made his name in engine building, making engines for the Cunard Line's first four liners in his factory at Lancefield in Anderston. In 1841 he began building ships in Govan and earned for himself one of the most illustrious reputations of all the Clyde's shipbuilders. Indeed, he became known as 'the father of Clyde ship-building' as so many of the next generation of engineers, such as John Elder and William Pearce (see pp.296 and 291 respectively), served under him. He became the main naval builder on the river and his ships included the warship *Black Prince* (1861). Another of his remarkable ships was the *Persia* which, when built for Cunard in 1855, was the world's largest ship.

Turn left at Orkney Street; on the right is the former **Govan Police Station 28**. The right hand side of this building was built in 1866-7 by John Burnet as the Govan Burgh Chambers and contained the police station, courtroom (housed in a large 600-seat hall) and other council offices. The southern extension was added in 1899-1901 and the council offices moved to the much larger Govan Town Hall (see p.286), leaving the police and the fire services with this building. The building's main external architectural feature are the first floor's tall decorated pilasters.

When the police station finally closed in 1998, the cells had changed little since the 1860s. They were arranged in three floors around a central well, with a total of thirty cells which could accommodate eighty prisoners. The cells' 'amenities' consisted of a raised concrete platform for a bed (though bedding was available) and a WC; the phrase 'Victorian conditions' could be correctly applied here! The barred windows of the cells can be seen at the south-western corner of the building.

One of the tasks the local police had to deal with was the care of those who were a bit the worse for wear of alcohol and many of the local drunks who were brought here were carried in on the station's 'Drunks' barrow'. A fee of a farthing or a halfpenny was paid for each use of the barrow and local tradition has it that a local lady called 'Black Mary' frequently highjacked the barrow and brought the drunkard to the station in order to claim the money for herself. In time, the police vehicles which carried prisoners were named 'Black Marias' after her. The barrow is on display at the People's Palace.

The station's most famous inmate was Rudolph Hess, Adolf Hitler's deputy; in 1941 he flew an aeroplane from Germany to Scotland, ostensibly in an attempt to secure the end of the war, and he was imprisoned here for a short time.

Return to Govan Road and turn left. The former **Savings Bank of Glasgow 29** (1906, Eric A. Sutherland) (now the Trustee Savings Bank) stands at 705 Govan Road. On both main walls are large carvings of royal coats of arms and the motto *In defence*. Tall columns above them rise through two storeys accentuating the height and dignity of this isolated example of early twentieth-century architecture. Locally, it is known as the 'potted-heid building' as the colour of the ground floor's granite resembles that of a type of old-fashioned meat paste.

Keep to the right hand side of Govan Road, passing to the right of **Govan Underground Station 30**. The route returns to this at the end of the walk, after going through Elder Park. On the right, just after the underground station, is the open area of Govan Cross.

GOVAN CROSS TO GOVAN UNDERGROUND STATION VIA ELDER PARK

Govan Cross ③① was once the centre of the burgh but redevelopment has removed its previous importance to the urban landscape. Between the cross and the river there once was a prominent earthwork known as **Doomster Hill**. This may originally have been a burial mound or a lookout post or perhaps a place where assemblies or courts were held. The hill was removed when the shipyards were built.

Today, Govan Cross' main feature is **New Govan Church** ③②, formerly St Mary Govan Free Church (1873, Robert Baldie).

Outside the church is the **Aitken Memorial Fountain** ③③ (1884, Cruikshanks & Co.), a well-decorated cast-iron fountain topped by an elaborate canopy. This was, as a plaque on it explains, *erected by the inhabitants of Govan in affectionate remembrance of John Aitken M.D.*, who was the burgh's first Medical Officer of Health. There are other plaques above the arches and they feature emblems such as the burgh's coat of arms (see p.286), and a badge connected with the Ancient Order of Oddfellows. Fish-like creatures form part of the canopy's internal decoration.

Beyond the fountain, at the corner of Govan Road and Water Row, is the former **British Linen Bank** ③④ (1897-1900, Salmon, Son & Gillespie), now the Bank of Scotland. The bank was originally founded in 1746 to develop the Scottish linen industry and, since it started life just after the 1745 Jacobite rebellion, its choice of name was a deliberate attempt to emphasise the 'British' rather than the 'Scottish' nature of the economy since the 1707 Union with England. The presence of the bank in Govan reflected the importance of weaving in the district.

The bank's doorway is topped by an elaborate sculpture of the prow of a boat. This is flanked by two winged wind gods who are blowing the boat forward; the sail bears the inscription *B L Co*. The seven columns around the building are topped by figures including a bee-keeper, a navigator, a fisherman and what might be the bank manager holding tightly onto a bag of money.

Water Row once led to a ford over the river and later to a ferry terminal which was just opposite the mouth of the River Kelvin. This operated until 1966 and remains of the terminal can still be seen. This must have been a picturesque place at one time as it attracted artists such as Sam Bough (1822-78) but the scene changed quite dramatically during the nineteenth century as the mouth of the Kelvin became the site of the Pointhouse shipyard of A. & J. Inglis. This was opened in 1862 and was eventually owned by Harland and Wolff (see p.288). Today it is remembered as the place where the paddle steamer *Waverley* (see p.149) was built.

Continue on Govan Road and the **Pearce Institute** ㉟ (1902-6, Robert Rowand Anderson) is soon found on the right. This was donated by Lady Dinah Pearce in memory of her husband Sir William Pearce (see below). Built in seventeenth-century Scottish Renaissance style, it provides social facilities (including the Macleod Hall) for local people. The two gables on the front are quite different in character; the western one is very Renaissance with lots of ornamentation (including a sailing ship at roof level), the eastern one is in the restrained Scots Baronial style. On the wall inside the entrance are the words *This is a house of friendship. This is a house of service. For families. For lonely folk. For the people of Govan. For the strangers of the world. Welcome.*

Just beyond the institute is a granite **First World War Memorial** ㊱. The burgh's coat of arms is on one face and on the others are the names of the battlefields where Govan men perished.

A statue of **Sir William Pearce** ㊲ (1894, Onslow Ford) stands opposite the institute. Locally, the statue is called 'the Black Man' due to the colour of the tarnished bronze. Pearce (1833-88) gained shipbuilding experience with Robert Napier (see p.288) and is best known for his stewardship of Fairfield shipbuilders (see p.295) in the 1870s and 1880s, during which time they built many world-class transatlantic liners. In 1885 he became Member of Parliament for Govan. He is also remembered in the city through his links with Glasgow University's Pearce Lodge, which is described on p.183.

Brechin's Bar ㊳ is next to the statue and a notice outside it states that it was established in 1798. The present building was erected in 1894 and boasts a tower in Scots Baronial style. Near the tower's conical roof is a stone plaque which features a shield with the date *1894*, two semi-clad men, a crown and a lion; its motto *Sans peur* means 'Without fear'. High up on the southern side of the building is a stone carving of a cat, immortalising one prolific rat catcher who killed large numbers of rodents which had been brought to Govan on vessels carrying flax for the local weavers.

The first floor contains the Cardell Hall, named after John Cardell who used the hall as a local headquarters for the Rechabites, a charitable organisation which espoused the virtues of temperance. A remarkable change of use for the building!

Behind the war memorial is the entrance to **Govan Old Parish Church** ㊴ (1883-8, Robert Rowand Anderson). The church may not be very well known outwith Glasgow, but it is historically important because of its collection of early medieval carved stones, indicating that this is a religious site of some antiquity. Tradition has it that a monastery was started here in the sixth-century by St Constantine who came from Cornwall. Whether this is correct or not, there was certainly a thriving religious community here before the end of the first millennium which

may have been dedicated to the cult of St Constantine. This was during the period in which Dumbarton was the capital of the kingdom of Strathclyde, and Govan may have been its spiritual centre and the burial place for the kingdom's nobility. As the Middle Ages approached this would have built around it the nucleus of what later became the agricultural village of Govan which was eventually overtaken by the much-later growth of the shipyards. The first parish church here was erected around 1136 and the present building continues the religious presence on what is certainly one of the city's most historic sites.

At first glance the church's exterior is rather unassuming and it was certainly never finished to the architect's plans as it lacks the planned western tower and the relief sculpture on the facade. In contrast, the church's interior is much richer than the exterior might suggest. It is quite cavernous, with the roof's substantial cross-members allowing a broad and uncluttered nave. The internal walls are of brick with stone arches by the side aisles and the walls soar upwards to the vaulted roof. At the northern end, the Choir has wooden choir stalls and some nice decorative ironwork. To the west of the Choir is the Steven Chapel named after Elizabeth and Grace Steven who donated money for the chapel and its decoration, including the provision of its stained-glass windows. To the east of the Choir is the Baptistry which has interesting stained-glass windows and some sculptured stones.

The church's stained-glass windows are of exceptionally good quality and many of them are from the studio of Charles Eamer Kempe (1837-1907), an English artist whose work was predominantly for Episcopalian

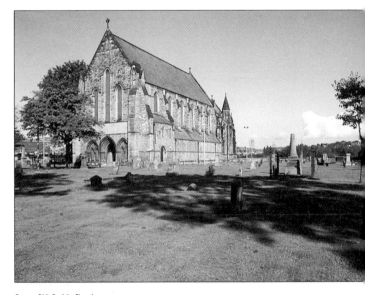

Govan Old Parish Church

churches. The windows were planned as a coherent collection by Dr John Macleod (1840-98) who was minister from 1875 to his death. He was a hard taskmaster and spent a great deal of time and effort in ensuring that the studios which produced the windows were able to carry out his detailed instructions; today's visitors will certainly be impressed by these beautiful works of art. The windows are generally very detailed and many of them are full of vibrant colours. In the Great East Window (at the church's geographical north), Kempe has depicted the risen Christ as High Priest and Intercessor encircled by angels and saints; St Columba and St Kentigern (St Mungo) are at the bottom of the window. The three windows below this represent the Incarnation, Passion and Resurrection of Christ. Between the Choir and the North Transcept are three more windows by Kempe from St Margaret's Church (in Polmadie) dedicated to Dr John Macleod. On the eastern side of the church, the North Transept windows (by Kempe) are on two levels: the six narrow lights show Noah, Faith, Abraham, Moses, Hope and Joseph; the two cinquefoil windows in the gallery above these represent Faith and Hope. Elsewhere in the church, there are other Kempe windows and a number by four other studios: Clayton & Bell; Burlison & Grylls; Heaton, Butler & Bayne and Shrigley & Hunt. Detailed information on all the windows is available in the church.

The church is best-known for its remarkable collection of pre-Christian and Christian **sculptured stones**, probably the best such group in the whole country; they were produced in the ninth, tenth and early eleventh centuries. Much debate (and speculation) has taken place over the nature of what has been called the Govan School of sculpture, particularly concerning the stones' similarities with styles found in England, Scandinavia and, intriguingly, the Pictish lands.

One of the most celebrated pieces is the lidless sarcophagus, which dates from the ninth or tenth centuries, and was presumably built to hold the body of some important person. Judging from the elaborate carvings the sarcophagus was presumably not intended to be buried and so it might have been made for display in whatever religious building stood here at the time. The front of this sandstone tomb has four carvings: two interlaced patterns; a hunter on horseback, a stag and what might be a dog; and a beast trampling another beast and a coiled serpent. The back also has four carvings: two interlaced patterns (one of them comprising the bodies of serpents); two pairs of beasts, the bottom pair lying upside down; and a pair of beasts with crossed necks. This fascinating piece of history was unearthed, lidless and empty, in the graveyard in 1855. By 1858 it was stored in a specially-built sarcophagus house until it was brought into the church in 1908.

Equally famous are the church's five remarkable hogback stones which were probably originally used as grave markers. These are about 2m (7ft) long and look a little like huge tortoises. All have head-like features and arched backs with a prominent ridge, and some have beasts carved at the ends. They have also been likened to Viking houses, with the 'scales' representing wooden shingles, a form of roof tile. One stone in particular also has intricate carvings below the 'scale' pattern on its sides; this, and its narrowness, may indicate that it was made in the middle of the tenth century. Interestingly, although it is made from local sandstone and was carved locally, it is related to the style of hog-backs which have been found in Cumbria.

Of the many other stones in the church, the best known is the Govan Cross. Only the shaft now remains of this old Celtic Cross which may have stood near the church for many centuries. The faces have various interlaced patterns and a relief sculpture of a person on horseback. One other well-decorated cross-slab is known as the 'sun stone' on account of one of its faces having a large boss from which radiate four curved snake-like bodies, complete with heads. The opposite face has a carved Latin cross below which is a horse carrying a rider who is holding what might be a spear.

The aisles of the church contain a large collection of recumbent stones which were carved in the tenth and eleventh centuries and which were originally used as grave slabs. They have a variety of decorations with many of them featuring a cross, incised bosses and interlaced patterns. The stones also have on them various dates, letters and names which were added long after the original carvings were made; an early example of recycling.

Govan Old Parish Church Graveyard **40** is described on p.368.

At the junction of Govan Road and the intriguingly named Harmony Row is **St Anthony's Roman Catholic Church** **41** (1877-9, John Honeyman). It is in Italian Romanesque style with unusual red horizontal bands.

From this point there are glimpses (and sounds) from the Kvaerner Govan shipyard (see below). At the far end of Howat Street (which is on the right) one of five large mosaic **murals** **42** (1994, Marion Brandis) erected on the yard's wall can be seen. To see them all, follow the loop of Howat Street, Taransay Street and Elder Street. These marvellous outdoor works of art are of various subjects, including Govan people and shipyard workers.

Back at Govan Road, a large steel sculpture stands at the entrance to the yard. The sculpture, ***Govan Milestone*** **43** (1994), by Helen Denerley, uses various engineering fittings such as nuts, bolts, chain and cable to produce intriguing models of living creatures.

The **Kvaerner Govan Shipyard** **44** has a long history – it was founded on Fairfield Farm in 1864 – and today it is the only merchant shipbuilder on the Upper Clyde. It was started by Charles Randolph (see p.182) and John Elder (see p.296) as Randolph, Elder & Company (later John Elder & Company) and built up a fine reputation for compound engines (which they had invented) and naval boat construction. It won many contracts from abroad including four ships for the American Confederates who used them as blockade breakers during the American Civil War (1861-5).

After Elder died in 1869, the yard was run by Sir William Pearce (see p.291) and it became known as the Fairfield Shipbuilding & Engineering Company; a long string of successful ships of various types allowed the yard to become one of the most important shipyards in the world. The yard produced many huge liners, including the *Athenia* (1922) and the *Empress of Japan* (1930), the fastest ship on the Yokohama to Vancouver route. It also built large naval ships such as the battleship *Howe* (1940) and the aircraft carrier *Implacable* (1942). Of all the ships, perhaps the strangest order was for the *Livadia* (1880) which was built as the Russian Czar's royal yacht; it was 'turbot shaped', 87m (285ft) long and a massive 47m (153ft) wide. A model of it exists in the Transport Museum (see p.211).

In 1986 the yard became part of UCS (see p.155), later emerging as Govan Shipbuilders and now Kvaerner Govan Ltd. More recently, its ships have included the large car ferry *Norsea* (1987) for North Sea Ferries and the remarkable *Sea Launch Commander* (1997) built for Sea Launch as a sea-going rocket assembly factory and control centre for launching satellites into space.

The entrance to the office building at Kvaerner Govan Shipyard

The office building (1889-91, John Keppie) at 1048 Govan Road is in French Renaissance style and is a good example of an industrial building built to impress. The doorway is flanked by statues of a shipwright and an engineer standing on prows of boats, and above the door are a couple of mermaids and a large winged head.

Elder Park is on the left and it is entered by the main gateway. The gates' ornamental stone pillars are decorated with carvings of plants, including thistles and oak leaves. The park was designed by John Honeyman in 1883-4 and opened in 1885.

Originally Fairfield Farm, the park was donated by Isabella Elder (see below) in memory of her husband John Elder (see below) and his father David Elder. It is a pleasant place away from the hustle and bustle of local industry and traffic. The park has been an important asset to the local community for a long time and in order to maintain decent standards of behaviour, the original by-laws regulating its use forbade anyone to 'read or recite any profane ballad or to expose wounds or deformities inducing giving of alms'.

Follow the path inside the park. On the right is the grey granite **K-13 Memorial** **㊺**, engraved *Sacred to the memory of those named who lost their lives in H.M. Submarine K-13 in the Gareloch 29th January 1917* and *Erected by the officials foremen and employees of the Fairfield Shipbuilding and Engineering, Co. Ltd*. Fairfield built this steam-powered submarine which sank while on sea trials in the nearby Gare Loch, drowning thirty-two men. The ship was eventually recovered and re-designated K-22. A later plaque is dedicated to Allied submariners lost in the Second World War.

To the right of the memorial, a path leads past the **model boat pond** to the **Italian Portico** **㊻**, originally the doorway to the mansion that stood at Linthouse, which is to the west of Govan. The house was designed by Robert Adam in 1791 and this structure was re-erected in the park in 1921.

Opposite the portico stands one of the original houses of Fairfield Farm.

There are many paths which can be followed to the Elder Library, but if the route is retraced back to the K-13 memorial and a right turn made, it leads to the statue of **John Elder** **㊼** by Sir J. E. Boehm (1887-8). Elder (1824-69) learned his shipbuilding skills under Robert Napier (see p.289) and was a co-founder of what is now the Kvaerner Govan Shipyard (p.294). His greatest achievement was the development in 1854 of the marine compound steam engine which cut ships' fuel costs by around one third by extracting more energy from the steam by passing it though additional low-pressure cylinders. This technological advance meant dramatic savings on long sea voyages and it led to the yard gaining many orders from shipowners such as the Pacific Steam Navigation Company which operated intercontinental services. See also p.356.

Continue towards the charming **Elder Library** ㊽ (1901–03, J. J. Burnet). This was gifted to the people of Govan by Isabella Elder (see below) and opened by Andrew Carnegie (1835–1918), himself a great benefactor of public libraries throughout the world. The building is influenced by French and Austrian Baroque styles, with a curved colonnade dominating the entrance, above which is the Govan coat of arms. A display on the history of Govan is exhibited inside.

To the west of the library is a pleasantly secluded little park in which stands a statue (1905-6) of **Isabella Elder** ㊾ (1828–1905) by A. MacFarlane Shannon. After John Elder died, Isabella used his substantial fortune for the benefit of the people of Govan and Glasgow. As well as donating the park, the library and a local hospital, she made provision for professorial chairs of civil engineering and naval architecture at Glasgow University and provided a building for Queen Margaret College (see p.236).

Within the same small park, and to the south-west of the Isabella Elder statue, is the **S.S. Daphne Memorial** ㊿ (1997, John McArthur)**.** The inscription explains: *Disaster on the Clyde. A vessel of 500 tons built by Alexander Stephen & Sons for the Laird Line's Irish Trade, Daphne, capsized at her launch on the 3rd of July, 1883. She heeled over and sank as she entered the water and 124 workers of various professions perished. Included, were a number of apprentices ages ranging from 14 to 20 years. Most workers were trapped below decks in holds, engine-room and cabins in which they were working.*

The ship had been launched from the Linthouse Yard (just downriver from Govan) and although the engines had been fitted, the boilers were still to be put in. When the ship rolled over the water poured through the large deck opening which had been left for the boilers. There is a duplicate memorial in Victoria Park, on the other side of the river, as many of the men who died came from nearby.

From the library, head eastwards along Langlands Road. The route passes to the left of the former **Abraham Hill's Trust School** ㊿ (1874, James Thomson), now used as council offices. The school was funded by Abraham Hill in order to provide education for children of poor families. In selecting pupils, preference was given to those with the surname Hill!

Cross Golspie Street and turn right. Pass to the right of the Govan Cross Shopping Centre and the bus terminal. On the left is **Govan Underground Station** ㉚ where the walk ends.

Pollok Country Park and The Burrell Collection

A walk through the large country park which houses
the world-famous Burrell Collection.

The Warwick Vase, The Burrell Collection

Main places of interest	Pollok Country Park **1**-**16**
	Pollok House **7** (18th-century house)
	The Burrell Collection 9 (museum)
Circular/linear	circular
Starting point	Countryside Rangers' Centre **1**
Finishing point	Countryside Rangers' Centre **1**
Distance	5 km (3 miles)
Terrain	paths around park, some of which are narrow and/or inclined
Public transport	Pollokshaws West Railway Station (C)
Sections	Pollok Country Park
	A walk through Pollok Country Park
	Pollok House
	The Burrell Collection
Architects	-
Nearby walks	10
Refreshments	Pollok House; Burrell Collection
Notes	Be aware of safety advice (see p.16) as some parts of the park can be very quiet at times.

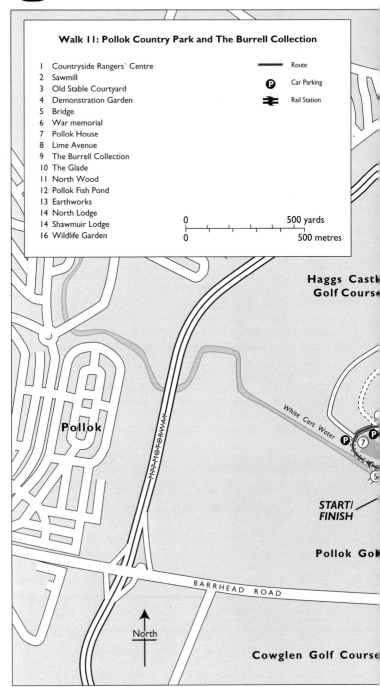

WALK

11

Walk 11: Pollok Country Park and The Burrell Collection

1 Countryside Rangers` Centre
2 Sawmill
3 Old Stable Courtyard
4 Demonstration Garden
5 Bridge
6 War memorial
7 Pollok House
8 Lime Avenue
9 The Burrell Collection
10 The Glade
11 North Wood
12 Pollok Fish Pond
13 Earthworks
14 North Lodge
14 Shawmuir Lodge
16 Wildlife Garden

- - - - - Route
P Car Parking
⇄ Rail Station

0   500 yards
0   500 metres

Haggs Castl
Golf Cours

White Cart Water **P** (7) **P**

Pollok

M77-MOTORWAY

5

START/
FINISH

Pollok Go

BARRHEAD ROAD

↑
North

Cowglen Golf Course

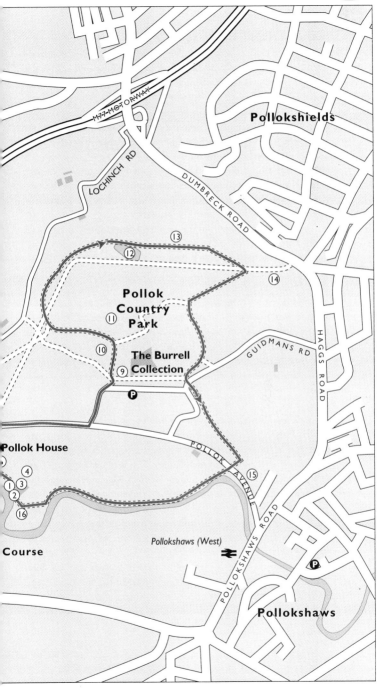

Pollokshields

M77 MOTORWAY

LOCHINCH RD

DUMBRECK ROAD

⑬

⑫

⑭

Pollok
Country
Park

⑪

HAGGS ROAD

⑩

GUIDMANS RD

The Burrell
Collection

⑨

P

Pollok House

④

① ③

② POLLOK AVENUE

⑯ ⑮

POLLOKSHAWS ROAD

Course

Pollokshaws (West) ⇌

P

Pollokshaws

 **WALK**

POLLOK COUNTRY PARK

The history of Pollok estate can be traced back to around 1124 when David I gave the land to Walter Fitzalan, the High Steward of Scotland. The estate came into the hands of the Maxwells in the mid-thirteenth century and belonged to the family until 1966 when the land (and Pollok House) was given to the city as a 'country' park. Although owned by Glasgow City Council, Pollok House is managed by the National Trust for Scotland. The Trust's links with the house go back a long time and in 1931 it was the venue for a number of meetings when Sir John Maxwell was involved in setting up the Trust.

Pollok estate was fairly small to begin with but at one time it covered a great swathe of countryside and its boundary even went beyond the River Clyde; one reason for the increased size of the estate was the 'sharing out' of church lands after the sixteenth-century Reformation. A number of castles were built on the estate: the first was by the banks of the White Cart Water, the site of the second is at the summit of the Demonstration Garden (see p.303) and the third was the laighe castle (see p.303); Haggs Castle (see p.280) and Crookston Castle (see p.344) were also Maxwell castles. However, by the eighteenth century, the area was peaceful enough for Sir John Maxwell (1686-1752) to erect Pollok House as a mansion rather than a fortified house. The gardens were established rather later and were created mainly by Sir John Stirling Maxwell (1866-1956) who was responsible for the Lime Avenue (see p.304), many of the trees and rhododendrons, and the seventeenth-century-style gardens near the house. He built up a collection of over one thousand species of plants and the present gardens owe much to his dedicated work.

The park is an important haven for wildlife in the midst of a busy city. With many different habitats including a river, lots of open grassland and a long-established wood, many varieties of plant and animal life have established themselves here. The White Cart Water (see p.304) is a particularly important area for wildlife. Many species of birds are attracted to it and grey herons and kingfishers might be spotted. In other parts of the park, sparrowhawks, kestrels and great-spotted wood-peckers are amongst some of the more unusual birds that can be seen, and in the case of the woodpecker, heard. A number of small mammals live in the park, amongst them voles, hedgehogs and, inevitably, lots of rabbits; grey squirrels are also very common. Mink, foxes and roe deer also live here as do two types of bat: the pipistrelle bat and the brown long-eared bat. There is a wide variety of flowering plants in the park, with the banks of the river and various areas of North Wood being particularly rich in wild flowers.

A WALK THROUGH POLLOK COUNTRY PARK

The walk starts from the park's **Countryside Rangers' Centre** ❶. This has displays which describe the park and what there is to see. This is also the place to obtain leaflets about the park's wildlife and to find out about any events which are taking place, including ranger-led walks.

Behind the centre is the **sawmill** ❷ (c. 1880) which was powered from the White Cart Water and the mill's substantial weir can still be seen in the river. Railway lines outside the building indicate how the estate's trees were brought here and there is a crane in the old woodyard which would have been used to load and unload wagons. Around 1890 the mill's waterwheel was replaced by a turbine which was also used to provide electricity for Pollok House, quite an innovation in its day.

Opposite the rangers' centre is the late eighteenth-century **Old Stable Courtyard** ❸ which was built on the site of the third castle, the laighe ('low') castle. A tower, which was added to the laighe castle in 1536, was incorporated into the courtyard complex and its remains can be seen on the outside of the north-eastern buildings. As well as the stables, the courtyard had houses, offices, workshops and storerooms in what must have been a noisy hive of activity. Look for the marriage stones (inscribed *SIM* and *DGB*) which are above some windows. Altogether, this is a good example of rural architecture and the buildings still maintain an air of country life, especially since the park's heavy horses are stabled here.

The Gardener's Bothy and the Demonstration Garden (see below) can both be reached via the north-eastern corner of the courtyard.

Above the arched entrance on the outside of the yard is a plaque on which is a head and four shields; this originally came from an older building and was placed here when the upper storey was added early in the nineteenth century.

Follow the White Cart Water downstream, towards Pollok House, past a gate on the right which leads into the gardens. These are divided into a number of sections, with walls or tall hedges separating the different areas. There is a large **Demonstration Garden** ❹ (sited within the old Walled Garden) which has a wide variety of trees, shrubs, alpines, vegetables, fruit and flowers arranged so that keen gardeners can see ideas for their own gardens. There are also glasshouses to walk through, formal gardens and a Rose Garden to sit in and, right at the back, a large Woodland Garden (well known for its rhododendrons) to stroll around. The second Pollok castle was erected at the hill's summit, now the highest point in the Woodland Garden. Its exact position is marked by an earth mound on which is a beech tree of enormous width.

The **Gardener's Bothy** is at the lowest point of the gardens; this small room was home to a gardener's family and it has been kept to show how gardeners may have lived in 1900; it's quite different from life in Pollok House!

Leave the gardens and continue walking beside the river, over which is a single-span stone **bridge** ❺. This carries the dates *1757* and *1758* on its sides and has handsome parapet walls featuring carved balusters. The **White Cart Water** rises on Eaglesham Moor (south of Glasgow), flows through Cathcart (see p.329), Pollok and Paisley then joins up with the Black Cart Water before it flows into the River Clyde just to the west of Renfrew.

On the other side of the river stood the medieval settlement of Polloktoun which housed people who worked on the estate.

Opposite the bridge is the **War memorial** ❻ which is *dedicated to the men from the tenantry and staff of Nether Pollok who served in the Great War 1914 -1919.* Unusually, it lists the men in alphabetical order, rather than by (decreasing) order of rank.

Follow the perimeter of **Pollok House** ❼ to its front gates. It is described on p.306.

On the left of the house (and opposite the gates) is a wide grassy area and the **Lime Avenue** ❽. This was planted in 1887 to celebrate the coming of age of Sir John Stirling Maxwell.

Go over the crossroads and walk along Pollok Avenue, heading away from Pollok House. The land beside the road was developed as a deer park but today these fields support a fold of prize-winning **Highland cattle**. These cattle were once very important in the Highlands and western islands as they could survive in the cold wet climate and live on a diet that was much poorer than that of the lowlands. To many visitors to Scotland these are fierce-looking beasts but they are usually very docile – although you do have to watch out for their horns!

Turn left and follow the signs to **The Burrell Collection** ❾, which is described on p.309.

After leaving the Burrell, turn right and pass to the left of Knowehead Lodge, opposite which is a little stone fountain decorated with lions' heads. Follow the road as it bends round to the right, passing the side of the house. On the left is the grassy area called **The Glade** ❿; its regular undulations are the remains of old rigs and furrows as this used to be farmland until the woods encroached upon it.

Turn left at a narrow path after The Glade and enter **North Wood** ⓫. A huge number of trees were planted in this area from the seventeenth to nineteenth centuries and timber has long been an important source of income for the estate. The original sessile oak woods had a number of different varieties added to it, including birch and rowan, and today the wood can be quite dense in places, making it a haven for wildlife.

Turn right at a T-junction and follow the surfaced road uphill. As the road levels off, the **Pollok Fish Pond** ⓬ will be found on the right.

This was where ornamental fish were kept, probably partly as a hobby and perhaps also for food. This is a good place to find insects, birds, amphibians and even a few fish.

A little later, some **earthworks** ⓭ will be seen on the left. These are in the form of two concentric circular banks, with higher ground in the centre. This may have been built as a defensive structure in the thirteenth or fourteenth century and might have had a wooden stockade on top of the inner bank.

At a junction of paths, the Renaissance-style **North Lodge** ⓮ (1892, Robert Rowand Anderson) is on the left. The building has the inscription *AD MDCCCXCII* (1892) and the Maxwell family motto *I am ready: gang forward* (*gang* = 'go'). The ornamental gates are guarded by two lions rampant (similar to those found at Pollok House) and two men's heads.

Return to the junction of paths and take the second path on the left. It heads downhill to a stream. Cross the bridge, go left at a crossroads and head downhill. The Burrell should soon be seen on the right. Continue until the path ends; this is just before the car park. Turn left, cross the road that comes from the car park and pass through a wood. This plantation is about one hundred years old and has lots of sycamore and horse chestnut trees with smaller numbers of beech and lime.

Turn left when Pollok Avenue is met, heading towards the estate's gates and **Shawmuir Lodge** ⓯ (1891, Robert Rowand Anderson). This is not so ornate as the North Lodge but it does have the date *MDCCCXCI* (1891) on it. The house is not in use at present. Above the two pedestrian gateways are carved the letters *GDC* and *MM*.

Retrace the route from Shawmuir Lodge and turn first left at the start of the riverside walk. This passes some tennis courts, the ground of Poloc Cricket Club, Strathclyde Police's training area for police horses and dogs – hence any barking that might be heard – and then a shinty field.

A tall beech hedge on the left marks the site of the **Wildlife Garden** ⓰. This is much wilder than the rest of the gardens and the habitats and the plants have been carefully selected and nurtured to attract small bugs, insects, birds and small mammals. Different types of habitat have been created in order to encourage a wide variety of creatures to make their home in this corner of the estate.

(Opposite the garden, a bridge over the stream on the right leads to another entrance to the gardens.)

Continue on the path past the Wildlife Garden. This passes the sawmill and the walk ends at the **Countryside Rangers' Centre** ❶.

POLLOK HOUSE

The original four-storey house was constructed in 1747-52 for Sir John Maxwell in a very austere style though the internal plasterwork and furnishings were more luxurious and quite modern for their day; indeed, in 1854 William Mure described the decoration as having 'more of taste and judgement than most other Scottish country residences of the period'. The next owner to contribute much to what we see today was Sir William Stirling Maxwell (1818-78) who, although he spent little time at Pollok, collected many of the superb paintings which are on display; the Spanish works are particularly fine. When the estate passed to Sir John Stirling Maxwell he asked Robert Rowand Anderson (1834-1921) to enlarge the house (1890) and he added two wings, substantial service quarters in the basement and the very grand entrance hall.

In many ways, the southern facade of the house is much finer than the northern. The two nineteenth-century wings make the house look less tall and more grand; the architectural detailing is more easily seen and the east-west balustrades help to emphasise the length of the whole structure. The addition of terraces, two pavilions and numerous staircases also ensured that this must have been one of the grandest houses of its day in the whole of the west of Scotland. One curious feature is that the two lions which guard the garden gate are licking their noses. (The lions were sculpted by Hew Lorimer in the 1940s.)

The addition of the chapel-like **entrance hall** radically changed the north facade's austerity and inside, its late nineteenth-century decoration is of a very high quality. The previous front doorway used to be where the entrance to the main corridor is now, but the original wooden door is now incorporated in the inside of the new entrance. Artistic works

Pollok House

displayed here include busts of the two Sir John Maxwells, Sir William Stirling Maxwell and portraits of other members of the Maxwell family.

The first floor contains the principal rooms. The **main corridor** is the house's thoroughfare and is dominated by large Ionic columns. Furnishings include a long case astronomical clock (*c.* 1760, John Craig) which indicates the time of high water at Glasgow Bridge and paintings including the sixteenth-century *St Ildefonso receiving the chasuble* (Jeronimo Cosida) and *Pieta* (*c.* 1498, Luca Signorelli).

On the left, the Morning Room (decorated with portraits of the Maxwell family) leads to the bright and airy **Library** of 1908. The books cover many subjects including Scottish history, art, architecture and gardening. Works here include *Portrait of a man* (*c.* 1590) and *Lady in a fur wrap* (*c.* 1577-9) by Domenikos Theotokopoulus, more usually known as El Greco.

The Print Room then leads to the very formal **Drawing Room** which has some nice delicate plasterwork. On either side of the fireplace are richly decorated gilt 'pier glasses' of *c.* 1740 and elsewhere on the walls are *Madonna and child with infant St John – 'La Serrana'* (*c.* 1645-50, Bartolomé Esteban Murillo) and the seventeenth-century *An allegory of repentance* (Antonio de Pereda y Salgado). There is also a spinet (a type of small harpsichord) of 1764.

On the other side of the main corridor is the **Dining Room**. The plaster decoration (by Thomas Clayton) is more grand here, with shells, fruits and flowers on the walls and ceiling, and hunting equipment (and recently shot birds) above the fireplace reflecting the room's use. Works include the eighteenth-century *St Peter's Chapel* (William Hogarth), a bust of Alexander Pope (*c.* 1740) and numerous portraits.

The **Cedar Room** was originally a serving area then became a smoking room. It now displays paintings including a number by William Blake including *Sir Jeffrey Chaucer and the nine and twenty pilgrims on their journey to Canterbury* (1808) and others by Francisco de Goya y Lucientes such as *Boys playing at soldiers* (*c.* 1780) and *Boys playing at see saw* (*c.* 1780).

The **Billiard Room** houses a number of interesting items of furniture, including a billiard table of *c.* 1909 and more portraits from the Spanish collection. Just outside, the lobby features the seventeenth-century *The adoration of the kings* (Luis Tristan). Close by, the Business Room has a lot of decorative plasterwork for such a functional place.

An oval staircase in the main corridor leads to the **Upper Landing** where paintings include *King Philip of Spain (1527-98)* (*c.* 1570, Alonso Sánchez Coello). This floor has a number of bedrooms and the most striking feature of the south-western bedroom is the brightly coloured handpainted Chinese wallpaper. Nearby rooms are used for displays which tell the story of Pollok House and its collection.

From the entrance hall, a stairway leads down to the **Basement Corridor** which runs the full length of the service area. This was redesigned by Rowand Anderson and it gives a fascinating insight into 'downstairs' life at the end of the Victorian era. Of particular interest is the large well-lit kitchen which is now used as the tea room. This has its original cast-iron range above which is an elaborate spit mechanism for turning meat in front of an open fire.

Other nearby rooms open for viewing include the Still Room, the China Closet and the Gun Room. The Still Room was where the housekeeper prepared such things as beverages and light meals and it has its original range; some distillation of herbal drinks also took place here, hence the room's name. The dry-goods store is next door. The China Closet was where the house's finest china was cleaned and kept, and some eighteenth- and nineteenth-century pieces are on display, including examples from Japan and China. The Edwardian Gun Room is furnished in the style of *c.* 1910 and it has displays of guns, stuffed animals and pictures of hunting scenes. As well as the extensive Pollok estate, the Maxwell family also owned the Highland estate of Corrour (to the east of Fort William), which provided opportunities for hunting expeditions.

THE BURRELL COLLECTION

William Burrell (1861-1958) was born in Glasgow and as a youth joined his father's shipping company (Burrell & Son) which was involved in building and owning ships as well as acting as international shipping agents. After his father's death in 1885, William and his brother George ran the company themselves. The shipping industry was in a slump at the turn of the century but instead of avoiding risks, the brothers bought numerous ships (at cheap prices) and later took advantage of an upturn in the market by having ships available for worldwide use. Each of the ships had British officers but the crews were often Chinese or East-Indian (called 'Lascars' in Glasgow). The demand for ships increased dramatically at the start of the First World War and in 1916 the brothers decided to take advantage by selling nearly all their ships and making a fortune in the process.

For much of this time, and especially after the ships were sold off, William spent a great deal of his time and fortune building up an enormous art collection comprising well over 8000 pieces. This was housed in various places, including his home on Great Western Road (see p.232) and Hutton Castle in the Borders (see p.309). In 1944 he donated his collection to the City of Glasgow but stipulated that it should be sited not less than 26km (16 miles) from the Royal Exchange, well away from Glasgow's noxious atmosphere. It was not until three decades later that a suitable site was found for it, when, with the improvement in the city's quality of air since then, the decision was taken to build a permanent home for the collection in Pollok Park.

Even though the building has been specially designed for the Burrell bequest, only about one-third of the items can be on show at any time, so changes may occur to the description below. This is probably the most important art collection built by an individual British person and although there is a wide variety of items, some fields (for example, ancient Egypt) are not broadly represented, whereas others (like European art) are very significant. Occasionally the Trustees use Sir William Burrell's fund to add new items, such as in 1978 when the Warwick Vase was acquired.

The fine building that houses **The Burrell Collection** (1972-83, Barry Gasson, John Meunier and Brit Andreson) took twelve years to design and construct and has numerous interesting features including medieval doorways collected by Burrell, not least of which is the entrance arch from Hornby Castle in Yorkshire. Even the museum's wooden entrance door came from the castle! Otherwise, the exterior of the building is of pink Dumfriesshire sandstone, stainless steel and glass. An unusual sundial stands just a little way to the right of the entrance and on its plinth are carvings of the sun, the moon and a star.

Once inside the building, walk past the information desks to the bright covered **Courtyard** on the right. Its main exhibit is the huge second-century Warwick Vase, the original parts of which came from the Emperor Hadrian's villa at Tivoli. Various sculptures, including *The Thinker* (1880, Auguste Rodin) also decorate the courtyard, three walls of which act as the 'exterior' walls of the Hutton Castle rooms (see below). In the wall which faces the museum's entrance is a large portal from Hornby Castle, a richly embellished early sixteenth-century doorway which has the original wooden door below it.

Burrell bought the fifteenth- and sixteenth-century **Hutton Castle** in Berwickshire in 1916 and transformed it in order to house his rapidly growing art collection. Three of the rooms, lavishly decorated and complete with furniture, are recreated in the museum and reflect Burrell's favourite art period – medieval European. The three rooms are reached by going through the Hornby portal and then keeping to the right. This allows the Drawing Room and the Hall to be viewed; after leaving the Hall, keep to the right, but ignore the narrow entrance to the courtyard. After visiting these three rooms, return to the courtyard.

The **Drawing Room** has many important stained-glass pieces, ranging from small shields and roundels to the large religious pieces which were made in England in the fifteenth century. Burrell also hung some of his best tapestries here and the two on the outside wall are early sixteenth-century Franco-Flemish examples which depict labours of the month. The stone fireplace is Late Gothic in style and around it are pieces of seventeenth- and eighteenth-century furniture with original coverings. The **Hall** has two walls which feature stained glass: the long wall has heraldic glass (sixteenth-century English) featuring royal badges and shields, while the short wall has well-detailed religious works (fifteenth- and sixteenth-century German). The stone fireplace is made up of various pieces and includes some graffiti of 1547. The very long oak refectory table (1581) dominates the centre of the room, Persian

carpets (seventeenth and nineteenth century) are on the floor and there are a variety of tapestries hung on the walls. The walls of the **Dining Room** are decorated with dark wood panelling of *c.* 1500. Made of oak, the lower part has a 'linenfold' pattern akin to folded fabric while the upper part has many carvings, including human figures and animals. The walls also feature three fifteenth-century tapestry altar frontals, probably from Germany. In the middle of the room is a long sixteenth-century Elizabethan oak refectory table which has elaborately carved bulbous legs and stands on a nineteenth-century Persian carpet.

From the courtyard, go through the Hornby portal again in order to reach the museum's northern wall. This is made of glass, allowing the woods behind the building to become an essential part of the collection's environment. Depending on the time of year, there are glorious wild flowers, rich autumn colours, plenty of birds, perhaps squirrels and possibly even the occasional roe deer. Follow the glass wall as it goes past three main areas: Ancient Civilizations, Oriental Art and Medieval and Post-Medieval European Art. It should be noted that the Near Eastern Carpets and Ceramics collections are on the east wall, beyond European Medieval Art.

The **Ancient Civilizations** collection is relatively small (it was not one of Burrell's specialisations) but it contains interesting items from Egypt, the Eastern Mediterranean and the Middle East. Of particular note are the Egyptian funerary items, including a collection of shawabtis, small figures which did any labouring work that the dead might be called on to do in the next world. Other interesting items include an Egyptian relief of a boy carrying a goose (*c.* 2420-2250BC), a Roman sculptured head (*c.* 320-330 but based on an earlier Greek bronze) showing either Zeus or Poseidon, and numerous Greek jugs decorated with human figures.

Oriental Art comprises quite a large part of the whole collection. The Chinese ceramics are beautifully decorated and as well as numerous plates and vases there are larger pieces such as the seated corpulent figure of a lothan (a Buddhist disciple) of 1484 and a pair of tall Fang-Xiang tomb figures of the eight century. The Chinese bronzes include many ritual vessels made as long ago as the twelfth and eleventh centuries BC and which still look in remarkably good condition considering they are over 3000 years old! There are many small Chinese figures, often made from earthenware, and some remarkably decorated commonplace articles such as roof ridge tiles. The jade collection contains intricately carved pieces, including small vessels and ornaments.

The **Near Eastern Carpets and Ceramics** are found in the eastern gallery, past all the European Medieval Art. The carpets come from a number of areas, such as the Caucasus, the source of the large seventeenth-century dragon carpet. This has lots of the ever-popular dragons on it, skilfully integrated as part of the overall design. There are also a number of prayer rugs, used by Muslims to kneel on while facing Mecca.

The very large section devoted to **Medieval and Post-Medieval European Art** is certainly the most important part of the whole collection and covers many different art forms, including religious statuary, books, armour, ceramics, silverware, furniture, paintings, tapestries, needlework and stained glass. There is even part of a ceiling (from Bridgewater in England) and large items such as gateways, decorated stone windows and a long screen from a great hall. A vast amount of material is on display and there is no set route through the interconnected galleries, but particular mention must be made of the tapestries as they are an important collection in themselves. The most massive tapestries are hung right in the centre of the museum and notable amongst these are *Triumph of the virgin* (early sixteenth century,

Stained Glass Gallery, The Burrell Collection

South Netherlandish), *Hercules initiating the Olympic Games* (*c.* 1450-75, Franco-Burgundian) and the amusing *The camp of the Gypsies* (early sixteenth century, Franco-Netherlandish). The stained glass gallery is nearby and in it is one of the oldest pieces of European stained glass showing the human figure, a panel showing the prophet Jeremiah (1140-5, France) from the abbey of St Denis near Paris. Its rich red and blue colours are still remarkably strong. There is a wide variety of religious material, reflecting the fact that churches were once the great storehouses of medieval art. One of the most celebrated pieces is also one of the smallest – the twelfth-century bronze-gilt Temple pyx (for holding sacrament wafers) made in England or Germany – which shows three sleeping soldiers. The larger religious pieces include alabaster panels, carved wooden statues and a set of fifteenth-century French choir stalls, complete with carved misericords (on which choristers partially sat while standing during services).

To continue looking at the medieval art collection, walk to the south-eastern corner of the museum, where the restaurant is situated. There can't be many eating places complete with sixteenth-century stained-glass armorial panels as part of the decoration! Now turn right and head towards the main entrance. On the left, lit by the strong southerly light, are more stained-glass panels, European in origin and from the thirteenth to sixteenth centuries. On the right are various pieces of wooden furniture (sixteenth and seventeenth centuries) including a splendidly decorated bed, complete with carved canopy.

The museum's mezzanine level has some small galleries featuring **paintings and drawings**. To reach this, go through the Hornby portal again and follow the wall on the right to a staircase. Burrell collected many paintings and the examples of the Impressionists are particularly worth looking at. These include *Women drinking beer* (1878, Edouard Manet), *The rehearsal* (*c.* 1877, Edgar Degas) and *The bell tower at Noisy-le-Roi* (1874, Alfred Sisley). Overall, these is great breadth to the collection as it also includes works such as the formal religious style of *Madonna and child* (*c.* 1488-90, Giovanni Bellini), the more relaxed-looking *Woman with auburn hair* (*c.* 1875, Pierre August Renoir) and the everyday scene of *The market stall* (1884, Camille Pissaro). In quite different style, there are a number of works by Joseph Crawhall, including *The aviary, Clifton* (1888) and *The flower shop* (*c.* 1894-1900).

Queen's Park

This short walk goes through the residential district of Queen's Park
and the park which shares its name.

Langside Battlefield Memorial

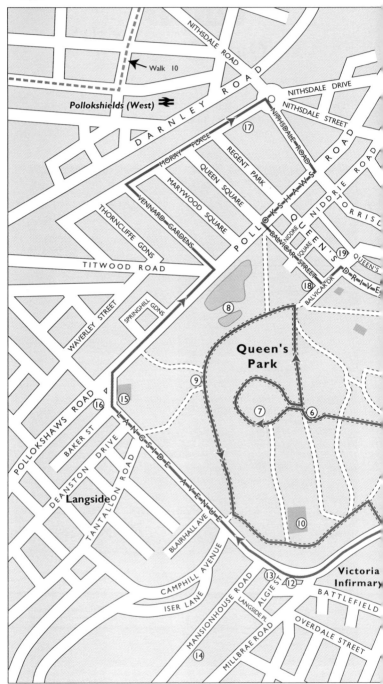

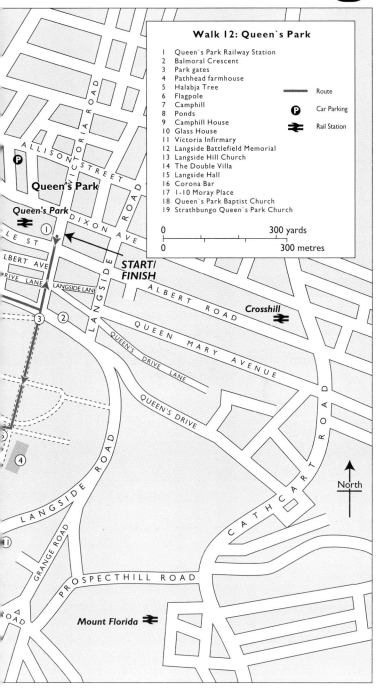

Walk 12: Queen's Park

1 Queen's Park Railway Station
2 Balmoral Crescent
3 Park gates
4 Pathhead farmhouse
5 Halabja Tree
6 Flagpole
7 Camphill
8 Ponds
9 Camphill House
10 Glass House
11 Victoria Infirmary
12 Langside Battlefield Memorial
13 Langside Hill Church
14 The Double Villa
15 Langside Hall
16 Corona Bar
17 1-10 Moray Place
18 Queen's Park Baptist Church
19 Strathbungo Queen's Park Church

―――― Route

P Car Parking

⇌ Rail Station

0   300 yards
0   300 metres

Queen's Park

P

Queen's Park
⇌
①

D I X O N   A V E

**START/
FINISH**

ALBERT AVE

RIVE LANE

LANGSIDE LANE

③

②

L A N G S I D E

A L B E R T   R O A D

Crosshill ⇌

Q U E E N   M A R Y   A V E N U E

QUEEN'S DRIVE LANE

QUEEN'S DRIVE

LANGSIDE ROAD

GRANGE ROAD

④

⑪

C A T H C A R T   R O A D

North ↑

P R O S P E C T H I L L   R O A D

Mount Florida ⇌

WALK

Main place of interest	Queen's Park –
Circular/linear	circular
Starting point	Queen's Park Railway Station
Finishing point	Queen's Park Railway Station
Distance	5.5 km (3.5 miles)
Terrain	hilly especially in Queen's Park itself and along Langside Avenue
Public transport	Queen's Park Railway Station (C) Pollokshields West Railway Station (C)
Sections	Queen's Park Railway Station to Queen's Park Queen's Park Queen's Park to Queen's Park Railway Station via Langside
Architects	Thomson: 'The Double Villa' 1-10 Moray Place
Nearby walks	10
Refreshments	Victoria Road; Pollokshaws Road
Notes	Be aware of safety advice (see p.16) as Queen's Park can be very quiet at times.

WALK 12

QUEEN'S PARK RAILWAY STATION
TO QUEEN'S PARK

The route starts from the exit from **Queen's Park Railway Station** ❶ on Victoria Road. The station dates back to 1886 when the Cathcart District Railway was built. In 1894 it became part of the Cathcart Circle and its development encouraged builders to erect new houses on what was then countryside. A plaque on the ironwork outside the Victoria Road exit records that the railway bridge was built by James Goodwin & Co. of Motherwell in 1885.

Turn right at Victoria Road. This is the **Queen's Park** area, named after Mary, Queen of Scots (see p.321). It was developed for housing in the nineteenth century (mainly with tenements) and many of the best tenements still remain, making the district a good example of a planned urban townscape. The Queen's Park district was originally part of the burgh of Crosshill but was swallowed up by Glasgow in 1891. Victoria Road is the district's main shopping centre and links the park to the city centre via Glasgow Bridge.

Head towards the gates of Queen's Park, but before entering the park, turn left at Queen's Drive to look at the grand block of tenements at **Balmoral Crescent** ❶ (1884-6, W. M. Whyte) at 78-118 Queen's Drive. The tenements are generally French influenced, especially in the tall and steeply pitched roofs, and they are amongst the finest buildings of their type in the city. They have unusually tall basements, making the entrance steps very steep and emphasising the importance of the doorways. Many of these are decorated with carved figures, some of which are very medieval-looking in appearance. A number of them are said to be representations of local people and the pair on the western end may be the architect and the builder. At the eastern end of the block is a roof-level sculpture of a female looking very like the *Statue of Liberty*.

Return to the end of Victoria Road and turn left to enter Queen's Park at the main gates.

QUEEN'S PARK

Plans for **Queen's Park** were drawn up in 1860 by Sir Joseph Paxton, the great Victorian landscape gardener. The present layout owes much to his ideas though some of his proposals, such as a music hall and a loch, were not pursued. The park was opened in 1862, and in 1872 John Tweed was impressed enough to report that 'In the summer months, when the shrubs are green and the numerous flower plots in bloom, there is much in the appearance of this favourite resort of the South-Siders to excuse their boasts of its beauty.' It would certainly have given local people a pleasant and peaceful place to walk around at a time when the city was full of noise, dust and dirt, and in 1886 the weekly magazine *Quiz* called the park 'that most bracing of the lungs of the city'.

Enter the park by the very fine **park gates ❸** which are Art-Nouveau in style and were erected in 1907. On the right as you walk along the main drive is the site of the former bandstand which, as well as being a music venue, was also where large May Day rallies were held as great crowds could sit on the grassy slopes to listen to the speakers.

The next part of the walk involves an ascent up the steep hill ahead; anyone wishing to avoid most of the park's steepest hills should turn right just inside the park gates, then take the wide path which heads towards the left of the spire of Queen's Park Baptist Church. The main route is rejoined close to the church.

Ascend the hill and pass the colourful formal gardens; this was where Paxton's proposed Winter Gardens (which incorporated a music hall) were to have been sited. To the left at a crossroads is the old **Pathhead farmhouse ❹**, now used as the park's offices. This nineteenth-century farmhouse stands beside what was the old route from Gorbals to Cathcart.

To the right of the crossroads stands the **Halabja Tree ❺**. This, as a notice informs, was planted by the *Friends of Kurdistan Society in remembrance of thousands of Kurdish civilians murdered in chemical bombing of Halabja by the Iraqi Ba'athist regime on 16th March 1988*. This Kurdish town in north-eastern Iraq near the border with Iran, lost 5000 of its people after Iraqi planes dropped poison gas on it.

Turn right at the crossroads and head towards the **flagpole ❻**, from which there is one of the city's finest views. The platform, which was erected on an artificial mound to give it an even loftier position, gives a wonderful view over the city, though summer foliage obscures many of the buildings. To the north are the Campsie Hills (see p.282) and beneath them can be seen many important buildings and structures such as (from left to right): Finnieston Crane, Glasgow University tower, the towers of Trinity College, Kingston Bridge, the glass-covered St Enoch Centre, Merchants' Steeple, Caledonia Road Church, Royal Infirmary, Glasgow Cathedral, Glasgow Necropolis and 'Paradise' (Celtic Park, the home of Glasgow Celtic Football Club). To the south-east are the Cathkin Braes with the tower blocks of Castlemilk just in front of them.

The view has certainly improved since the demise of the big factories and the introduction of smokeless fuels because in 1872 John Tweed reported that the whole city *was overhung, it must be confessed, by a dense canopy of smoke.*

Continue heading west, passing to the right of some allotments. On the right are the low grassy walls of **Camphill ❼**, a substantial earthwork measuring some 100m by 120m (330ft by 390ft). The surrounding land has been marshy for a very long time and this site would have been a superb defensive position for a settlement or military camp (hence the name). It may possibly date from the Iron Age but it was certainly in use in Medieval times and traces of linear 'rigs' and 'furrows' provide evidence that the site was used for agriculture. It has an earth rampart and a ditch, and in the centre there is a collection of large boulders, though it is not certain when these were introduced.

Walk clockwise round Camphill and head back towards the flagpole. Turn left immediately before the flagpole and walk down a long steep slope. Bear left at a wide driveway and head towards the park gates beside Queen's Park Baptist Church. Turn left before the gates and walk along a broad path, to the right of which will be seen two **ponds** ❽. The nearer pond is a duck pond while the pond farther away, which is much larger, is used for boating.

Continue on the main path to **Camphill House** ❾ (David Hamilton?). This two-storey building was built early in the nineteenth century and its entrance boasts two pairs of fluted Ionic columns. The house and its grounds were bought by the council in 1894 and it became the park's museum with fine exhibits from the city's notable collection of costumes. It is now converted into flats.

Pass to the left of Camphill House and follow the wide driveway on the left. To the right is a maze of paths through gardens which can be explored at leisure. Turn left just before the park gates at Langside Avenue and climb the steep hill to the glasshouses found on the left.

The Glass House ❿ (1905) has a delightful domed entrance behind which is a large collection of individual glasshouses containing displays of a wide variety of plants (and animals). The Temperate Corridor is just inside and leads to the other glasshouses and to a Japanese Garden. The corridor contains displays of various colourful plants, many with attractive foliage. It also contains a pond with a collection of cold water fish.

   Glasshouse 1 contains a collection of cacti and succulents. These range from ground-hugging species to those which almost touch the roof. Glasshouse 2 is very warm and humid as it is devoted to numerous tropical and economic plants. Glasshouse 6 is the insect and reptile house, though many of the insects are there as food for the reptiles! The reptiles include snakes, iguanas and many exotic species. There are also small mammals and birds. A veritable zoo!

Turn left after leaving The Glass House and follow the path to the park gates at Langside Road, opposite the Victoria Infirmary. Leave the park and turn right.

QUEEN'S PARK TO QUEEN'S PARK RAILWAY STATION VIA LANGSIDE

The **Victoria Infirmary** ⑪ stands opposite the Langside Road park gates. The building in front is the Administration Block (1888-90, Campbell Douglas & Sellars), a handsome structure made of white Giffnock sandstone which has a central pedimented gable flanked by rooftop towers. The facade has a large coat of arms of Queen Victoria with the motto *Dieu et mon droit* ('God and my right'). Above that is a puma, an emblem associated with medical care. Below the two towers are the coats of arms of Glasgow and Renfrewshire.

The 'Vicky' is one of the city's smaller hospitals and was the Southside's first hospital (excepting the small Govan Poorhouse). A local doctor, Ebenezer Duncan, started a campaign for the hospital in 1878 and it was started as a voluntary hospital with bequests from people such as Robert Couper (see p.332). When built, it incorporated many state-of-the-art features such as the ability to completely change all the air in the building in only eight minutes. This was to ensure that 'none of the inmates will ever breathe air which had previously passed through the lungs of any of the other occupants'. The infirmary has expanded greatly since then and one of its most notable design features are the open air verandas on the southern buildings.

Turn right at Langside Road and follow it to the 18m (58ft) tall **Langside Battlefield Memorial** ⑫ (1887-8, Alexander Skirving). A plaque explains that *the battle of Langside was fought on this ground on 13 May 1568 between the forces of Mary Queen of Scots and the Regent Moray, and marked the queen's final defeat in Scotland.*

The lion at the top of the memorial rests his paw on a cannonball and faces Clincart Hill where the forces of Mary, Queen of Scots were positioned. Just below the lion are badges with thistles or lions on them. Next down, the tall ornate column is decorated with a spiral design of thistles, roses and fleur-de-lis. Below this are eight carvings; each alternate carving has a targe (a shield) with crossed swords, and the four others have a cannon, a set of bagpipes, a targe with a variety of battle weapons, and an iron helmet with a crossed sword and axe. The four eagles at the corners of the monument's plinth are preparing to fly. When being built, plans of the monument, a copy of *The Abbot* (by Sir Walter Scott, 1820), and newspapers and coins of the day were placed under the structure.

The Battle of Langside was fought between Mary's forces and those of the Regent Moray. He was based in Glasgow while Mary had come from Hamilton via the southern bank of the River Clyde. Moray managed to position his troops on Langside Hill, while Mary's troops were on the lesser Clincart Hill (now the site of Langside College), 1km (½ mile) to the east. Mary herself watched from Cathcart Hill (see p.330). After an unsuccessful cavalry charge, Mary's foot soldiers approached Langside Hill up what is now Battlefield Road, but they were met by gunfire as well as other forces coming down from the site of Pathhead Farm. Between these two wings of Moray's forces, archers and then the cavalry attacked the oncoming army. One hundred of Mary's men were killed and her army fled; the battle had only taken three quarters of an hour. Mary turned southwards and headed into England.

Mary, Queen of Scots (1542-87) is one of the most controversial characters in Scottish history and countless articles and books have discussed her life and deeds. The daughter of James V, she was declared queen at the tender age of one week when he died. From then on she was in the centre of all sorts of intrigue involving religious and dynastic disputes at home as well as the ambitions of the French and English crowns. She spent the years 1548-61 in France and married the Dauphin, who later became Francis II. He died in 1560 and she prepared to return to Scotland, a country whose leaders had just recently renounced the power of the Roman Catholic church and were intent on establishing Protestantism as the dominant religious force. Once home, Mary continued exercising her Catholic beliefs to the obvious infuriation of her enemies, notably the outspoken Protestant reformer John Knox (see p.358). In 1565 she married Lord Darnley (1545-67) who was later involved in the murder of David Rizzio, Mary's private secretary. Darnley later fell ill and his end was hastened by the blowing up of the Edinburgh house in which he lay. Mary then married the Earl of Bothwell (*c.* 1537-78), generally reckoned to be one of the conspirators in Darnley's murder. By this time, Mary's powerful enemies were intent on destroying her and they felt confident enough to move against her. She was captured and then taken to Loch Leven where she was imprisoned in the castle on an island. She was forced to abdicate in favour of her son (the future James VI, 1566-1625) and her half-brother, the Earl of Moray (1531-70), took over as Regent. However, Mary escaped from her island prison and fled to Hamilton, where she gathered an army of 6000 men and prepared for a showdown here at Langside. After her defeat she fled to England where she was held prisoner by Queen Elizabeth. This did not stop her from being involved in further intrigue and, after being found guilty of being linked to a plot against Elizabeth, she was executed at Fotheringay.

To the west of the memorial stands the former **Langside Hill Church** ⓭ (1894-6, Alexander Skirving). This grand Graeco-Roman building takes full advantage of the sloping ground to impose its presence; its height is emphasised by placing its portico (with six fluted Ionic columns) above the entrance doors. The little towers at the side contain the stair-ways. Skirving was chief draughtsman to Alexander Thomson (see p.395) and the latter's influence can clearly be seen in the design. The church was built for the Free Church of Scotland and was the last Classical church to be built in Glasgow. It was left unfinished as there were plans to add sculptures. It is now converted into a pub (the 'Church on the Hill').

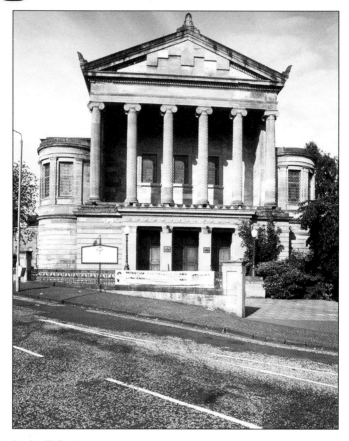

Langside Hill Church

This is the district of **Langside**, which had only twenty to thirty families in it in the mid-seventeenth century. It remained a country estate for another two centuries until it was turned over to housing, the first villa being Alexander Thomson's famous 'Double Villa'. At the end of the nineteenth century, the construction of tenement blocks started and this brought many thousands of people to the area.

Pass to the right of the church, following Langside Avenue downhill to Pollokshaws Road. On the way, Mansionhouse Road is passed on the left. At 25 Mansionhouse Road is **The Double Villa** ⓮ (1856-7, Alexander Thomson) which is described on p.399.

Langside Hall ⓯ stands on the right at the junction with Pollokshaws Road. This well-proportioned Palladian-style building was originally the National Bank of Scotland (1847, John Gibson) which stood in Queen Street in the city centre. It was rebuilt here in 1902-03.

At the top of the building is a royal coat of arms and the motto *My defence*. This is flanked by two figures representing *Peace* and *Plenty*. There is a lot of exceptionally fine detailing at cornice level (including swags of sculpted fruit and the head of a crowned woman) and the tall decorated pilasters emphasise the height of the upper storey. At ground floor level, the windows' keystones have five bearded faces representing the great rivers of the Clyde, Thames, Severn, Tweed and Humber, and various emblems such as fish, a boat and plants are used to decorate the heads. Handsome tall pilasters and the city's coat of arms decorate the ground floor. The sculpture is by John Thomas.

Opposite the halls is the **Corona** bar **16** (1912-13, Clarke & Bell), an unusual-looking single-storey pub with a clocktower at the street corner. This has been the site of a pub since 1817 and this one has the date *1912* on it. Above each of the two doorways are two faces and a hand holding a cross. The hand refers to the (disputed!) story that at the time of the Battle of Langside (see p.320) Mary, Queen of Scots was fleeing to Dumbarton. She took her crucifix in her loof (hand) and swore that *By the cross in my loof, I will be there tonight in spite of yon traitors*. The nearby district of Crossmyloof may owe its name to this tale.

Turn right at Pollokshaws Road and follow the edge of Queen's Park into the district of Strathbungo. Turn left at Vennard Gardens and right at Moray Place. This is followed along to the end, to see **1-10 Moray Place** **17** (1958-9, Alexander Thomson) which has been called *the finest of all Grecian terraces*. It consists of ten two-storey houses, with pedimented pavilions jutting out at each end. As with many of Thomson's buildings, the upper floor is less tall than the ground floor and its relatively narrow windows are set well back into the stonework, so that from an oblique angle the upper floor seems to consist entirely of a long series of pillars. The blank panels on the facade of this floor are used to indicate the divisions between the individual houses. Above this, the roof is very shallow pitched, allowing the stone cornice to dominate the top of the building; the only parts of the roof that can readily be seen are the chimney-pots which are in the shape of Egyptian-style lotus flowers. Carved decoration on the facade includes many of Thomson's classical motifs, including anthemia and a key pattern.

Thomson stayed in number 1 (see p.393) and the house was extended around 1930 in the same style. The terrace was part of the area once known as Regent's Park which was a promotion by Thomson, John McIntyre the builder (see p.372) and Alexander Stevenson, operator of the Giffnock stone quarry (who lived at number 5). Some of the other terraces in Moray Place have similarities to numbers 1-10.

Turn right at Nithsdale Road and right at Pollokshaws Road, then left at Balvicar Street. The **Queen's Park Baptist Church** **18**, originally the Camphill United Presbyterian Church (1875-83, William Leiper) is on the right, at the junction with Balvicar Drive. This French Gothic church has two large windows between which is a large sculpture (by John Mossman) of an angel with outspread wings holding a book. Another carving depicts a group of angels playing musical instruments. The spire, which was finished well after the rest of the church, is tall and slender and is one of the finest on the Southside. Some of the interior design was done by Daniel Cottier (see p.234).

Turn left at Balvicar Drive and right at Queen's Drive. **Strathbungo Queen's Park Church** ❶ (1873-5, James Thomson) stands at this corner. This Gothic church boasts a tall and slender spire.

Continue on Queen's Drive then turn left at Victoria Road. Walk up to **Queen's Park Railway Station** ❶ where the walk ends.

Queen's Park Baptist Church

Cathcart and Linn Park

This is another walk off the normal tourist trail through
the suburb of Cathcart and Linn Park, which is just on
the edge of the city.

Cathcart Old Parish Church

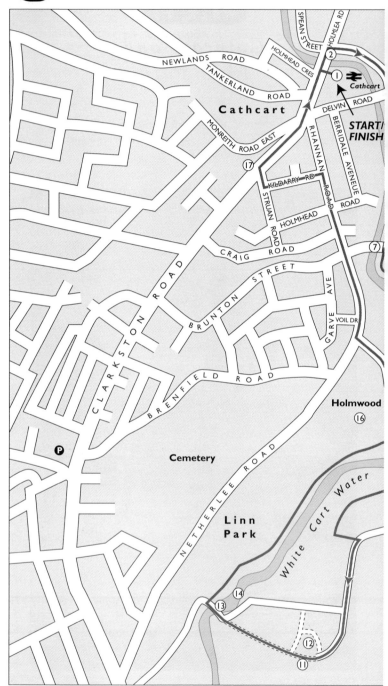

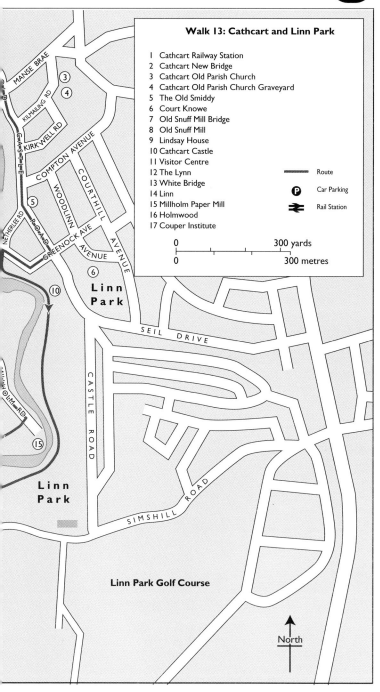

Walk 13: Cathcart and Linn Park

1 Cathcart Railway Station
2 Cathcart New Bridge
3 Cathcart Old Parish Church
4 Cathcart Old Parish Church Graveyard
5 The Old Smiddy
6 Court Knowe
7 Old Snuff Mill Bridge
8 Old Snuff Mill
9 Lindsay House
10 Cathcart Castle
11 Visitor Centre
12 The Lynn
13 White Bridge
14 Linn
15 Millholm Paper Mill
16 Holmwood
17 Couper Institute

▬▬▬▬ Route

P Car Parking

⇌ Rail Station

| 0 | | | 300 yards |
| 0 | | | 300 metres |

MANSE BRAE

KILMAILING RD

KIRK-WELL RD

COMPTON AVENUE

COURTHILL AVENUE

WOODLINN AVENUE

GREENOCK AVE

NETHERLEE RD

Linn Park

SEIL DRIVE

CASTLE ROAD

Linn Park

LINN RD

SIMSHILL ROAD

Linn Park Golf Course

↑
North

WALK

Main places of interest	Cathcart Old Parish Church Graveyard **④** Linn Park **⑥** and **⑩**-**⑭** **Holmwood ⑯** (19th-century house by Alexander Thomson)
Circular/linear	circular
Starting point	Cathcart Railway Station **①**
Finishing point	Cathcart Railway Station **①**
Distance	4.5 km (3 miles)
Terrain	generally hilly, especially in Linn Park (including the riverside walk which has steep steps); level near Clarkston Road
Public transport	Cathcart Railway Station (C)
Sections	Cathcart Railway Station to Linn Park Linn Park Linn Park to Cathcart Railway Station via Holmwood

Architects	Thomson: Cathcart Old Parish Church
	   Graveyard **④** (monument)
	   Holmwood **⑯**

Nearby walks	-
Refreshments	Clarkston Road
Notes	Be aware of safety advice (see p.16) as the graveyard and the park can be very quiet at times.

Cathcart Railway Station to Linn Park

From **Cathcart Railway Station** ❶, descend the stairs from the station's platform, turn right to walk through a passageway and then go left to meet Clarkston Road. The half-timbered **Margaretta Buildings** are on the right at this junction.

This is the district of **Cathcart**, named after the Cathcart family who built their castle here in the fifteenth century (see p.331). Over the next couple of hundred years the village prospered in the relatively small area between the castle, the White Cart Water and the old church but it was not until the eighteenth century that the village started to become important in its own right. This was as a result of mills being built to exploit the power of the river and these brought many people into the expanding community. In the late nineteenth century, the establishment of the railway line improved communications with the city and this allowed the village to develop as a residential area; but, partly as a result of this success, it was annexed by the city in 1912. By that time, the main thoroughfare was no longer what is now Old Castle Road and the old village (Old Cathcart) became a bit of a backwater, allowing it to retain rather more peace and quiet than is normally found in today's suburbs.

Turn right and cross the granite-topped **Cathcart New Bridge** ❷ (1900-2) over the White Cart Water (see p.304). Turn next right at Old Castle Road and pass under two railway bridges to reach a major junction. Go straight across, still following Old Castle Road, and head into Old Cathcart. Pass Edith Cottage (Cathcart Old Men's Club) on the right. Turn left at Kilmailing Road and follow it uphill.

The original **Cathcart Old Parish Church** ❸ (1831, James Dempster) stands at the end of the road. This now-ruined church was described by Hugh MacDonald in 1854 as 'an elegant building in the Modern Gothic style of architecture', but it was demolished in 1931, leaving only the tower and belfry standing. The main doorway has an information plaque above it and a sculpted head either side of it. This is an old-established religious site, dating back to at least 1707, though the graveyard is certainly older than that.

Cathcart Old Parish Church Graveyard ❹ is described on p.371.

Retrace the route back to Old Castle Road and turn left. Although the street has some tenements, there's something of a village air about this district; there's even **The Old Smiddy** ❺ pub. The blacksmith lived and worked in these buildings when the village was surrounded by farms. In those days, horses were the motive power on the land and on the roads and canals, and the smith, Robert Peddie, must have been in great demand as he also acted as the local veterinary surgeon.

Continue on Old Castle Road, cross Greenock Avenue and ascend the steps on the left which lead into a small section of Linn Park. Climb the steep grassy slope on the left to reach **Court Knowe** ❻ on Cathcart Hill where Mary, Queen of Scots is said to have watched the Battle of Langside (which is described on p.320). The stone that marks the spot is dated *XIII of May 1568* and has the initials *MR* ('Mary Regina').

The view from here in mid-nineteenth century was described by Hugh MacDonald in typically Victorian romantic terms:

> *The landscape seen from this station is extensive and beautiful, including,*
> *as is well known, an excellent prospect of the battle-field of Langside. The*
> *blue smoke of Cathcart is seen close at hand curling through the trees;*
> *beyond is the church and the shadowy burying-place; and in the distance*
> *the spires of Glasgow, relieved against the towering Kilpatrick hills.*

The view from here is now obscured by the trees' dense foliage. However, even in summer, a pair of binoculars can be used to pick out the domed glasshouse in Queen's Park (just to the west of north) and the very top of the Langside Battlefield Memorial (a little to the left of the glasshouse).

Retrace the route back to Greenock Avenue and turn left. Follow this road down to the **Old Snuff Mill Bridge** ❼ (Cathcart Old Bridge) which crosses the White Cart Water. This narrow two-arch bridge was probably built in the late eighteenth century but, very confusingly, a 1624 datestone has been built into the outside of the right hand wall; it possibly belonged to an earlier bridge. This used to be a very important river crossing as it was on the main road from Glasgow to Ayr. It is now pedestrianised.

The low buildings immediately upstream of the bridge are the remains of the **Old Snuff Mill** ❽. The original mill was built in the seventeenth century to grind corn, but in 1812 Solomon Lindsay converted it to make cardboard for bookbinding. Two years later, part of the premises were used by Stephen Mitchell (the benefactor of the Mitchell Library) to grind tobacco into snuff – hence the name. None of the original buildings remain but some of the later mills' buildings have been converted into houses.

The tall and elegant tenement opposite the old mill (at 38 Snuff Mill Road) is **Lindsay House** ❾ (1863-4, John Baird II). This was built by David Lindsay, son of Solomon Lindsay, as accommodation for himself and the people who worked in the mill. Above the doorway to his flat and at the top of the house can be seen intricate carvings comprising all the letters of his surname. The date 1863 is also carved on the building.

Walk a short distance back up Greenock Avenue. On the right, immediately after the houses, will be found Linn Park's entrance gate.

LINN PARK

Linn Park, centred on the mansion of The Lynn, has been in the hands of the city council since 1919. It is a much 'wilder' park than others in the city, with more grassy areas left uncut, thus allowing many varieties of wild flowers to grow. There is also a wide variety of animal life here, with numerous types of insects and birds; mammals such as squirrels will be seen in the woods. Broadleaf woodlands are found on both sides of the White Cart Water and there are open grassy spaces on the eastern side. There is a 'Walkaboutabit' trail on both sides of the river indicated by wooden posts – the route of this walk follows the trail from the Old Snuff Mill to Millholm Road.

Enter the park gate and follow the riverside path. Part of the river's weir which served the Old Snuff Mill can be seen on the right. On top of the steep cliffs on the left stand the remains of **Cathcart Castle** ❿. It can be reached by taking the first path on the left, passing to the left of a children's playpark, and then following a narrow path on the left which is found just before the park gates. However, the area around it is very overgrown and there is a precipitous drop beside the ruins. You have been warned!

This stone structure dates back to about 1450 when it was built by the Cathcart family on a prominent cliff above the White Cart Water. It was a strongly built castle, based on a five-storey rectangular keep with walls in some places over 3m (10ft) thick. Around 1740 it was sold for building material but still managed to retain its height for the next hundred years. Eventually it deteriorated so much that in 1980 it was partly demolished and the rubble was used to help fill in the River Clyde's Queen's Dock in order that the SECC could be built (see p.152). The walls are now only 2m (7ft) high but the keep's layout and its imposing position may still be appreciated.

Continue on the riverside path and bear left when the path splits in order to gain height. As the path bends to the right there is a view of a weir and the buildings associated with Millholm Paper Mill (see below). There are some particularly fine beech trees beside the path here.

The path is now high above the river and it splits just before Low Wood. Keep to the right and enter the wood. This contains many conifers, the most interesting being the Scots pine which is readily identified by its reddish bark. Turn left at the brow of the next hill and go straight through the wood to a road beyond which is Linn Park Golf Course. Turn right and follow Lime Avenue; this runs behind The Lynn and leads to the park's **Visitor Centre** ⓫ and the **equestrian centre**. The Visitor Centre organises various activities such as ranger-led walks.

The Lynn ⓬ (c. 1828), often just called 'the Mansionhouse', was originally built for city-dweller Colin Campbell who wanted a peaceful country retreat far away from the stench of Clydeside. This two-storey mansion has been much altered since then and is presently unused.

A path leads downhill between the equestrian centre and the mansionhouse; follow this down to the river. The **White Bridge** **⑬** (c. 1835) is then crossed. This is the oldest iron bridge in Glasgow and is often called the Halfpenny Bridge, probably on account of the circular holes in the bridge's ribs.

Turn right immediately after the bridge and follow the major path (the White Cart Walkway) as it keeps near the river, passing the **linn** **⑭**. Waterfalls in Scotland are sometimes called linns, hence the name of this estate and its house. Salmon may be seen here in late autumn when they are leaping upstream to reach their spawning area, while smaller and more common fish attract birds such as kingfishers.

Ignore any turns to the left, keeping to the main path which follows the course of the river. The path gradually climbs away from the river and passes through an area of planted horse-chestnut and beech trees. It then follows the perimeter of Holmwood (see below) and meets Millholm Road. The White Cart Walkway crosses this road and continues following the course of the river to the Old Snuff Mill Bridge, but the route of this walk leaves the park here and takes a right turn towards the old mill buildings.

Linn Park to Cathcart Railway Station via Holmwood

Turn right at Millholm Road to see the ruined buildings of the **Millholm Paper Mill** **⑮**. A Frenchman, Nicholas De Champ, set up a papermill here around 1729, turning rags into 'lily-white paper'. After his death, his son-in-law converted it into a snuff mill but it later reverted to papermaking and was bought by Robert and James Couper in 1853. They had been tenants for a few years beforehand and had been making paper by hand but they now installed machinery and produced good-quality writing paper in quantity. The mill had various uses after the Couper brothers left and the buildings were partially dismantled in the 1950s, though the weir remains; see also pp.334 and 372.

Ascend Millholm Road, passing the Walkway, to Netherlee Road. Turn left and left again to enter the driveway to **Holmwood** **⑯** (1857-8 Alexander Thomson).

James Couper (see above) chose this elevated site just above his mills for a new home and he gave Thomson great freedom to build an exceptionally fine piece of architecture. The house was lived in for one hundred years and then used as a school by the Sisters of Our Lady of the Missions but it is now owned by the National Trust for Scotland. This is an important building for the Trust, as it is generally regarded as

Thomson's finest house. It has been extensively restored by the Trust and visitors may be fortunate enough to watch the internal conservation work being carried out. As this work progresses, the richness of Thomson's original colour scheme is being revealed, making the house once more visually stunning. Thomson also designed the house's furniture but, unfortunately, it is all lost; perhaps some of it will turn up one day.

The driveway leads *up* to the house, giving the building that extra air of importance. The front of the building is asymmetric and quite complex, the most interesting feature being the almost circular bay window to the left of the main door. The glazing is set well behind the tall stone columns that support the heavy stonework above this projecting feature. This is the parlour; the dining room is on the other side of the entrance. Other external features of particular interest are the glazed circular lantern (which allows the internal stairway to be brightly lit) and the large amount of Classical incised detailing on the stonework. Many of the designs used on the stonework are repeated on the woodwork around the windows and they are used again with great effect inside the house. The complex roof is topped by numerous chimney-pots in the shape of Egyptian-style lotus flowers.

Inside, many of the walls are decorated with brightly coloured stencilwork which employs Classically-inspired geometric patterns. The plasterwork too, has many repeated patterns, and various stretches of otherwise plain plasterwork are studded with decorative bosses. Light is very important in Holmwood and, as well as using the circular lantern above the staircase to light the centre of the house, Thomson placed mirrors in various rooms in order to increase the feeling of spaciousness.

The **hall** features a horseshoe-shaped white marble chimney-piece topped by a cherub and a barometer; this was probably carved by George Mossman.

Holmwood

The **parlour** is well-lit by the large amount of glass, and the circular bay at the window has its own detailed plasterwork cornice. The main elements of the room's decoration are an elaborate plaster cornice and colourful stencilled patterns on the walls.

The **dining room** also has large windows which allow a lot of light in, and there is in addition a skylight at the end farthest away from the windows. This was specially designed to throw light onto an elaborate sideboard which was placed in the alcove below. When the house was used as a school this room functioned as a chapel, and the altar was placed in the alcove. Probably the most interesting feature of the room is its fascinating frieze which is in the form of a large mural with brown-painted figures on a blue background. The frieze shows twenty-one scenes from the Greek epic *Iliad* inspired by the work of John Flaxman (1755-1826). When the room was used as a chapel the frieze was covered over with anaglypta wallpaper, no doubt because the pictures of semi-clad figures were thought to be inappropriate! Above the frieze is a three-dimensional cornice composed of a series of elaborate plaster anthemia. The room's woodwork is another important feature, with the substantial doors in the form of tall Egyptian pylons. The chimney-piece is of black marble.

The **staircase** is top lit by means of the elaborate lantern, the inside of which is decorated with numerous plaster lion chimerae. The stairs lead to the spacious **drawing room**. This has a large white marble chimney-piece which is decorated with Thomson's hallmark incised details. Elaborate plasterwork, woodwork and wall decorations add to the room's interest and originally this would have been the most richly decorated room in the house.

A wall, now rebuilt, running from the house to the former stables and **coachman's lodge**, emphasizes how all the elements of the structure are fitted together into one grand design.

After leaving Holmwood, turn right at Netherlee Road (which later becomes Rhannan Road) and left at Kildary Road. Turn right at Struan Road in order to reach Clarkston Road directly opposite the Couper Institute.

The **Couper Institute** **⑰** (1887-8, James Sellars) was financed by money left by Robert Couper (see p.332). The public library was added later (1923-4, J. A. T. Houston) and a new hall was built, giving the local people a fine set of community facilities. The city's coat of arms is engraved on both wings. The local library is housed here and contains displays of local history.

Follow Clarkston Road northwards to the entrance to the railway station on the right, just after passing under the railway bridge.

The walk ends at **Cathcart Railway Station** **❶**.

CHAPTER 5

Places to Visit

Glasgow has a remarkable range of museums and galleries and their number (and quality) grows every year. They range from the very large (and extremely popular) Kelvingrove Art Gallery and Museum to small galleries featuring the work of young artists. Glasgow City Council and Glasgow University operate the main museums and galleries, while a number of smaller organisations have specialist collections on a wide variety of subjects.

The large table ('Glasgow at a glance') on p.18 lists lots of places in Glasgow that may be of interest to the reader. This chapter is intended to give general information specifically on the city's museums, galleries and other interesting places that can be visited.

The lists below indicate a number of these places according to the organisations that control them. All are open to visitors and most are described in the walks. Those not on the walks are described in this chapter.

The amount of information this book gives on each place varies considerably and depends on the building, its contents and what the author considers readers may find most interesting. Generally, the description can only give a flavour of each museum's collection but, hopefully, enough to allow the reader to get a good idea of what is available and what to look out for. Museums and galleries often change their exhibits so there may be some differences between the description given in the text and a venue's current displays. Where the buildings themselves are of importance, the interesting architectural details are mentioned.

The number in parenthesis following the name of the museum, gallery or other place to visit, refers to the number of the walk in which it is described. As with the table 'Glasgow at a glance', the most important sights are listed in bold.

GLASGOW CITY COUNCIL
St Mungo Museum of Religious Life and Art (1)
Provand's Lordship (1)
People's Palace (2)
City Chambers (3)
Gallery of Modern Art (3)
McLellan Galleries (4)
Kelvingrove Art Gallery and Museum (6)
Museum of Transport (6)
Scotland Street School (10)
The Burrell Collection (11)
Fossil Grove (see p.341)

Glasgow University

Hunterian Museum (6)

Zoology Museum (6)

War Memorial Chapel (6)

Hunterian Art Gallery (6)

Mackintosh House (6)

Other Museums, Galleries and Places to Visit

Glasgow Cathedral (1)

Collins Gallery (Strathclyde University) (1)

Glasgow Print Studio (2)

Sharmanka (2)

Glasgow Herald Building (3)

The Piping Centre (3)

Centre for Contemporary Arts (4)

Glasgow School of Art (4)

Tenement House (NTS) (4)

Royal Highland Fusiliers Museum (4)

Police Museum (4)

Queen's Cross Church (9)

House for an Art Lover (10)

Rangers Football Club (10)

Govan Old Parish Church (10)

Pollok House (NTS) (11)

Holmwood (NTS) (13)

602 Squadron Museum (see p.342)

Celtic Football Club (see p.342)

Crookston Castle (NTS) (see p.344)

Provan Hall (NTS) (see p.344)

The Scottish Mask and Puppet Theatre Centre (see p.345)

Springburn Museum (see p.346)

General Notes

• Generally, all the council and university museums and galleries have free entry. However, there may be charges levied for special (temporary) exhibitions. Other museums and galleries may charge. Contact the Tourist Information Centre for further information.

• The places marked 'NTS' are owned or managed by the National Trust for Scotland.

• Many of the places listed here publish their own guidebooks and the city's own museums often provide floor plans.

• Some of the council's museums arrange guided tours — details of these will normally be given just inside the building.

• Some of the buildings can only be seen if you are taken on a guided tour for which a fee may have to be paid.

- The Visitor Centre at Glasgow University will be able to give details of guided tours around the university; in some cases these provide the only opportunity to visit particular buildings.

OPENING TIMES

The following table indicates the opening dates and times of the places listed in the above table. These times can, of course, vary from those given here so the appropriate telephone numbers are given in order that up-to-date details can be obtained.

The Tourist Information Centre will also be able to provide details of current opening times. Their telephone number is (0141) 204 4400.

Burrell Collection 649 7151
closed Dec 25 & 26, Jan 1 & 2
Mon-Sat: 10.00-17.00 Sun: 11.00-17.00

Celtic Football Club 556 2611
closed Dec 25 & 26
tours (booking necessary):
during season: Mon-Fri: 10.00-14.45 Sat: 10.00-15.00
outside season: Mon-Fri: 10.00-14.45 Sun: 10.00-15.00

Centre for Contemporary Arts 332 7521
Dates/times: see note 1 on p.340
Mon-Sat: 11.00-18.00 Sun: 12.00-17.00

City Chambers 287 2000
closed public holidays
tours : Mon, Wed & Fri at 10.30 & 14.30 (also some Thursdays)

Collins Gallery (Strathclyde University) 548 2558
closed on public holidays and while exhibitions are being changed
Mon-Fri: 10.00-17.00 Sat: 12.00-16.00

Crookston Castle 226 5922
Dates/times: see note 1 on p.340

Fossil Grove 287 2000
open Easter – end of September
daily: 12.00-17.00

Gallery of Modern Art 229 1996
closed Dec 25 & 26, Jan 1 & 2
Mon-Sat: 10.00-17.00 Sun: 11.00-17.00

Glasgow Cathedral 552 6891
open all year
Apr-Sep: Mon-Sat: 09.30-18.00 Sun: 14.00-17.00
Oct-Mar: Mon-Sat: 09.30-16.00 Sun: 14.00-16.00

Glasgow Herald Building ('The Lighthouse')
not yet open

Glasgow Print Studio 552 0704
closed bank holidays
Mon–Sat: 10.00–17.30

Glasgow School of Art 353 4526
closed during the Christmas/New Year period and on other occasions
tours: Mon–Fri: 11.00 & 14.00 Sat: 10.30

Glasgow University Visitor Centre 330 5511
closed during the Christmas/New Year period
Mon–Sat: 09.30–17.00 also May– Sept: Sun: 14.00–17.00

Govan Old Parish Church 445 1941
Wed & Sat: 10.30–12.30 & 14.00–16.00
(telephone no: Pearce Institute)

Holmwood 637 2129
Dates/times: see note 1 on p.340
daily 13.30–17.30

House for an Art Lover 353 4770
irregular openings
times vary from week to week

Hunterian Art Gallery 330 5431
closed during the Christmas/New Year period and on other occasions
(mainly public holidays)
Mon–Sat: 09.30–17.00

Hunterian Museum 330 4221
closed during the Christmas/New Year period and on other occasions
(mainly public holidays)
Mon–Sat: 09.30–17.00

Kelvingrove Art Gallery and Museum 287 2700
closed Dec 25 & 26, Jan 1 & 2
Mon–Sat: 10.00–17.00 Sun: 11.00–17.00

Mackintosh House (Hunterian Art Gallery) 330 5431
closed during the Christmas/New Year period and on other occasions
(mainly public holidays)
Mon–Sat: 09.30–12.30 & 13.30–17.00

McLellan Galleries 331 1854
only open during special exhibitions

Museum of Transport 287 2720
closed Dec 25 & 26, Jan 1 & 2
Mon–Sat: 10.00–17.00 Sun: 11.00–17.00

People's Palace 554 0223
closed Dec 25 & 26, Jan 1 & 2
Mon–Sat: 10.00–17.00 Sun: 11.00–17.00

Piping Centre   353 0220
Dates/times: see note 1 on p.340
daily: 10.00–16.30

Police Museum   532 2000
open by prior arrangement only

Pollok House   616 6410
closed Dec 25 & 26, Jan 1 & 2
(Note: entrance is free during Nov–Mar)
Nov–Mar: 11.00–16.00 Apr–Oct: 10.00–17.00

Provan Hall   771 4399
closed during the Christmas/New Year period when events
are in progress
Mon–Fri: 09.00–16.30

Provand's Lordship   553 2557
closed at present

Queen's Cross Church   946 6600
closed on public holidays
Mon–Fri: 10.30–17.00 Sun: 14.30–17.00

Rangers Football Club   427 8500
Dates/times: see note 1 on p.340
tours: Sun: 09.45–16.30

Royal Highland Fusiliers Museum   332 0961
Dates/times: see note 1 on p.340

Scotland Street School   429 1202
closed Dec 25 & 26, Jan 1 & 2
Mon–Sat: 10.00–17.00 Sun: 14.00–17.00

Scottish Mask and Puppet Theatre Centre   339 6185
closed Dec 25 & 26, Jan 1 & 2 and July
Mon–Fri: 10.00–17.00 Sat: 13.30–17.30

Sharmanka   552 7080
Dates/times: see note 1 on p.340
Sat & Sun: 12.00–16.00

602 Squadron Museum   810 6002/6204
closed Dec 25 & 26, Jan 1 & 2
Jan–Jun & Sep–Dec: Wed & Fri: 19.30–21.30
also Apr–Sep: first Sunday in each month: 14.00–17.00
also groups by special arrangement
(telephone no: Rolls-Royce)

Springburn Museum   557 1405
Dates/times: see note 1 on p.340
Tues–Fri: 10.30–17.00 Sat: 10.00–16.30
bank holidays: 14.00–17.00

**St Mungo Museum of Religious
Life and Art** 553 2557
closed Dec 25 & 26, Jan 1 & 2
Mon–Sat: 10.00–17.00 Sun: 11.00–17.00

Tenement House 333 0183
open Mar 1 – Oct 31
daily: 14.00–17.00

War Memorial Chapel (Glasgow University) 339 8855
closed during the Christmas/New Year period and on other occasions
(mainly public holidays)
normally Mon–Fri: 09.00–17.00 and Sat 09.00–12.00
except during services (including weddings)
(telephone no: University's main switchboard)

Zoology Museum 330 5506/6630
closed during the Christmas/New Year period and on public holidays
Mon–Fri: 09.00–17.00

Note 1: Contact the place for details, especially if you wish to find out
about the Christmas and New Year period and public holidays.

Note 2: The offices, cafés and restaurants in these venues may have
different opening times from those listed above.

PLACES TO TAKE CHILDREN

The following table gives some suggestions for places which might be of
particular interest to children. The museums may be particularly useful
on rainy days.

Museums and galleries	Parks	Miscellaneous
People's Palace	Pollok Park [2]	Sharmanka
Gallery of Modern Art	Queen's Park [3]	Rangers Football Club
Kelvingrove Art Gallery and Museum [1]	Linn Park [4]	Celtic Football Club
Museum of Transport		The Scottish Mask and Puppet Theatre
Scotland Street School		Centre
Zoology Museum		

Notes
1. The Natural History section is recommended. In addition, a
    number of the temporary exhibitions are aimed towards children.
2. There is an interesting Wildlife Garden and there are also some
    Ranger-led activities.
3. There is a small zoo in The Glass House.
4. The park has an equestrian centre and there are also some
    Ranger-led activities.

PLACES NOT INCLUDED ON THE WALKS

The following places of interest in the Glasgow area are not encountered on any of the walks but may well be of interest to readers.

Fossil Grove
(in the south-western corner of Victoria Park, off Dumbarton Road)

Although Fossil Grove is not the best-known of the city's tourist attractions, it's certainly the oldest with a collection of fossil tree trunks that date from around 330 million years ago. This is important enough to be officially classed as a SSSI (Site of Special Scientific Interest) and is the only place in the world where a collection of fossil trees are preserved *in situ*.

The trees lived during the Carboniferous (i.e. coal-producing) Period, when Scotland was situated near the equator and the warm and humid climate encouraged huge tropical forests to grow. When the trees eventually died and fell into swamps they were covered with water-borne debris and the remains were slowly compressed into coal. The eleven trees in this particular location represent a small area of a large forest that grew in a freshwater lowland swamp and they are known as Lepidodendron, a type of giant club moss which grew to a height of 30m (100 ft) or more. When these trees died the upper part of their trunks broke off, leaving behind the stumps, the soft interior of which soon rotted away. Sand then filled the interior of the stumps and the roots and eventually covered all that we see today. Around 40 million years later a volcanic eruption occurred in the district and this covered the site with lava which eventually cooled to form a very hard rock called whinstone (or dolerite). Happily, this lava preserved the stumps from later erosion. The eruption also pushed lava underneath the site, lifting it up and tilting it, leaving the sloping forest floor that is seen today.

The whinstone was quarried for road making during the nineteenth century and in 1887, when the disused quarry was being landscaped as part of the new Victoria Park, workmen discovered the trees. Fortunately the fossils were preserved as what the Victorians would probably have called a 'curiosity'.

Some of the fossil tree stumps are very large (up to 1m (3 ft) across) although they are sandstone casts of the insides (rather than the outsides) of the trees' trunks. The bark is not preserved as it would have been compressed by the weight of the covering rock and then turned into coal which was subsequently removed during the excavation in order to expose the underlying sandstone fossils. The root system is clearly visible and there is also a fossil of a large tree trunk lying near the entrance. One rock (about halfway along the site) carries the impression of the trees' easily recognised bark which is covered with diamond-shaped leaf scars. Another rock carries fossil ripple marks, indicating that water must have been flowing over the land; this rock is on the left and is quite near the viewing balcony. One curious feature of the fossils is that the trunks are not circular but ellipsoid in shape. As the ellipses generally point in the same direction it is thought that this change may have been produced by the pressure of flowing water which forced the rotting tree stumps to take on a more streamlined profile.

602 Squadron Museum
(Queen Elizabeth Avenue, Hillington Industrial Estate)

This small museum was opened in 1983 and is dedicated to the RAF squadron whose full title is the 602 (City of Glasgow) Squadron Royal Auxiliary Air Force. It is situated beside the Rolls-Royce aircraft engine factory which has had its own 2175 (Rolls-Royce) Squadron Air Training Corps since 1946, the staff and cadets of which set up the museum.

The 602 Squadron was originally formed in 1925 and was the first of the RAF's twenty-one auxiliary squadrons; it was based at the nearby Moorpark airfield at Renfrew. In May 1939, just a few months before the start of the Second World War, the squadron converted from bombers to fighter aircraft and were equipped with Spitfires which were powered by Merlin engines produced in the Rolls-Royce factory. The squadron was soon involved in action as German aircraft bombed Scotland from early on in the war and this squadron was the first to bring down an enemy plane onto British soil; this happened on the Lammermuir Hills to the south of the stategically important Firth of Forth. In 1940 the squadron moved south to the Portsmouth area where it was involved in the Battle of Britain. Other activities during the war included protecting the naval base at Scapa Flow in Orkney and bombing raids against German V2 rocket sites. The squadron was disbanded at the end of the war but was later reformed and flew from Abbotsinch, now Glasgow Airport. The final disbandment took place in 1957.

The museum's collection includes parts of aircraft (including a Merlin engine), uniforms, equipment, photographs and other items that deal with the squadron's history and aircraft engineering. The Rolls-Royce Heritage Trust Museum can also be visited to view a collection of aircraft engines.

Celtic Football Club
(Kerrydale Street)

Celtic was founded in the impoverished East End in 1888 by a Marist brother called Walfrid to raise money for the district's poor children. Walfrid was Irish and he hoped that by using the name 'Celtic' this would encourage the city's Irish community to support the club and help them integrate more fully in the sporting and social life of the city. Many (but certainly not all) of the first players were of Irish Catholic origin and the Irish tradition is still very important for the club. Its most obvious manifestation is the use of the green shamrock as the club's symbol and the green and white team strip. The stadium's interior decoration is, not surprisingly, predominantly green in colour.

Celtic's first match was on 28 May 1888 when they defeated Rangers 5-2 in front of a crowd of 2000 spectators, and in 1890/1 they took part in the first season of the Scottish Football League. The club's first ground was close to the Eastern Necropolis and in 1892, when it moved to the present (adjacent) site, it was remarked that the club had left the graveyard for 'Paradise', the name Celtic Park is often called to this day. The site, a waterlogged quarry, was in a terrible state when it was acquired, to the extent that it needed 10,000 cartloads of infill to level it. However, the new stadium soon became a great success and was large enough to hold the 46,000 spectators who attended a Scotland-England international here in 1894. Hampden Park later took on the role of the national stadium.

The worsening of British-Irish relations at the beginning of the twentieth century was unfortunately accompanied by sectarianism in the city and, in many cases, blatant discrimination against Catholics. Social tensions were reflected in the polarisation of football supporters, with Celtic's support being overwhelmingly Catholic and Rangers' Protestant. The history of Rangers is described on p.285.

Celtic won many honours in the first half of the twentieth century, including six consecutive League Championships in 1904-10 and four in 1913-17; they also won the Scottish Cup twelve times in the first half of the century. In the 1936/7 season Celtic defeated Aberdeen in front of 146,433 spectators, with another 30,000 outside Hampden, unable to get inside! However, for many supporters, the greatest achievements took place between 1965 and 1975 under the management of Jock Stein, a former Celtic player of the 1950s. During this time the team won nine consecutive League Championships, won the Scottish Cup seven times and the League Cup six times. Success at national level won them a place in European championships and in 1967 Celtic became the first British team to win the European Cup when they beat Inter Milan 2-1 in Lisbon, earning the players the nickname the 'Lisbon Lions'.

The stadium's modern red brick frontage carries the inscription 'Celtic Football Club 1888' and on either side of the entrance can be seen the external framework of the new stands which were erected in the late 1990s. A tour of Celtic Park includes a visit to the club's museum and trophy room and an opportunity to see the pitch. The stadium has tier upon tier of seats and can accommodate just over 60,000 spectators; inevitably, most of the seats are either green or white. The museum contains many footballing momentoes including trophies, players' strips, newspaper cuttings, photographs and numerous displays outlining the history of the club and the people associated with it. One of the most poignant momentoes is the handsome silver cup won by Rangers in the competition arranged during the city's 1888 International Exhibition. In 1901 a tragic accident took place at Ibrox (Ranger's ground) during a match and in order to raise compensation money for the victims, a competition was organised with this cup being offered as the prize. Celtic won the competition, hence the appearance of the cup here.

Crookston Castle
(Brockburn Road)

Considering that Glasgow has few castles open to the public, this one is not all that well known, probably because it is situated well away from the normal tourist trail. A castle was built on this prominent hill by Sir Robert Croc of Neilston in the twelfth century but the present structure was erected around 1400. It was originally in the form of a three-storey block with tall square towers at each of its corners and guarded by substantial earth banks and a deep ditch. In the thirteenth century it passed into the ownership of the Stewarts of Darnley who, in 1489, were involved in the rebellion against King James IV. The king's forces laid seige to the castle with the result that a substantial part of it (notably the towers) was destroyed. It later belonged to Sir John Maxwell of Pollok who gave it to the National Trust for Scotland in 1931 though today it is under the guardianship of Historic Scotland.

The castle's small arched entrance is protected by a portcullis and there is a guard chamber (which leads to an underground dungeon) just inside the main doorway. A second and smaller doorway leads into a barrel-vaulted cellar. Directly above the cellar is the vaulted Great Hall which is now roofless; it has a massive fireplace and some stone seats by the windows. A doorway leads from the hall into the north-eastern tower's spiral staircase, off which is a latrine which has its own opening to the fresh air outside.

This north-eastern tower is still intact and it contains three bedrooms and a narrow stairway leading to a rooftop platform which gives a good view of the south-west of the city. To the west can be seen the tall tower of Leverndale Hospital and to the north-west is Paisley, with Paisley Abbey and the Thomas Coats Memorial Baptist Church being two of the town's most prominent landmarks.

Provan Hall
(Auchinlea Park, Auchinlea Road)

This fifteenth-century building is not very well known outside Glasgow (in fact, it is not known by many Glaswegians either), but it is one of the city's most interesting buildings which served as a country retreat for the Prebendary of Lanark, one of the canons of Glasgow Cathedral. His town house was in St Nicholas Hospital, now popularly known as Provand's Lordship (see p.42). There are similarities in the designs of the two buildings, notably the rubble walls, crow-stepped gables and the fireplaces, and it is possible they were both constructed by the same group of craftsmen. The church sold the hall's large estate in 1565 and it was bought by Glasgow Burgh in 1667. It is now owned by the National Trust for Scotland but it is in the care of the council. It is situated in Auchinlea Park, hence the very pleasant gardens to the west of the building.

The 2000 acre (800 hectare) estate was known as the Bishop's Forest and was regarded as one of the country's best hunting grounds. There were many lochans and marshy areas between here and Glasgow and it is

Provan Hall

said that it was once possible to travel by boat between the two places. Part of this wet ground was later used as part of the Monklands Canal, itself replaced by the busy M8 motorway. The higher ground was used as the site of the massive Easterhouse housing scheme which was started in the 1950s.

The hall is essentially a small but well-defended country house with a walled courtyard which is entered by an arched gateway. Downstairs there are three barrel-vaulted rooms: a kitchen (with a massive fireplace), a dairy and a hallway; upstairs, there is a dining room and a bedroom. All the rooms have stone floors. A circular stair turret on the outer wall has a number of shot-holes in its walls which would allow those inside to fire on any unwelcome visitors that might be approaching. The external stair to the upper rooms was a later addition and just off it is a narrow flight of steps leading to a lookout platform above the gateway. On the outside of the gateway is a projecting stone plaque which bears the date *1647*, the letters *RH* (for a one-time owner Sir Robert Hamilton) and the Hamilton coat of arms.

On the southern side of the courtyard stands an eighteenth-century house which faces towards the Clyde Valley. This was once known as Hall Mailing as it was a halting place for the Glasgow to Edinburgh stagecoach (which carried the mail) but now it acts as the hall's visitor centre and exhibition area. Its displays tell the story of the hall and the people associated with it, including Mary, Queen of Scots (see p.321), James IV and not one, but three (!) ghosts.

The Scottish Mask and Puppet Theatre Centre
(Balcarres Avenue)

The Centre, which is the only one of its kind in Scotland, uses puppets, marionettes and masks to entertain children and grown-ups alike. Many adults probably remember being enthralled by Punch and Judy shows on seaside beaches during their childhood but the theatre's wide repertoire encompasses much more than traditional British puppet entertainment as it uses tales from many countries and a diverse range of cultures. Puppetry is essentially a form of folk art as it employs hand-crafted models to act out traditional tales and legends, and it has long been a popular means of telling stories to children.

There is also a large collection of puppets which come from many countries, with a significant number from the Far East where puppetry is a highly-regarded art form. The museum has displays of these remarkable puppets, together with masks and shadow masks from around the world. Some puppets will be readily recognised, such as Punch, Judy and Parker who was in the television series *Thunderbirds*; others, especially those from overseas, are dressed in marvellous costumes which will delight children.

The Centre was founded in 1981 and as well as staging performances and running the museum, it organises workshops and courses. It also maintains a very high profile in the world of puppetry. The theatre and museum sections of the Centre will be moving to Martyrs' School in the near future.

Springburn Museum
(Ayr Street)

The museum is situated within Springburn Library which was originally built with money donated by Andrew Carnegie (1835-1918). Carnegie was born in Dunfermline, made a massive fortune in steelmaking in America, and on his return to Scotland in 1901 provided the finance to build public libraries up and down the country.

Springburn was once the home of many very important factories which made a bewildering variety of products such as pottery, chemicals, beer and ironware. But in the minds of most Glaswegians the area is best known for railway engineering and it is fitting that the public square in front of the library was the site of the Hydepark Locomotive Works which was founded in 1862. At one stage, and after various amalgamations, this was part of the North British Locomotive Company, the largest locomotive manufacturer in the world; their nearby offices are now used by the North Glasgow College. The history of the city's locomotive industry is described on p.210.

The museum, which is run by a local trust, acts as a community museum for Springburn and much of the north of the city. Its frequently changing displays cover the social history of the area – housing, social life and working lives – as well as the engineering and other products that the people produced in such a downtrodden corner of the city. Thirty thousand people once lived in less than 3¼ km^2 (1¼ square miles) before the bulldozers moved in. Much of Springburn has been 'redeveloped' in recent years, so much so that the area is almost unrecognisable to those who left it before the factories closed and the slum tenements came down. However, if a museum sets itself the task of capturing memories of people's lives then this is what would be called 'a wee gem' by Glaswegians.

The *Springburn Statue* by Vincent Butler stands outside the museum and features two figures. The man is a worker from Springburn's locomotive factories and symbolises the area's pride in past achievements; the small girl represents hope for the future.

CHAPTER 6

Glasgow's Graveyards

Graveyards offer an exceptionally interesting insight into our history. Their monuments not only record the names, dates and relationships of the people buried there, but they also often have carvings and inscriptions which record occupations, interests and achievements, forming a telling social commentary. However, the evidence is often selective in that it has been wealthier people who have been able to afford the large, prestigious and well-built monuments which survive best of all.

Before the sixteenth-century Reformation, the wealthy were often buried inside churches and had monuments to them erected within the walls of these churches. After the Reformation burials were invariably made in churchyards, the most prestigious plots being those in the aisles attached to the church, in old and perhaps redundant chapels, or in specially built mausoleums. Monuments of various styles were built and the most lavish were intended to serve as a reminder of the wealth, rank or achievements of the incumbents. In other cases, a flat gravestone was laid over the grave, while others stood vertically against the inside of the churchyard wall. In contrast, the poor were generally interred to the north of the church, as were unbaptised children; this often accounts for the paucity of monuments in these areas of some graveyards.

With the predominance firstly of the Roman Catholic Church and then the Church of Scotland, burials normally took place on church property. But while control over churchyards after the sixteenth-century Reformation was nominally in the hands of the local churches, the real power (up until the 1920s) was often exercised by the heritors (the local parish's landowners) who, as well as controlling such matters as the appointment of a new minister to a church, would also determine who could be buried in the churchyard. Gradually, the churches' role in burials diminished over the centuries, partly because their 'hold' over the people was loosened and also for the practical reason that many of the churchyards had become filled. This led to non-denominational cemeteries being established, some of them originally private undertakings such as the Glasgow Necropolis, although today they are almost invariably under the care of the local council.

In many cases, monuments erected during the last couple of centuries took the form of vertical headstones, usually of sandstone, granite, marble or occasionally iron. More elaborate designs such as obelisks, Greek columns, Celtic Crosses or the addition of sculpted urns or statues were used to show off a person's wealth. Many monuments carry clues to the occupations of those buried there. For example, a carving of a pair of shears would denote a tailor, though generally this type of carving is less common in Glasgow than in rural graveyards; Govan Old Parish Church Graveyard is a notable exception. More common are symbolic carvings which have particular meanings. Symbols of mortality include the skull and crossbones, Father Time, an hourglass ('the passage of time') and an urn. Symbols of immortality include angels, a sunburst, a torch (either upwards or downwards), a heart, scales and a phoenix. Sculptors often combined these and other symbols to produce grander symbols such as a winged hourglass – which represents the 'rapid passage of time'! The lettering styles used on monuments have changed over the centuries and some of the early styles may be rather difficult to decipher. Sometimes J is written as I, S is written as Z, U is written as V and W is in the form of two overlapping Vs. In some cases, letters are run together, such as with the letters TH in the word THE, or LL becomes L$^\text{L}$.

It is worth noting that it is not unusual in Scotland for a wife's maiden name to be used on a burial monument and many memorials described in this chapter follow this old tradition.

In some graveyards a small watchkeeper's hut still exists, harking back to the days when body-snatchers dug up fresh corpses on which medical students could practise. With its large teaching hospitals, Glasgow was troubled by these macabre deeds on many occasions and the exploits of Burke and Hare in Edinburgh in 1828-9 resulted in many graveyards being guarded during the night. Cathcart Old Parish Church Graveyard has one of these huts while the Ramshorn Graveyard has the remains of an iron mort safe which was used to deter would-be grave-robbers. Even more protection was given by erecting railings around a grave or by building an expensive mausoleum.

Glasgow's most elaborate monuments (to say nothing of the large mausoleums) are to be found in the Glasgow Necropolis, though the other graveyards have numerous well-carved and interesting monuments. The graveyards in this chapter are included either for the interest of the actual monuments or because of the people whose lives they celebrate. In the larger graveyards, the text is given in the form of a route past these monuments to give the reader the opportunity to wander around and study other monuments at leisure. In a book of this nature, only a very small proportion of the monuments can be dealt with, so the reader is encouraged to find those monuments which are described and in so doing, discover many more which are worth examining.

Personal safety must be carefully considered while walking around the graveyards. Some of them may be very quiet, while others may be busy with visitors. However, some graveyards may be a meeting-place for some of the city's less pleasant individuals. The location, the time of day and the weather are all factors to consider, as well as the reader's own possible vulnerability. Please take care. If in doubt, don't go.

Two other important places in which to study the city's gravestones and funerary architecture are inside Glasgow Cathedral and Govan Old Parish Church. The latter has the country's most fascinating collection of sculptured stones, dating back to the ninth, tenth and eleventh centuries.

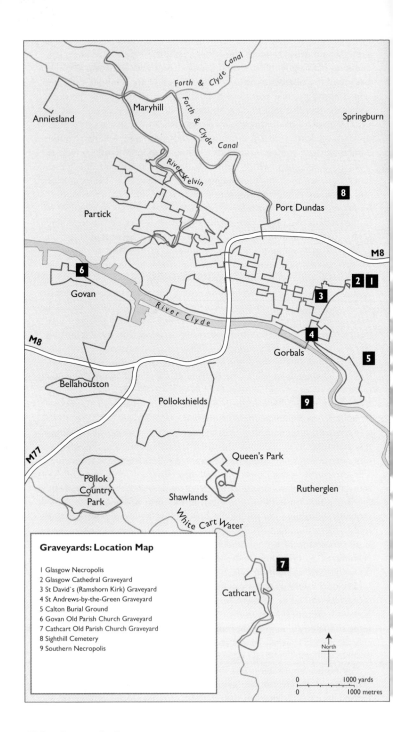

Graveyards: Location Map

1 Glasgow Necropolis
2 Glasgow Cathedral Graveyard
3 St David's (Ramshorn Kirk) Graveyard
4 St Andrews-by-the-Green Graveyard
5 Calton Burial Ground
6 Govan Old Parish Church Graveyard
7 Cathcart Old Parish Church Graveyard
8 Sighthill Cemetery
9 Southern Necropolis

North

| 0 | | 1000 yards |
| 0 | | 1000 metres |

These two churches are described on p.38 and p.291 respectively.

Nine graveyards are described in this chapter and they are listed below. Seven of them are encountered in the course of the thirteen walks described in this book.

The map opposite shows the locality of each of the nine graveyards.

GLASGOW NECROPOLIS

This graveyard is situated to the east of Glasgow Cathedral and can be reached from John Knox Street. Its precise location is described on Walk 1 (see p.34).

The Necropolis is the city's most spectacular graveyard, not just because it has so many fine monuments, but also because of its position on a prominent hill from which there are excellent views of much of the city. The land had been owned by the Merchants' House since 1650 and in 1825 a monument to John Knox was erected at the highest point. The merchants then decided to make this hilltop site their lasting memorial and its grand name ('Necropolis' means 'City of the dead') reflected the importance its founders intended it should have. It was modelled on Paris' Père-Lachaise cemetery and a total of 50,000 burials have taken place here, with 3500 tombs being built. Most of the burials took place in the nineteenth century, and consequently most of the monuments reflect the dominant architectural styles of that time. After the first few decades of the twentieth century there were few interments and in 1966 the Merchants' House handed the graveyard over to the city council. The graveyard is only very occasionally still used for a burial.

There is a small separate section for Jewish burials, but otherwise there was no discrimination, except against those who couldn't afford it. Styles of tombs and mausoleums vary considerably, including Greek, Roman, Arabic and Gothic; indeed, it has been said that the style of many of the

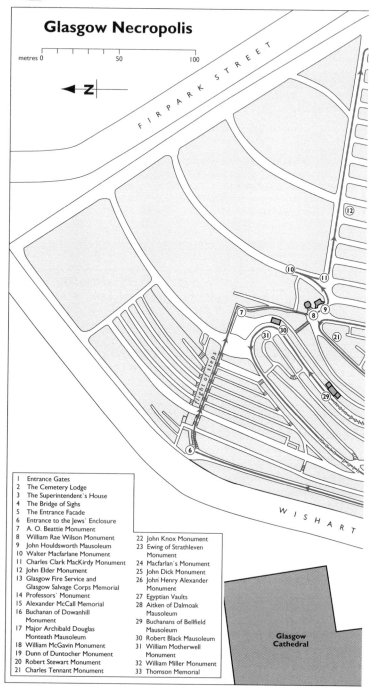

Glasgow Necropolis

metres 0   50   100

WISHART

Glasgow Cathedral

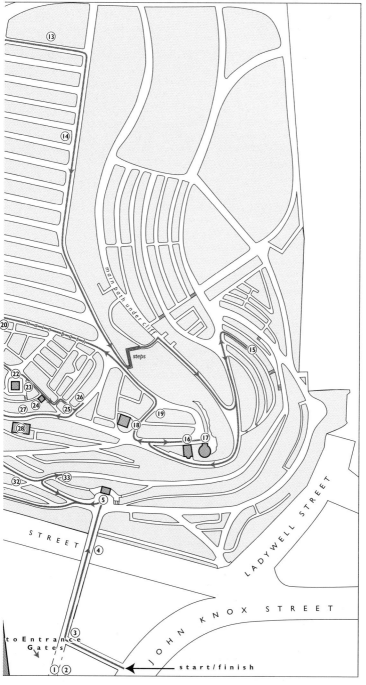

tombs reflected where the person made their money. Certainly, each occupant of the different lairs must have vied with their prospective neighbour to ensure a fitting tribute to their own worthiness.

The route described below visits the best-known monuments and mausoleums but there are many other interesting pieces of sculpture (and history). The route takes the reader from the Entrance Gates to the Entrance Facade, then leftwards to the Jews' Enclosure. This allows access to a long and steep flight of steps which leads to the uppermost area, from which there are fine views. From there, a circuitous route leads back downhill to the Entrance Facade. Most of the memorials are relatively easy to find, except for the McCall Monument (which is nearly thirty paces away from the gravel path) and the Aitken of Dalmoak Mausoleum (the exact position of which can be ascertained from the Egyptian Vaults).

❶ Entrance Gates (1833, James Hamilton)

These heavy and elaborate cast-iron gates have in the centre the symbol (a sailing ship atop a globe) of the Merchants' House with their motto *Tòties redeuntis eodem* ('So often returning to the same place'). The history of the Merchants' House is given on p.88.

❷ The Cemetery Lodge (1839-40, David Hamilton)

This squat stone building was erected as the cemetery superintendent's office.

❸ The Superintendent's House (1890)

This traditional single-storey dwelling was erected as the cemetery superintendent's house.

Glasgow Necropolis

❹ The Bridge of Sighs (1833-34, James Hamilton)
This was originally built to cross the ravine through which the stinking Molendinar Burn once flowed. This stream, which flows from Hogganfield Loch, was once very important to the city and two dams were built near here in order to provide water for a couple of mills. The burn was culverted in the 1870s and its route below this bridge is now followed by Wishart Street, named after Robert Wishart whose exploits are mentioned on p.40. The bridge takes its name from the number of sad occasions when funeral parties have crossed it into the graveyard.

❺ The Entrance Facade (1835-36, John Bryce)
At the eastern end of the bridge is an ornamental gateway behind which is a tunnel. It was originally envisaged that subterranean vaults could be built here for 'secure' burial, safely away from graverobbers. Building these catacombs would have involved expensive tunnelling as the Necropolis is on one of the few hills in the city composed of solid rock. Most of the hills in Glasgow are drumlins which are essentially great piles of debris (comprised of stones, sand and clay) which were produced by the local glaciers; the hills were then shaped by thick sheets of ice which passed over them.

❻ Entrance to the Jews' Enclosure
This is sited at the foot of a long flight of stairs. The tall monument (by John Bryce) is styled after Absalom's Pillar in the King's Dale, Jerusalem. To its right is the rather small entrance to the burial ground (by John Park) while on the left are two gravestones with Hebrew inscriptions. This plot of land was purchased by Jewish people in 1830 solely for the interment of Jews.

❼ A. O. Beattie Monument (1858, Alexander Thomson)
Alexander Ogilvie Beattie (1793-1853) was the first minister of the St Vincent Street Free Church of Scotland (described on p.158) which was also built by Thomson. Situated on sloping ground, it consists of a plinth and a tall obelisk topped by an urn.

❽ William Rae Wilson Monument (J. A. Bell)
Wilson (1772-1849) travelled in the Middle East and wrote the book *Travels in the Holy Land*. This interest is reflected by the octagonal monument which is in the Moorish style found in Palestine.

❾ John Houldsworth Mausoleum (1854, John Thomas)
Marble statues of Hope (resting on an anchor) and Charity (holding a small child) stand outside, while Faith (with angels on either side) shelters inside.

❿ Walter Macfarlane Monument
This famous manufacturer of cast-ironwork lived from 1817 to 1885 and his achievements are described on pp.64 and 222. This large grey granite monument has a bronze plaque featuring a bust of Macfarlane.

⓫ Charles Clark MacKirdy Monument (1891, James Thomson)
This monument is based on the Choragic Monument of Lysicrates in Athens.

It is made of granite which has allowed it to retain its fine detail and it is topped by an urn.

⓬ John Elder Monument

The achievements of this important engineer and shipbuilder are described on pp.294 and 296. His wife Isabella Ure is also buried here – her role in Glasgow life is described on p.297. So too is his father, David, who also played an important part in the development of the city's shipbuilding industry.

⓭ Glasgow Fire Service and Glasgow Salvage Corps Memorial

For a long time Glasgow earned the title 'tinderbox city' because of the number of fires which claimed so many lives. Fires in houses and factories alike brought real terror to a great number of people and the city has always been grateful to the firefighters who risked their own lives to rescue others.

This tall granite memorial honours those who lost their lives in two terrible fires. One side declares that the monument is *in proud and loving memory of the officers and men of the Glasgow Fire Service and the Glasgow Salvage Corps who perished in the Cheapside Street Fire 28th March 1960.* This street is just to the west of the Kingston Bridge and these nineteen men died in a fire in a bonded warehouse which was used for storing whisky. On another side is an inscription which is in remembrance of seven firemen who were killed on 25 August 1972 in a fire at Kilbirnie Street which is near West Street Underground Station.

⓮ Professors' Monument

The academics of the Old College in High Street and their families were buried in the nearby Blackfriars Churchyard. However, when the college site was sold to the railway company the burial ground was also taken over and the bodies were reinterred here in 1876.

⓯ Alexander McCall Memorial (1888; Charles Rennie Mackintosh)

This monument's great interest lies in the fact that it is the first documented solo piece by Mackintosh and his name (*Chas. R. McIntosh*) can be seen on the left of the plinth. (The spelling 'Mackintosh' was used from 1892, around the time when his father remarried and changed his own name.) On the right of the plinth is the inscription *Peter Smith, S.*, the name of the mason who sculpted the work for the Mossman firm of monumental sculptors and who, incidentally, took over that firm in 1890. This tall white granite Celtic Cross is decorated with traditional interlaced patterns and bosses and its style is quite unlike the designs Mackintosh is so well known for. In contrast, the lettering used for the text and the architect's own name show that Mackintosh was willing to use his own style even when designing something as sombre as a memorial.

McCall was the city's second Chief Constable and his personal assistant was none other than William McIntosh, the architect's father. A plaque, which was sculpted by Pittendrigh Macgillivray, carries the words *In memory of Alexander McCall for 18 years Chief Constable of Glasgow. Born at Ayr 12 Feb 1836 died 29 March 1888. This monument was erected by the Police Commissioners, a few friends and the force of which he was so long the honoured chief.* The memorial used to have a brass plaque but this is now in the care of Glasgow Museums and it has been replaced by a fibreglass replica.

⓰ Buchanan of Dowanhill Monument (1844, James Brown)
This monument is also based on the Choragic Monument of Lysicrates and is one of the more finely carved monuments in the cemetery. The top half was toppled over by a storm in 1856 and replaced with the cylindrical centrepiece to give it more stability. The lower set of fluted Corinthian columns are based on the Tower of the Winds in Athens. It was built for John Buchanan (d.1844).

⓱ Major Archibald Douglas Monteath Mausoleum
(1842, David Cousin)
This is the cemetery's most elaborate mausoleum. Its circular base (in the style of a Knights Templar church) features variously decorated Romanesque windows while the ornamented doorway has a series of grotesque animal faces. The upper storey is in the form of an octagonal lantern and is supported from ground level by eight substantial pillars.

It was erected for Archibald Douglas Monteath (d.1842). It is said that while working in India he chased an elephant that had escaped from a maharajah's procession. He caught the beast and kept its burden of jewellery and precious stones. Not bad for a day's work.

⓲ William McGavin Monument (1834, John Boyce)
This is in the Flemish Mannerist style and is topped by a statue of McGavin (d.1832), merchant, preacher and author of *The Protestant*.

⓳ Dunn of Duntocher Monument (John Thomas Rochead)
This substantial domed Roman Doric monument was erected to the very wealthy manufacturer William Dunn (1770-1849).

⓴ Robert Stewart Monument (James Brown)
Stewart (1811-66) was Lord Provost of Glasgow and is best known for his work in bringing clean water supplies to the city (see p.202).

㉑ Charles Tennant Monument (1838, Patric Parc)
This white Carrara marble sculpture shows the seated Tennant (1768-1838). He worked with Charles MacIntosh (see p.361) to produce a 'chloride of lime' (a dry bleaching powder) which was produced at the St Rollox Chemical Works in Springburn just north of here and was in great demand in the textile industry. In the 1830s this became the largest chemical factory in the world — and probably also one of dirtiest, especially when it started to produce vast quantities of sulphuric acid. A massive chimney, at 139m (455ft) high Europe's tallest, was built to carry the noxious gases eastwards, away from the city to unsuspecting recipients of acid rain who lived elsewhere, like Edinburgh.

㉒ John Knox Monument (1825, Thomas Hamilton)
Standing at the top of the Necropolis, and with an 18m (58ft) column

to support him, Knox has one of the best views there is over the city. He is depicted dressed in a Geneva gown and holding a bible. John Knox (*c.* 1513-72) was Scotland's most important reformer during the period of the Reformation. He was initially a Catholic priest but later studied law and held various teaching posts. He became a follower of the Lutheran George Wishart but eventually took up the ideas of John Calvin. For many years he travelled between Scotland, England and various continental countries, becoming very involved in the political intrigue of the day. He eventually became minister of St Giles' High Kirk in Edinburgh and clashed with the Catholic Mary, Queen of Scots on many occasions. After Papal authority was abolished, his contributions to the *First Book of Discipline* (1560) were very influential in matters of religion, church politics, education and general social organization.

㉓ Ewing of Strathleven Monument (1857, John Baird I)
This consists of a sarcophagus of pink Peterhead granite on a sandstone base. It is to James Ewing (1744-1853), who was one of the city's richest merchants and was involved in the establishment of the Necropolis.

㉔ Macfarlan's Monument (1861, J. A. Bell)
This elaborate High Gothic monument is to Duncan Macfarlan (1771-1857). The inscription refers to him as *Principal Macfarlan* as he was Principal of Glasgow University (when it was in the High Street) and minister of Glasgow Cathedral. Macfarlan is also depicted on a plaque in George Square (see p.87).

㉕ John Dick Monument (1838, Robert Black)
This Ionic rotunda is based on the Choragic Monument of Lysicrates. Dick (1764-1833) was minister of Greyfriars Church which stood near the High Street.

㉖ John Henry Alexander Monument (1851, James Hamilton)
This finely-sculpted monument to Alexander (d.1851) celebrates his achievements as both an actor and the proprietor of the Theatre Royal in Dunlop Street. Hence the poetic inscription:

> *Fallen is the curtain – the last scene is o'er:*
> *The favourite actor treads life's stage no more,*
> *Oft lavish plaudits from the crowd he drew,*
> *And laughing eyes confess'd his humour true.*

A theatre proscenium fills the centre of the monument, while to the sides are the words *Tragedy* and *Comedy*. Cerubs, musical instruments and a profile of the man are found higher up.

㉗ Egyptian Vaults (1837, David Hamilton)
This was built to provide temporary accommodation before lairs could be opened for burial. Despite its name, it has a Greek gateway, with pairs of inverted torches and a winged hourglass (which represents the rapid passage of time).

28 Aitken of Dalmoak Mausoleum (*c.* 1875, James Hamilton II)
The domed roof of this mausoleum stands opposite and at a lower level than the Egyptian Vaults. It is on a minor path and is hidden by surrounding trees. With four cast-iron gates, eight pink granite pillars and guarded by an attendant angel, this is the cemetery's largest mausoleum. It has four lairs inside.

29 Buchanans of Bellfield Mausoleum (mid-nineteenth century, ? J. Stephen)
The (three) misses Buchanan are buried in this severe Greek-style mausoleum. The draped urns on either side of the entrance were sculpted by Mossman.

30 Robert Black Mausoleum (*c.* 1837)
This Greek Doric temple has a frieze of wreaths above the doorway. The inscription inside notes that Black died in 1879, aged eighty-six; in comparison, five of his six children died before they were twenty-one.

31 William Motherwell Monument (1851, James Fillans)
Motherwell (1797-1835) was a poet and at various times the editor of both *The Paisley Advertiser* and *The Glasgow Courier*. His poetry often featured 'heroic deeds' and the monument's frieze (which faces the path) shows two knights in combat. Unfortunately, the monument's inscription has broken off.

32 William Miller Monument
William Miller (1810-72) is described on the monument as *The laureate of the nursery* as he wrote the children's poem 'Wee Willie Winkie'.

> *Wee Willie Winkie*
> *Rins through the toun*
> *Upstairs and doon stairs*
> *In his nicht-goun,*
> *Tirlin' at the window,*
> *Crying at the lock,*
> *'Are the weans in their bed?*
> *For noo it's ten o'clock.'*

(For those who need help with the translation: rins = runs; doon = down; nicht-goun = night-gown; tirlin' = rattling; weans = children; noo = now.)

Miller was a woodworker by trade and some of his poems were written down on sandpaper — the smooth side, of course.

33 Thomson Memorial
This stone was erected by Dr James Thomson (1786-1849) in memory of his son John, a medical student, who died in 1847 aged twenty. James Thomson was Professor of Mathematics at Glasgow University from 1832 until his death. His eldest son, also James Thomson (1822-92), was the university's Professor of Civil Engineering from 1873 to 1889. To complete a trio of profs in one family, the base commemorates another son, William Thomson, better known as Lord Kelvin; see pp.185 and 203.

GLASGOW CATHEDRAL GRAVEYARD

This is situated around the Cathedral and is encountered on Walk 1 (see p.38).

There are two graveyards here. The old graveyard surrounds the cathedral; most of its memorials are in the form of large slabs of stone sunk into the ground but there are also a number of very interesting monuments built into the perimeter wall. The new graveyard is to the north of the old graveyard and a large wall separates the two. This latter graveyard has few interesting monuments; in any case, it is overgrown and unkempt.

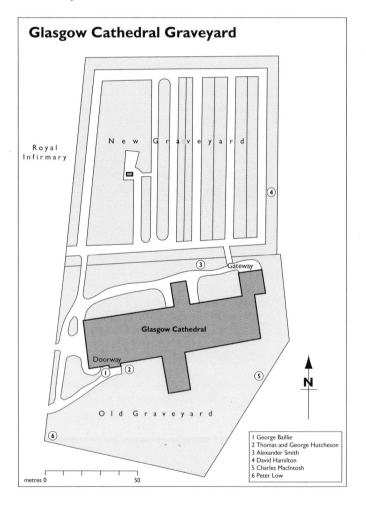

Glasgow Cathedral Graveyard

Royal Infirmary

New Graveyard

Gateway

Glasgow Cathedral

Doorway

Old Graveyard

N

metres 0   50

1 George Baillie
2 Thomas and George Hutcheson
3 Alexander Smith
4 David Hamilton
5 Charles MacIntosh
6 Peter Low

❶ George Baillie (John Burnet, sculpted by John G. Mossman)
Baillie (1784-1873) was a wealthy lawyer who, as the monument's inscription explains, *some years before his death divested himself of all his large Fortune to endow Baillie's Institution, for promoting the intellectual culture of the Operative classes in Glasgow, by means of Free Public Libraries, Reading Rooms, and Unsectarian Schools.* Baillie's Library is now housed in the Mitchell Library. A small bust of the man has been placed near the top of the monument.

❷ Thomas and George Hutcheson (before 1670)
A skull and crossbones and a winged hourglass are among the tomb's decorations. The benevolence of the Hutchesons is described on p.49.

❸ Alexander Smith
This very unusual monument shows off the man's trade – he was a tiler and slater — and there is a wonderful display of highly coloured encaustic tiles, many of which have survived well in Glasgow's none-too-pure atmosphere.

❹ David Hamilton
The monument's design blends into the wall, with only the inscription *The property of David Hamilton, architect* to catch the eye. Hamilton (1768-1843) designed Hutcheson's Hall (described on p.49) and also worked on what is now the Gallery of Modern Art (described on p.89).

❺ Charles MacIntosh
MacIntosh's monument is sandwiched between two much grander memorials. MacIntosh (1766-1843) was an industrial chemist whose most famous discovery was that rubber could be dissolved in the solvent naphtha. When this was spread over clothing material and allowed to dry the rubber so deposited made the material waterproof – hence the so-named (and misspelt) 'mackintosh'. He was also involved with David Dale (whose work is described on p.364) in developing turkey-red dyeing and with Charles Tennant (whose work is described on p.357).

❻ Peter Low
Low (or Lowe) (*c.* 1549-1612) was a surgeon at the time when barbers performed various surgical operations. He pressed for a charter allowing only doctors to perform surgery and this led to the Faculty of Chirurgerie being established in 1599. This later developed into what is now the Royal College of Physicians and Surgeons, whose history is described on p.159.

The plinth carries the following inscription:

Ah me I gravell am and dust
And to the grave deshend I most
O painted peice of liveing clay
Man be not proud of thy short day.

St David's (Ramshorn Kirk) Graveyard

The two graveyards here are situated beside St David's (Ramshorn Kirk) on Ingram Street in the Merchant City, descibed on Walk 1 (see p.47). The older of the two is very small and is close to the church. The very much larger new graveyard is reached either from the east side of the church or by its own entrance which is farther east of the church. The graveyard was established here in 1719 in the orchard of Hutchesons' Hospital (whose history is given on p.49) and the last interment took place in 1915.

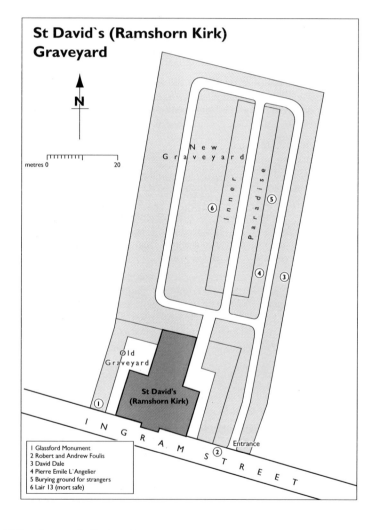

St David`s (Ramshorn Kirk) Graveyard

N

metres 0   20

New Graveyard

Inner Paradise

Old Graveyard

St David's (Ramshorn Kirk)

INGRAM STREET

Entrance

1 Glassford Monument
2 Robert and Andrew Foulis
3 David Dale
4 Pierre Emile L`Angelier
5 Burying ground for strangers
6 Lair 13 (mort safe)

The old graveyard has only a few lairs and the most interesting is the **Glassford Monument** ❶ which is the first on the left after the gate. John Glassford of Dougalston (1715-83) made a fortune from the tobacco trade and at one time owned over twenty-five ships, trading tobacco for the Scottish-manufactured goods he shipped to the Americas. He was instrumental in setting up the appropriately named Ship Bank in 1750 and his wealth allowed him to patronize the arts, including supporting the efforts of the Foulis brothers (see below).

The next memorial of interest is not even in the graveyard; it is *on* the pavement outside, between the eastern side of the church and the entrance to the new graveyard. This is the memorial to **Robert** and **Andrew Foulis** ❷ which is marked by a cross and the letters *RF* and *AF*. Robert (1707-76) and Andrew (1712-75) set up an Academy of Fine Arts in the city in 1754. This was intended as a teaching institution and a place where Scottish artists could study and produce works of art including paintings and engravings. Only a few benefactors helped them, notably the merchants John Glassford (see above) and Archibald Ingram. Without sound financial backing, the academy's renowned printing and publishing activities were not enough to maintain the hopes of the two brothers and it closed in 1775. Examples of their work are on display in the People's Palace.

The two brothers were well known beyond Glasgow and during the famous 1773 tour of Scotland by Dr Samuel Johnson and James Boswell, the four men met in the Saracen's Head Inn in the Gallowgate. The two brothers obviously made some sort of impression as the biographer Boswell recorded that 'Though good and ingenious men, they have that unsettled speculative mode of conversation which is offensive to a man regularly taught at an English school and university. I found that instead of listening to the dictates of the sage [Dr Johnson], they had teased him with questions and doubtful disputations.' The comment probably says more about the two travellers' attitudes than it does about the brothers!

Their grave is located outside the graveyard as the widening of Ingram Street led to the Ramshorn losing some land and forty-two tombs were either moved to the crypt or to the burial ground at the back of the church. However, the brothers' resting place was not disturbed so they still lie here, below the pavement.

The new graveyard has many merchants' lairs, but none have particularly large or flamboyant memorials. Most are marked by plaques in the walls (giving the lair's number), others are in the form of large flagstones flush with the ground. Many small, unmarked, stones are scattered about. The inner walled enclosure ('Inner Paradise') was originally for poor people but lairs were later sold and in time this became the 'in' place to be buried. This peaceful graveyard, which is hemmed in by tall office blocks, is now a quiet lunching place for people working in the city.

On the eastern wall, at lair 113, is a plaque inscribed *This burying ground is the property of David Dale, merchant in Glasgow 1780*. Part of Glasgow's great wealth was built on the cotton trade and **David Dale** ❸ (1739-1806) and Richard Arkwright had a large mill operation at New Lanark, using the power of the River Clyde. In 1793 these were the largest water-driven mills in Britain. A great number of his 1500 employees were very young, with one-third of them under fourteen years old, many of them orphans. History has given most of the credit to Dale's son-in-law Robert Owen for the far-reaching social and educational provision for the employees, especially the children, but it was Dale who started the benevolent treatment which was looked at in fear by other mill owners, lest their own employees demanded similar housing, educational and social facilities. Dale was also involved in banking, local politics and the founding of the 'Old Scotch Independent Church'.

Lair 5 is the resting place of members of the Fleming family and it is inscribed *In memory of Janet Fleming, wife of Thomas Kennedy, merchant, Glasgow, who died 16th March, 1869, aged 71 years*. It is also the (unmarked) grave of **Pierre Emile L'Angelier** ❹ (d.1857), whose poisoning Madeleine Smith was tried for in the scandal described on p.117. L'Angelier was a friend of Thomas Fleming Kennedy, a member of the Fleming family, which is why he was buried here.

A little farther northwards, near lair 14, is a large horizontal slab on which is carved ***Burying ground for strangers, 1815*** ❺. This lair was reserved for the interment of people who died within the city boundary but who did not belong to Glasgow. However, since the Ramshorn's administrators refused to bury paupers, strangers could only be accommodated if the requisite fee was paid. A similar slab will be seen in front of lair 16.

A 'caged' lair, Ramshorn Graveyard

A number of lairs in the graveyard have substantial iron railings (called 'cages') round them. These were designed to stop Resurrectionists from stealing newly buried bodies which were in great demand in medical circles. Outside the Inner Paradise's western wall, at **lair 13 ❻**, can be seen the rusty remains of a 'mort safe'. Instead of going to the expense of erecting a large and expensive railing, families wishing to stop a body being stolen could hire a strong and very heavy metal cage which fitted over the grave. This only needed to be in position long enough to allow the body to partly decompose so it would no longer be of use to students.

St Andrew's-by-the-Green Graveyard

This small graveyard surrounds the former Episcopalian church of St Andrew's-by-the-Green on Greendyke Street (north of Glasgow Green) which is described on Walk 2 (see p.60). None of the graveyard's monuments are very elaborate, but there are a few well-carved memorials and some which carry interesting inscriptions.

Just beside the north-western corner of the church (i.e. to the left of the church's door) lies a flat stone on which is inscribed *Here lie buried the mortal remains of* **Capt. Wemys Erskine Sutherland** *and* **Sarah G. Duff** *his wife, a most aimable, handsome, and worthy young couple, who, ardently attached for years, had only been united a few short weeks before they were unfortunately drowned in the Clyde on the XXI, October MDCCCXXV; when the Comet steam boat was run down, and its passengers inhumanly left to perish, by the Ayr !*

This *Comet* was built in 1821 and it was the second Clydebuilt ship of that name to be constructed by Henry Bell. The collision with the steamship *Ayr* took place near Greenock.

On the southern side of the church (opposite Glasgow Green) is a well-carved monument to **Richard Curtis** (d.1839), a musical instrument maker, which carries a wide variety of sculptured details such as a cloth-draped urn, a winged cherub, an hourglass, inverted torches and some musical instruments.

At the rear of the church is a memorial to **Jane Eliza Madden** (1859-71) who was *killed by being run over by an omnibus* – streets were dangerous places in 1871 too! Below it is the warning:

> *All little children that survey*
> *The emblem'd wheel that crush'd me down,*
> *Be cautious, as you careless play,*
> *For shafts of death fly thick around.*
> *Still rapid drives the car of time,*
> *Whose wheels some day shall crush us all.*
> *The cold low bed which here is mine,*
> *Shall somewhere be of great and small.*
> *– Death is certain; the hour unseen. –*

CALTON BURIAL GROUND

This graveyard is situated on Abercrombie Street to the north-east of Glasgow Green (Walk 2). It can be reached by following Arcadia Street northwards, but its position tucked away off a side street means that few people, other than locals, tend to notice it. It is quiet, with many mature trees, and has a number of well-made monuments, some placed horizontally on supporting pedestals. None of the monuments are grand but the memorial to the Calton Weavers is very well known as it celebrates an important event in the city's often-turbulent labour history. Many of the other monuments here mention the occupation of the incumbent and these include weaver, pastry baker, bookseller, wright, stay maker, portioner (a small landholder) and even a straw-hat manufacturer!

Weavers' Memorial (1)

Once inside the graveyard's southmost gate, turn right and the memorial's two monuments are almost immediately on the right; they stand against the roadside wall.

In the eighteenth century there were many thousands of weavers living in this part of the city and in 1786 the Calton Incorporation of Weavers established this graveyard though it was not used solely by them. The weavers were engaged in the manufacture of cotton webs which they wove at home for the merchants who organised the trade; this was a very successful industry and the cloth was sold all over the globe. In 1786, as a result of the import of cheap cloth from India, the manufacturers cut the rates paid to the weavers and further cuts were planned for the next year. At the end of June 1787 a bitter strike began. In September, the local magistrates intervened and called in the military (the English-based Dorset Militia). The weavers marched through the city and after some skirmishes, the soldiers fired on the workers, killing six of them. The magistrates then declared a curfew, pronouncing that 'parents and masters are hereby strictly required to keep their children, servants and apprentices within their quarters, in the evening and in the night time, as they shall answer at their highest peril.' Two days of further trouble on the streets was quelled by reinforcements from the West Suffolk Militia who were stationed in Ayr. It was presumably not coincidence that both sets of troops were English; otherwise the soldiers may possibly have mutinied.

Three of the men who died are buried here and the memorial to John Page, Alexander Miller and James Ainslie has two monuments. The right hand stone is very worn but it records that *This is the property of The Weaving Body under charge of the five districts of Calton.* The second stone records that *These memorial stones were renovated by the Glasgow Trades Council and re-dedicated by an assembly of trade union delegates on the 27th June 1931 to the memory of the martyred weavers named on the adjacent stone and also to the memory of those named for their trade union activities and zeal for the welfare of their fellow workers.* Below that is a very worn inscription which has been copied onto yet another monument (see below).

In 1987 the People's Palace commissioned paintings by Ken Currie to mark the bicentenary of the weavers' struggle.

Weavers' Memorial (2)

This modern memorial is located on the northern side of the tall internal wall which almost splits the burial ground in two. The stone, which is made from blue/grey larvikite, bears the words which were originally on the older weavers' memorial:

> They,
> though dead,
> still liveth. Emulate them,
> we'll never swerve,
> we'll steadfast be
> we'll have our rights,
> we will be free
> they are unworthy
> of freedom,
> who expect it from hands,
> other than their own.

The tallest monument in the northern portion of the burial ground has a granite obelisk and a base which carries a dedication to the **Reverend James Smith** (1798-1871). This records that he was *a minister of the gospel for forty years in the United States of America; in his declining years he was appointed U.S. consul at Dundee by Abraham Lincoln, whose pastor he had been.*

Between the Smith monument and the burial ground's internal path stands a memorial dedicated to **Elspeth Gartly** (d.1829), aged twenty-five, and Margaret Leitch, her two-year-old daughter who died two months after her mother. The very sad inscription reads

> Like lovely plant that decks the verdant lawn,
> Spreads its bright leaves in summer's early dawn,
> Its tufted branches rob'd in blossoms fair
> Each bloom diffusing sweetness through the air.
> But ah! the stem which all the sap supplies
> Is early nipt – its blossoms fade – it dies:
> Even so art though consign'd to lonely tomb,
> Cut off 'midst beauty's blaze, in virtue's bloom. –
> But hark! – another knell – thy infant too,
> A father's hope – is call'd to follow you:
> And we must follow soon – ah! follow – whither?
> Hope points to Heaven and fondly answers thither.

The monument also records that Elspeth Gartly was married to John Leitch and that the stone is *the property of George Gartly, portioner, Bridgeton.* It is dated *MDCCXCVI* (1796). Another Gartly family memorial stands alongside.

GOVAN OLD PARISH CHURCH GRAVEYARD

This graveyard is situated on Govan Road and is encountered on Walk 10 (see p.294). It has much more of the air of a countryside grave-yard than most other cemeteries in the city as it has a very long history, with many of the graves dating back to the seventeenth and eighteenth centuries. Indeed, of the graveyard's 240 or so memorials, about forty per cent of them were erected before 1800. The rounded shape of the site is itself a clue to its antiquity and the burials of important people probably took place here in previous centuries.

There is a good variety of monuments although, in comparison with the Glasgow Necropolis, none are particularly flamboyant. This reflects the fact that only a few substantial landowners or merchants are buried here and many of the most interesting stones relate to minor merchants or skilled tradespeople, such as weavers, who were living and working in what was a riverside agricultural village. The graveyard has many examples of well-known symbols carved on the stones which include skull and crossbones, hourglasses, bells, angelic faces, shells, flowers, masonic symbols such as the square and dividers, and tools and crowns denoting various trades. One unusual group of grave markers are the low 'double-bedders' which have been used to indicate one side of the burial plot. The fact that these are more often found in rural districts helps cultivate the 'countryside atmosphere' of the site. However, this atmosphere can be rudely shattered by the noise from the nearby shipyard!

The graveyard is well worth exploring and a number of the most interesting monuments are described here. The site is conveniently divided by two paths running from the entrance gate to the door of the church; after first describing a stone which is sited just outside the perimeter fence, this description of the graveyard deals with the side to the west of the paths and then the side to the east of them.

Just outside the graveyard's entrance gate is a tall **Celtic Cross** which stands on top of a large stone plinth. The front has interlaced patterns and a carving of a rider on horseback while the back has some lovely complex interlaced patterns. It was carved in the 1930s and is a replica of one of the cross shafts which stands inside the church.

Enter the main graveyard. On the west side, near the path and about one-third of the way to the church, is a headstone to someone probably called **James**. This was erected in 1773 and is inscribed *He was an honest man and as such respected by all that knew him his son Archibald in greatful remembrance of his deceased father, caused this stone to be set up* [up]. Its main interest is that on the other side there is a carving of a death mask flanked by two roses (representing Paradise), then under that is a shell (the symbol of St James of Compostella, in northern Spain), an hourglass and a skull and crossbones.

A little farther along the path, there is the substantial horizontal **Gibson** monument. This is supported on a base whose legs are carved in the

Headstone to 'James', Govan Old Parish Church Graveyard

shape of the tops of pointed windows. It is *sacred to the memory of James Gibson of Hillhead* (1800-62), his wife (Elizabeth Smith) and their daughter. Gibson was a member of the family who took over the Hillhead area (see p.218) from the Roman Catholic Church after the Reformation and he is buried here as Hillhead was at that time part of the large parish of Govan. Gibson's coat of arms, displayed on the monument, includes a pelican, three keys and the motto *Pandite cœllestes portæ* ('Open wide ye heavenly gates'). The stonework is quite worn and it can be difficult to recognise some parts of the design, but the pelican is traditionally shown stabbing her breast in order to feed the brood with her own blood; this is a medieval symbol representing piety. Around the edge of the stone are the words *Blessed are the peacemakers for they shall be called the children of God. Matthew Chap V Verse IX.*

Closer to the church is the finely carved sandstone **Fleming** monument which has beautifully inscribed writing on it. It has the words *Malcom Fleming Gardner died the 6th of April 1788 aged 72 years*, together with a scallop shell between two roses. On the other side is the inscription *This is the burying Place of James Fleming and Helen Hill his spouse and their children.*

Monuments occasionally tell how people died and can provide useful evidence of local social history. The tall **McDonald** obelisk is close to the west side of the church and details two family tragedies. On one side the weathered sandstone inscription records that Donald McDonald (aged 46) died of sunstroke in New York in 1872 and on another side, a granite plaque notes that James McDonald (aged 26) accidentally drowned in the River Kelvin in 1877.

Near the site's western edge stands the tall **George Bissett** memorial. It records that he lived at Three Mile House and the names of many of his family are given. At the top of the pedestal are four winged cherubs and lower down is the verse

> *By Jordans stream we parted here*
> *A scene of grief and pain.*
> *But mourn no more on Canan's shore*
> *We soon will meet again.*

The graveyard's eastern side contains some very old memorials, particularly in the group of large flat stones lying close to the path. The oldest of the graveyard's 'modern' monuments is here and it is inscribed *Here lies **John Rouan** [Rowan] of Greenhead, who died 1624 his age 76. Also his wife … Gibson & John their son who died 1614.* The Rowans were part of the 'Govan gentry' and a number of other monuments to the family can be found in the graveyard.

About halfway between the path and the eastern boundary wall is an upright stone about 70cm (30in) high. It is most easily recognized by the crown sculpted on the side facing the path; this emblem was used by the hammermen (metalworkers) to represent their claim to be the highest-ranking trade. As well as the royal crown, the stone has carvings of a hammer, a bell, three flowers, the initials *JM* and the date *1731*. On the back of the stone are the words *This is the property of **George Murdoch** smith [in] Partick, Margaret King his spouse and their heirs.*

The graveyard's most substantial monument is in the form of a tall obelisk with a tapered fluted column. The four tall cast-iron pillars around it mark the corners of the railed fence which originally guarded this large grave.

The eastern side of the monument's plinth bears the inscription *This is the private property of **John Mair** and his family.* John Mair was one of the local landowners and as a wealthy heritor (see p.348) he was able to erect such a large monument in this very conspicuous location. In the 1790s he purchased Plantation, an estate to the east of here, which had been given its name by the previous occupant who had owned a sugar and cotton plantation in the West Indies. The monument's rather worn inscriptions also record that the grave is the resting place of Lieutenant General Sir William Paterson, who was Mair's grandson.

A little to the east of Mair's monument is a memorial to **Dr Matthew Leishman** (1794-1874) and his wife (Jane Elizabeth Boog) who died less than a month after her husband. Leishman was the church's minister for fifty-three years, during a time when Govan changed dramatically from being a small village to an important industrial centre. The appointment of Dr Leishman to this church in 1820 caused quite a stir in Glasgow University's Divinity faculty as the university owned the patronage to the church and were thus entitled to appoint a new minister whenever a vacancy occurred. However, in April 1820 the Paisley grain dealer Thomas Leishman made an offer of £2100 for the patronage and this was seriously considered as the university was short of funds and the minister's stipend had just been increased by the considerable sum of £200 a year. The university had previously sold off the patronage of the Gorbals but after great debate they declined this particular offer. Eventually, the university appointed Matthew Leishman to the post, thus saving his father the £2100 he had been willing to spend in order to acquire the job for his son.

An adjoining horizontal stone lists the couple's children and grandchildren and it particularly mentions William Leishman (1834–94) *fifth son of the late Rev. Dr. Leishman, of Govan for 25 years Regius Professor of Midwifery in the University of Glasgow.*

CATHCART OLD PARISH CHURCH GRAVEYARD

This graveyard is situated on Kilmailing Road (off Old Castle Road), and its location is described on Walk 13 (see p.329). It is an old-established graveyard which lacks the grandeur of some of the other graveyards in this chapter and has few carvings that give clues about people's occupations, but it does have some monuments of importance to Glasgow.

Immediately to the west of the church is a very low and narrow **carved stone** with three ridges running along its length. On one side is carved a sword in a scabbard and on the other a spear. The design suggests a mid-thirteenth century origin and it may be connected with the Order of Knights Templar which was active in Scotland from 1153 to 1312. The carved date of 1707 is a later addition.

To the west of the church (near Kilmailing Road) is **The Martyrs' Tomb**. The horizontal stone on top of the tomb carries a long inscription (in old lettering and spelling) which tells of the death of two Covenanters: *This is the stone tomb of Robert Thome Thomas Cooke and John Urie martyrs for ounng the covenanted work of reformation the 11 of May 1685. The bloody murderers of these men were Magor Balfour and Captain Metland. With them others were not free caused them to search in Polmadie as soon as they had them out found they murthered them with shots of guns. Scarce time did they to them allow befor ther maker ther knies to bow many like in this land have been whos blood for wingance crys to heavn this cruell wickedness you see was don in lon of Polmadie. This may a standing witness be 'twixt prisbytrie and prelacie.*

Cooke and Urie were weavers who were hunted down by the government troops for their religious beliefs and this monument is a grim reminder of the sad story of the seventeenth-century Coventanters. These were people who believed in the presbyterian form of Protestant worship and organisation, and who had signed the various National Covenants. This was as much a political act as a religious one as it flew in the face of the beliefs and power of the British monarchy. Scotland was intent on keeping its church independent from the English-based state machine and its episcopal church and this led to a political crisis as signing the Covenant was seen as treason. The resulting strife between the Scots and the government came to a head in the three decades up to 1690, during which some 18,000 people died in battles and persecutions, such as the infamous 'Killing Times' of the 1680s organised by John Graham of Claverhouse.

To the west of The Martyrs' Tomb stands a nineteenth century **watch-house** (complete with fireplace) which would have been used to guard the graveyard at night in case graverobbers were at work, looking for bodies to sell to medical schools.

The centre of the graveyard features a gabled **Gothic mausoleum** (to the Gordons) and a circular **Byzantine mausoleum**.

The **John McIntyre Memorial** (1867) stands against the southern wall which is at the opposite end of the graveyard from the church tower. This is in the form of a Greek sarcophagus and it was designed by Alexander Thomson, initially for John McIntyre's son Donald, then for the father. The upper part of the monument is very well decorated with incised carvings which are similar to those Thomson used in his buildings.

Walk eastwards from the McIntyre memorial towards Carmunnock Road. On the left will be seen the very large memorial to **James Couper** (1818-77), whose local connections are described on p.332. The inscription *Resurgam* on the monument means 'I shall rise again'.

SIGHTHILL CEMETERY

This graveyard is situated on Springburn Road, which is to the north of Glasgow Cathedral. The entrance is about 1.5km (1 mile) north of the Cathedral and can be reached from there by bus.

The cemetery, which was opened in 1840, occupies a prominent hill, the summit of which offers a good view over the northern part of the city and towards the Campsie Hills. The monuments are generally interesting with a wide variety of styles but the primary reason most people come here is to see the Martyrs' Monument.

The cemetery is entered by a gate designed by John Stephen in an early Greek Revival style and just inside the gate stands a former chapel which was also designed by Stephen. Once past the chapel, continue along the main drive, leaving it at the first junction on the right.

At the start of the fourth row of trees on the left is a large red granite memorial with the name *Curle* on it. This is a monument to the shipbuilder **Robert Curle** ❶ (1813-79). He worked with Robert

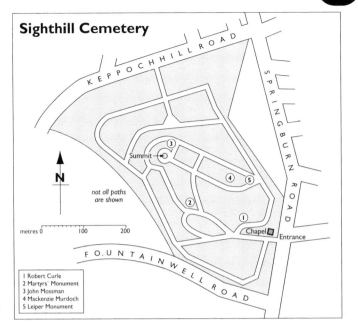

KEPPOCHHILL ROAD

SPRINGBURN ROAD

N

Summit

*not all paths
are shown*

metres 0   100   200

Chapel ■ Entrance

F O U N T A I N W E L L ROAD

1 Robert Curle
2 Martyrs' Monument
3 John Mossman
4 Mackenzie Murdoch
5 Leiper Monument

Barclay and their Glasgow firm of Barclay, Curle & Co. was an important shipbuilder, although it was better-known for manufacturing ships' engines in their factory at Whiteinch. A winged beast and the phrase *une foi* ('one time') are at the top of the monument.

Return to the main drive. Two roads will be found on the right; follow the upper road. Stop at the next junction and cross the grassy area ahead to a tall light-coloured monument topped by a sculpted urn. This is the cemetery's most-famous memorial, the **Martyrs' Monument** ❷, which is dedicated to John Baird and Andrew Hardie, leaders of the 1820 Radical Rising.

There was a wave of political agitation in the country in 1819 which led to events such as the Peterloo Massacre in England when eleven people listening to a radical speaker were killed by soldiers. Also that year, a large demonstration took place in Glasgow and the town council reacted by calling for a cavalry force to be sent to the city. All this took place in the aftermath of the Napoleonic Wars, with standards of living falling and the government reacting by invoking repressive measures. Against this troubled background, Baird and Hardie led a small group of armed men towards the Carron Ironworks (near Falkirk) which produced armaments. About thirty of them were attacked and captured by government soldiers and many of them were subsequently charged with high treason. This resulted in the two leaders being hanged and beheaded in Stirling. Nineteen other men were originally sentenced to death but were transported to New South Wales in Australia and later

Martyr's Monument, Sighthill Cemetery

pardoned in 1835. In 1847 the bodies of the two executed men were removed from their graves in Stirling to be reinterred here and an inscription on the monument describes that event.

The main inscription uses poetry to celebrate their martyrdom:

Here lie the slain, and mutilated forms,
Of those who fell, and fell like Martyrs true.
Faithful to freedom through a time of storms,
They met their fate as Patriots always do,
Despising death which ne'er can noble souls subdue.

Calmly they view'd deaths dread and dark array,
Then heaven directed, turn'd their prayerfull eyes,
Serene in hope they triumphed o'er dismay,
Their countrys wrongs alone drew forth their sighs,
And those to them endear'd by natures holiest ties.

But truth and right have better times brought round,
Now, no more 'traitors' scorn'd by passing breath,
For weeping Scotland hails this spot of ground,
And shrines, with all who fell for freedom's faith,
Whose sons of her's now fam'd made glorious by their death.

The memorial has a relief sculpture depicting two figures with wreaths at a tomb. Further inscriptions record that it was erected in 1847 and repaired in 1865, 1885 and 1986. This is obviously a highly regarded monument and an inscription records one particular gathering here: *On September 5th, 1920 100 years after the execution of John Baird and Andrew Hardie a great assemblage of the common people met here at the call of the Glasgow Independant Labour Party to honour the memory of those two working class martyrs in the cause of liberty.*

Follow the path that is just below the monument to the nearby junction. Take the upper path and head towards the nearby tall blocks of flats. This goes uphill gradually, opening up views of the hills to the north of the city. There is a wide variety of monuments here, and while most are made of sandstone, one very badly eroded monument of white marble will be seen on the right and a tall, rusty, cast-iron monument is passed on the left. In this exposed position, the granite monuments last much better.

Skirt the top of the hill and when the path heads eastwards and there is a stand of trees below on the left, look for a grey granite monument on the right with the name *Mossman* on it. This is the memorial to **John Mossman** ❸ (d.1914), the son of John G. Mossman (1817-90) who worked on so many of Glasgow's finest buildings and became the city's most famous sculptor. Some of his work is mentioned on p.383.

Turn right immediately after this monument and climb a narrow path up the grassy slope to reach the cemetery's summit. (If the slope is too steep, then continue on the path and take the next turning on the right in order to reach the main path to the summit.) The monuments here are amongst the best in the cemetery, particularly those in the summit's circular grassy area; funerary urns and Celtic Crosses are well represented here. There is an extensive view, especially to the Campsie Hills which are described on p.282. The view to the west is obscured by high flats but a number of prominent buildings in the city centre can be seen. They include the Royal Infirmary, Caledonian University and the former Trinity College on Woodlands Hill.

Head eastwards along the ridge of the hill. As the path heads downhill, there are interesting monuments on both sides and, on the right, the green roof of Glasgow Cathedral becomes visible. Just as the path begins to bend round to the left, the monument to **Mackenzie Murdoch** ❹ (1870-1923) can be found on the left. It is two rows away and is in the form of a tall decorated Celtic Cross sitting on a roughly hewn block of stone. The inscription (which is on the northern face) hails him as *The most renowned interpreter of the soul of Scotland's music in his day. Erected by admirers whom he charmed by the magic of his bow. Unveiled by Sir Harry Lauder.*

Lauder (1870-1950) was one of the country's most famous stage performers. He started as a comic but became famous as a singer of Scottish songs such as *Roamin' in the Gloamin'*. He was particularly popular in the USA and Murdoch accompanied him on his tours.

Murdoch composed Lauder's well-known *Hame o' mine* as well as many violin tunes with evocative names such as *Glencoe* and *Culloden*.

Regain the path and continue downhill to the **Leiper Monument** ❺ which is on the left immediately before a junction of paths. William Leiper (d. 1867) ran the Commercial College in the city centre and he and his partner described themselves as 'writing masters and teachers of arithmetic'.

His son, the architect William Leiper (1839-1916), is also buried here. He was responsible for numerous important buildings in Glasgow, including Templeton's Carpet Factory (described on p.66), the Sun, Fire and Life Building (described on p.109) and Dowanhill Church (described on p.234).

Turn right at the junction and head downhill, passing the Curle monument. Turn left and head towards the main gate.

SOUTHERN NECROPOLIS

This graveyard is situated in Hutchesontown to the south of the River Clyde. The entrance is on Caledonia Road, which can be reached by going south from Albert Bridge (on Walk 2, see p.69). From the bridge, go along Crown Road, Laurieston Road and Hospital Street to Caledonia Road Church, then turn eastwards. In total the graveyard is about 1.5km (1 mile) from Albert Bridge.

The Southern Necropolis was established in 1841, with the large entrance archway (by Charles Wilson) erected in 1848. This leads into the central section; the eastern section was added in 1846 and the western (the largest section) in 1850. All three sections have their own perimeter path, and the central and western sections have a central hub. A central passageway, parallel to Caledonia Road, links the two hubs and all three sections.

The graveyard is large and very exposed to the elements – and to the vandals who have knocked down many of the monuments. There are few grand monuments, but many are substantial memorials marking a whole family's grave. The monuments described here can be a bit difficult to find.

Sir Thomas Lipton ❶
Lipton (1850-1931) was born in the Gorbals and in 1865 he sailed to the USA, where one of his jobs was in a grocer's shop. On his return to Scotland in 1870 he opened his first of many grocer's shops (in Anderston) and used unique advertising gimmicks to help sell his goods. For one such stunt, he had an enormous cheese made with gold sovereigns (a pound coin) in it and this was driven with due ceremony from the docks to his shop. Crowds clamoured to buy pieces of cheese, hoping their slice contained one of these valuable coins. He also had two pigs driven through the streets each day with banners on them reading 'I'm on my

Southern Necropolis

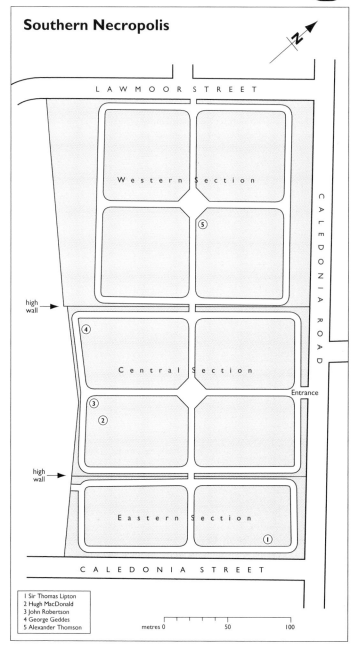

LAWMOOR STREET

Western Section

⑤

high wall →

④

Central Section

③

②

Entrance

high wall →

Eastern Section

①

CALEDONIA STREET

CALEDONIA ROAD

1 Sir Thomas Lipton
2 Hugh MacDonald
3 John Robertson
4 George Geddes
5 Alexander Thomson

metres 0   50   100

way to Lipton's, the best place in town for bacon'. He probably became best known for his Lipton's Teas which came from his own plantations in Ceylon, now Sri Lanka. Eventually, his large chain of shops stretched throughout Britain and at one point he employed ten thousand people, an enormous number for a retail organization in those days.

In 1899 he made his first of five unsuccessful attempts to win the Americas Cup with his yacht *Shamrock I*. The boats, named *Shamrock I* to *V*, celebrated his Irish parentage. His collection of yachting trophies can be seen in the Kelvingrove Art Gallery and Museum and the People's Palace.

The grave is marked by a decorative slab and a well-made monument which is topped by a funerary urn.

Hugh MacDonald ❷

MacDonald (1817-60) worked for the *Glasgow Citizen* newspaper and wrote a series of articles called *Rambles Round Glasgow* under the name Caleb. In 1854 these were published in a book (of the same name) which became one of the best-known guides to the area. The walks he described were full of antiquarian detail as well as information on local history, wildlife and the people he met.

MacDonald often wrote for the left-wing Chartist press and he also wrote poetry (see p.63). His monument (in grey granite and shaped like a scroll) describes him simply as *poet*.

John Robertson ❸

Robertson (1782-1868) was an engineer who is best remembered for the steam engine he built for Henry Bell's paddleship called the *Comet*. This wooden ship was Europe's first working sea-going steamship and in 1812 it took three and a half hours to travel from Glasgow's Broomielaw to Port Glasgow, about 30km (19 miles) down the river. Her top speed was 6.5 knots (12kmph (7.5mph)). Unhappily, it was wrecked in 1820 in Argyll but the engine was salvaged and used in a sugar mill until it was presented to the Science Museum in London.

In 1912 the roughly hewn grey granite monument was further decorated when a commemorative plaque was erected by the Institute of Engineers and Shipbuilders in Scotland.

George Geddes ❹

This sandstone monument honours George Geddes (1859-89), described on the memorial as the [Glasgow] *Humane Society Officer . . . a faithful public servant for 45 years and rescuer of over 100 persons from drowning. A life of honour and of worth.* The grave also holds his grandson George Geddes (d.1928) who drowned while trying to save a man who had jumped from St Andrew's Bridge into the River Clyde. The society's story is told on p.69.

Alexander Thomson ❺

Alas, the monument is no longer extant but the base still remains. To find it, walk along the graveyard's central passageway; the plot is immediately to the right of the passageway and it is the very last plot before the central hub of the western section is met. The life and work of Thomson (1817-75) is described on p.392.

CHAPTER 7

Glasgow's Architecture and Architects

The great wealth of fine buildings in Glasgow is firmly based on the Victorian period (1837-1901) which generally coincided with the city's heyday as 'The Second City of the Empire'. This chapter briefly outlines some of the processes which helped to shape Glasgow's built environment, especially the rapid changes which took place in Victorian times, in order to help the reader understand the present layout of the city. Readers wishing a fuller analysis of these developments should consult architectural texts such as Gomme & Walker and Williamson, Riches & Higgs (see Bibliography).

Glasgow owed its importance during medieval times to its cathedral (described on p.38) which is sited near the summit of one of the city's many hills. The present building dates back to at least the thirteenth century and over the succeeding centuries a number of important ecclesiastical buildings were established around it. However, their only survivor is the fifteenth-century Provand's Lordship. Over the centuries, the city developed along either side of High Street, the main thoroughfare which ran past the cathedral and down towards the ford across the River Clyde. Gradually, the city expanded to the east and west of the High Street axis with much of the industry gathering to the east and the western side enjoying the better housing and civic amenities.

Compared to Edinburgh, Glasgow has few pre eighteenth-century buildings, but there are some well-preserved examples on the city's outskirts such as Haggs Castle and Provan Hall. Within the present city centre, the oldest buildings outside the Cathedral area which have withstood the ravages of time (and the property developers) are the Tolbooth Steeple (1625-7) at Glagow Cross, the Merchants' Steeple (1665) on Bridgegate, the Trades Hall (1791-4, Robert Adam) on Glassford Street and the Tron Kirk (1793-4) on Trongate. Sadly, the mid seventeenth-century Old College in High Street was almost completely lost when the university moved westwards in the 1860s. Many other good eighteenth- and nineteenth-century buildings were undoubtedly sacrificed in the late nineteenth century to make way for the large-scale city redevelopment undertaken by the City Improvement Trust which started its work in 1866.

The city expanded rapidly in the second half of the eighteenth century, due in great measure to the prosperity brought about by the trade in tobacco, sugar and cotton, and many of the richer merchants moved a short distance westwards from the High Street. A number of them became developers and they built on their own land, thus encouraging the emergence of what we now call 'The Merchant City'.

Glasgow's gridiron street layout dates from this time and this regular rectangular pattern was maintained as the city expanded westwards. However, this design failed to spread to the east and south of the city because of the growth of industry in these areas and also because of the exploitation of local deposits of iron ore and coal. Speculative 'superior' housing developments were started in a number of the city's peripheral areas, notably Carlton Place (1802-18) and Blythswood Square (1823), and these provided the wealthy with large and comfortable terraced houses. The tall tenement buildings which became so common in most parts of the city were built for a wide range of tenants and most of those we see today were built in the second half of the nineteenth century. The role of tenement housing in the city is described on p.128.

As in many cities, the growth in prosperity was reflected in the construction of elaborate churches. St Andrew's Parish Church (1739-56) was erected in what was then a very fashionable area, though the substantial houses which surrounded it were built at a later date. In time, a number of church architects adopted the Gothic style; Thomas Rickman who built St David's (Ramshorn Kirk) in 1824-6 is such an example. The early nineteenth-century public buildings also reflected the growing importance of the city; amongst the most notable of these are the riverside Custom House (1840) and the massive County Buildings and Courthouses (1841-71). In addition, the merchants started to invest huge sums of money in their own workplaces and imposing buildings such as the Royal Exchange (1827) were lavishly decorated in order to show off the merchants' wealth and taste; in comparison, the Tobacco Lords worked from rather spartan premises.

At the same time as the city was expanding from its historic centre, the outlying districts (which later became independent burghs) grew in importance, some of the most notable being Partick, Springburn, Anderston, Govan and Gorbals. They grew rapidly as tens of thousands of people came to the city in search of work, and some of these important communities developed around specific industries such as railway locomotives (Springburn) and shipbuilding (Partick and Govan). In time, they were all annexed by the city, willingly or otherwise. As the nineteenth century progressed there was a rapid expansion of large-scale industry, especially engineering, shipbuilding and chemicals, which meant that houses and factories coexisted side by side. Inevitably, this led to overcrowding and appalling social conditions and great swathes of the city centre, inevitably the oldest parts, became disgusting slums. Many of the original tenements had to be swept away by the City Improvement Trust and were replaced by new tenements, many of which still remain. The survival of this second generation of tenements is testament to the superior building materials and techniques which were used, and in many ways it is the retention of these 'new' buildings which has allowed a number of the city's older districts to maintain their social cohesiveness in the face of the many economic changes which took place in the twentieth century. Indeed, a number of these tenement buildings, notably St George's Mansions (1900-1) near Charing Cross

St George's Mansions, near Charing Cross

and McConnel's Building (1906-7) on Hope Street, can be classed among the most important buildings in the city as they represent municipal determination to provide good quality housing.

While large-scale urban renewal was taking place in the second half of the nineteenth century (predominantly in and around the city's historic centre) the newly developed western area had already become the new administrative and commercial centre. Many examples of fine Victorian architecture were erected, the most significant of which was the City Chambers (1882-90, William Young), the rich and imposing exterior of which was matched by the lavish interior which features two quite outstanding marble staircases. As time went on, the well-to-do moved even farther west (maintaining a comfortable distance from the squalor of the city centre and Clydeside) and large-scale planned developments were undertaken, the most notable of which was that on Woodlands Hill which was designed by Charles Wilson in the 1850s. The transfer of Glasgow University to Gilmorehill in the 1860s and the subsequent erection of its substantial buildings by Sir George Gilbert Scott and his son J. Oldrid Scott then established the West End as the most prosperous area of the city. Some of the district's spectacular terraces, such as Alexander 'Greek' Thomson's Great Western Terrace (1869), rank among Glasgow's finest examples of very expensive middle-class housing.

The westward moves of both the city's commercial interests and middle class housing went hand in hand, and at various times many of the houses of the Merchant City, Buchanan Street, Blythswood Hill and Woodlands Hill were either replaced by or converted into commercial buildings. In addition, banks and insurance companies expressed their own self-confidence in the magnificent buildings which were erected in the mid and late nineteenth century. Among the best-known bank buildings are those of the Royal Bank of Scotland in Exchange Square (1827) and Gordon Street (1853-7) and the Ingram Street banking hall of the Savings Bank of Glasgow which J. J. Burnet built in 1894-1900. Insurance companies played an important role in the development of the commercial life of the city and they also erected a number of large offices which were almost invariably embellished by numerous statues. These buildings are some of the most eye-catching pieces of Victorian architecture in the city centre and they include the Sun, Fire and Life Building (1889-94, William Leiper) and the Liverpool & London & Globe Insurance Building (1899-1901, J. B. & W. A. Thomson). Outwith the city centre, the banks erected a number of fascinating buildings; these were often deliberately placed at busy junctions and were well-endowed with elaborate carvings in order to catch the attention of passers-by. Good examples of this type of building still exist at Govan Cross (British Linen Bank) and in Cowcaddens and Anderston, both of which had branches of the Savings Bank of Glasgow.

As the nineteenth century progressed, many significant cultural, professional and social institutions were established and the best-supported of these were housed in buildings which reflected the particular institution's importance and influence. A good early example is the Western Club (1839-42, D.& J. Hamilton) in Buchanan Street; later notable buildings include the Royal Faculty of Procurators' Hall (1854-6) in Nelson Mandela Place, the Merchants' House Buildings (1874) in George Square, the New Club (1877-9) in West George Street, The Athenaeum (1886), also in Nelson Mandela Place, and the Royal College of Physicians and Surgeons (1892-3) in St Vincent Street. The growth of the West End encouraged the erection of important cultural buildings in that area such as the very grand St Andrew's Halls (1873-7, James Sellars) and the Kelvingrove Art Gallery and Museum (1891-1901). The People's Palace (1893-8) was opened in the East End a few years later to provide some sort of geographical balance in the provision of 'culture'.

The nineteenth century was also a time when many fine churches were built; a number were French-influenced, though Greek and Italian influences can be clearly seen in other delightful buildings. The churches were often treated as works of art in themselves and their towers and spires were always prominent in contemporary pictures of the urban landscape; indeed, they are still important landmarks around the city, especially on or near Great Western Road and on the northern side of Queen's Park. A number of these churches were lost in the twentieth century but some of the survivors are particularly outstanding, especially Alexander Thomson's St Vincent Street Free Church of Scotland (1857-9). Other important (and exceptionally varied) examples from the second half of the century are Dowanhill Church (1865-6) on Hyndland Road, Barony Parish Church (1886-9) at the top of High Street and Queen's Cross Church (1897-9) on Garscube Road.

A large proportion of the churches, and many public and commercial buildings, were adorned with sculptures and other embellishments.

Some of the finest of these were produced by the prolific Mossman studio, with John G. Mossman (1817-90) responsible for a remarkable number of the city's most outstanding sculptures, including figures on the City Chambers, Glasgow High School and The Athenaeum. Other sculptors who made important contributions to buildings or who created significant individual sculptures include William Birnie Rhind, Baron Carlo Marochetti and Francis Derwent Wood.

The wealth of the Victorian middle class was generally reflected in the large houses built in the West End and in some enclaves in the Southside such as Pollokshields. In addition, the large disposable income of the well-off led to the development of bustling shopping areas such as Buchanan Street where substantial warehouses (the forerunners of today's department stores) were established. Consumerism isn't a recent phenomenon in Glasgow! The best example of this type of shop still exists at 45 Buchanan Street (1883-5) but elsewhere in the city centre there are fine examples of exuberant Victorian architecture which represent the confidence and flamboyance of the city's main retailers in the late nineteenth century.

The best-known architects of the city's schools were Hugh and David Barclay, partly because they built so many schools for the Govan School Board whose area covered parts of the West End as well as Govan itself. The best-known individual school of the Victorian period is the very grand Glasgow High School (1846-7, Charles Wilson) on Elmbank Street. Charles Rennie Mackintosh's Scotland Street School (1904–6) was built only sixty years later but it is radically different from not only Wilson's building but also the more usual school designs such as Woodlands Public School (described on p.219). Other public institutions such as hospitals were sometimes afforded the luxury of fine buildings; both the Royal Infirmary and the Western Infirmary still have vestiges of older buildings but these are now dwarfed by their more modern counterparts.

Just outside the city, the surrounding burghs benefitted greatly from the city's manufacturing successes and they erected large public buildings such as Govan Town Hall (1879-1901), which were intended as statements of the wealth and independence of the local people. However, the independence often didn't last very long and between 1846 and 1912 many populous outlying districts were annexed by Glasgow, giving the city a population which peaked at over 1,100,000 just before the Second World War.

The dawn of the twentieth century heralded a new era in Britain. The country's great political, military and economic strength was being challenged by many other countries and the First World War marked a sea change in Glasgow's fortunes. The major manufacturing and commercial companies were far less self confident during this period and the important buildings of the time had less of the 'over the top' flamboyance of previous decades. The most significant building of the turn of the century was Charles Rennie Mackintosh's Glasgow School of Art; the first phase was erected in 1897-9, towards the close of the

Victorian period, and the second phase followed in 1907-9. Some traditional elements of Scottish design were used in the building but, overall, the design was quite startlingly 'modern', with the functional shape of the building being far more important than any ornamentation. The nature of the building is even more astonishing when it is compared with other buildings of the same era, such as the Argyll Chambers (1902-4) in Buchanan Street and the third phase of the Central Thread Agency (1901) in Bothwell Street.

After the First World War, with Britain's position in the world undergoing tremendous changes, new types of building were introduced into the city. Some architects drew inspiration from cities such as Chicago and a number of Glasgow's commercial buildings, such as the massive Scottish Legal Life Assurance Society Building (1927-31) on Bothwell Street, reflect this American influence. Important changes were also taking place on the outskirts of the city and in the 1920s and 1930s Glasgow continued to annexe new areas, many of which were used for houses. These were often relatively small buildings, thus allowing low population densities, and they were quite different from the traditional tenements of the older parts of the city. As the middle decades of the century passed, and with the Depression and the Second World War taking its toll of the city's once-proud role as The Second City, the fabric of the city slowly but surely deteriorated. As in the nineteenth century, many of the old tenement areas became slums and, as had occurred one hundred years previously, wholescale demolition was undertaken. The Comprehensive Development Areas of the 1950s and 1960s were very ambitious attempts to revitalise many of the older parts of Glasgow, and at the same time huge new housing schemes were built on farmland well outside the traditional limits of the city. 'Deserts wi' windaes' was how the Glasgow comedian Billy Connolly described these new areas on the city's outskirts. Tall skyscraper blocks of flats were erected in some of these new communities, as well as in the older (and newly redeveloped) parts of the city; the dominating height of these tall structures has radically changed the overall appearance of the city.

Despite all the problems of living through what has been termed the 'post-industrial age', the city has changed considerably (and for the better) in the last three decades of the twentieth century. A huge amount of public money has been invested in new houses, the refurbishment of older buildings and in improving the sprawling housing schemes. But for many people, the most significant improvement has been the stone-cleaning of many of the city's Victorian buildings. At last a century's deposit of soot and grime has been removed from countless tenements and public buildings, allowing them once more to sparkle in the sunlight.

Detail of the facade of the Royal Bank of Scotland, 8 Gordon Street

GLASGOW'S ARCHITECTS

The following table includes the names of many of the most important architects who worked in Glasgow up until the middle of the twentieth century. Most of them belonged to Glasgow architectural practices but a small number of them were based in Edinburgh (e.g. Robert Rowand Anderson) or London (e.g. George Gilbert Scott and John Oldrid Scott). A glance at the table, which is generally arranged in architectural practices, clearly indicates the most prolific designers of the city's built environment: the Burnets (father and son); Honeyman, Keppie and Mackintosh; James Miller; Alexander Thomson; Charles Wilson. These men designed important buildings in numerous districts and the table shows the range of buildings with which they were involved. All of the buildings listed in the table are arranged according to which of the book's walks they are in. In addition, each of the buildings' Place Numbers are given to allow ready access to the text's description of a building.

Robert Adam (1728–92) and
James Adam (1732–94)

Walk 1   **7** Babbity Bowster
         58 Trades Hall
         59 Tron Kirk

Walk 2   **9** McLennan Arch

Walk 10 **46** Italian Portico

Robert Rowand Anderson
(1834–1921)

Walk 5   **57** Central Station
         Hotel

Walk 10 **35** Pearce Institute
         39 Govan Old Parish
         Church

Walk 11 **7** Pollok House
         14 North Lodge
         15 Shawmuir Lodge

John Baird I (1798–1859)

Walk 3   **33** Argyll Arcade
         39 Princes Square

Walk 5   **6** A. Gardner & Son's
         Warehouse

Walk 7   **31** Claremont Terrace

John Baird II (1816–93)

Walk 3   **40** Glasgow Herald
         Office

Walk 12 **9** Lindsay House

Robert Baldie (d.1890)

Walk 10 **2** Pollokshields Parish
         Church
         32 New Govan Church

Hugh Barclay (1828–92) and
David Barclay (1846–1917)

Walk 1   **44** Royal College

Walk 3   **34** 106–14 Argyle Street

Walk 4   **14** Cumming and Smith
         Building

Walk 5   **47** Central Thread
         Agency

Walk 7   **10** Hillhead
         Congregational
         Church
         28 Glasgow Academy

R. Bell & D. Miller

Walk 2   **27** Albert Bridge

Walk 6   **71** Partick Bridge

Walk 7   **26** Great Western Bridge

James Boucher (c. 1832–1906)
and **James Cousland** (c. 1832–66)

Walk 5   **5** Teacher's Offices
         60 Forsyth's

Walk 7   **18** 22 Park Circus
         36 Kibble Palace

Robert Alexander Bryden
(1841–1906)

Walk 1   **37** Glasgow Royal
         Maternity Hospital

Walk 3   **74** Ocean Chambers

Frank Burnet (1848–1923),
William Boston (1861–1937)
and **James Carruthers** (b.1872)

Walk 1   **9** City Improvement
         Trust Tenement

Walk 4   **34** St George's Mansions

Walk 5   **34** 188–92 St Vincent
         Street
         35 Commercial Union
         Building
         37 140–2 St Vincent
         Street

Walk 6   **5** Kelvinhaugh Primary
         School

John Burnet (1814-1901),
John James Burnet (1857-1938)
and **John Archibald Campbell**
(1859-1909)

William Clark (1809-89),
George Bell I (1814-87) and
George Bell II (1854-1915)

Norman Aitken Dick
(1883-1948)

Neil Campbell Duff
(c. 1861-1934)

(Charles) Formans & McCall

James Miller (1860-1947)

Walk 1 ㉕ Royal Infirmary

Walk 3 (81) Commercial Bank of Scotland
(90) Anchor Line Building

Walk 4 ㊼ Strathclyde Police Headquarters

Walk 5 ③ Travel Centre
㊷ Bank of Scotland
㊻ National Commercial Bank Building
(61) Cranston's Picture House and Tea Rooms
(65) Caledonian Chambers

Walk 6 ㉕ Natural Philosophy Building
㉘ Materia Medica and Physiology Dept. Building
(59) Sunlight Cottages

Walk 7 ㉗ Caledonian Mansions

Walk 8 ㉗ Kelvinbridge Railway Station

Alexander Nisbet Paterson (1862-1947)

Walk 3 (54) Liberal Club

Walk 4 ④ Royal Bank of Scotland

John More Dick Peddie (1853-1921)

Walk 3 (84) National Bank Chambers
(86) Scottish Provident Institution Building

John Thomas Rochead (1814-1878)

Walk 1 (57) 74-92 Trongate

Walk 3 (83) John Smith & Son

(91) Bank of Scotland Building

Walk 7 ⑰ Park Church
㉜ Buckingham Terrace
㊾ Grosvenor Terrace
(61) Northpark House

James Salmon I (1805-88), **James Salmon II** (1873-1924) and **J. Gaff Gillespie** (1870-1926)

Walk 61 ⑧ British Linen Bank

Walk 3 (67) Lion Chambers
(79) West Regent Street

Walk 5 ㉕ Savings Bank of Glasgow
㊱ Hatrack Building
㊸ Scottish Temperance League Building
㊽ Mercantile Chambers

Walk 6 ㉝ University Gardens

Walk 10 ㉞ British Linen Bank

George Gilbert Scott (1810-78) and **John Oldrid Scott** (1841-1913)

Walk 6 ⑧ Glasgow University Main Buildings
⑩ University Tower
⑫ Bute Hall
⑬ Randolph Hall
⑯ Engineering Building
㉑ Professors' Square
㉔ Botany Building

Walk 7 ㉔ St Mary's Episcopal Cathedral

James Sellars (1843-88)

Walk 3 ㊲ 45 Buchanan Street
㊵ Glasgow Herald Office
(63) Piping Centre
(77) James Sellars House

Walk 4 ㊷ St Andrew's Halls

Walk 6 ㊹ Gilmorehill Hall

Baptist Church
㉑ Garnetbank Primary
School

Walk 6 **㊺** Wellington Church

Robert Whitworth (d.1799)

Walk 9 **❾** Kelvin Aqueduct
❿ Maryhill Locks
⓰ Stockingfield
Aqueduct
㉞ Possil Road
Aqueduct

Charles Wilson (1810-63)

Walk 2 **⓴** Greenhead School

Walk 3 **㊼** Royal Faculty
of Procurators' Hall

Walk 4 **㊲** Queen's Rooms
㊳ 2-5 La Belle Place
㊻ Glasgow High
School

Walk 7 **⓰** Trinity College
Park Circus
⓲ 22 Park Circus
⓳ Park Terrace
⓴ Granite Staircase
㊿ Kirklee Terrace

Edward Grigg Wylie
(*c.* 1885-1954)

Walk 4 **⓴** Dental Hospital

Walk 6 **㊿** Scottish Legal Life
Assurance Society
Building

Walk 7 **❾** Hillhead High
School

CHAPTER 8

Alexander Thomson
(1817-75)

Alexander Thomson was a highly respected Glasgow architect whose work is now being recognised as being of great importance. In particular, his St Vincent Street Free Church of Scotland is attracting admirers from around the world. His style is unique – and as a result his buildings are very recognisable – and his work is an important bridge between 'Classical' and 'Modern' ideas. Although many of his designs have a strong Greek flavour (which led to him being known as Alexander 'Greek'Thomson) he borrowed and developed ideas from other ancient civilisations, including Egypt and Assyria. This, and his use of new building materials such as cast iron, allowed him to combine tried and tested (but not necessarily fashionable!) ideas with the building techniques of the day.

Thomson was born in the village of Balfron, to the north of Glasgow, but after his father's death (when Alexander was only seven years old) the family moved to the outskirts of the city. In 1834 he entered the architectural practice of Robert Foote whose great love of classical architecture obviously had a profound effect on the young Thomson. In 1836 he joined the practice of John Baird I, an innovative firm in which Thomson would have been able to learn about modern construction techniques. Perhaps surprisingly, he did not take time to travel widely and he never ventured abroad to study the Greek buildings he admired so much. However, he thought highly of the Royal High School (1825-9, Thomas Hamilton) in Edinburgh, Scotland's 'Athens of the North', and St George's Hall in Liverpool; indeed, these were considered by Thomson as 'unquestionably the two finest buildings in the kingdom'.

In 1847 Thomson married Jane Nicholson (whose grandfather Peter Nicholson had designed Carlton Place) and he went into partnership with John Baird II (no relation to John Baird I) who, incidentally, married Jane's sister. Thomson now started to design buildings himself, including small villas in the then-fashionable Late Gothic or Italian Renaissance styles. In 1852-3 he designed the first portion of The Knowe (described on p.278), a villa with Romanesque details. There are also some traces of Greek style in that building and about a year later he started serious experiments with Greek ideas, including designs for warehouses with regularly spaced external pillars and a very obvious lack of arches. His harsh and uncompromising attitude towards this long-popular means of supporting heavy loads was explained thus in 1874: 'the arch is essentially a bricklayer's contrivance… the great monumental builders of Egypt and Greece, although quite familiar with it, wisely avoided its use in their more important structures, knowing well the destructive nature of this most mischievous and absurd of building contrivances.' Indeed, he went as far as claiming that 'the adoption of the arch by the Romans has strewed Europe with ruins'!

The partnership with John Baird II ended in 1856 and Thomson then worked with his brother George in the firm A. & G. Thomson, with Alexander concentrating on the design work and George being responsible for supervising the construction of the buildings. In 1857 Alexander and his family moved from the Hutchestown-Gorbals area to Shawlands, mainly because of the outbreaks of cholera and other diseases which had spread rapidly through the district, caused mainly by unclean drinking water and poor sanitation. Sadly, four of his children died during the various epidemics.

The Thomson brothers' first building of note was 'The Double Villa' (1856-7, described on p.399), a remarkable design the idea for which was Alexander's own invention. The Caledonia Road Church (1856-7, described on p.401) then followed; both Thomson and John Baird II were trustees of the church, but Thomson was given the commission and he later also built the two adjoining tenement blocks. A studio for the sculptor John G. Mossman and various tenements came next but, alas, the studio and most of the tenements have since been demolished although Walmer Crescent (1857-62, described on p.399) still remains from this period.

Around 1856-7, the congregation of the Gordon Street United Presbyterian Church sold their church, the city-centre site of which had greatly increased in value, and bought land in St Vincent Street. Not only did the brothers win the commission for the large St Vincent Street United Presbyterian Church (1857-9, described on p.158), but they also bought the Gordon Street site for themselves and erected the Grosvenor Building (1859-61, described on p.167). In 1857-8 Thomson designed the large villa of Holmwood (described on p.332), a building now under the ownership of the National Trust for Scotland which will become a centre for the study of the architect's work. The office block at 99-107 West Nile Street (1858, described on p.103) was his next important commission, to be followed by various now-demolished buildings.

In 1858-9 he started another speculative project, this time for the terrace of houses at 1-10 Moray Place (described on p.323), and the family moved into number 1 in 1861. In 1862 he produced an (unsuccessful) design for the Albert Memorial in London and in 1862-3 he built the Buck's Head Building (described on p.94), two years later erecting a warehouse on the adjacent site in Dunlop Street. In 1864 he had another attempt at winning a large London competition, this time for the South Kensington Museum; although his design was quite stunning (it included huge sculpted elephants!) it was unsuccessful.

Back in Glasgow, his next buildings were the addition to Lilybank House (1863-5, described on p.190), the terrace at 41-53 Oakfield Avenue (1865, described on p.218), Sauchiehall Street's Grecian Buildings (1865, described on p.119) and Northpark Terrace (1866, described on p.235); the second terrace is notably more 'severe' than the first and it can be seen as a step towards his later – and more famous – grand terraces. By now his designs were becoming very recognisable and there are distinct 'hallmarks' which he included in his buildings. They often had a regular rectangular appearance – the curves, arches and circular windows which his contemporaries used were eschewed, with rectangular pillars and lintels above doors and windows being used instead. In addition, there was very little flamboyant detail; most elements of his designs had a purpose and the artistic decorations were often kept to a minimum. Classical symbols such as anthemia were used as decorations and regular patterns were incised in the stonework as a means of uniting the various sections of the building into one coherent structure. His next major work was for the Queen's Park Church (1867), a massive and very 'classical' building which was unfortunately destroyed in 1942 during a Second World War air raid.

Glasgow's City Improvement Trust started its work in the 1860s rehousing thousands of people who were living in the squalor of the old city centre. Many architects were involved in this work and between them they put forward many different plans. Thomson supported the idea of continuing to use the tenement as the main type of building in the redeveloped parts of the city and he worked on many tenements, including buildings with 'single-ends' (see p.128) – quite a change from his designs for villas for the rich. His most remarkable proposal (which was never realised) was for the erection of 'galleria' which involved placing glass roofs between blocks of tenements, thus protecting the street below with a wide transparent canopy. The design he submitted was to provide houses for over ten thousand people and he explained that the glass roofs would provide 'playgrounds for the young, where they may run about under shelter'.

In 1869 Thomson started another speculative venture with John McIntyre which resulted in his most famous domestic building, Great Western Terrace (described on p.232). He had already developed his ideas of how middle-class terraced housing should look and now he turned his talents to designing a grand set of houses for the very wealthy. The terrace sits well above the street and so imposes itself on its surroundings, all the better for showing off the rhythmic and monumental character of this outstanding building. In 1870 he designed Castlehill (described on p.398), surprisingly his first villa since Holmwood, and while it was being built he was asked to design a house for the adjacent plot. This resulted in Ellisland (1871, described on p.398) and although he used many of his usual 'hallmarks' there is no overwhelming similarity between the two neighbouring houses.

Thomson's finest commercial building, the Egyptian Halls (described on p.169), was designed in 1871-3 and followed the popular city centre plan of ground-floor shops with offices placed above. However, what makes this block so startlingly different is that the facade of the upper floors are extravagantly decorated with various styles of pillars. Thomson's last building of note was Westbourne Terrace (1871, described on p.233). This is close to Great Western Terrace and it shares some of its features, such as the decorative ironwork, but it is on a less grand scale.

George Thomson left the practice in 1871 and became a missionary in Africa, leaving his brother to look after the construction of the buildings as well as their design. Alexander had no further major commissions but was generally kept busy with various relatively smaller undertakings. The publisher Robert Blackie asked him to carry out the interior design at 1 Great Western Terrace and in 1872 he designed the substantial Kelvinside Terrace Steps, showing that he could turn his hand to various types of structures. As well as being a practising architect, Thomson was also a 'committee man' and he worked hard at raising the architectural and building standards in the city. He gave lectures too, and his series of talks at the Haldane Institute in 1874 ranged widely over art and architecture

He suffered from asthma all his life and his health deteriorated in the bad winter of 1874-5. He died on 22 March 1875 at Moray Place and was buried in the Southern Necropolis but unfortunately his memorial stone is no longer there. However, as a tribute to his work, a marble bust of him was sculpted by John G. Mossman and this is on display in the Kelvingrove Art Gallery and Museum. In addition, the Alexander Thomson Travelling Studentship was established to allow architecture students to travel abroad – a very imaginative prize as Thomson, who had loved Greek buildings so much, had never managed to see any of them. What makes this prize so interesting in the history of Glasgow architecture is that in 1890 its second recipient was the young Charles Rennie Mackintosh.

After his death, a number of his unfinished buildings were executed by his partner Robert Turnbull, and other Scottish architects used some of his ideas in their own designs. One notable example was his former assistant Alexander Skirving who later designed Langside Hill Church (1894-6), but by the turn of the century the dominance of new fashions such as Art Nouveau meant that the Classicism so admired by Thomson was pushed aside.

In recent decades, a number of Thomson's buildings have been demolished. While some of these were in very poor condition, others might have been saved if his work had been given due recognition much earlier – hindsight is a wonderful gift! However, Glasgow is graced with a number of his fascinating buildings and the city is much richer architecturally because of them.

The table on p.397 lists all of Alexander Thomson's works which are described in this book. The map on p.396 indicates the location of the places listed in the table.

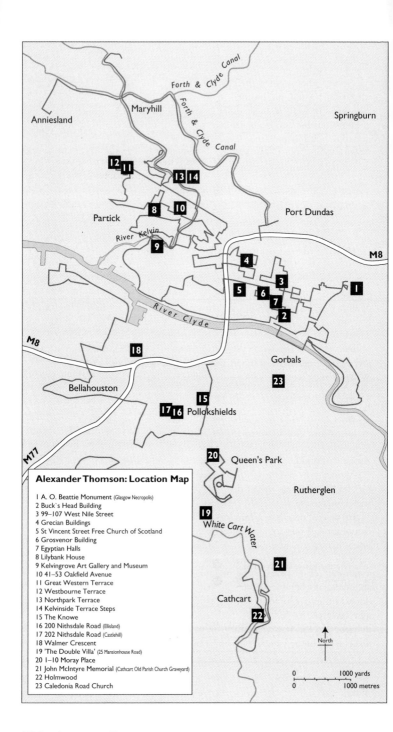

Alexander Thomson: Location Map

1 A. O. Beattie Monument (Glasgow Necropolis)
2 Buck's Head Building
3 99–107 West Nile Street
4 Grecian Buildings
5 St Vincent Street Free Church of Scotland
6 Grosvenor Building
7 Egyptian Halls
8 Lilybank House
9 Kelvingrove Art Gallery and Museum
10 41–53 Oakfield Avenue
11 Great Western Terrace
12 Westbourne Terrace
13 Northpark Terrace
14 Kelvinside Terrace Steps
15 The Knowe
16 200 Nithsdale Road (Ellisland)
17 202 Nithsdale Road (Castlehill)
18 Walmer Crescent
19 'The Double Villa' (25 Mansionhouse Road)
20 1–10 Moray Place
21 John McIntyre Memorial (Cathcart Old Parish Church Graveyard)
22 Holmwood
23 Caledonia Road Church

41-53 Oakfield Avenue, Hillhead: details of Thomson's stonework

The following Thomson buildings are described here as they are not included on any of the book's walks. Please note that both houses on Nithsdale Road and 'The Double Villa' are private houses with no public access.

200 Nithsdale Road (1871)
Ellisland is a one-storey villa which is very different from Thomson's other houses as it is essentially square in plan and the facade is symmetrical. There are important Egyptian influences in the overall design, especially at the doorway which is flanked by a pair of lotus-headed columns, the capitals of which were originally painted in terracotta, gold, blue and black. The entrance is made all the more imposing by the placing of substantial stone plinths on either side of the wide steps and the use of these to support tall cast-iron lampstandards. The doorway and the windows on either side of it are sunk into the facade, thus allowing the stonework to dominate the overall design. This is emphasised by the long low stone walls (with their decorative ironwork) which stretch out from either side of the facade to the boundary walls.

Thomson often gave his villas broad overhanging eaves and in this case he placed a decorative cast-iron screen above them. Behind this embellishment is a low pitched roof (only 18°) which incorporates a large glazed area allowing lots of light to enter the hallway. Other points of interest include the lotus flower chimney pots.

202 Nithsdale Road (1870)
Castlehill is a handsome two-storey asymmetric building which was built as a house and later converted for use as a school; it is now occupied as a private house. It is situated on a prominent ridge and the principal

rooms face south to take advantage of the sun and the view. Unlike many of Thomson's other houses, this one lacks a dominating entrance, nor does it have much external decoration; instead, it relies on its overall shape for its interest. The general outline of the house follows a technique he used in other villas, with the building being low on the left (part of the single-storey portion contains the dining room) and generally rising to the right. The tall central portion of the house protects the doorway from the prevailing wind and on the far right of the building is a large billiard room, a common component of many middle-class houses in the late nineteenth century.

Walmer Crescent (1857-62)

Thomson built a number of tenement blocks in Glasgow which ranged from those built for the slum-clearance work of the City Improvement Trust to more expensive housing such as here at Walmer Crescent. This may have been his first tenement building and, sadly, is the only one that survives. This three-storey curved block of tenements was built in what were open fields in the 1860s and the very large flats were described as being 'occupied exclusively by rich merchants'. They stand a little way back from Paisley Road West and were separated from that busy thoroughfare by private gardens but these have since been developed for shops.

The ground floor has groups of three doors, with the door to the close in the middle and the entrances to the main-door houses on either side. The ground and first storeys have bold rectangular bay windows and the second floor is in the form of a continuous colonnade. Thomson added numerous subtleties into the stonework's design to ensure that this was the most important feature of the whole building. He emphasised the horizontal lines of the building by recessing the ground floor's horizontal joints and, on the first floor, by using alternating bands of broad and narrow blocks. This technique was also used on the Caledonia Road Church (see p.401) which he built around the same time, and here again he has made the narrow bands jut out slightly. In addition, there is a narrow (but prominent) string course between the ground and first floors and there is also an unusual band of stonework around the first-storey windows which acts as (horizontal) lintels and (vertical) jambs.

The austere overall look is lessened by cast-iron railings, circular emblems at the doorways and the incised decoration on the first-floor bay windows' mullions.

'The Double Villa' (25 Mansionhouse Road) (1856–7)

This was the first building that Thomson designed when in partnership with his brother and it was intended as the forerunner of a number of such buildings in this newly laid out housing area, but unfortunately no others were constructed. At first glance this building appears to be a large asymmetric two-storey sandstone villa with features which are also found in some of his other villas. However, this unique structure comprises two smaller semi-detached houses which stand side by side and face in opposite directions — one to the west, the other to the east. No matter which particular side of the building is viewed, each is

'The Double Villa', Langside

identical with the front (of one house) on the left and the back (of the other house) on the right. The routes of the local roads were not settled when this house was built, so that the northern house has its front door relatively near what became Mansionhouse Road while the southern house has its front door facing a long garden that sweeps down towards Millbrae Road.

The facade's dominant feature is the vertical combination of the house's two principal rooms, the ground-floor dining room and the first-floor drawing room. Thomson used a Greek temple style here, with the dining room's bay window jutting out boldly with its windows set well back from the tall external pillars, a feature he used in many of his buildings. The upper room's pillars continue the vertical lines of the lower pillars and this helps to emphasise the height of this part of the building. External decoration does not play an important role in this building but some incised patterns are used on the capitals of the pillars and around the doors. The eaves have a substantial overhang and, above them, the roof has a very shallow pitch (only 18°), allowing the tall lotus flower chimney pots to become a feature themselves.

Internally, the houses were given a number of interesting features, one of which was the dining room's store. This is in the single-storey structure at the gable end and was built with trapdoors in the floor allowing access to suspended metal wine bins.

Caledonia Road Church (1856-7)

The Caledonia Road United Presbyterian Church was Thomson's first church and it has many design features which he subsequently used in later — and more elaborate — structures such as St Vincent Street Free Church of Scotland. He was a member of the church and his regular visits to it must have given him the ideal opportunity to see his building in operation, allowing him to learn more about how well his novel design actually worked. The whole building (the church plus the narrow wedge-shaped hall which is on the west side) occupies only a small plot of land but Thomson employed an elevated temple and a tall bell tower to ensure that the whole structure was as prominent as possible. Fortunately, no buildings were ever erected directly in front of the church so it was able to dominate the space around it and it was the Gorbals' finest building until disaster struck in 1965 when it was gutted by fire. Since then it has remained as a sad-looking, empty shell with an air of desolation particularly heightened during those years when the neighbouring district was subjected to wholescale 'comprehensive redevelopment'.

At the southern end, the church's very austere podium is pierced by the two main doorways which are in the form of tall tapering Egyptian pylons decorated with numerous Classical ornaments. The facade's stonework is unusual as the sandstone blocks are arranged in alternating broad and narrow bands, with the narrow bands projecting slightly. This pattern, which helps to relieve the otherwise featureless wall between the doors, is continued on the building's other main walls. A Greek temple is placed above the podium and this has six Ionic columns supporting a pediment which has small Classical decorations.

Thomson was quite prepared to mix different architectural styles and as well as having the Egyptian doorways and the Greek temple, he included a tall Lombardy-style bell tower. At the lowest level it contained the stairs to the gallery, farther up (and on the west side) is a tall Egyptian-style opening and much higher up, each of the sides is pierced by three vertical bell-openings above which are incised geometric patterns. The tower supports a decorated lantern-like structure on top of which is a cross.

Inside, the church featured a fine timber roof and the wood and plaster work was colourfully decorated in red, green and gold. The interior's main lighting came from the portico and the numerous windows in the (now lost) clerestory.

CHAPTER 9

Charles Rennie Mackintosh (1868-1928)

For many decades after his death, the work of Charles Rennie Mackintosh was little known outside Glasgow, but the unstinting work carried out by his admirers have now borne fruit. Today, he is a household name in Glasgow, his Glasgow School of Art is world-famous and his paintings, interior designs and furniture are recognised by an ever-growing number of people. The 1996 exhibition of his work in the city's McLellan Galleries drew in visitors from all over the world and today there are possibly more books written about him than any other Scotsman other than Robert Burns.

Glasgow is fortunate in having a number of his buildings in very good condition which allow people to see his work for themselves, and in addition his reconstructed house can be visited at Glasgow University. While Mackintosh started his professional life as an architect, he developed into an interior designer and his house contains rooms designed by Mackintosh and his wife Margaret; the starkness and use of black and white in these rooms means few visitors leave without having formed an attitude (favourable or otherwise) about the Mackintoshes' work. In recent years there have been many imitators of Mackintosh's style and although he never designed jewellery, 'Mockintosh' pieces of jewellery which employ his lattice-work patterns, rose emblems or some other eye-catching detail are widely found. Perhaps imitation *is* the sincerest form of flattery.

This chapter is intended to offer a very brief introduction to Mackintosh's career and to give some background details about his buildings encountered on this book's walks.

Charles Rennie Mackintosh was born in Glasgow on 7 June 1868, the son of William McIntosh (a policeman) and Margaret Rennie. The couple had a total of eleven children but four died in infancy. Charles' first home was at 70 Parson Street, just a short distance west of Glasgow's Royal Infirmary, but when he was six the family moved a little eastwards, to a bigger flat at 2 Firpark Terrace in Dennistoun, and stayed there until 1889. Margaret Rennie died in 1885 and her husband (who remarried seven years later) died in February 1908.

After attending Reid's Public School and Allan Glen's School, the sixteen-year-old Charles joined the architectural practice of John Hutchison in 1884 and also began attending classes at the Glasgow School of Art where he studied art and architecture. Towards the end of his apprenticeship he won his first solo commission which was for a memorial to Alexander McCall (1888, described on p.356) which still stands in the Glasgow Necropolis. Once qualified he left Hutchison and joined the practice of John Honeyman and John Keppie, at the time one of the leading practices in the city.

In 1888 Herbert McNair joined the practice as a draughtsman and the two students attended classes together at the Art School. There they were introduced by the school's Director, Francis Newbery, to two sisters, Margaret and Frances Macdonald, and the group later became well known as 'The Four'. The sisters both studied art at the school and produced drawings and other works often using ultra-slim women whose stylized shapes formed part of the overall image. Mackintosh was later to use some of the sisters' Art Nouveau figures in his work, notably in posters, wall decorations (especially in the tea rooms) and even in stonework.

In 1890 he won the Alexander Thomson Travelling Studentship (see p.395) and early the next year set off for Italy for a study and sketching tour that took him to many famous cities such as Rome, Venice and Florence. On his return he worked as a draughtsman for the Honeyman and Keppie practice, but in his spare time he entered many architectural competitions in order to get his name and his designs seen by a larger audience. He was also developing his own architectural philosophy and as well as looking back at traditional Scottish architecture, he cast a critical eye over the new ideas that were being tried out in various countries. In 1891 he spoke to the Glasgow Architectural Association on the subject of Scottish Baronial architecture and, after describing some aspects of Scottish architecture up to the eighteenth century, he went on to suggest that

> Since then we have had no such thing as a national style, sometimes we
> have been Greek, sometimes Italian and again Gothic… It is a matter
> of regret that we don't find any class of buildings but domestic in this style
> [Scots Baronial], whether the style can be developed beyond this or not is
> a point which our forefathers left for us to decide. From some recent buildings
> which have been erected it is clearly evident that the style is coming to
> life again and I only hope that it will not be strangled in its infancy by
> indiscriminate and unsympathetic people who copy the ancient examples
> without trying to make it conform to modern requirements.

His first important architectural work was in helping to design the Glasgow Herald Building (1893-5, described on p.98) and a number of his own personal touches can be seen in the building. After that he was engaged on the Martyrs' Public School (1895, described on p.412) which, coincidentally, stood on the same street as his first home. As well as working as an architect, Charles was involved in many other aspects of art and design and he developed his talents in posters, watercolour paintings and furniture. In time, these were to become as important as his buildings as he gradually became more a designer than simply an architect.

Mackintosh's great opportunity came in 1896 when the practice was invited to compete for the new Glasgow School of Art (1897-9 and 1907-9, described on p.125), which gave the young architect the chance to design what is now regarded as a world–class building. Newbery had already been impressed with his talents in a variety of disciplines and this project allowed him to express his ideas in the design of the interior and furniture as well as the building itself. Whilst Keppie supervised the construction of the first phase of the Art School, Mackintosh continued on other work and also exhibited furniture at the 1896 London Arts and Crafts Exhibition. However, Mackintosh was never really taken seriously in England and may well have been regarded as being a bit too 'provincial' to be of interest.

His next important venture was in designing stencil wall decorations for the tea rooms in Buchanan Street which were being opened by Kate Cranston, whose work is described on p.123. Cranston's main designer at that time was George Walton but she hoped that the interest generated by Mackintosh's startlingly different posters and drawings would bring more custom to her tea rooms. And she was right. Mackintosh's designs for the tea rooms included peacocks, clouds (very appropriate for the Smoking Gallery!) and tall slim women posing amid decorative roses.

Queen's Cross Church (1897-9, described on p.264) was Mackintosh's next building. This has a modern, uncluttered interior within a structure which owes much to an English medieval church Mackintosh once

Queen's Cross Church, Garscube Road

visited. When it ceased its function as a church the building was given a new lease of life as the headquarters of the Charles Rennie Mackintosh Society. However, it was not his buildings but his furniture and interior decorations that were getting Mackintosh noticed outside Britain. The group of artists known as The Glasgow Boys (see p.209) had exhibited in Munich in the 1890s and that city's interest in Glasgow's thriving artistic life led to an article on The Four and Talwin Morris in the periodical *Dekorative Kunst* and to Mackintosh being invited to furnish the publisher's dining room.

Back home, in 1898 Mackintosh was responsible for drawing the practice's unsuccessful entry for Glasgow's 1901 Exhibition. Then came Ruchill Parish Church Halls (1898-1900, described on p.262), Kate Cranston's tea rooms in Argyle Street (1898-9) and the Daily Record Building (1900, described on p.162). His first important commission for a house came in 1900 when William Davidson asked him to design Windyhill in Kilmacolm. This was an L-shaped house which drew on many of the country's architectural traditions (such as the use of harling) while carrying elements of the Modern Movement forward, particularly in the internal decoration. Mackintosh had already done some work for Davidson, including designing some furniture in 1894, and in years to come the close relationship between the two men was to help Mackintosh find new contracts and extricate him from financial difficulties.

Charles and Margaret Macdonald married in 1900, just a year after her sister Frances had married Herbert McNair. The couple worked on numerous commissions together, with Margaret being responsible for aspects of a building's interior decoration; indeed, in many cases, work that is ascribed to Mackintosh should properly be jointly credited to both of them. They moved into a large Victorian flat at 120 Mains Street (now 120 Blythswood Street) and set about redecorating it to their own very distinctive taste. In many ways this was not so much a home as a gallery, with each room a work of art in itself. Photographs of the rooms show them as being quite devoid of the usual Victorian middle-class 'clutter' – there were few paintings, few items on the mantelpieces and few pieces of furniture – but there was lots and lots of space. The flat was furnished with a number of Mackintosh's pieces of furniture and while these are fascinating to look at and admire, to many people they appear very uncomfortable.

Kate Cranston provided the next major commission when she asked Mackintosh to add extra rooms to her Ingram Street Tea Rooms. The interior designs included features such as large gesso panels, and a few of the chairs were in the famous high-back style for which Mackintosh is so well known. (Fortunately, these striking interiors are in the care of Glasgow Museums but they are still awaiting a permanent home in which to display them.) Some pieces from Ingram Street and Mains Street as well as some new items of furniture were exhibited in the 1900 Vienna Secession exhibition. In inviting the couple to design a complete room, the exhibition's organisers were recognising their special expertise in interior design. Their overall approach was that the interior design of a house or room should be a piece of art in its own right and this was very evident at Mains Street and Ingram Street where the lighting, furniture, fixtures and wall decorations were all carefully chosen to complement each other. The couple were able to build upon this technique in Mackintosh's competition entry for the House for an Art Lover (described on p.282); this remarkable building has now been constructed in Bellahouston Park, providing a large-scale example of the joint talents of the Mackintoshes.

In 1901 Mackintosh became a partner in Honeyman and Keppie and in 1902 he drew their (unsuccessful) competition entry for Liverpool's Anglican cathedral; for this he used a Gothic design which employed ideas borrowed from Durham Cathedral. Later that year the Mackintoshes exhibited 'The Rose Boudoir' in Turin as part of a Scottish entry organised by Newbery. This, as the name implies, had roses as one of its main features and this was the most extensive use they made of the motif; high-backed chairs were also included in the room's design. In 1902 the couple designed a music room for a German client while Mackintosh began work on The Hill House in Helensburgh. This substantial harled house, which has views over the Firth of Clyde, was built for the publisher Walter Blackie and is now in the care of the National Trust for Scotland. It is larger than Windy-hill (and it cost over twice as much) and was designed with all the stark originality that Mackintosh is famous for. In many ways it is a development of Windyhill but its size and the generous amount of internal space available gave Mackintosh an even greater opportunity to show off his abilities.

Kate Cranston's patronage was important in ensuring that the Mackintoshes' work was seen daily by Glaswegians and in 1903 they started creating The Willow Tea Rooms in Sauchiehall Street (described on p.120). Although they were not Cranston's biggest tea rooms they are the best known today as they still function, complete with much of the (reconstructed) original interiors. Mackintosh's second school building, Scotland Street School (1904-6, described on p.277) was designed around the same time. Its overall design is very different from other city schools and the school board and the architect had some very heated arguments over various matters. This (and the overspending) was presumably the reason why the practice was not asked to do any more buildings for the school board! The school is another of the architect's buildings which has been preserved for public use and it now serves as Glasgow's Museum of Education. The next commission from Kate Cranston was to redesign the interior of her mansion Hous'hill. This house dated back to the seventeenth century so the new interiors had to be a little more restrained than those he had put into new houses such as Windyhill and The Hill House. However, his 'hallmark' bold stencilling was there, so also were white-painted wooden features and dark-stained furniture. Sadly, the furniture collection was split up in 1933 and the house was demolished.

By this time Mackintosh's work was getting better known and in a letter of 1904 Margaret wrote (very prophetically!) 'It is very amusing –

and in spite of all the efforts to stamp out the Mackintosh influence [from the Art School] – the whole town is getting covered with imitations of Mackintosh tea rooms, Mackintosh shops, Mackintosh furniture etc – It is too funny – I wonder how it will end.' Indeed.

Mackintosh's last major exhibition entry in Europe was in 1905 in Berlin where he showed a dining room fitted with dark walls and furniture. Although his work was seen in exhibitions in Vienna and Paris in later years, only individual objects were put on display. While he was alive none of his work (either drawings or furniture) was ever put on display in America nor were any articles published there about his or the couple's work; however, that situation changed quite dramatically at the tail-end of the twentieth century.

1905 was generally a quiet year, though it was enlivened by the arguments over Scotland Street School, and the high point was probably the commission for the Dutch Kitchen in Kate Cranston's tea rooms in Argyle Street. Unlike much of his earlier work for Kate Cranston, this interior was dark (and not very Dutch, either); black and white squares, as used in The Hill House and Hous'hill, were employed and colour was virtually banished, though the chairs were bright green.

In 1906 the couple purchased 78 Southpark Avenue (see p.218), then called 6 Florentine Terrace. This was a large end-terrace house of the 1850s and they moved in many items, including fireplaces, from their house in Mains Street. The interior design of the new house was generally based on their work in Mains Street, but since they now owned a house (rather than renting one) they could make more radical changes to the fabric of the building. This included knocking down walls, removing cornices and inserting new windows. It is this home which has been reconstructed at Glasgow University's Hunterian Art Gallery and which is described on p.194.

Early in 1907 the practice was given the task of building the second phase of the Art School and the first half of the year was taken up with work on that project – his last important work in Glasgow. This was followed by work on further interiors for the Ingram Street Tea Rooms. With the completion of the Art School, a job which was frequently punctuated with disagreements with the governors, the practice hit a lean patch with a substantial drop in the amount of business coming in. This situation persisted from 1909 right through to 1914 and during this time Mackintosh only worked on half a dozen new commissions although there was work completed on other projects. Mackintosh was also going through a professional crisis of his own as he was unable to find clients willing to accept his avant-garde designs. In 1913 he worked on drawings for the new teaching training college at Jordanhill but these were never completed. Shortly after that he resigned from the partnership and set up his own business which never managed to win any work.

In February 1914, just before the First World War started, the couple went on holiday to the Suffolk fishing village of Walberswick. Mackintosh was depressed; he had no work in Glasgow and he felt that

The Mackintosh House at the Hunterian Art Gallery, Glasgow University

his talents were not being given the recognition they deserved. The holiday turned into a protracted stay and the couple put the time to good use, with Margaret working on large oil paintings and Charles producing around forty flower pictures using pencil and watercolours. The change of scenery and activity was doing the trick and Margaret was able to write, 'Already Toshie is quite a different being and evidently at the end of the year will be quite fit again.' But their stay was not all peaceful. He was regarded as a bit of an eccentric (after all, he was an artist) and it was known that he had travelled in Germany, with whom Britain was now at war. He was reported to the military authorities and various papers of his, including some recent letters from Germany, were taken away for inspection. The powers-that-be were very suspicious and ordered him to leave the area, forcing the couple to move to London.

They spent the next eight years in Chelsea and were involved socially and professionally with many artists who lived in that area. In 1915-6 Wenman J. Bassett-Lowke asked him to alter and completely redecorate 78 Derngate, a nineteenth-century four-storey house in Northampton. The design was radically different from the likes of Mains Street and The Hill House; in places the house was awash with colour, with black and white chequerwork, latticework with coloured glass inlays, and bright yellow was used on the hall's stencilled wall decorations. The sinuous curves that Mackintosh had used with great effect in his earlier work were absent and were replaced by squares, triangles and dazzling eye-catching patterns. It is said that Bassett-Lowke was colour blind and the stunning colours, including the bright yellow in the hall and deep blue in the guest bedroom, were chosen because he could discern these colours more readily than others. The dramatic guest bedroom (1919) has fortunately been saved for posterity and is on display in the University's Mackintosh House; the decoration is described on p.195. Soon after this job, Kate Cranston asked Mackintosh to add a new interior to her Willow Tea Rooms and this basement addition (which was called the Dug-Out) was decorated with motifs he had been using at Derngate.

During the Chelsea years most of his time as an artist was taken up with flower painting, but these new paintings were far more detailed and elaborate than those executed at Walberswick. The techniques he now employed were also used for textile designs, a number of which were used by William Foxton of London and this provided him with a new outlet for his skills. Although the Mackintoshes had income from a number of sources, in 1919 they were facing financial difficulties and Mackintosh wrote to William Davidson to tell him, 'I find myself at the moment very hard up and I was wondering if you could see your way to buy one of my flower pictures or landscapes for £20 or £30… my rent of £16 is overdue and I must pay or leave.' Davidson duly sent him £30. His last architectural commission was in 1920 when he was asked to do design work for some proposed artists' studios and living areas in Chelsea's Glebe Place. Unfortunately, not much came of that work but the resulting fees were very welcome.

In 1923 the couple headed farther southwards and stayed four years in France. Late in 1925 they were in Port Vendres, a busy town on the Mediterranean coast which was just 3km (2 miles) from Collioure where Matisse and many other artists painted. Mackintosh produced numerous watercolours while at Port Vendres, many of them depicting the landscape and seascape around him; people were excluded. The fascination of these paintings is the clarity of the detail in the buildings, demonstrating his great skills as an architectural draughtsman.

In autumn 1927 he became seriously ill with cancer of the tongue and throat (he had been a smoker for much of his life) and he went back to London for treatment. After a spell in hospital and in a nursing home, he died in Paddington on 10 December 1928. Margaret never really settled down after her husband's death and stayed at Port Vendres a few times as well as visiting Normandy. Eventually, she went back to Chelsea and died on 7 January 1933.

In May 1933 the ever-faithful William Davidson (who was Mackintosh's executor) organised a Mackintosh Memorial Exhibition in Glasgow's McLellan Galleries. In 1920 Davidson had purchased 78 Southpark Avenue from the Mackintoshes and on Davidson's death in 1945 the house was bought by the University of Glasgow. In addition, the Davidson family presented the university with the contents of the house, and the Mackintoshes' heir, Sylvan McNair, gave furniture, drawings and paintings to the university. These gifts now form the basis of the wonderful collection on display in the university's Mackintosh House.

The table below lists all the architect's works which are described in this book. The list includes a number of buildings where Mackintosh was not the principal architect but where he assisted someone else; the relevant description of the building mentions where this is the case. Much more information is available from the Charles Rennie Mackintosh Society in Queen's Cross Church.

Name	Walk no.	Place no. in walk	Open to public	Notes
Glasgow Herald Building	3	41	in 1999	also known as 'The Lighthouse'
The Glasgow Society of Lady Artists Club	4	4		
The Willow Tea Rooms	4	13	yes	
Glasgow School of Art	4	19	yes	
Daily Record Building	5	44		
Mackintosh House, Hunterian Art Gallery (Glasgow University)	6	38	yes	a reconstruction of his own house
Kelvingrove Art Gallery and Museum	6	68	yes	furniture exhibits
Queen Margaret College	7	62		
Ruchill Parish Church Halls	9	21		
Queen's Cross Church	9	29	yes	HQ of the Charles Rennie Mackintosh Society
Scotland Street School	10	2	yes	
House for an Art Lover	10	16	yes	
Alexander McCall Memorial (Glasgow Necropolis)	1	15	yes	monument described in the graveyard chapter
Martyrs' Public School	1	26	not yet	described in this chapter
140-2 Balgrayhill Road	–	–		described in this chapter

The map opposite indicates the location of the places listed in the table.

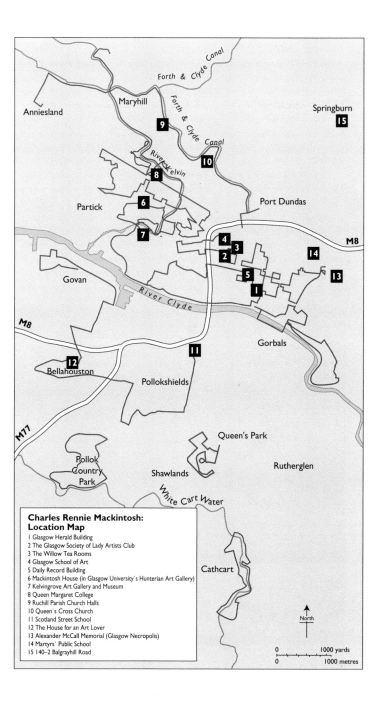

**Charles Rennie Mackintosh:
Location Map**

1 Glasgow Herald Building
2 The Glasgow Society of Lady Artists Club
3 The Willow Tea Rooms
4 Glasgow School of Art
5 Daily Record Building
6 Mackintosh House (in Glasgow University's Hunterian Art Gallery)
7 Kelvingrove Art Gallery and Museum
8 Queen Margaret College
9 Ruchill Parish Church Halls
10 Queen's Cross Church
11 Scotland Street School
12 The House for an Art Lover
13 Alexander McCall Memorial (Glasgow Necropolis)
14 Martyrs' Public School
15 140–2 Balgrayhill Road

Martyrs' Public School (1895-8)

Mackintosh was senior assistant in Honeyman and Keppie when this Scots Renaissance building was designed and it incorporates many ideas that he developed in later buildings such as the Glasgow School of Art and Scotland Street School. The school was given its name in memory of three Covenanters, James Lawson, James Nisbet and Alexander Wood, who were executed on this site for their beliefs in 1684. It is situated in Parson Street, the very street Mackintosh lived in for the first six years of his life.

The best view of the school is from the pedestrian bridge which links Parson Street to the Royal Infirmary complex and from there the layout of this red sandstone building can be appreciated. It is essentially a rectangular building onto which has been attached a block containing the northern classrooms. It is almost symmetrical (the tall chimney beside the southern door spoils the symmetry) and there are two entrances (one for boys, the other for girls) on the northern side. Within the design constraints that would have been laid down by the school board, Mackintosh added a number of Art Nouveau features to the

Martyrs' Public School

exterior such as the detailing at the entrances and the curved projecting stonework around some of the windows. There is also variety in the window styles, with some of them being sash-type and others leaded. Another unusual feature is the design of the three rooftop ventilators which are in the form of cupolas.

Like many Glasgow schools of the period, the building has a large central well lit by a huge skylight. This allows the classrooms, which are arranged around the well, to be lit from both inside and outside, making the whole building very bright. While this standard layout was used by many architects in the city, there are many features which indicate where Mackintosh was involved in the design. For example, it was not unusual to use white tiles in the central well in order to reflect light, but Mackintosh added coloured tiles as a bold border to link the doors and windows, and also to provide splashes of colour which break up the clinical appearance of the white tiled surface. Above the main hall, the two upper floors have balconies supported on steel beams which rest on stone corbels and the relative plainness of the balconies is relieved by Mackintosh's addition of a series of curved brackets which project into the well. Mackintosh supported the roof using wooden trusses as in a number of his later buildings but these trusses are unusual as he deliberately left their wooden pegs jutting out, possibly in order to draw the observer's attention to the woodwork. There are similar trusses over the two stairwells.

The first two floors of the building are used by The Scottish Mask and Puppet Theatre Centre and the top floor is used by Glasgow Museums' conservation department.

140-2 Balgrayhill Road (1890)

Mackintosh built this pair of semi-detached houses for his uncle and this is a very early example of his ideas on house design; indeed, there are very few details that mark this out as a Mackintosh building. Perhaps the most notable features are the large canted bay windows and the use of a horizontal band of stonework to divide some of the bays' windows into two parts.

St Mungo at the Kelvingrove Art Gallery and Museum

St Mungo and the Glasgow Coat of Arms

Many buildings in the city, especially in the city centre, carry a Glasgow coat of arms and although there are variations in the design, they all incorporate the same important features. These are the city's motto *Let Glasgow flourish*, its patron saint St Mungo and four objects associated with his life: a bird, a tree, a bell and a fish.

A twelfth-century biography of Mungo was compiled by Jocelin, a monk from Furness Abbey, but there are many conflicting stories about his life which are very difficult to resolve. Mungo may have been born around 530, the son of Princess Thenew, but the identity of his father is not known. It is said his mother believed that Mungo had no earthly father but another story claims that she was raped by Prince Ewen, the son of the king of Cumbria. Her father, Loth the king of Lothian, was horrified by the pregnancy and he had her thrown off the top of Traprain Law, a prominent hill in East Lothian. She survived this ordeal so she was cast adrift in the Firth of Forth in a flimsy coracle. Eventually she came ashore at Culross in Fife, where she subsequently gave birth, and was taken in by St Serf who christened the child Kyentyern which is today spelled Kentigern. Some sources claim that St Serf gave him the pet name Mungo, which means "Dear one", while others state that it was the people of Glasgow who called him this out of their affection for him.

The young Mungo joined a group of boys who were being educated by St Serf but they grew jealous at all the special attention he was given. This feeling became malicious and on one occasion the boys decapitated a pet robin belonging to St Serf and Mungo was given the blame for this deed. However, Mungo performed a miracle on the bird and returned it to life. On another occasion the boys decided to interfere with Mungo's church duties and one evening, just before Mungo was to keep the church's lights burning through the night, the boys put the flames out. Undaunted, Mungo took a bough from a hazel tree, made it burst into flames, and thus relit the fire.

When Mungo eventually left St Serf's community he headed westwards from Culross and happened to come across an old holy man by the name of Fergus who was on the point of death. After Fergus died, Mungo placed the body on a cart which was hauled by two untamed bulls and they continued westwards until they stopped at the banks of the Molendinar Burn. This was the site of a cemetery which had been consecrated by St Ninian and there he laid Fergus to rest. The local king later persuaded him to stay and had him installed as the bishop of the area centred on the town, then known as Glesgu. Mungo was later to build his church beside the old cemetery and thus establish Glasgow's first cathedral exactly where the present-day cathedral stands.

Some time later Mungo left Scotland for a period but he was asked back by King Rhydderch Hael whose kingdom was based in Dumbarton, farther down the River Clyde. Glasgow's coat of arms takes its symbol of a salmon with a ring in its mouth from this period and the ring was a present from the king to his wife Languoreth who was having a relationship with a young soldier. She foolishly gave him the ring and one day the king found the soldier asleep, saw the ring, removed it from the soldier's finger and threw it into the River Clyde. He then challenged his wife to show him the ring and when she was unable to do so she was cast into a cell. In her desperation she asked Mungo for help and he had someone catch a salmon from the river. And, yes, the ring was found inside the fish.

The square metal bell on the coat of arms may possibly have been given to Mungo by the Pope when he visited Rome but unfortunately it no longer survives. Priests' bells were important many centuries ago as people would leave an endowment to pay for the bell to be rung to call people to pray for their soul.

Mungo continued to perform miracles during his time as Glasgow's bishop and after he died (*c.*612) his shrine in the cathedral became a place of pilgrimage.

The city's motto is a shortened version of the inscription on a bell that was made in 1637 for the Tron Kirk: *Lord let Glasgow flovrichse throvgh the preaching of thy word and priasing thy name.* In 1663 this motto became *Lord let Glasgow flourish through the preaching of thy word* and in 1699 this was shortened to *Let Glasgow flourish.*

Glasgow coat of arms, Annan Fountain, Cowcaddens

APPENDIX 2

Glossary of Architectural Terms

This glossary lists a number of architectural terms which are used in the book. The definitions are necessarily brief and they refer to many common features found in Glasgow's buildings.

acanthus	a plant with thick scalloped leaves used as a Classical sculptural decoration
alabaster	a translucent form of the mineral gypsum
ambulatory	an aisle in a church which often encloses an apse or sanctuary
anthemion (plural: anthemia)	a Classical sculptural decoration similar in shape to a honeysuckle flower
aqueduct	an artificial channel for carrying water
arcade	a series of arches resting on columns or a covered passage enclosing shops
arch	a structure that spans an opening and which does not have a horizontal lintel
Art Deco	an artistic and architectural style of the 1920s and 1930s that was popularised by a Paris exhibition of decorative and industrial art in 1925
Art Nouveau	an artistic and architectural style popular around the beginning of the twentieth century which often employed natural wave-like forms
Arts and Crafts	an artistic and architectural style popular in the second half of the nineteenth century which used traditional techniques and designs
astragal	a wooden moulding that supports a pane of glass in a window
atlantes	male sculptural figures used as decorative supports or part of a building
balustrade	a railing supported by a series of vertical balusters
Baroque	an artistic and architectural style popular in the seventeenth and eighteenth centuries which employed exceptionally flamboyant decoration
barrel-vaulted ceiling	an arched ceiling with semicircular or pointed sections without cross-members
bay window	a curved or angular projection from a building which is filled by windows
Beaux Arts	an artistic and architectural style of the late nineteenth century named after the École des Beaux Arts in Paris
boss	an ornamental projection placed at the intersection of ribs in a vault or ceiling

bow window	a curved bay window
campanile	a bell tower which may be separate from the main building
canopy	a suspended or projecting hood
capital	the topmost part of a column
caryatid	a female sculptural figure used as a decorative support for part of a building
chancel	the eastern end of a church in which an altar is placed
cherub	a winged child
clerestory (or clearstorey)	the upper storey of a church's wall which is pierced by windows
colonnade	a series of columns supporting a structure
column	an upright structural member (or sometimes just on its own as a monument) which is circular in section and may be tapered; see also *order*
cornice	a projecting ornamental moulding at the top of a building or the decorative moulding in the angle between a room's wall and its ceiling
cornucopia	a symbol of plenty which consists of a goat's horn overflowing with flowers, fruit and corn
crow-stepped gable	a gable of a building which is protected from rainwater by a series of stone steps placed on top of it; often used in sixteenth- and seventeenth-century Scottish houses
cupola	a small dome placed at the top of a circular or polygonal structure
dormer window	a window placed vertically in a sloping roof and protected by its own roof
eaves	the underpart of a sloping roof which overhangs a wall
electrolier	an ornamental pendant or stand which carries electric lamps
facade	the front of a building
faience	glazed terracotta blocks
finial	an ornament (sometimes pointed) placed at the top of part of a building
flèche	a slender spire which rises from the ridge of a roof
fluting	concave grooves which run vertically along the shaft of a column
frieze	a decorated band along the upper part of a wall
gable	the (often triangular) part of a wall at the end of a pitched roof
Glasgow Style	an artistic and architectural style that was popular at the end of the nineteenth and beginning of the twentieth centuries

Gothic	a style of architecture which was used in the twelfth to fifteenth centuries and which featured elements such as tall pillars, spires, pointed arches and rib vaulting
hammerbeam roof	a design employing horizontal brackets projecting into the roof space which support vertical posts that help support the weight of the roof
incised pattern	a pattern which is cut into a solid face
key pattern	a geometric pattern used to decorate a building which employs horizontal and vertical lines joined together to form a repeated band
keystone	the central stone of an arch or vault
lantern	a circular or polygonal turret, often at the top of a roof, which has windows all round it
mansard roof	a roof with a double slope, the lower of which is longer and steeper than the upper
nave	the western end of a church, often the longest part
niche	a vertical recess in a wall designed to contain an object
obelisk	a tall shaft of stone which is tapered and topped by a pyramid
order	This refers to the designs of Classical columns – the main orders found in Glasgow are Doric, Ionic and Corinthian. The orders differ in their styles of base, shaft, capital and entablature. Doric: relatively plain fluted shaft, with the Greek style having no base; Ionic: base, fluted shaft and a capital with curly 'volutes'; Corinthian: base, fluted shaft and a very elaborate capital with lots of fussy detail.
Oriel window	a bay window that does not start from the ground floor
palazzo	an Italian palace
parapet	a low wall guarding a sudden drop on a bridge, building, etc.
pavilion	often used to describe a projecting part of a large building
pedestal	the supporting base of a column or the support for a statue
pediment	a low-pitched gable above a portico
pilaster	a column with a rectangular cross section which projects only slightly from a wall
pilastrade	a series of pilasters
pillar	a vertical member which need not be cylindrical or conform to one of the orders
plinth	the projecting base of either a column's pedestal or a wall
podium	a platform

porch	a covered entrance to a building
portico	the roofed entrance to a building with columns supporting a pediment
putto (plural: putti)	a representation of a naked child (often a cherub)
pylon	an Egyptian pyramidal tower which may flank a doorway; it may surround the doorway itself
relief sculpture	a sculpture in which the design stands out from a surface
reredos	the wall or screen behind a church's altar
Renaissance	literally the rebirth of the use of Roman forms of art and architecture, this style originated in Italy in the fifteenth century and its ideas were taken up and modified in other European countries
rib vault	a framework consisting of diagonal arched ribs which carry the weight of a ceiling or roof
Romanesque	a style of architecture used before the development of the Baroque, it employed features such as round arches
rose window	a circular window with decorative tracery radiating outwards
rotunda	a circular room or building which may also have a dome
roundel	a circular decorative medallion
Scots Baronial	A style of architecture that was developed from the fortified tower houses built by Scottish barons in the fifteenth and sixteenth centuries. As time went on, the defensive nature of towers, turrets, small windows, gun-ports and battlemented wall-walks gave way to their use as decorative features. In later centuries, large country houses and some town buildings used these elements in their design.
scroll	a sculptural decoration in the form of a partly rolled scroll of paper
spandrel	in a bridge or archway, the roughly triangular space between the arch and the superstructure; it is often pierced in order to reduce its weight
terracotta	fired clay that has not been glazed
transept	the side arm of a cross-shaped church
turret	a small slender tower
tympanum	the space enclosed by the pediment above a portico
undercroft	a vaulted space below an upper room or building
vault	an arched ceiling or roof

Bibliography

This short selection of books about Glasgow is intended to assist readers wishing to find out more about the city. The list is divided into a number of sections and many of these books also contain good bibliographies. A short description of each book is given and those particularly recommended are marked with an ★.

All these books (and lots of others) are held in the Glasgow Room of the city's Mitchell Library.

General descriptions and history of Glasgow

Cunnison, J. and Gilfillan, J. B. S. (eds.) *Third Statistical Account of Scotland: Glasgow, The,* (1958) Collins, Glasgow.
> ★ A wide-ranging description of the city, its history, economy, services and community life. Extensive bibliography.

Daiches, David, *Glasgow,* (1986) Grafton Books, London.
> ★ A very readable history of the city. It includes a bibliography.

Devine, T. M. and Jackson, Gordon (eds.), *Glasgow. Volume I: Beginnings to 1830,* (1995) Manchester University Press, Manchester.
> A detailed history of the early development of the city. Extensive list of references.

Fisher, Joe, *Glasgow Encyclopaedia, The,* (1994) Mainstream Publishing, Edinburgh.
> ★ Articles on numerous subjects covering all aspects of the city. Good bibliography.

Fraser, W. Hamish and Maver, Irene (eds.), *Glasgow. Volume II: 1830 to 1912,* (1996) Manchester University Press.
> A detailed history of Glasgow including the time when it was "The Second City". Extensive list of references.

Lindsay, Maurice, *Glasgow,* (1989) Robert Hale, London.
> A general history of the city.

Miller, Ronald and Tivy, Joy, *Glasgow Region, The,* (1958) British Association.
> A wide-ranging survey of the Glasgow area including its geography, history and economy.

Oakley, C. A., *Second City, The,* (1967) Blackie & Son, Glasgow.
> ★ A readable and well-illustrated account of the city's history especially during the nineteenth century.

Local histories and guides

Berwick, Allan, *Park Circus Heritage Trail*, Glasgow.
A small guide to many places of interest in the Park Circus area.

Bell, G.T. (ed.), *Third Time Lucky?: The History and Hopes of the Gorbals*, (?1994) The Gorbals History Research Group, Glasgow.
The history of the Gorbals.

Boyce, David, *Bridges of the Kelvin: Partick to Kirklee*, (1996) Glasgow City Libraries Publications Board, Glasgow.
A description of the bridges over the River Kelvin between Partick and Kirklee.

Cooper, John N., *Simply Anderson*, (?1973) Vista of Glasgow, Glasgow.
The history of the area.

Curtis, E. W., *Guide to the Glasgow Botanic Gardens, A*, (1979) City of Glasgow Parks Department, Glasgow.
A technical description of the Botanic Gardens' plant collection.

Donnelly, Patrick, *Govan on the Clyde*, 1994) Glasgow City Libraries, Glasgow.
A collection of photographs illustrating the history of the Govan area.

Eunson, Eric, *Old Queen's Park*, (1995) Richard Stenlake, Ochiltree.
A collection of photographs illustrating the history of the Queen's Park area.

Gault, Rob and Gault, Linda, *Govan Heritage Trail, The*, (1995) Govan Reminiscence Group, Glasgow.
A small guide to many places of interest in the Govan area.

Glasgow District Council, *Glasgow City Chambers*, (1985) Glasgow District Council Public Relations Department, Glasgow.
A history of the city's most important civic building and a description of its most important rooms.

Greene, Margaret, *From Langside to Battlefield*, (?1993) Phil Greene, Glasgow.
A description of the districts of Langside and Battlefield.

MacQueen, Loudon and Kerr, Archibald B., *Western Infirmary, The, 1874-1974*, (1974) John Horn, Glasgow.
A history of the infirmary over a period of one hundred years.

Marshall, Ian and Smith, Ronald, *Queen's Park: Historical Guide and Heritage Walk*, (1997) Glasgow City Council, Glasgow.
A guide to many places of interest in the Queen's Park area.

Morris, William J, *Walk through Glasgow Cathedral, A*, (1995) The Society of Friends of Glasgow Cathedral, Glasgow.

A detailed guide to the city's most historic building.

Morton, Henry Brougham, *Hillhead Album, A*, (1973) The Trustees of the Late Charles A. Hepburn, Glasgow.
  The history of the Hillhead district. It contains lots of fascinating reminiscences.

Ogilvie, Sheila M., *Pollokshields Pastiche*, (1989) Glasgow.
  A miscellany of information on the Pollokshields area.

O' Neill, Mark, *Springburn Heritage Trail*, Springburn Museum, Glasgow.
  A small guide to many places of interest in the Springburn area.

Rush, Sally Joyce, *Stained Glass Windows of Govan Old Parish Church, The*, (1990) Friends of Govan Old, Glasgow.
  A detailed description of a very interesting set of windows.

Smart, Aileen, *Villages of Glasgow, Vol. 1*, (1988) John Donald Publishers, Edinburgh.
  ★ A very readable account of a number of old districts north of the River Clyde which were eventually annexed by Glasgow. It contains a bibliography.

Smart, Aileen, *Villages of Glasgow, Vol. 2*, (1996) John Donald Publishers, Edinburgh.
  ★ A very readable account of a number of old districts south of the River Clyde which were eventually annexed by Glasgow. It contains a bibliography.

Guides to museums and galleries

Allan, C. J., *Guidebook to the Hunterian art Gallery of the University of Glasgow, A*, (?1990) University of Glasgow, Glasgow.
  An illustrated guide to the gallery.

Auld, Alasdair A., *Stirling Maxwell Collection, Pollok House, The,* (?1968) Museums and Art Galleries Department, Corporation of Glasgow, Glasgow.
  A detailed description of the house's collection of paintings.

Glasgow Museum, *Fossil Grove, The*, (1995) Glasgow Museums, Glasgow.
  An illustrated guide to this geological wonder.

Glasgow Museums, *Gallery of Modern Art, Glasgow*, (1966) Scala Books, London.
  An illustrated guide to the gallery.

Glasgow Museums, *Glasgow Art Gallery and Museum*, (1994) HarperCollins Publishers, Glasgow.
  ★ An extensive guide to the city's principal museum at Kelvingrove.

Glasgow Museums, *People's Palace Book of Glasgow, The*, (1998) Mainstream Publishing, Edinburgh.
  An illustrated social history of the city encompassing the themes covered by the Palace's collections.

Glasgow Museums, *St Mungo Museum of Religious Life and Art, The*, (1993) W & R Chambers, Edinburgh.
  An illustrated guide to the museum.

Kinchin, Juliet, *Pollok House: A history of the house and gardens*, (1983) Glasgow Museums & Art Galleries, Glasgow.
  A short description of the history of the estate.

King, Elspeth, *People's Palace & Glasgow Green, The*, (1995) W & R Chambers, Edinburgh.
  ★ A very readable account of the importance of the Palace and the Green to the city. It contains a list of references.

Marks, Richard et. al., *Burrell Collection, The,* (1983) William Collins, Glasgow.
  ★ An illustrated guide to the collection.

Robinson, Peter and Ritchie, W. K., *Tenement House, The*, (1990) The National Trust for Scotland, Edinburgh.
  An illustrated guide to the contents of the house.

Architecture and architects

Doak, A. M. and Young, Andrew McLaren, *Glasgow at a Glance*, (1977) Robert Hale, London.
  A profusely-illustrated handbook to a large number of buildings of architectural interest.

Gomme, Andor and Walker, David, *Architecture of Glasgow*, (1987) Lund Humphries, London.
  ★ The authoritative analysis of the city's architecture. It contains an extensive bibliography, maps, a detailed list of all important buildings and notes on architects and their buildings.

Hume, John R., *Industrial Archaeology of Glasgow, The*, (1974) Blackie, Glasgow.
  A very detailed listing of a large number of industrial sites. Contains maps.

Kenna, Rudolph, *Glasgow Art Deco*, (1985) Richard Drew Publishing, Glasgow.
  A description of the city's Art Deco buildings.

Lawson, Judith, *Building Stones of Glasgow*, (1981) Geological Society of Glasgow, Glasgow.

A detailed account of the building stones used in a number of the city's buildings.

McKean, Charles; Walker, David; Walker, Frank Arneil, *Central Glasgow*, (1993) Royal Incorporation of Architects in Scotland, Edinburgh.
An illustrated guide to many of the most important buildings in the city centre and the West End.

Reed, Peter (ed.), *Glasgow: The Forming of the City*, (1993) Edinburgh University Press, Edinburgh.
An account of the development of the city. It contains an extensive bibliography.

Teggin, Harry; Samuel, Ian; Stewart Allan; Leslie, David, *Glasgow Revealed*, (1988) Heritage Books (Scotland).
An illustrated guide to the sculpture on some of the city's best-known buildings.

Walker, Frank Arneil, *Glasgow*, (1992) Phaidon Press, London.
An illustrated technical guide to some of the city's most notable buildings.

Ward, Robin, *Some City Glasgow*, (1988) Richard Drew Publishing, Glasgow.
This contains sketches and notes on some of the city's most important landmarks.

Williamson, Elizabeth; Riches, Anne; Higgs, Malcolm, *Glasgow*, (1990) Penguin Books, London.
★ A highly-detailed book which describes every single building of note in the city.

Wordsall, Frank, *Victorian City*, (1982) Richard Drew Publishing, Glasgow.
A very readable description of a number of the city's most interesting buildings.

Charles Rennie Mackintosh

Crawford, Alan, *Charles Rennie Mackintosh*, (1995) Thames and Hudson, London.
★ A very readable account of his life. It contains a bibliography, lists of references and a note of all Mackintosh's buildings and interiors.

Howarth, Thomas, *Charles Rennie Mackintosh and the Modern Movement*, (1977) Routeledge & Kegan Paul, London.
An important and very detailed biography. A large bibliography.

Macleod, Robert, *Charles Rennie Mackintosh: Architect and Artist*, (1983) William Collins, London.
An illustrated biography.

Moffat, Alistair and Baxter, Colin, *Remembering Charles Rennie Mackintosh: An Illustrated Biography*, (1989) Colin Baxter Photography, Lanark.
> An illustrated biography consisting of quotes from Mackintosh and those who knew him.

Neat, Timothy, *Part Seen, Part Imagined*, (1994) Canongate Press, Edinburgh.
> A study of the symbolism in the work of Mackintosh and his collaborators. It contains lists of references and a bibliography.

Alexander Thomson

McFadzean, *Life and Work of Alexander Thomson, The*, (1979) Routledge & Kegan Paul, Henley-on-Thames.
> An illustrated biography with notes, bibliography and a list of Thomson's works.

Sinclair, Fiona, *Alexander Greek Thomson: The Glasgow buildings*, (1990) City of Glasgow District Council Planning Department, Glasgow.
> A small guide to the architect's buildings in Glasgow.

Stamp, Gavin and McKinstry (eds.), ' *Greek' Thomson*, (1994) Edinburgh University Press, Edinburgh.
> A collection of essays on the architect's work. It contains notes and a bibliography.

Glasgow University

Brown, A. L. and Moss, Michael, *University of Glasgow, 1451-1996, The:* (1996) Edinburgh University Press, Edinburgh.
> The history of the university.

Coutts, James, *History of the University of Glasgow, A*, (1909) James Maclehose and Sons, Glasgow.
> A detailed history of the university and its place in the development of the city.

Ross, Anne and Hume, John, *"A new and splendid edifice": The architecture of the University of Glasgow* (1975) University of Glasgow Press, Glasgow.
> A description of the university's buildings of architectural interest.

University of Glasgow, *University of Glasgow Through Five Centuries, The*, (1951) University of Glasgow, Glasgow.
> An illustrated history of the university.

Forth and Clyde Canal

Carter, Paul (ed.), *Forth & Clyde Canal Guidebook*, (1985) Strathclyde District Libraries & Museums, Bishopbriggs.
 A guide to the canal.

Cooper, Tony; McCann, Linda; McIntyre, Angus, *Scotland's Grand Canal*, (1988) Woodside & North Kelvin Local History Project, Glasgow.
 A guide to the part of the canal which runs through Glasgow.

Lindsay, Jean, *Canals of Scotland, The*, (1968) David & Charles, Newton Abbot.
 This contains a history of the canal. It includes a number of useful references.

Graveyards

Berry, James J., *Glasgow Necropolis: the city of the dead, The*, (1985) Mackintosh School of Architecture, Glasgow.
 A small guide to many of the monuments in the city's most famous graveyard.

Black, Jimmy, *Glasgow Graveyard Guide, The*, (1992) Saint Andrew Press, Edinburgh.
 A guide to a number of monuments in the city's main graveyards.

Charlotte Hutt (ed.), *City of the Dead: The Story of Glasgow's Southern Necropolis*, (1996) Glasgow City Libraries and Archives, Glasgow.
 The history of the cemetery and information on notable people buried there. It contains a bibliography.

Willing, June A. and Fairie, J. Scott, *Burial Grounds in Glasgow: A Brief Guide for Genealogists*, (1986) Glasgow and West of Scotland Family History Society, Glasgow.
 Technical details on the city's cemeteries. It contains a bibliography.

Literature

Burgess, Moira, *Glasgow Novel, 1870-1970: A Bibliography, The*, (1972) Scottish Library Association, Glasgow.
 A useful source, giving information on novels of this period as well as a list of relevant books and articles on literary history and criticism.

Burgess, Moira, *reading Glasgow*, (1996) Book Trust Scotland, Edinburgh
 ★ This interesting guidebook describes the literature of the city and the places associated with various authors and books. It

contains an extensive list of authors connected with the city and a list of their works.

Carswell, Catherine, *Open the Door!*, (1996) Canongate Books, Edinburgh.
  This novel is also partly autobiographical and it describes Glasgow life in the days of "The Second City".

McArthur, A. and Long, H. Kingsley, *No Mean City*, (1990) Corgi Books, London.
  A novel set in the brutal world of Glasgow gangland.

McLaughlin, Brendan (ed.), *A Spiel amang us*, (1990) Mainstream Publishing, Edinburgh.
  A collection of short stories which were entered for the Scotia Bar Writers' Prize.

Scientific studies

Dickson, J. H., *Wild Plants of Glasgow*, (1992) Mercat Press, Edinburgh.
  This describes the plants that are found growing wild in the city. It includes a bibliography.

Lawson, J. D. and Weedon, D. S. (eds.), *Geological Excursions around Glasgow and Girvan*, (1992) The Geological Society of Glasgow, Glasgow.
  This includes a description of the building stones used in the city's buildings and the geology of Fossil Grove.

Nineteenth and early twentieth century descriptions

MacDonald, Hugh, *Rambles Round Glasgow*, (1910) John Smith & Son (Glasgow), Glasgow.
  ★ This reprint of MacDonald's well-known guidebook of 1854 contains an introductory essay by G. H. Morrison.

MacGeorge, Andrew, *Old Glasgow: The Place and the People*, (1888) Blackie and Son, Glasgow.
  A detailed history of the city from the Roman occupation to the eighteenth century.

MacIntosh, Hugh, *Origin and History of Glasgow Streets, The*, (1902) James Hedderwick & Sons, Glasgow.
  This contains notes on many of the city's streets, giving their history and explaining how they got their names.

Muir, James, *Glasgow Streets and Places*, (1899) William Hodge, Glasgow.
  A collection of brief notes on many old places in the city.

"Nestor", *Rambling Recollections of Glasgow*, (1880) John Tweed, Glasgow.

A collection of numerous small articles on various facets of Glasgow life.

Renwick, Robert, *Glasgow Memorials*, (1908) James Maclehose and Sons, Glasgow.
  A collection of articles on the history of the old parts of Glasgow.

Senex, *Old Glasgow and its Environs*, (1864) David Robertson, Glasgow.
  This contains numerous essays on various topics dealing with the city's history.

Tweed, John, *Tweed's Guide to Glasgow and the Clyde*, (1979) The Molendinar Press, Glasgow.
  This is a reprint of the interesting 1872 guidebook.

Miscellaneous

Barr, William W., *Glaswegiana*, (1990) Richard Drew Publishing, Glasgow.
  ★ An interesting collection of stories about the city's history.

Berry, Simon and Whyte, Hamish (eds.), *Glasgow Observed*, (1987) John Donald Publishers, Edinburgh.
  ★ This contains extracts from newspapers, magazines and books from 1773 to 1986 which describe life in Glasgow.

Brooke, Marcus and Bell, Brian (eds.), *Glasgow*, (1992) APA Publications, London.
  An "Insight Guide" which has numerous articles of interest.

Castle, Colin M., *Legacy of Fame, A*, (1990) Murdoch Cadbury Publishing, Erskine.
  This describes the city's shipping lines and the docks. It also includes descriptions of a number of famous Clyde-built ships.

Cowan, James, *From Glasgow's Treasure Chest*, (1951) Craig & Wilson, Glasgow.
  An interesting collection of accounts of the author's exploration of the city. It includes a history of the Tontine Faces.

Devine, T. M., *Tobacco Lords, The*, (1975) Edinburgh University Press, Edinburgh.
  A study of these eighteenth-century merchants. It contains an extensive bibliography.

Edward, Mary, *Who Belongs to Glasgow?*, (1993) Glasgow City Libraries Publications Board, Glasgow.
  An account of the immigrants who came to the city during the last two hundred years. It contains a bibliography.

Foreman, Carol, *Did You Know?*, (1996) Glasgow City Libraries and Archives, Glasgow.
> This has short notes on a number of Glasgow subjects.

Gourlay, James (ed.), *Provosts of Glasgow from 1609 to 1832, The*, (1942) James Hedderwick & Sons, Glasgow.
> This contains notes on the city's Lord Provosts, among whom were some of the city's most influential men of the period.

House, Jack, *Heart of Glasgow, The*, (1982) Richard Drew Publishing, Glasgow.
> ★ A very readable account of many aspects of Glasgow history.

House, Jack, *Square Mile of Murder*, (1984) Richard Drew Publishing, Glasgow.
> This tells the stories behind four murder trials, the accused being Madeleine Smith, Jessie McLachlan, Dr Edward Pritchard and Oscar Slater.

Irvine, Peter and Kelling, Graeme, *Glasgow the Best!*, (1998) HarperCollins Publishers, Glasgow.
> A guide to the city based on the authors' recommendations on places to visit.

Jeffrey, Robert and Watson, Ian (eds.), *Images of Glasgow*, (1995) The Breedon Books Publishing Company, Derby.
> A fascinating collection of photographs of the city which were taken by photographers of *The Herald* and the *Evening Times*.

Kinchin, Perilla, *Tea and Taste: the Glasgow Tea Rooms 1875-1975*, (1996) White Cockade Publishing, Oxford.
> An account of the tea room phenomena in Glasgow. It contains references, a bibliography and a list of buildings that housed tea rooms.

Kinchin, Perilla and Kinchin, Juliet, *Glasgow's Great Exhibitions: 1888, 1901, 1911, 1938, 1988*, (1988) White Cockade Publishing, Bicester.
> A well-illustrated account of the city's five great exhibitions.

Munro, Michael, *Patter: A guide to current Glasgow usage, The*, (1985) Glasgow District Libraries, Glasgow.
> A fascinating "dictionary" giving the English translation of lots of Glaswegian words and phrases.

Oakley, Charles, *Dear Old Glasgow Town*, (1975) Blackie, Glasgow.
> A series of articles about various streets in Glasgow. The text is accompanied by numerous sketches.

Osborne, Brian D., Quinn, Iain; Robertson, Donald, *Glasgow's River*, (1996) Lindsay Publications, Glasgow.
> ★ A guide to the River Clyde, from Victoria Bridge downstream to Gourock.

Pateman, Rachael and Robertson, John, *Glasgow Pubs*, (1988) The
Glasgow File, Glasgow.
   A series of articles on some of the city's best-known watering
   holes.

Spring, Ian, *Phantom Village*, (1990) Polygon, Edinburgh.
   A study of Glasgow culture. It contains many references.

Thomson, Willie and Hart, Finlay, *UCS Work-in, The*, (1972) Lawrence
& Wishart, London.
   An account of the world-famous fight against shipyard
   redundancies.

Wordsall, Frank, *Glasgow Keek Show*, A,(1981) Richard Drew
Publishing, Glasgow.
   An amusing collection of extracts from newspaper and magazine
   articles during the period 1600 to 1900.

Babbity Bowster, Blackfriars Street

Index